THE LEADING MAN

THE LEADING MAN

*Hollywood and
the Presidential Image*

Burton W. Peretti

RUTGERS UNIVERSITY PRESS
NEW BRUNSWICK, NEW JERSEY, AND LONDON

Library of Congress Cataloging-in-Publication Data

Peretti, Burton W. (Burton William), 1961–
    The leading man : Hollywood and the presidential image / Burton W. Peretti.
        p.   cm.
    Includes bibliographical references and index.
    ISBN 978-0-8135-5404-4 (hardcover : alk. paper) —
    ISBN 978-0-8135-5405-1 (e-book)
    1. Presidents in motion pictures.   2. Motion pictures—Political aspects—
United States.   3. Historical films—United States—History and criticism.
4. Motion pictures and history.   I. Title.
PN1995.9.P678P47   2012
791.43′658—dc23   2011053241

A British Cataloging-in-Publication record for this book
is available from the British Library.

Visit our website: http://rutgerspress.rutgers.edu

Manufactured in the United States of America

For Jenny, Catherine,
and Elizabeth

CONTENTS

ACKNOWLEDGMENTS

George Cotkin is responsible for the writing of this book. By his own strong example as an intellectual historian, and through his kind solicitations and enthusiasm, he has guided a series of books through Rutgers University Press that illuminate American culture in the late twentieth century. I am proud to be a part of his project, and I am also indebted to George for his thoughtful critiques of an early draft of the manuscript. Elliott Gorn also provided valuable advice at the proposal stage three long years ago.

I am happy to join the many authors who have praised the virtues and skills of Leslie Mitchner, editor in chief at Rutgers. Leslie also has been enthusiastic about my work, and she has brought her rich experience in book editing to the thornier aspects of the project. She has kindly accommodated my rather tortuous schedule for completing it. Lisa Boyajian, the editorial assistant, Marilyn Campbell, the prepress director, and above all Peter Strupp, the excellent copy editor, were also instrumental in helping to complete this book in fine style.

My research was supported in 2010 by a Connecticut State University–American Association of University Professors faculty research grant, administered through my employer, Western Connecticut State University. I am grateful to my former provost, Linda Rinker, for her support of this project, and to numerous colleagues who have offered bits of advice and encouragement during my work. My greatest debt lies with Martha May and Leslie Lindenauer, fellow faculty members in the Department of History, who embarked on their own fascinating exploration of representations of the presidency on the Internet at the same time I began my work. Through our discussions and joint appearances on conference panels, Marcy and Leslie enriched my sensitivity to many aspects of the general subject that I had heretofore ignored. They are also great friends. Like many other scholars, I am consistently delighted by the cooperation and generosity of archivists at five US presidential libraries, who were instrumental to the success of my research into primary sources. The Historians of the Twentieth Century United States in the United Kingdom and the Social Science History Association permitted me to present portions of this book at their annual conferences.

Finally, I continue to be sustained and enriched in countless ways by my family, to whom *The Leading Man* is dedicated.

THE LEADING MAN

INTRODUCTION

From 1958 to 1963, the scene was repeated on countless occasions across the United States, in parking lots and motorcades, on airport tarmacs and in hotel ballrooms. John Fitzgerald Kennedy, first a candidate and later the president of the United States, appeared in public. When the crowds saw him, they reacted viscerally and emotionally.

Tanned, well-built, smiling, with a full head of brown hair, Kennedy especially elicited a powerful reaction from women. His campaign staff called the excited young women the "jumpers." In Manhattan in 1960, when the publisher Henry Luce welcomed the candidate to the Time-Life building, "there was a big crowd, especially of teenagers, the first good whiff I had had [of the jumpers]. . . . There was very little public announcement of it, or none. In the lobby and outside in the street there wasn't a huge crowd, but there certainly were several hundred, maybe a thousand, people, with the teenagers . . . really jumping." Later in the campaign Kennedy visited Waterbury, Connecticut, at three o'clock in the morning. Elizabeth Simpson, then fifty-three years old, ran "up South Main Street alongside his motorcade. . . . He was so handsome. I thought my husband was going to kill me; he was a Republican." As president, Kennedy was captured in a vivid photograph taken on the beach in Malibu, California, standing in soaking wet swim trunks amid a group of surprised and adoring young women. Nancy Greene recalled seeing Kennedy in Tampa, Florida, in November 1963: "He looked so young and was so handsome . . . a knight in shining armor." Men agreed; "He was certainly charismatic," William Davenport of Tampa remembered.[1]

1

Four days after his visit to Tampa, President Kennedy was killed by an assassin. Years afterward, JFK's private life and his effectiveness as president became the subjects of controversy, but even his detractors continued to acknowledge the primacy of his personal appeal to Americans. In 1998 the journalist Seymour Hersh, a merciless critic, claimed that Kennedy's life had illustrated "the power of beauty," which in this case became a deceptive and even evil force. "Kennedy's beauty made him more corrupt," Hersh argues. "He was above the law; he didn't think anything could stop him. Kennedy was a very seductive man and a very pretty man, and a lot of people responded to that." In a society made up of plain-looking people, such beauty endowed those who possessed it with a strangely superhuman—even a godlike—arrogance and power. The former Kennedy White House aide Fred Dutton was privy to the late president's extensive sexual activity. "We're a bunch of virgins, married virgins. And he's like God, fucking anybody he wants to anytime he feels like it." Echoing Dutton, the motivational speaker Tony Alessandra, author of a book about charisma, has asserted generally that "our personalities consist . . . of a series of containers, like cups or glasses. Some are nearly empty, some brimming, yet others are partially filled to varying degrees. Together, they constitute our potential charisma. If all the glasses were filled to the top, you'd be so charismatic people would think you were a god . . . and you'd probably think so, too."[2]

In twentieth-century America, godlike beauty and attraction was marketed most effectively by the motion picture industry. The Hollywood "dream factory," as it was often called, left a powerful mark on Kennedy. He had grown up around Hollywood actors and image makers, a legacy of his father's early career as a movie producer and his family's continuing social ties to the industry. Indeed the potent mixture of desire and envy—and repulsion—that Kennedy aroused in Americans resembled the impact of the movies on their hopes and dreams. Rising from their modest origins as the purveyors of three-minute novelty movies unspooled in nickelodeons, American film studios became the nation's most skilled fabricators of fantasies that, in their deceptively realistic guises, seemed to fulfill wishes in real life. As Kennedy (who was born in 1917) learned from childhood, no one in America could embody average people's hopes and fantasies as powerfully as leading men and women in motion pictures. Character actors and talented comic and musical performers might become film stars, but the most potent cultural forces were the lead actors; it was they who largely defined the mystique of the silver screen.

Through an elusive blend of talent and personal and sexual attractiveness, actors and actresses who achieved lead stardom hit upon the combination of looks and behavior that dramatized what spectators wanted their own lives to be like. The stars' power transcended that of product advertisers and leisure professionals, who merely promised to add spice to people's lives. On movie screens and in their highly publicized, pampered "private" lives, stars dramatized people's fantasies of living without fear, repression, or the threat of failure. Here the religious gift of charisma seemed to reappear in everyday guise, bestowing a vaguely superhuman quality on these celluloid figures. As the novelist Mario Puzo put it, "movie star[s'] charisma is so powerful that it seems as if their adult images as heroes, as beauties, had sprung full grown out of the head of Zeus."[3]

From the early years of the twentieth century, presidential politics and motion pictures coexisted as complementary pillars of mass communication. Presidents administered the daily life of the nation and symbolized its structure and organization; movie stars epitomized the desire of citizens to break free of that very structure and organization. The movies, like other artistic genres that had preceded them, expressed what Norman Mailer (in a 1960 essay on Kennedy) called the "subterranean river of untapped, ferocious, lonely and romantic desires, that concentration of ecstasy and violence which is the dream life of the nation."[4] It may seem surprising to claim that a president or other politician could cross over to the fantasy world of the movies, but it has happened. Such transformations have, in fact, been a major development in American political history. This book tells their story.

The divide between everyday politics and government and the movies' fictional worlds of fantasy can be vast. Bureaucratic routine and ossified official functions can seem to be the antithesis of wish fulfillment. However, as Kennedy's career vividly shows, bridges across the divide have been built, and they have been significant. JFK even earned the admiration of leading film stars, who appreciated his mastery of a cinematic brand of leadership. Princess Grace of Monaco, the former Grace Kelly, recalled after Kennedy's death that "he was almost too good to be true—he was just like the All-

American boy, wasn't he, handsome, a fighter, witty, full of charm."[5] Kennedy's was a paragon of the cinematic presidency, but his was not the only example. Presidents, above all other US politicians, often sought to benefit from the workings of the cultural dream factory that has been dominated by Hollywood.

The history of the presidential image in the decades before movies arrived, covered in chapter 1 of this book, shows us how the chief executive was positioned early to assume the mantle of cultural leading man. It is perhaps surprising to note that the presidency, which predated Hollywood by more than a century, created a cultural role for the office's holders that prefigured aspects of the cinematic leading man. As an early star figure in the young republic, the president served as a symbol of national survival and of wish fulfillment. Filling an exalted office that had him functioning as both head of government and head of state, the president at least had the potential to enact a powerful and charismatic role. Certainly there were strong countervailing forces—many Americans feared a government ruled by dominant personalities—but before 1900 many of the attitudes that fed the growth of the cinematic presidential image had already emerged.

During the nineteenth century, the rise of the Washington, D.C., social scene, the print media, and the professional theater helped to build up and define the president's cultural function as a lead actor in society. Leaders thus in part became followers, as presidents studied how actors and publicists captured the attention and the allegiance of the mass audience. As popular entertainment grew in influence, the White House increasingly adapted the publicity techniques used in show business to the president's own ends. In the print media, political and theatrical leaders acquired a roughly similar celebrity. The process was uneven; some presidents resisted a performing role, and even those who embraced such a role interacted with show business in different ways. Nevertheless, by the 1920s, when motion pictures claimed the dominance in the popular performing arts that they retain to this day, presidents were already familiar with the flashbulbs of publicity, the benefits of well-rehearsed public performance, and the political effectiveness of well-turned speech, dress, and mannerisms. Subsequent decades only enhanced their eagerness to understand and to emulate Hollywood's claim on the popular imagination.

———

The Leading Man explores the development of the cinematic presidential image since the 1920s. Occasionally, for the sake of providing context, it also discusses politicians who never made it to the White House, as well as movie actors who dabbled in politics without making a run for office or a having a major impact on public affairs. These supporting figures helped to define the cultural terrain with which presidents had to contend. At the center of the story are the fourteen presidents of the cinematic era, from Herbert Hoover to Barack Obama. Since the 1920s the president, like the lead actor in a movie, has been given the central place on the political stage, under the intense glare of a spotlight. As we have already seen, though, presidents were spectators as well as performers. Most of them, like Kennedy, were dedicated members of the movie audience. Like other American men, future presidents were taught by lead movie actors how to look and behave, what to say, and how to say it. Through their cultural education in darkened theaters, and through their involvement in Hollywood's and Washington's complex institutional interactions, male politicians destined for the White House made use of the effective techniques of self-presentation demonstrated by the movies' leading men.

The cinematic presidential image has been heavily influenced by the definition of masculinity in American culture. To date, all US presidents (as well as all presidential nominees of major parties) have been male. Americans before 1900 developed assumptions about how their leaders might represent the ideal white man, and they passed those assumptions on to politicians and popular artists of the early twentieth century. Presidents in the 1700s and 1800s were characterized variously as military commanders on horseback, or prudent attorneys, or bourgeois husbands and fathers. In the past century—the era of the movies—feminism has transformed society, but stubborn vestiges of male domination exist, especially in the ranks of leadership and in roles that allegedly depend on physical intimidation and strength. America's heritage as a land of exploitation and aggressive conquest helped to validate outsized concepts of masculinity, and when an individual such as Andrew Jackson put them on display in the presidency, they became attached to the office. In the twentieth century, global hot and cold wars enhanced the president's powers and thus inspired an updating of the old aggressive persona. Movies played a concomitant role in glorifying extreme American masculinity, and the oversized ambitions, egos, and earnings of men in Hollywood (behind and before the cameras) helped to integrate it into the broader national arena of aggressive striving and conquest.

Women have fought for attention in such a cultural landscape. From the beginning they were central to Hollywood, and it can be argued that Florence Lawrence (the first actor ever to receive star billing in a movie) and Lillian Gish, among others, established film stardom years before their male counterparts emerged. Male executives, however, have always dominated the industry; by the 1920s they had pushed out the few powerful women remaining in the studios. As a reflection of this trend, for decades even the most hard-driving female movie stars were typecast as the submissive helpers and love interests of leading men. In society and politics, women faced similar oppression. As half of the population, they were central to family and community life, but until the 1970s they only sporadically won positions of power and influence. Today, in an era of unprecedented advancement by women in so many other fields, the persistence of a strong male image in the presidency shows the resilience of the cinematic tradition, as well as the influence of sexism dating back to the 1700s. A female president may be elected in the near future, but the long wait for this breakthrough illustrates the pervasive sexism underlying American culture, in which both Washington and Hollywood have been complicit. Much the same could be said about racial barriers to the presidency, which were overcome only in 2008. The generic American hero's whiteness has been as central to his identity as his gender.

Yet *The Leading Man* also shows that women and the so-called feminine cultural sphere have exerted an important influence on the presidential image, even during the cinematic era of the past century. In the early 1800s First Ladies were already celebrities in Washington society, and they appeared in print as paragons of fashion and etiquette. As newspaper and magazine circulation grew after the Civil War, the largely passive presidents of the Gilded Age acquired a celebrity status that derived from that of their wives; for the first time, their clothing and mannerisms were displayed and debated. Many presidents joined the celebrity elite, socializing with well-known business people and with stars of the theater. The United States' rise to the status of a world power encouraged presidents, beginning with Theodore Roosevelt, to play up the office's masculinity and the president's rugged image as a "man on horseback," but the ever-expanding mass media also continued to implicate the president and his family in society news that was largely crafted for female readers. Later, in the wake of the Women's Movement of the 1960s and 1970s, "feminized" news about celebrities became central to mass-media journalism. The contemporary cult of celebrity encourages the melding of a feminized presidential image with the more traditional masculine depictions found in Hollywood films and older media. Particularly in the empathic and seductive figure of Bill Clinton, the result has been an intriguing re-articulation of the masculine cinematic image of the president.

Within these parameters of gender and race, the relationship between politicians and movies deepened. As already noted, presidents beginning with Hoover have tended to be movie fans. Some of them took a keen interest in actors' techniques of self-presentation. This was especially true of the more recent presidents who grew up watching motion pictures. John F. Kennedy and Richard M. Nixon took particular care to learn from the grooming, gestures, movements, and vocal inflections of film actors, and they applied what they learned in significant ways to their political careers. As a young man Ronald Reagan became a professional actor, and like many of his colleagues in Hollywood he was a careful student of other actors' work. Bill Clinton, a child of the post–World War II Baby Boom, may have been the biggest movie fan of all presidents. Reagan and Clinton's careful construction of likeable self-images modeled on movie personas helped them to maintain their personal popularity with voters during politically stormy times in the White House. Yet not all presidents of the past half century were devotees of film. Chief executives such as Lyndon Johnson and George H. W. Bush generally ignored popular culture and its lessons for politicians, and their disinterest contributed to their inability to retain the public's personal admiration when the political climate worsened.

Presidents' interest in the movies mattered because, of course, politics is the most social of professions. Like their other preferences, politicians' tastes in films either resonated with the mass of voters or signified their distance from average people. The movies came late to the "fame game" that politicians and other leaders had been playing for millennia. Would-be leaders have used every trick at their disposal to persuade governments and the masses to support them. These run the gamut from Cicero's oratorical gimmicks to elaborate displays of royal power such as the *lit de justice* (a parliamentary gathering) in medieval France and the *grand lever* (meetings with official callers) of King Louis XIV. Beginning in the late eighteenth century, revolutionary politics in America and Europe, the mass print media, and improved means of transportation democratized public awareness of, and participation in, the business of leadership. After 1900, motion pictures contributed to this democratizing process.

The movies were a mass-culture industry that based its livelihood on incorporating vastly different subgroups and individuals into one paying national audience. Politicians turned to them to learn new techniques for reaching and uniting the public and for inculcating diverse subgroups with the same message and ideology. Movie actors, like political leaders, sought to fuse polyglot audiences into a single mass following, albeit at the box office rather than the ballot box. Movies—and their stepchildren, television and mass publicity—helped presidents to make themselves more palatable and accessible to a large and pluralistic population. After 1941, the president was transformed into a more imperial figure, a leader with global responsibilities, often working in secret and becoming increasingly isolated from average voters. The wealth and exclusive social lives of film stars similarly helped to isolate them from most audience members. The tension between maintaining a common touch and existing in an insulated and rarefied milieu affected leading men in both Hollywood and Washington.

Through such developments, citizens have come to perceive Hollywood and Washington as similar capitals of ambition, power, and celebrity. Since 1990 it has become common for Americans to joke that Washington politics is "show business for ugly people." Jack Valenti, a man with rare experience in both government (as Lyndon Johnson's top aide) and movies (as the longtime president of the Motion Picture Association of America), expressed the similarity another way. "I have become convinced that movie people and politicians spring from the same DNA," Valenti said. "They are both unpredictable, sometimes glamorous, usually in crisis (imagined or otherwise), addicted to power, anxious to please, always on stage, hooked on

applause, enticed by publicity, always reading from scripts written by someone else, constantly taking the public pulse, never really certain, except
publicly. Indeed, it's difficult to say which deserves more the description of
'entertainment capital of the world,' Hollywood or Washington, D.C."[6]
Valenti suggests not only that the people in both professions share similar
personalities, but also that in the glare of publicity and mass marketing, they
behave in much the same way.

Today, well into the era of movies, the processes and the products of
Washington increasingly resemble those of Hollywood. As this book makes
clear, the closely matched public roles of the politician and the film actor
bred similar efforts at publicity, advertising, and public relations; scripting,
and the consequent need to create the illusion of spontaneity; and an other-
directed obsession with reading the moods of the audience. The history of
motion picture publicity can thus be compared with the evolution of campaign advertising, presidential appearances on radio and television, and the
White House communications office to detect ways in which Washington
has been influenced by Hollywood.

From the perspective of the audience—or the electorate—the movies
have updated older concepts of fame and celebrity. Since the dawn of recorded
history individuals have striven to be known widely for their deeds. As Leo
Braudy has observed in his cultural history of fame, Alexander the Great set
out to make himself the best-known person on earth. He succeeded; long
after the Greek Empire collapsed and ceded Alexander's conquests in India
and the Middle East, his name, image, and reputation persisted. Rulers in
succeeding centuries pursued similar strategies to keep their names in the
public mind, but time also gradually democratized fame. Writers in the
Middle Ages, including commoners such as St. Augustine and Chaucer,
could win renown because of the high quality of their work, while in the
modern era merchants and inventors hoisted their names and visages into
public view.[7]

The true democratization of fame came in the 1700s, with the dawn of
modern celebrity. As Fred Inglis has shown, celebrity depended upon ever-
expanding communications, beginning with the robust and argumentative
newspapers of cities such as London and Paris. Elite "society" sought above
all to be mentioned in print, and journalists yearned to discover society

"news" worth printing (in other words, news that would sell copies of their publications). Celebrity separated deeds from fame and magnified the force of personality or novelty in the public eye. Talent in a field remained helpful; Sarah Bernhardt and Charles Lindbergh, to name two examples, leveraged their real achievements to gain celebrity status through the machinery of publicity.[8] Once such achievers reached the popular pantheon, though, their accomplishments were obscured by the very fact of their fame, their ubiquity in the press and in other media. Gradually the new celebrity culture claimed public officials as well, especially those with "personality" whose personal qualities attracted widespread attention. Colorful politicians' fame as celebrities overshadowed their accomplishments in office. Thus Jimmy Walker, a lackluster mayor of New York City in the 1920s, dazzled the newspapers and the newsreels with his dapper attire, quick wit, and frequent appearances in Manhattan nightlife.[9]

Movie studio publicity departments were uniquely successful in promoting movie stars, and beginning in the 1920s presidents took notice. Herbert Hoover and Franklin Roosevelt were the first presidents to exploit the public relations benefits offered by the studios. They cultivated personal connections in Hollywood and took advantage of the movies' new resources for enhancing their own presence and effectiveness in the mass media. Harry Truman and Dwight Eisenhower served in office during a time of decline for Hollywood studios, but through their encounters with the new medium of television they made the cinematic mode of presidential self-presentation a more consistent concern in the West Wing. John F. Kennedy brought his family's experience in the movie industry into a campaign for the White House that crafted what might be called the first fully cinematic presidential image. His success inspired a generation of younger politicians to market their own charisma as leadership. Lyndon Johnson struggled to project an appealing image in the mass media, but he was more successful in enhancing his party's fundraising apparatus in Hollywood.

The liberal dominance of the 1960s gave way to a new conservative version of cinematic presidential leadership. Richard Nixon created the first major presidential image making operation and labored mightily—and futilely—to use it to overcome the deficiencies in his public reputation. Ronald Reagan and George W. Bush oversaw improvements in the operation which exploited the public's ever-increasing fascination with movie-inspired celebrity and spectacle. Between these two presidents, Bill Clinton nurtured a close relationship with Hollywood and became entwined in the public mind with the numerous cinematic representations of the presidency that appeared during his term. Barack Obama's meteoric rise to the White House in 2008 was a classic tale of the triumph of celebrity politics, although Hillary Rodham Clinton's strong showing and Obama's presence gave the tale new gender and racial twists. Obama's subsequent troubles in office, though, demonstrate the limits of the cinematic presidential image—and possibly even its staleness—in the early years of the twenty-first century.

In *The Leading Man* I have built on the findings and approaches of excellent earlier studies of the interaction of Washington and Hollywood by Ronald Brownstein, Kathleen Hall Jamieson, and Alan Schroeder, among others.[10] In the chapters that follow, I analyze the evolution and the significance of this interaction and trace the somewhat convoluted history of the cinematic presidential image. "The leading man" is a legacy of old and new cultural forces, of structural and financial tendencies in Washington and Hollywood, and of the efforts of elites in both towns to perpetuate their bond with the diverse public that resides on the continent between the two capitals. The cinematic presidential image has also been centrally shaped by the remarkable individuals who have attained the Oval Office, who have used their imagination and their power to revise the image in important ways. Despite the heightened cynicism and divisions in today's political culture, Americans of all persuasions perceive the president through the amorphous yet familiar cinematic image that has developed over the past century. It is an image we must understand and critique if we are to understand our political culture more clearly, and if we are ever to come close to realizing effective and wise self-government.

CHAPTER 1

"THE TORMENTS OF DESIRE"

PRESIDENTS AND PERFORMANCE BEFORE 1929

For a century before the 1890s, when Thomas Edison produced his first moving picture and William McKinley became the first president to be filmed, the president of the United States was being primed for his debut in the movie spotlight. This preparation came about through a series of developments that defined how the presidency was to be performed. On the speaker's rostrum, at social occasions, in theater boxes, and even on vacation, the president became a cultural performer, a figure who at times transcended politics. During the nineteenth century, professional performing artists were earning increased status and prestige among Americans. At the same time, presidents were more frequently likened to these performers. This entwining of the president and the performing artist accelerated during the early twentieth century, in part due to the efforts of a new class of professional manipulators of public opinion—but the trend also illustrated how the two cultural institutions spoke similarly to the desires and aspirations of the American people.

———

The Constitution, a mechanistic and legalistic document, enumerated the basic powers of the new presidency but left almost everything else out. As in the rest of the document, the vagueness of Article II was pragmatic—intended to help ensure its ratification by the states—but it also illustrated the framers' conviction that the new federal government would "go of itself" and naturally develop its own traditions.[1] Some of the Founders, though, most notably John Adams, looked to the past for models of presidential behavior. The president, Adams thought, ought to be the New World's version of royalty. At the other extreme, antifederalists such as George Mason and Patrick Henry hoped that the sovereignty of the states would check all federal power, and in particular render the chief executive a figurehead.

It is well known that this ambiguity about the nature of the presidency heavily burdened the office's first occupant. George Washington, first president by acclamation, lived in fear of making the wrong decisions—of saddling his successors with disastrous procedural and substantive precedents, landing the new government in the middle of the next European war, and above all dying in office and initiating a possible hereditary presidency-cum-monarchy. Serving at a time when transportation and communication had barely progressed beyond medieval conditions, Washington worked in the capital cities of New York and Philadelphia, out of the view of almost all citizens. Most of his presidential "firsts" were set down in writing. He created the military and civilian machinery of the federal government, but it was small and thinly distributed across the vast new nation. While citizens across America memorialized Washington in portraits, allegories, woodcuts, and statues, they barely noticed much of his actual work as president.

Nevertheless, even in this dark age, more than a century before electronic communications became the norm, George Washington also established the visual component of the presidency. Inspired by colonial and European tradition and motivated by the challenges of his office, Washington exploited the unique impact of the physical presence of the chief executive on the political process. He thus originated "presidential performance" in its most literal sense. The Virginian had been thrust into positions of leadership since early adulthood. More than any other Founding Father, therefore, Washington felt in his bones what Adams had grasped only intellectually: that he, as the first president, was a kinglike embodiment of the hopes and values of the new nation.

Medieval European rulers, drawing upon religious imagery of the Christian church as the ever-vital body of Christ on Earth, began to proclaim their own bodies to be extensions of their kingdoms, and vice versa. Since the mid-

1600s, Louis XIV, Frederick the Great, and other would-be "absolute monarchs" had spent lavishly to enshrine their images in the perceived heart of their lands, through art, architecture, and regular ritual.[2] George Washington's experiences in the colonies and during the Revolution were humbler, but they taught him the value of this mystical aspect of the leader's presence among his people. Through calculated self-presentation, Washington established such a presence among his fellows. Circumstance and luck helped to define his leader's profile as well. In 1775, as the first and as yet the only member of the Continental Army, Washington purposely strode down the streets of Boston, a tall commander full of swagger and resolution. The performance worked; crowds gasped in awe, and men enlisted in large numbers.

During the Revolution Washington suffered many reversals in battle but won the priceless allegiance of his regular troops by facing down musket fire—leading a charmed life atop a succession of horses who were less fortunate—and enduring miserable winter encampments along with them. The general was enough of a literary stylist to convey the desperation of his ill-equipped force in stark terms to Congress, and his occasionally self-pitying eloquence was magnified by the worshipful officers on his staff. The Marquis de Lafayette, Alexander Hamilton, and others were in a sense the forerunners of modern political image makers. Hamilton and other former lieutenants propagated the image of Washington's revolutionary legend. It helped of course that the general had been present for the final British defeat at Yorktown (although the epochal nature of that defeat became apparent only months later, in a British surrender that was decided in London, not in America). His forsaking of a dictatorship for a return to Mount Vernon allowed his promoters to stoke the legend of Washington as the American Cincinnatus. When the Confederation fell into crisis and the constitutional conventioneers launched a semisecret, elite rebellion in favor of an entirely new national government, Washington reentered national life and resumed his performance as the embodiment of the nation, chairing the convention. After ratification, he was unanimously selected by the Electoral College to assume the new presidency.[3]

Washington's tenure was fraught with perils both foreign and domestic, and posterity generally has credited him with making wise decisions and utterances that ensured the survival of the nation and government. On a daily basis, though, the president was passive, allowing Congress to initiate policy and the cabinet officers to make most of the important decisions. Washington perceived that his most important role was to embody his office and to enact unity and tranquility. This he did through two kinds of action that set important precedents: official travel and entertainment. On his celebrated tour of the thirteen states, as well as at his "levees" or Friday evening social events in the capital city, Washington allowed himself to be seen as the steady, even immovable cornerstone of the US government. The formality of the levees owed something to the stiff etiquette of royal occasions, and they struck plain-acting Americans as a social oddity. Each levee began with the president and "Lady Washington," as she was officially styled, greeting selected guests in an anteroom of the presidential residence and then making a slowly paced, statuesque passage through the ballroom, barely acknowledging the crowd. Nothing else in the nation matched this distant, regal behavior, but few complained; the president was Washington, maintaining the inspiring public role he had assumed twenty years before.

After the general's retirement to Mount Vernon, political divisions immediately set in. John Adams could never convincingly assume a regal bearing (though he approved of, and came to crave, the splendid insulation that aristocracy provided), and he forsook any pretense to unity by plunging into the arena, grappling with the Jefferson-Madison faction over states' rights, freedom of the press, and neutrality in the European wars. Thereafter, the president would always be seen as part of the calculating rabble—first among public men, to be sure, but a politician nonetheless.

———

In 1800 President Adams's household and office were transplanted to the new capital city on the banks of the Potomac. For the next century, the physical dimensions of the presidency, as well as many of the intangible elements of the image of national leadership, would be shaped by the gradual design and construction of Washington, D.C. The capital was assembled stone by stone in a succession of official as well as commercial architectural endeavors, but its significance as the seat of political culture was built through social events. Thus was created "Washington society," a weirdly artificial and seasonal phenomenon which nevertheless became an essential medium of communication for politicians, a forum for the development of political alliances and power. The physical symbol of the presidency, and the site of its social function, was the executive mansion. The evolution of the drafty, white stone house during the 1800s partially illustrated the transformation of the office. During the Democratic-Republican era the mansion began as a nearly empty and lonely pile, but it became a showcase for elite housewares and cuisines (usually European in origin). Beginning with Andrew Jackson's presidency, the mansion became the site of informal mass social occasions that welcomed common voters, as well as a glorified employment agency for the endless stream of job-seeking partisans who called on the president.

Upon his election as president in 1801, Thomas Jefferson promised a true republican revolution at the top. Jefferson was the great American philosopher of natural rights and the consent of the governed, and now he seemed poised to bring the spirit, if not the sanguinity, of France's Jacobin revolution to the presidency. The power of the office, in the view of Jefferson and his partisans, grew entirely out of the wishes of the people. For President Jefferson, as Robert Wiebe has noted, "there would be no monarchic glitter of 'birthdays, levees, processions to parliament, inauguration pomposities, etc.'" The third president held levees only on New Year's Day and the Fourth of July, and his entertainment of the diplomatic corps in Washington— which initially numbered four during his first term—was notoriously paltry. Yet wealthy citizens and congressmen strove to create a semblance of society in the village-like capital city, and gradually the foundations of Washington society were laid.[4]

Wives and other prominent women were central to this process. The widower Jefferson depended upon the wives of his associates to guide such activity, and it fell to Dolley Payne Todd Madison, spouse of the secretary of state, to establish the tone and protocol of official social events. Energetic, ebullient, and eager to achieve pride of place, Dolley Madison accompanied her husband, James, the fourth president, into the executive mansion in 1809 and proceeded to make her unofficial position into the most theatrical element of the presidency. Mrs. Madison assumed a similar position long after her husband left office. After his death in 1836 she returned to Washington and quickly earned recognition as the city's most celebrated hostess. On the occasion of her passing in 1849, President Zachary Taylor described her as the "first lady" of the federal government, coining a term that has persisted in American political life. In the 1850s and 1860s the cult of the First Lady grew in fits and starts, hindered by a succession of widower presidents and invalid or shut-in presidential wives. But its steady growth from the Dolley Madison years onward provided the presidency with much of its early theatricality. As in the monarchies of Europe, women lacked formal political power, but their influence on their husbands, arbitration of disputes regarding fashion and etiquette, and dominance of social functions helped to make the president's mansion a stage for the display of powerful men and women.[5]

The capital's growing and disputatious corps of journalists tried to implicate presidents in social disputes—rich in entertaining gender conflicts—in order to sell newspapers. Notable among these was President Andrew Jackson's vehement defense in 1829 of the honor of Peggy Eaton, a sailor's widow and the former tavern-keeping wife of his secretary of state, against the public scorn of other prominent Washington wives. Technological and political trends conspired to turn leaders of republics into widely followed exemplars of fashion and etiquette. Steamships and modern printing presses brought newspapers and women's magazines to a mass audience; the magazines, especially, popularized new trends in clothing from the urban fashion centers on both sides of the Atlantic. As parliamentary power grew across Western Europe, royal families increasingly became relegated to the role of pampered figureheads, leaders of the leisure class whom the popular press turned into arbiters of the latest styles. The reporting in the mass print media of the sexual and social antics of aristocrats and wealthy commoners helped to make them some of the first modern celebrities.[6]

The effect of these trends on US leadership is exemplified by the brief career of Julia Gardiner Tyler, who served as First Lady for less than one year. In 1844, at the age of twenty-four, Gardiner eloped to New York City with the widowed President John Tyler. After their return to Washington, Mrs. Tyler promoted herself in ways that eerily anticipated the methods of later generations of celebrities. She enlisted the *New York Herald* correspondent F. W. Thomas as her publicist, "to sound Julia's praises far and near" and to promote her as "a spirit of youth and poetry, and love, and tenderness, and riches, and celebrity, and modesty." Hardly modest were Julia Tyler's preferred term of address, "Lovely Lady Presidentress," retinue of servants, and coach pulled by six Arabian horses. As more reticent presidential wives had done, she used feminine self-presentation to advance her husband's policy goals and acted as his confidante, but in the view of the newspapers and of Washington society, her queenly theatricality overshadowed her apparent devotion to republican virtue.[7]

The early evolution of First Ladyhood best illustrates how antebellum celebrity culture began to make claims on the presidency. In the mid-nineteenth century the presidents themselves, especially those who lacked illustrious military backgrounds, were far less likely to excite the mass imagination. Andrew Jackson was a towering exception to this trend, for reasons that both transcended and exploited the journalists' new practice of creating celebrities out of politicians. A moderately successful planter and elected official in his younger years, Jackson exploited his military achievements in the War of 1812 to become an owner of vast properties (he seized massive tracts of land from the Native American groups he conquered) and a national political figure. His rise to the presidency, which included a stint as virtual dictator of the West Florida territory, resembled the ruthless career of a Caesar or di Rienzo more than that of any republican tribune. As president, in the manner of a European monarch, Jackson seemed to bend the national agenda to his passionate will, attacking entities he hated, such as the Bank of the United States and Native Americans, selectively enhancing federal power, and knitting together the Democrats into America's first national organized political party.

Traditionalists were horrified by Jackson's tone and rhetoric, and they especially feared his wild popular appeal. To Whigs, as Daniel Walker Howe has noted, Jackson's "charisma threatened the social order." Ralph Waldo Emerson wrote in his journal in 1840 that "The Best are never demoniacal or magnetic but all brutes are. The Democratic Party in this country is more magnetic than the Whig. Andrew Jackson is an eminent example of it." The twenty-nine-year-old Illinois Whig Abraham Lincoln, in his Springfield Lyceum address of 1838, similarly warned against the new havoc that charismatic, Jackson-style leaders with vaulting ambition might wreak upon the sober and mechanistic workings of republican government. "A seat in Congress, a gubernatorial or a presidential chair" would not satisfy "the family of the lion, or the tribe of the eagle," Lincoln argued; "think you these places would satisfy an Alexander, a Caesar, or a Napoleon? Never! Towering genius distains [sic] a beaten path." As Howe has shown, the American Whigs embraced the prudent and restrictive rule-writing of the Constitution's framers and clung as tenaciously as Washington and Hamilton to rituals and symbols of national unity. Their ideal America was a nation of Protestant lawyers and shopkeepers. Jackson's vivid counterexample both revived memories of bloody European dictatorships and stoked fears of an American future out of their control, in which demagogues goaded classes and nationalities to seize the corridors of power and to roam unchecked across the American continent.[8]

Other cultural and political trends, however, conspired to make mid-nineteenth-century presidents a rather docile lot. In the 1840s and 1850s slavery and expansion caused American leaders to split along sectional lines and finally to plunge the nation into secession and civil war. Partly as a result of this, and partly in reaction to Jackson's example, citizens remained deeply ambivalent about the merits of strong individual leadership. The examples of forceful executive performance provided by James K. Polk and Abraham Lincoln did not sway voters' continued preference for "leadership" that acquiesced to majority opinions in the houses of the national legislature. In its messy way Congress largely continued to set policy, thrashing out the issues of the day and passing laws. The newspapers as a result chronicled the regular doings of Congress in far greater detail than those of the president. Governing in America largely had come to represent the general desire to expand and protect commercial markets, and workaday politics—as well as its daily coverage in the papers—shared the deal-making, horse-trading, profit-oriented qualities found in business. Lofty ideals and leadership were exceptions, and often impediments, in such a political culture.[9]

The president's profile as a leader was diminished further by the two leading parties, which imposed a second, extra-constitutional framework onto American politics and government. To stand any chance of winning a national contest, a party had to cobble together a rough agreement among most, if not all, of its state organizations before its nominating convention could settle on a presidential candidate. The Democrats' requirement that two-thirds of all convention delegates approve any presidential nomination (a concession made to the South in the 1830s) made it especially difficult for any politician of strong opinions to be nominated for the presidency. The result was the "dark horse" candidate, the little-known man whose nomination was engineered by the party factions because they found him to be the least disagreeable option. The cult of the dark horse, also known as the "available man," began with the Democrats' nomination in 1844 of James K. Polk (who went on to defeat the much better-known Henry Clay), and it held sway for the rest of the century. The parties were at the height of their influence, effectively transforming millions of adult white males into voters—occasionally through corrupt practices, but usually through persuasion, parades, rallies, and the forms of indoctrination that persuaded men that they belonged to a large and great cause.[10] As a result of these cultural dynamics, for most of the nineteenth century the character and the deeds of the man at the top of the ticket proved far less consequential than they had been in Washington's day.

The alignment of these political trends with the manufacture of celebrity in the mass media, in the view of the presidential descendant and historian Henry Adams, resulted in the glorification of increasingly ordinary and unremarkable White House aspirants. The available man bore little resemblance to his grandfather and great-grandfather, John Quincy Adams and John Adams, or to Washington or Jefferson. Ulysses S. Grant, he observed, "was archaic and should have lived in a cave and worn skins. . . . That, two thousand years after Alexander the Great and Julius Caesar, a man like Grant should be called—and should actually and truly be—the highest product of the most advanced evolution, made evolution ludicrous." In his novel *Democracy,* the product of fifteen years of observation of Gilded Age Washington, Adams parodied conventional images of the president in a scene depicting a White House reception: "Two seemingly mechanical figures, which might be wood or wax. . . . The President and his wife . . . stood stiff and awkward by the door, both their faces stripped of every sign of intelligence, while the right hands of both extended themselves to the column of visitors with the mechanical action of toy dolls. . . . There they stood, automata, representatives of the society which streamed past them."[11]

The British politician and historian James Bryce, also writing in the 1880s, agreed to an extent with Adams, averring that "great men are not chosen presidents" because of political exigencies such as availability and the parties' need, created by the Electoral College, to win populous states. However, Bryce also cited the limited nature of the president's constitutional duties and tendencies in the national culture. "A president need not be a man of brilliant intellectual gifts. . . . Four-fifths of his work is the same in kind as that which devolves on the chairman of a commercial company or the manager of a railway, the work of choosing good subordinates, seeing that they attend to their business, and taking a sound practical view of such administrative questions as require his decision. Firmness, common sense, and most of all, honesty, an honesty above all suspicion of personal interest, are the qualities which the country chiefly needs in its chief magistrate." Bryce was far more approving of Ulysses S. Grant than Henry Adams had been, and today we can appreciate to some extent the merits of the Gilded Age construction of the presidency. During that era, in fact, the parties did a reasonably good job of insulating presidential nominees from the rampant corruption afflicting politics, choosing for the most part men from their ranks who conformed as closely as possible to an ideal of honesty. Recent biographers of Rutherford B. Hayes and Benjamin Harrison in particular put forth this favorable analysis, celebrating the fact that these presidents' ordinariness was coupled with their determination in office to do a minimum of civic harm.[12]

Similarly, it might be argued that Adams's dismissive portrayal of the president as an automaton was accurate but incomplete. The robotic blandness of the fictional chief executive in *Democracy* may have been reflective of a real-life defensive mechanism, developed by presidents over the decades, which protected them from the crush of office seekers and numerous others who sought the chief executive's hand and attention. At a human level, such mechanical behavior was the president's strategy to preserve himself against the onslaught of a populace that held unrealistic expectations. By the late nineteenth century, presidents adopted a public mask that expressed little of Washington's heroic virtue or Jefferson's republican simplicity. The mask instead symbolized the president's withdrawal in public settings from meaningful contact with other human beings. The journalist William Allen White, for example, recalled tellingly that William McKinley, the last president of the century, "became galvanized with a certain coating of publicity. He lost his private life and his private view. . . . He became as one 'affected by public use.' He walked among men a bronze statue, for thirty years determinedly looking for his pedestal."[13]

As the twentieth century dawned, the fragile republic sired by George Washington and his compatriots had survived disunion and civil war and now thrived as a continental power. The United States was becoming an international leader in industry, technology, and the production of wealth. In the process of this evolution Washington's office had undergone a curious metamorphosis. The nation which the president protected and defended now possessed vast power and wealth, and it was poised to gain much more. In certain cases the chief executive had proven willing to use his office boldly to advance the nation's fortunes. Jackson and Lincoln used the force of their personality and intellect and exploited national crises to exercise truly powerful presidential leadership. The presidency itself bestowed a certain gravity on even its meekest incumbents. In the early 1800s, when private fortunes were insubstantial, the office and the executive mansion conferred a measure of majesty on their occupants. Politics and precedent, though, generally minimized the chief executive's political influence. Voters, as well as most presidents themselves, perceived the office as a check on the recklessness and ambitions of Congress and an embodiment of republican virtues that made government pleasingly weak.

In spite of these trends—or perhaps because of them—presidents in the 1800s, like First Ladies, were increasingly perceived as celebrities, as famous for their social life and fashion as for their official duties. Like Western European monarchs in these increasingly democratic and parliamentary times, US presidents were cloaked in the often-criticized but ever-expanding mantle of public fame. Julia Gardiner Tyler, a short-tenured First Lady who is barely remembered today, approached publicity, fashion, and self-promotion in ways that, more than a century after her time in the White House, have become commonplace methods of presidential image making. "Celebrity," the Oxford English Dictionary tells us, emerged as a common term in the 1830s, as lithography mass-reproduced images of leaders and tastemakers. The business of promoting celebrities, and of profiting from their fame, was becoming a large one. The renown of political leaders in the Old World, as Leo Braudy has shown, preceded mere celebrity by millennia.

Some traditional monarchical and military trappings of fame had accrued to the US presidency. Now, though, the mass public's thirst for the more cosmetic, sartorial, and literally theatrical fame that constituted modern celebrity shaped perceptions of occupants of the office.[14]

————

The theatrical profession helped to drive the growth of the celebrity promotion industry, and it also benefited magnificently from it. Increasingly during the nineteenth century, US presidents both great and small would be attracted to the imagery, the fame, the excitement, and the narrative power that inhered in the world of theatrical make-believe. This attraction set an important precedent for public figures in the next century who would interact with the movies.

Theater evolved slowly at first from meager origins in the thirteen colonies, mostly due to the censorious attitudes of Puritans and Quakers. North of the Potomac, theatrical performances in the 1700s were regularly banned on the grounds that they were a threat to public morality. Nevertheless, as Jay Fliegelman and Timothy Raphael have shown, the drama inherent in Americans' expansion across a continent and in their revolt against the crown and establishment of a modern republic inspired them to think about themselves more theatrically—to adopt the Shakespearean concept (which actually dated back to ancient Greece) that all the world was a stage.[15]

The dramatic events of independence and revolution, set against the impressive backdrop of the wild "new" continent, inspired the first presidents to make theatrical analogies. When he resigned from the Army in 1783, Washington wrote that "The Citizens of America. . . . are from this period to be considered as actors on a most conspicuous Theatre, which seems to be peculiarly designed by Providence for the display of human greatness and felicity." "The Declaration of Independence," John Adams confessed to Benjamin Rush, "I always considered a theatrical show" in which "[Thomas] Jefferson ran away with all the stage effect . . . and all the glory of it." Washington's early exposure to the stage (in Barbados in 1751), as well as Adams's frequent playgoing during his diplomatic missions to France and Britain, helped to explain such language, as did the concern they shared with other Enlightenment thinkers about the need for public figures to display natural authenticity. As Jay Fliegelman has argued, the naturalistic revolution in stage acting led by the British performer David Garrick in the late 1700s had a direct analogue in the deliberately plain public speaking of revolutionary orators such as Patrick Henry—whose mysterious power over crowds stunned and worried Thomas Jefferson—and the conscious plainspokenness of Benjamin Franklin, Thomas Paine, and Jefferson himself. Fliegelman notes significantly that the Declaration of Independence was composed by the latter to be declared orally, and that declamatory pauses were inserted in prints to assist public speakers.[16]

In the early national period, elites in most cities became more permissive toward the theater, and some of them spoke in favor of official, national dramatic institutions. As Thomas Bogar's exhaustive survey shows, virtually every American president attended the theater at some time in his life. Some evangelical Christians, such as James K. Polk, objected on moral grounds to stage performances and rarely witnessed them, but these men were exceptions. The Adamses were particularly fond of the stage. John and Abigail Adams frequently attended plays during their years in Paris and London, and their daughter Nabby entered into a short-lived engagement to Royall Tyler, author of *The Contrast,* the first successful play produced in the new nation. Nabby's brother John Quincy Adams was perhaps the most dedicated playgoer, and certainly the most prolific amateur theater critic, of all US presidents.[17]

Much of this play attendance by political luminaries, of course, can be classified as leisure activity that was typical of white Americans of their particular classes and eras, of no more political significance than their daily diets or other leisure habits. Nevertheless, much presidential playgoing in the nineteenth century was shaped by the particular fortunes of the theatrical industry in Washington, D.C. Although many early theaters in the capital failed and closed, the industry gradually became enmeshed in the city's social scene. Washington theaters increasingly became sites at which chief executives presented themselves to the public; and, beginning especially in the 1830s, the workings of the new celebrity culture began to bring presidents and stage performers together more frequently and to interweave their public functions more tightly.

Just as President John Tyler's second wife Julia had originated many aspects of First Ladyhood, the first "accidental" president (achieving the office upon the death of his predecessor) was also a pioneer in associating the presidency intimately with the theater. Shortly before Tyler became president, his son Robert married the New York actress Priscilla Cooper, who had taken to the stage as an adolescent to support her family during the depression of 1837. When her father-in-law took office in 1841, Priscilla Cooper Tyler became the "presidentress" or official hostess in the mansion, filling in for Tyler's ailing first wife Letitia. Priscilla Tyler's acting career ended, but she applied the skills of self-presentation and social interaction she had learned onstage to her official social duties. Her efforts, as well as those of Julia Gardiner Tyler (who succeeded Priscilla as hostess upon her marriage to the widowed president), were strongly motivated by the need to curry favor with Congress, to enhance John Tyler's fragile legitimacy as the first accidental president. Washington "society," including would-be and future presidents in the political ranks, took note of the amalgamation of the presidency and the theater through Priscilla Cooper Tyler and of Julia Gardiner Tyler's monarchical pretensions.[18]

In the antebellum era, in addition, famed performers began the practice of making calls on the president. Fanny Kemble, the British actress who married a politically well-connected southern planter, initiated the trend when she visited Andrew Jackson in Washington in 1833. The opening of the new National Theatre in Washington in 1835, which first established the capital city as an important stop for touring theatrical troupes, made social calls paid by actors to presidents a regular occurrence. As the Robert Tyler–Priscilla Cooper marriage indicated, the occasional social mingling of presidential relations with acting folk also attracted the latter to the president's house. Robert Tyler was preceded in this sense by John Van Buren, the son of President Martin Van Buren, who in 1840 escorted the Austrian dancer Fanny Elssler from New York to Washington. Her entire tour—which introduced ballet dancing (and, provocatively, female legs encased in tights) to the United States—caused a popular sensation, as did her call upon the president at his residence.

Fraternization between political and theatrical denizens reflected the emergence of greater similarities between these two very public and prominent occupations. Politicians and actors shared the heritage of naturalistic speech that emerged in both their arenas during the revolutionary age, and now, in the mid-1800s, each profession was required to publicize itself in the mass media and to court coverage in the newspapers. Also, in what was largely a coincidence, actors and politicians began to mingle during the same years in which the modern spoils system and machine politics generally reduced the moral reputation of politicians. Falling from Washingtonian heights of civic virtue, elected officials increasingly found themselves likened to the morally disreputable. Performers had traditionally been disdained by clerics and other elites for their nomadic employment, professional involvement in fantasy and fiction, and alleged disdain for a stable family life. The result, these critics alleged, was a profession dedicated to immorality. In similar fashion the highly partisan US press mercilessly attacked the purported moral failings of political leaders, such as Martin Van Buren's love of domestic luxury, Henry Clay's vanity, and Daniel Webster's greed.

Perhaps as a reaction to this opprobrium, presidents in the mid-nineteenth century were far more willing to welcome musical performers than dramatic actors to the executive mansion. Jenny Lind, the pianists "Blind Tom" Bethune and Teresa Carreño, and other musicians who called or performed at the mansion benefited from the fact that classical music had received the stamp of genteel approval quite early from organized elite philanthropists (who withheld kind words for the theater until the decades following the Civil War).[19] The fact that the theater remained a purely commercial enterprise, which elites felt pandered to the low tastes of the masses, helped to ensure that actors as a group were seen as problematic companions for presidents, who as we have seen were expected to transcend the moral depravity of less exalted politicians.

Gilded Age presidents did not seek out actors for coaching in oratorical skills. Before the Civil War, elite politicians (or those, such as Lincoln, who aspired to join the elite) had made a study of classical oratory, while the plainspoken tradition exemplified by Patrick Henry continued to find favor in the culture of Jacksonian democracy. Generally without the aid of professional actors, politicians made nineteenth-century America a hotbed of entertaining, lengthy, and emotive public speech. Such oratory was celebrated for its power to persuade audiences. Like the ancient Greeks, American neoclassicists such as Edward Everett wrote appreciations of both the intellectual power of oratory and its dangerous ability to sway listeners with illogical passion. Throughout the history of oratory, actors have occasionally coached public men in effective gestures and vocal techniques. Cicero was aided by the actors and writers Roscius and Aesop. During the French Revolution, performers dabbled in politics by delivering addresses from soapboxes, and Napoleon Bonaparte received coaching in oratory from his friend, the noted actor François-Joseph Talma. In Washington, D.C., famed orators such as Daniel Webster apparently did not often avail themselves of coaching by actors, but they studied the history and lore of political oratory and proved so compelling, in the halls of Congress and elsewhere, that professional actors were said to consider them competitors.[20]

For the rest of the nineteenth century, some US presidents sought to master various speaking skills and the tricks of the best political orators. Generally, though, cultural preferences conspired to render presidents mute in public. George Washington's statuesque appearances before crowds led him to make only the briefest of remarks, and for a century after Jefferson's uncomfortable efforts in the well of the Congress, no president would appear before the legislative branch to speak. Presidents almost never campaigned for themselves, and aside from their inaugural addresses, they largely confined public speaking to innocuous opening remarks on ceremonial occasions and canned responses to gatherings outside on the mansion lawn.

The president, in fact, had no constitutional duty to speak before anyone. In a seeming act of revenge against the oratorical zest of the Revolution, Article II largely envisioned the president as an administrator sitting at a desk, and that is what the nineteenth-century chief executive largely became. There is some merit to this bureaucratic concept of the office. As Arthur Schlesinger Jr. has noted, the impact of oratory in these years was overrated both by observers and by future historians.[21] Listeners in the 1800s admired and were transported by brilliant speaking, but in the halls of government plain talk and skillful politicking proved far more effective in achieving goals. Oratory thus was allied with the theater in providing transcendent, often inspiring emotional entertainment to grateful audiences, while the president's official duties were divorced in the public mind from such entertainment.

While the president rarely behaved theatrically, the echoes of royal pageantry in the image of the executive, coupled with the nascent celebrity status and high-society membership he enjoyed by virtue of his office, kept presidents in a quasi-theatrical limelight. This was most evident on the rare occasions when they embarked on extended tours of the nation. James Monroe and every antebellum president from Andrew Jackson to Franklin Pierce followed in Washington's carriage tracks—which were eventually lined with railroad tracks—embarking on long trips that they justified for a variety of administrative and political reasons (although only Monroe, Jackson, and Tyler made "official" national tours). As Richard Ellis has noted in his study of presidential travel, republican-minded Americans criticized the increasing levels of ceremony attached to these trips, but "a funny thing happened on the way to the modern presidency. The monarchical side of the presidency proved remarkably resilient. Just as pomp and ceremony did not in fact give way to republican simplicity, so the ideal of a president above party survived even after the nation accepted that parties and partisanship were necessary to democracy." Lacking broadcast media, Americans strained to see the leader in the flesh, gathering in enormous crowds at his appearances. Two hundred thousand New York City residents turned out to greet Jackson, and Tyler was welcomed by a similar vast audience. Fifty thousand welcomed Jackson in Philadelphia, and nearly ten thousand citizens met Zachary Taylor in Lancaster, Pennsylvania.[22]

These appearances before huge crowds held the potential of transforming the nature of the presidency. In willing hands, such events might encourage a chief executive to sway popular passions, perhaps through the exploitation of the histrionic techniques used by stage actors. The potential that such a possible "theatrical presidency" might be used to poison the nation's political life was a central and long-held concern of the most sensitive, complex, and visionary president of the nineteenth century—a man who, in a terrible irony, was robbed of his life in a theater. Abraham Lincoln's persistent interest in the theater as a spectator and his fascination with the psychological motivations of certain dramatic characters were harbingers of cultural trends that would typify American political culture in the movie-dominated twentieth century, decades after his death.

Unlike privileged predecessors such as John Quincy Adams, Lincoln came to playgoing late in life, and he made the vast majority of his trips to the theater during his years as president. As a young man in Illinois, he had already keenly read Shakespeare's plays and studied classical oratory. While he relied as much as any other politician on backroom and boardinghouse talk to advance his career, Lincoln was the rare aspirant to high office who also regularly gambled on painstakingly prepared and rehearsed addresses. At the same time, he had a rich introspective life of which only his closest male friends were aware. He wrote poetry about madness and isolation on the prairie, pondered the defects of organized religion, and struggled regularly with bouts of depression. As we have seen, Lincoln began his oratorical career with a meditation in 1838 on the threat posed to democracy by leaders possessing boundless ambition, but he himself spent the next twenty years stoking his own enormous drive for success, in the face of numerous failures and obstacles. Ever since George Washington had struggled as a young man to master his volcanic temper and strike the pose of the immovable warrior, and Andrew Jackson had allowed his personal hatreds to dictate many of his policies, the struggle of leaders to maintain self-control brought an inherently dramatic or theatrical subtext to American political life. Lincoln was fascinated by this, and after a long career drought, he rose quickly and was given the chance to wield unprecedented presidential power—including military might that dwarfed the fears of earlier generations.

In addition, Lincoln proved to be a canny student of the new currents of celebrity and theatricality in mid-nineteenth-century America. His wife shared in this skill. Mary Todd Lincoln was instrumental in assisting her husband's political rise, through the usual social venues available to wives in that era. As First Lady, she reintroduced the social flamboyance of Dolley Madison and Julia Tyler to the executive mansion after a period of relative torpor. Courting journalists and spending lavishly on interior decorating, Mary Lincoln reasserted the First Lady's role as an outsized paragon of Victorian female domesticity. Her husband, of course, realized his ultimate career ambition at the cost of the dissolution of the nation itself—a tragic irony that could not have been lost on this devotee of Shakespeare. As Thomas Bogar notes, though, despite wartime conditions that rocked the capital throughout his term, Lincoln's patronage of musical and theatrical entertainment was not dissimilar from that of previous presidents.[23] Moreover, the war swelled Washington's population, and government spending inflated local incomes and bank coffers. The result was an expansion of theatrical and musical activity in the city.

Abraham Lincoln's engagement in the theater as president illustrated both his desperate need to escape from the pressures of office and his introspective exploration, through reading and theatrical attendance, of themes in the great tragedies. Both Lincoln's leisure reading and his playgoing were heavily weighted toward the humorous, a preference that reflected his own winning facility at telling jokes and entertaining stories (a legacy of a frontier heritage that differentiated him from all of his predecessors). Humor helped Lincoln combat his melancholia, and as his friends in Washington observed, time in the theater box allowed him to be alone. While on many evenings Lincoln was too exhausted even to follow the action on stage, he nevertheless cherished opportunities to hide in the dark, away from the relentless stream of office seekers and war news.

Among friends in the executive mansion, Lincoln revealed his fascination with playacting and Shakespeare. The artist Francis Carpenter memorably recorded how the president recited soliloquies with dramatic skill and offered perceptive criticisms of some actors' approaches to these speeches. Carpenter also related Lincoln's preferences in Shakespeare, most tellingly his fascination with depraved and destructive leaders such as Richard III, Macbeth, and Claudius of Denmark (as well as Cardinal Richelieu, the subject of one of Lincoln's favorite contemporary plays). In these craven figures, it seemed, Lincoln kept returning to the theme of reckless ambition that had animated him throughout his political career. We can assume that Shakespeare's recurring invocation of the blood spilled through the designs of these tyrants made an impression on Lincoln, who regularly watched cartloads of maimed soldiers coming down Pennsylvania Avenue and met convalescents lying in the East Room of the executive mansion. Often melodramatically, Lincoln told acquaintances that the burdens of the war were consuming him, and he described to them dreams that foretold of his death or departure across a stormy sea. The biblical cadences of Lincoln's late public statements were matched by his growing sense of his own martyrdom for the cause, on the march toward a fateful Good Friday.[24] Lincoln's remarkable self-dramatization has helped to enshrine his presidency, to the latest generation, in the annals of the neo-Shakespearean, gothic romantic imagination of the mid-nineteenth century. Not incidentally, though, it also worked theatricality more deeply into the cultural grain of the US presidency.

The final scene of the Lincoln drama contains more irony than any self-respecting playwright would have committed to paper. John Wilkes Booth's father, the great British-born actor Junius Brutus Booth, bore an assassin's name. Junius Booth had worn out his welcome in the capital city thirty years earlier by writing a letter to President Andrew Jackson threatening his life, only weeks after Jackson had survived the first assassination attempt ever made on a US president. The Booth family, like Mary Todd Lincoln's, had split almost evenly between the Union and the Confederacy. The Lincolns were fans (to use an anachronistic but entirely appropriate term) of Junius's celebrated acting sons, Edwin, John Wilkes, and Junius Jr. During the war, Edwin—in the most far-fetched irony of all—saved the life of Robert Todd Lincoln when the latter nearly fell in front of a moving train at a railroad station. John Wilkes Booth's descent into infamy was driven by ideology, alcoholism, and sibling rivalry; his motives cannot be characterized as inherently theatrical, or as some kind of analogue to Lincoln's fascination with theatrical villainy. Nevertheless, he committed the deed in Ford's Theater, timed his pistol shot to coincide with the biggest laugh line in *Our American Cousin,* and brought down the curtain himself from the stage, breaking his leg in the process. To the Founders, the American Revolution was metaphorical theater; the war to repair the Union now ended with an actual bloody deed in a real theater. The assassin yearned for good publicity. He left behind an apologia for the newspapers, and during his flight from justice he wrote in his diary, "I struck boldly, and not as the papers say."[25]

Even though all would-be regicides seem to thirst for the maximum amount of fame that they could earn in their place and time, the peculiar capacity of the Lincoln assassination to meld the worlds of politics and entertainment would not be matched until the attempt on President Ronald Reagan's life more than a century later. In the long run, the incident in Ford's Theater disrupted, but did not derail, the social bonding of presidents and actors. As Benjamin McArthur has shown in his study of actors in American culture, the decades after the Civil War saw the most intensive effort to date by leading performers to enhance the reputation and the prestige of their profession. Male actors indicated the seriousness of their endeavor by largely excluding (allegedly disreputable) actresses from their social climbing. They bonded with politicians, businessmen, and male writers in

masculine enclaves such as the saloon and the private club. In the 1880s
Joseph Jefferson, beloved for his stage portrayal of Rip Van Winkle, went
fishing with President Grover Cleveland during their vacations at Buzzards
Bay, Massachusetts, and Cleveland also befriended William J. Florence, who
like Jefferson was best known for his comic roles.

Central to this effort to enhance actors' social reputation was Edwin
Booth. Booth counteracted his many family misfortunes by achieving a brilliant career in tragic stage roles and by thoughtfully championing the virtues
of professional performers. Lamenting that actors were perceived as "a set
of mere vain, selfish, brainless idiots" addicted to "happy-go-lucky, Bohe-
mian habits," Booth promoted moral paragons in their ranks and encouraged all performers to become respectable citizens of the republic. In 1888
he established a new men's club, The Players, in his home in Manhattan's
Gramercy Park, for the purpose of cultivating "frequent intercourse with
gentlemen of other arts and professions, who love the stage and appreciate
the value of the drama as an aid to intellectual culture." Nontheatrical char-
ter members of The Players included the New York politicians Abram
Hewitt and Chauncey Depew, as well as William Tecumseh Sherman, Mark
Twain, and John Singer Sargent; Grover Cleveland later joined as well. As
Benjamin McArthur notes, The Players replicated earlier efforts by actors
(such London's Garrick Club) and men of letters to integrate themselves
with influential public officials and businessmen.[26]

The founding of The Players also symbolized the entry of some American
actors into big business. By 1888 Augustin Daly, Edwin Booth's longtime
manager, was the wealthy owner of a "combination" company, a prestigious
concern that mounted dignified touring repertory productions. For the top
dramatic performers, the theater had become a rationalized big business.
The "well-made plays" of Clyde Fitch and others codified a formula for successful stage writing; Broadway in New York City became the thriving center
of all theatrical arts; Wall Street invested in the leading companies; and the
railroads brought the combinations to cities and towns across America. Just
as a nascent brand of "realism" brought more true-to-life themes to new
plays and commonplace mannerisms to acting, a hard-headed attention to
the bottom line characterized the most successful theatrical concerns.[27]

———

Entertainment, in short, became big business in the late 1800s. Theatrical producers had to secure substantial capital and good connections, but if they succeeded in the national market, the potential profits were unprecedented. The industrial employment market gradually increased the average worker's free time and discretionary spending, setting the stage for the consumer-driven national market of the twentieth century. Technology began to change show business as well; Edwin Booth was among the first American actors to record his recitations on Edison wax cylinders. Entertainment took part in the transformation of American culture in the industrial age. Henry Adams, disappointed for so long by the apparent decline in the mentality and forti-tude of human leadership, was staggered and awed by the power of electricity and new technology to rule modern life—forces that, in his view, had over-thrown Christianity as the guiding principle of Western civilization. Old-stock Americans found their country fundamentally transformed by millions of newly arrived Catholic, Jewish, and other non-Anglo-Saxon immigrants. The United States' ethnicity and complexion—as well as its technology, faith, and average wealth—were undergoing revolutionary changes.

The complexion of show business was also changing. Far beneath The Players and the president's social circle on the American status hierarchy, humble new entertainment businesses were thriving, in urban dance halls, saloons, and amusement parks. Massive new immigration and Gilded Age wealth, in combination, nurtured unprecedented entrepreneurial forces among the urban working classes, who sought a share of the riches that the new consumer society seemed to promise. The working and immigrant classes' thirst for the good life, simply put, would become an elemental force in both the politics and the entertainment business of the twentieth century. Upward class mobility in America would carry poor young people into pros-perous careers as politicians and performers; such mobility also would be central to the plots of countless new dramatic presentations. Politicians sought votes by pledging to enhance the American Dream, as it came to be called, for all. These trends, coupled with ongoing innovations in communications and other technology, obscured nineteenth-century perceptions of politi-cal theatricality and changed the scale, tone, and reach of the interactions between politicians and entertainers. In short, these changes paved the way for the movies and for a cinematic image of American politicians.

This transformation was best illustrated by the alliance that grew up in New York City between Tammany Hall and Broadway. In the mid-1800s, political ward heelers and entertainment entrepreneurs alike toiled to win the allegiance of the average people in New York's streets and tenements. Saloons were among the most important gathering places for Tammany Hall operatives, as they urged workers on break to vote for the Democratic ticket in return for social services, extra income, and a sense of belonging to the American electorate. Some of these sites were converted into concert saloons, where song-and-dance acts entertained customers close to their tables. In some instances, concert saloons were also Tammany Hall club-houses, headquarters for the ward bosses who owned or leased the saloons and profited from their operation. Henry Miner, the Tammany leader in the Bowery in the 1880s, was the owner of five early vaudeville houses, and Miner passed on both his post and his knowledge of show business to Timothy "Big Tim" Sullivan, who became the most influential and wealthiest patron of popular theater in Tammany Hall.

Sullivan's clubhouse in the Bowery presented regular entertainment and served as the meeting point of politicians, businessmen, and gamblers. While Sullivan pursued a respectable political career that put him in the state legislature and the US House of Representatives, he was also Tammany's most effective racketeer, controlling gambling and prostitution across a wide swath of Manhattan. Racketeers were Jewish and Italian as well as Irish, and their illegal activity complemented Tammany's efforts to attract these ethnic groups to the Democratic ticket. As the historian Daniel Czitrom has argued, "Sullivan hitched electoral politics to the commercial flash of the Bowery."[28] Sullivan also employed singers and dancers in his clubhouse, invested in Broadway revues, and fathered illegitimate children by actresses in his acquaintance. Sullivan's headquarters was a key meeting place for show-business people; here they struck deals and gave performers their first breaks on the New York stage. James J. Walker, an indifferent young law student who frequented the clubhouse, parlayed his contacts into a steady career as a Tin Pan Alley song lyricist. Years later, Walker was elected a Tammany mayor of New York.

At the turn of the century, as New York City gained new prominence as the capital of popular entertainment, the working-class origins and nouveau riche wealth found on Broadway helped to set the tone of both urban entertainment and politics. Jimmy Walker was only one of the Tammany politicians who shared Tim Sullivan's theatrical style and bluster. Before he became a Tammany operative, governor of New York, and presidential candidate, Alfred E. Smith pursued a dramatic career in the small playhouses of the Lower East Side, specializing in playing villains. A politician's ability to sing to a crowd, relate the latest vaudeville routine, or shift from the stage brogue of one ethnic group to that of another were highly valuable in city vote-getting efforts (in which the oratory was decidedly nonclassical in nature, but no less important than in other American settings). Even the Republican anti-Tammany crusader Fiorello H. La Guardia, who was first elected to office in the 1910s, relied on his background as a musician in his father's military band to hone a theatrical speaking style, which he used to campaign in at least five different languages.

From the same streets emerged the Jewish retail merchants who pioneered the founding of nickelodeons, moving picture viewing rooms, and movie studios in New York City. Men such as Samuel Goldwyn, Adolph Zukor, William Fox, and Carl Laemmle mated the symbiosis of street politics and street entertainment with a new medium of communication. It was not coincidental that virtually the first motion picture biography made of a politician, filmed in the Bowery and released in 1914, about a year after the subject's death, was *The Life of Big Tim Sullivan; or, From Newsboy to Senator.*[29]

———

In the early twentieth century, the new energy of the urban masses, expressed in many genres of popular entertainment, helped to shape the behavior and communication methods of politicians far beyond Tammany Hall. At the presidential level, the spirit (if not the substance) of vaudeville, ragtime, and the nickelodeon shaped the self-presentation of a group of presidents who prided themselves on restoring virtue and good government to Washington: the progressives Theodore Roosevelt and Woodrow Wilson, and, to a lesser extent, the conservative William Howard Taft.

The progressive movement has often been represented as the antithesis of the roistering urban culture of the new immigrants. Progressives, largely middle-class Americans of British stock, did battle with political machines and attempted to "Americanize" immigrants by making them conform to Anglo-Saxon behavior and values. Similarly, progressives' roots in the professionalization movement of the late nineteenth century—which sought to impose rational methods and university credentials on the law, medicine, business, and government (among other fields)—qualified them as the heirs of Jefferson and other advocates of republican virtue and sobriety. The progressives were a diverse lot. Their ranks included prohibitionists; moralists (Jewish and Catholic as well as Protestant) who campaigned against the theater, the amusement park, and the nickelodeon; businesspeople who promoted regulation and efficiency over pure market competition; suffragists who support the vote for women but opposed legal birth control; and reformers who found social salvation in western European–style, bureaucratic social democracy.[30]

The wildly popular Chautauqua lecture circuit, which brought week-long tent events to small towns and millions of spectators every year, might be characterized as a cultural wing of the progressive movement. White Protestant Chautauquans kept alive the Puritan disdain for the theater by characterizing their tent platform performances as educational or spontaneous "readings" or "elocution." Chautauqua events thus were allied more with political oratory and classroom instruction than with the theater, turning political and educational speeches into a sober and substantive kind of live "entertainment."[31]

Yet, especially in larger cities, progressives were also children of their times, subject to the pull of the new tolerance and intimacy of urban life. Like immigrant workers, they too were exposed to modern new behavior, ideas, and sentiments. Young middle-class white women might still aspire to marriage and motherhood, but they were also newly athletic and college-educated, and roaming freely on city streets. Politicians, social scientists, and social workers might have been raised on farms according to the strictures of the county parish, but their professions brought them into the city, where old values were eroded by a new tolerance and by ethnic and religious diversity. So, too, despite their trademark Protestant moralism and occasional stance against city amusements, progressives inherited the tradition of American political theatricality. Influenced by the fast-paced and varied new culture of the early twentieth century, they also made their own revisions to the tradition.

A leading national progressive politician, Theodore Roosevelt embodied the paradoxes of the movement and projected its curious blend of moralizing and theatricality more fully than any other individual. Arriving at the White House—a designation for the mansion he made official while in office—from a station of wealth and high class, Roosevelt was on a trajectory that was the opposite of Abraham Lincoln's steady rise from poverty. Nevertheless, as Leo Braudy has argued, TR was the first president since Lincoln to infuse the presidency with cultural significance. As a result he became the first president to be aware of and responsive to dynamic new trends in entertainment. He also reinterpreted both the republican and the monarchical aspects of the presidency in light of these trends.

As a very moralistic Protestant, Roosevelt had little use for the informal masculine affinities that had brought recent political figures into social contact with entertainers, either at Grover Cleveland's cabin on Buzzards Bay or at Big Tim Sullivan's clubhouse in Manhattan. Roosevelt had theatrical acquaintances, but they did not occupy a prominent place in the large crowd of people from all fields that he cultivated. He did not smoke and rarely drank, and excepting his passionate interest in literary fantasy (and the rare whimsical play such as *Peter Pan*), his social and artistic excursions were almost always by-products of his political and literary activities. (He was the most prolific author ever to become president.) Roosevelt famously indulged in bruising "masculine" sports and pastimes, but he rejected the passive spectatorship of the theater or the sporting park, possessing, in Edward Wagenknecht's words, "a William James–like sense of the dangers of stimulation without expression." TR moralistically condemned the sedentary passivity of spectators that increasingly characterized the new US mass culture.

These qualities showed Roosevelt taking a critical and revisionist stance against complacency old and new. While he disapproved of some new trends, such as spectatorship, he vigorously embraced many dynamic new tendencies in American life. When we explore how Roosevelt changed the behavior of the presidency—and he did more to change it than virtually any other occupant of the office—his representativeness in the new twentieth-century culture becomes more highly defined. Despite his filiopietism and boasts of adhering to a warrior's ancient code of conduct, he absorbed modernity more fully than any of his predecessors, in part simply by having been born late (in 1858) and coming of age entirely during the factory era. While Roosevelt would later disparage spectatorship at both motion pictures and sporting events, he was probably the first future president ever to watch a movie, viewing in 1897 Thomas Edison's kinetoscope restaging of the Corbett–Fitzsimmons championship fight. After he left the White House, during World War I, Roosevelt effected a rapprochement with motion pictures by serving as an adviser to the pro-preparedness feature film *The Battle-Cry of Peace,* produced by a neighbor in Oyster Bay, New York. TR disparaged the telephone, but he was the first president to travel by submarine, to visit another country, and to ride regularly in an automobile, and after he left office he became the first chief executive to fly in an airplane.[32]

Roosevelt also revolutionized the president's political role. He took the lead in addressing domestic political issues. He was the first president to confide in newspaper reporters (speaking off the record) and to persuade editors to print headlines and stories that advanced his interests. TR possessed an almost instinctive grasp of how to use publicity to advance his career. As a young man working on a Dakota ranch in the mid-1880s, he recreated for a photographer the moment on the prairie when, after a lengthy pursuit, he apprehended a couple of rowboat thieves and held them captive at gunpoint. As Karen Russell and Carl Bishop have shown, the modern concept of "publicity" emerged in the United States exactly during TR's formative years in politics. In 1896, for example, the *New York Times* reported that Democratic presidential candidate William Jennings Bryan (who was even younger than Roosevelt) sought out "his old college chum, Will Block," a publicist for a theatrical company, to join his campaign as a press agent. The Republican-leaning *Times* mocked Bryan for being "familiar with the duties of a press agent, which is to construct all sorts of tales that will keep the star well in the public mind."[33] As president, Theodore Roosevelt popularized the term "publicity" in its more traditional meaning, with reference to bringing secrets of industrial combination out into public scrutiny, but his trust-busting activism served as the culmination of his self-publicizing in the political arena. (Ironically, trust-busting also stimulated the growth of the first sophisticated public relations efforts by American corporations, which hoped to improve their images in the wake of TR's lawsuits.)

Most vividly, Roosevelt revolutionized the image of the individual in the presidency. Andrew Jackson possessed a more intimidating personality than TR, but he made little attempt to promote it himself; one has to look back to George Washington to find a president who relied as much as Roosevelt on self-presentation to maintain his legitimacy in office. Many biographers have noted TR's special qualities: his self-confidence, encyclopedic curiosity, powerful sense of noblesse oblige, hatred of all who violated his genteel moral and ethical code, and love of nature. In the context of our survey of presidential imagery, two aspects of Roosevelt's self-presentation stand out. First, his aggressive public persona was in part a response to his own deep anxiety (shared by many wealthier Americans) about the perceived effeminacy of office careers for males. TR hunted, rode horses, boxed, and fought wars, and the "bully pulpit" he fashioned out of the presidency was a highly theatrical reaction to the recent image of the president as a paunchy man sitting behind a desk. As president Roosevelt rarely seemed to be seated, and he proposed legislation, barnstormed the country, gave speeches, and otherwise strained to project an image of strenuous leadership. Millions of anxious middle-class men, fearing the onset of neurasthenia in their office-bound labors and urban enclaves, responded with visceral approval to Roosevelt's canny self-promotion.[34]

Through a mixture of instinct and calculation, TR innovated by wielding his personality as a prime political weapon. The use of "personality" as a noun, referring to the distinctive general impression created by an individual, had expanded gradually throughout the nineteenth century, but the Roosevelt years saw the arrival of personality as a topic of fascination in middle-class American culture. In those years, the first generation of psychological and career-success manuals popularized the notion that personality was "worn" by a person to define herself socially, and to an extent realistic stereotypes (both literal and metaphorical) fixed categories of people in the popular imagination. (Theater and vaudeville, which employed char-

acter actors and others who specialized in particular behavioral types, helped
to popularize this categorizing tendency as well.)

Acquaintances of TR wore out the term "personality" in describing their
impressions of him. Richard Washburn Child remarked that the president
"so crowds the room that the walls are worn thin and threaten to burst out-
ward. . . . You go to the White House, you shake hands with Roosevelt and
hear him talk—and then go home to wring the personality out of your
clothes." William Allen White "was afire with the splendor of the personality
I had met. . . . [H]e poured into my heart such visions, such ideals, such
hopes, such a new attitude toward life and patriotism and the meaning of
things, as I had never dreamed men had." Woodrow Wilson, Roosevelt's bitter political enemy, was nonetheless "charmed by his personality; there is a
sweetness about him that is very compelling. You can't resist the man." Face
to face, Roosevelt enacted a charismatic brand of leadership that seemed,
again, to harken back to the personal political appeal of a Washington or a
Jackson.[35]

Roosevelt's key innovation, though, was in marshaling his ebullient personal qualities to make himself a unique political force. As Greg Goodale
and Carol Gelderman have noted, he did this largely by turning the president once again into an industrious orator. This development epitomized
the recent revival of oratory in American political culture after a period of
decline during the Gilded Age—a revival best symbolized by William Jennings Bryan's Cross of Gold speech in 1896. As president, Roosevelt's purpose was to go over the heads of a reactionary Congress to persuade voters
to govern by plebiscite, to ratify industrial regulation, conservation, and his
other favorite programs. To achieve this end, Goodale argues, Roosevelt
rejected the "orotund" style of speaking from the nineteenth century, with
its exaggerated arm gestures and feigned facial emotions, in favor of an
"instructional" style that laid out the issues in a more controlled emotional
fashion. For decades American theatergoers had been ambivalent about the
orotund style of visiting British actors, admiring its magnetic eloquence
while despising the aristocratic condescension it seemed to express. By 1890
vaudevillians, as well as writers such as Mark Twain, were viciously parody-
ing the orotund style. Simultaneously, the Chautauqua tent shows channeled passion into the service of instructional talks on a range of topics.[36]

Theodore Roosevelt had strong personal reasons for adopting this speaking style. As a young politician, he battled working-class voters' prejudices against him as a wealthy dilettante running for office. Besides stressing his stint as a cowboy and his advocacy of manly pastimes, Roosevelt met crowds of commoners halfway by cultivating the instructional manner of speaking of new-style professionals such as college professors and Chautauqua lecturers. The fact that TR *restrained* his personality on the stump, to assert the primacy of ideas over his obvious passion, indicated the new prevalence of objectivity, professionalization, and pragmatism (in the sense of the term popularized by William James) in American culture. The new instructional speaking style introduced an element of restraint into what otherwise was a rather raucous rising tide of fame-seeking and outsized personalities in the pools of early twentieth-century celebrity culture.

———

In the 1910s and 1920s, decades that witnessed the explosive growth of the American motion picture industry, the disparate elements of political theatricality displayed in Theodore Roosevelt's presidency were amplified and became commonplace. Even trends that Roosevelt tended to avoid flourished in the rich soil of increased publicity and mass communication. Edith Carow Roosevelt was a private First Lady, but her stepdaughter Alice Roosevelt, an outspoken socialite, relished and expanded the publicity efforts involving female residents of the White House, staging events for the newspapers such as her famous, fully-clothed jump into a swimming pool in Honolulu in 1906. Nellie Taft and Ellen Wilson hoped to benefit from the intense new press interest in the First Lady, but both were stymied by serious health problems. After Ellen Wilson's death, the orgy of publicity surrounding Woodrow Wilson's courtship of Edith Bolling Galt, who became his second wife during his presidency, belatedly brought First Ladies into the orbit of modern publicity and established them as de facto arbiters of (white) female identity, thought, and style in the mass media.[37] This promotion, of course, helped to channel citizens' anxieties about the rapidly changing social position of women in the era of suffrage, birth control, and the rising average age of first marriages, just as Roosevelt's measured bluster addressed fears about the fate of contemporary masculinity in the era of the office career.

Diffident, juridical, and sedentary, William Howard Taft nevertheless
strove to give his best imitation of Theodore Roosevelt in at least one way,
by traveling often and speaking frankly (and often ill-advisedly) about current political disputes. In 1912, while campaigning for reelection, Taft was
outshone by his two major opponents, Roosevelt and Woodrow Wilson. An
academic political scientist who had devoted much of his career to the study
of presidential leadership, Wilson also theatrically created and performed a
new kind of leader's role. Listeners may have expected that Wilson, the
academic, would speak in the new instructional style that Roosevelt had
made prominent, but they were unprepared for the force and charm which
Wilson brought to his oratory as well. Even as early as 1910, when New Jersey
Democratic bosses chose Wilson as their candidate for governor, they
seemed to sense that he fit the role uncannily. Boss Bob Davis was heard to
say of Princeton's president, "How the hell do I know whether he'll make a
good governor? He will make a good candidate, and that is the only thing
that interests me." Democratic state senator Joseph P. Tumulty, an opponent of Wilson and the party machine, was converted to a supporter (and
later became a close confidant) after hearing the latter's acceptance speech:
"The personal magnetism of the man, his winning smile, so frank and so
sincere, the light of his gray eyes, the fine poise of his well-shaped head, the
beautiful rhythm of his vigorous sentences, held the men in the Convention
breathless under their mystic spell. Men all about me cried in a frenzy:
'Thank God, at last, a leader has come!'"[38]

As president, Wilson continued Roosevelt's strategy of using presidential
oratory to appeal for popular plebiscites. In fact, as Robert Kraig has argued,
Wilson "relied on oratory more than any president before him."[39] Scholarly
looking yet forceful, the president actually drew on popular oratorical models from the Chautauqua circuit and from theater and vaudeville to craft a
confident stride, winning arm gestures to the crowd, and ringing yet almost
colloquial phrasing. As president Wilson also revived the practice, dead for
a century, of appealing to Congress by speaking in person at the Capitol. His
success in 1913–1914 as an advocate of progressive legislation seemed to validate triumphantly his study of modern presidential leadership and his
exploitation of the new speaking style.

Wilson's executive effectiveness was put to a severe test when war broke out in Europe. World War I proved to be a watershed era in the development of the mass-marketed presidency, but it also threw the progressive model of leadership into confusion and decline. Beset by huge pressure from all sides over the question of joining the great conflict, Wilson pioneered the modern political campaign in his bid for reelection in 1916, employing public relations and advertising executives to craft an effective general message. The journalist George Creel figured most prominently in this group. Creel, who was married to the Broadway actress Blanche Bates, had been a flamboyant but short-lived police commissioner in Denver, and his promotional abilities caught Wilson's eye. It was Creel who crafted the president's effective and highly disingenuous 1916 campaign slogan: "He Kept Us Out of the War."

In his second term, after he quickly reversed course and led the United States into the war, Wilson recruited Creel to lead a propaganda campaign, under the guise of "educating the public," as head of the new Committee on Public Information (CPI). As Elmer Cornwell notes, Creel's dissemination of war information often involved "a general tie-in of the appeals and information with the President as national leader and prime mover in the war effort," creating a powerful image of a guiding hand in the White House.[40] The growth of American involvement in foreign affairs, initiated under Theodore Roosevelt and expanded greatly by Wilson, created a corresponding increase in the power and visibility of the presidency. The CPI's application of new advertising and public relations techniques, though, oversimplified the complexity of the war and of the peace negotiations that followed it, trapping Wilson rhetorically and robbing him of much of his power to persuade voters. The marathon series of speeches he gave across America in 1919 in favor of the Treaty of Versailles and the League of Nations demonstrated the limits of the rhetorical presidency and of his personal touch—indeed, it drove him into a full physical collapse.

———

Wilson's demise, and the simultaneous weakening of progressivism, prefigured the nature of the presidency and its public image in the 1920s. On

the one hand, George Creel and Bruce Barton extolled the virtues of advertising as the new way in which corporations could "educate" the public about
their products, and public relations specialists such as Ivy Lee (in the employ
of John D. Rockefeller) and Edward Bernays exalted their ability to change
how the masses thought about their corporate clients. In their view, public
relations mediated between corporations and citizens who could barely comprehend the complexity of modern life, and created something called "public
opinion"—the simple set of perceptions that most people could be persuaded to share. These new concepts would have a major impact on enterprising politicians. Simultaneously, the disillusionment and shell shock of
many US war veterans indicated a new crisis in American masculine identity
and purpose. Wilson's rhetorical failure and physical collapse, along with
the death of Theodore Roosevelt in 1919, created a similar crisis for the image
of the presidential leader, an image that (thanks especially to Roosevelt) had
been bound up in traditional concepts of masculinity. This crisis of the
presidential image was one that even the public relations wizards might find
difficult to resolve.

More than those of any of his predecessors, both Warren G. Harding's
election as president and his subsequent popularity were manufactured by
a comprehensive advertising campaign, financed by his promoters in big
business. When subsequent scandals completely overshadowed the ongoing
PR campaign on Harding's behalf, the president (in an ominous echo of
Wilson in 1919) seemed to lose his will to continue in office, and in 1923 he
succumbed to physical ailments. His successor, Calvin Coolidge, avoided
scandal and dialed back on the public's expectations of the presidency.
Coolidge also had the good fortune of serving during the extended economic boom of the mid-1920s, and of facing an opposition party that was
deeply divided and bereft of leadership.

But it was perhaps a third element that proved decisive in making
Coolidge a popular and successful president. The quiet New Englander
enhanced Harding's reliance on public relations techniques for his own
political benefit. After Harding, he was the second president to rely heavily
on a full-time speechwriter (Judson Welliver, later replaced by Stuart Crawford), and the flow of pronouncements coming from the White House
increased accordingly. Coolidge also expanded presidential contact with

journalists and cleverly scheduled his vacations during slow periods in the political calendar. The newspapermen appreciated both the change of scenery at carefully chosen sites such as the Black Hills and the president's curious habit of communicating freely with them. Coolidge filled slow news days with photographic opportunities that cleverly contradicted his reputation as a taciturn New Englander, showcasing him in cowboy gear, fishing waders, and an Indian headdress, and in the weight room. He also was the first president to grasp the power of radio, delivering six nationally broadcast addresses—no mean feat in the years before radio networks—in a voice that was well suited to the medium. Thus Coolidge, in Elmer Cornwell's words "the weakest of modern day weak Presidents," "did nearly as much as any of the strong Presidents of this century to bring the office to its present peak of prestige and popular deification."[41]

Calvin Coolidge was also acted upon by the forces of public relations, most evidently on October 17, 1924, when a trainload of Broadway performers visited the White House for breakfast. The visit was the idea of the public relations pioneer Edward Bernays. This brash Austrian immigrant had begun his career as an agricultural journalist, in part to please a father who ardently endorsed Theodore Roosevelt's conservationism. Drawn more to city life and to the arts, Bernays became a P. T. Barnum–style promoter of a French play, *Damaged Goods,* which shocked Americans with its frank depiction of the effects of syphilis when it arrived on Broadway in 1913. He went on to specialize in publicizing foreign artists such as the Ballets Russes and Enrico Caruso. These experiences persuaded Bernays that virtually any obscure product could be turned into a topic of general conservation, or into a household staple, through imaginative stunts that compelled consumers to perceive elements of everyday life in new ways. Thus Bernays was credited with popularizing the combination of bacon and eggs for breakfast, cigarette smoking outside the parlor, Ivory soap, and having walls of bookshelves in family rooms—credit that came above all from Bernays himself, who tirelessly promoted his own image as the founding genius of the public relations profession.[42]

The actors' breakfast with Coolidge, in Bernays's view, was a creative juxtaposition of two formerly disparate occupations in American life. "In 1924 this was a startling idea, for actors and actresses still were tainted with a 17th Century reputation," Bernays recalled, but the breakfast made compelling sense for the president's campaign, since "there was no disputing that [performers] also carried a strong connotation of humanness, warmth, extroversion and camaraderie." The publicist had passed over delegations of female novelists or well-known mothers (his initial ideas) because of this perceived association of actors with personal warmth and other good feelings. For the campaign, the stars of the stage were an antidote to the personal shortcomings of the dour president, who, Bernays claims, "recogniz[ed] the implications of this venture into imagemaking." Al Jolson, John Drew, Ed Wynn, Charlotte Greenwood, and a dozen other celebrated stage performers took the midnight train from New York, "after the curtain fell on Broadway," and were ready to visit the White House the next morning. Bernays introduced each performer to the president and Mrs. Coolidge. His payoff, he would note proudly until his death in 1995, was the stories about the event that appeared in newspapers nationwide.

Bernays's "event"—actually a non-event, or a publicity stunt—turned the White House into a set for a carefully staged tableau. Many such occasions now filled empty spots in the president's schedule. Groups posed with the chief executive in what we would now call photo opportunities, feigning camaraderie in an attempt to leverage the prestige of the office to achieve political success in the Congress. Bringing the actors to the capital city to counteract Coolidge's sour personality, Bernays himself was surprised to perceive the aura of the presidency surrounding Coolidge. "What really impressed me was the potency the office conferred on the man . . . that is what Mr. Coolidge was, a symbol of government that embodied the majesty conferred on him by millions of people." The slender Vermonter incongruously possessed some of the intimidating and elusive power wielded by the Hapsburg royalty in Bernays's native city of Vienna.[43]

The 1924 breakfast proved to be a pivotal event in Bernays's life and thought. Before then his career had been largely in the arts, and his thinking had been informed by the rich Viennese culture of ideas he had enjoyed as a child. Central to his upbringing was the intellectual influence of his uncle, Sigmund Freud, who encouraged Bernays to perceive culture in its entirety through the perspective of the mostly submerged consciousness that Freud labored to define. After 1924 Bernays increasingly worked with corporations to produce stunts, contests, and advertising designed to influence consumer behavior, persuading Americans that the trifles and novelties manufactured by his clients were indispensable staples of contemporary existence. His skills also formidably aided in the creation of entertaining events of no consequence—non-events, like the breakfast for Coolidge and the actors—which existed largely to call attention to themselves.

Bernays's successes, along with the folly of World War I, deepened his conviction that manipulation of the public was required in order for any major new trend to take hold. Business trusts, in his view, were "friendly giants and not ogres." Bernays's endorsement of corporate propaganda as a positive good probably horrified psychoanalysts, but it reflected Freud's pessimistic belief that the mind could not resist seductive suggestion. Even though there is no evidence that the 1924 White House breakfast aided in Coolidge's election, Bernays and his colleagues were persuaded that actors and presidents were similar shapers of public opinion, who could to be employed in similar ways by public relations elites. Thus it was that Bernays stage-managed Herbert Hoover just as effectively as he had Coolidge, coaching the last president of the 1920s to hit his marks properly during the half-centenary celebration of Thomas Edison's perfection of the light bulb—a celebration that Bernays himself produced at the behest of his client, the General Electric Corporation.[44]

Like Bernays, the diligent and inquisitive Hoover was highly capable of perceiving the impact of orchestrated persuasion on the mass public. In 1925, while serving as secretary of commerce, he told a convention of advertisers that they "have taken over the job of creating desire. . . . In economics *the torments of desire* in turn create demand, and from demand we create production, and thence around the cycle we land with increased standards of living." Hoover, a Quaker by birth and a mining engineer by training, hardly seemed the kind of man to indulge in (as a Lincoln or a Wilson might have) a consideration of the effect on people of irrational "torments of desire." Still, he had worked to ease the starvation of millions in wartime Europe, and at Commerce he was an almost frantic student of the exuberant new consumer economy of the 1920s. "The advertiser has full swing," Hoover argued, "in stimulating 'desire' for better food, better clothing, better shelter, entertainment and so on over the whole range of the ten thousand and

one things that go to make up superimposed layers of living standards."
Hoover's addition of entertainment to the basic necessities of life testified to
the vitality of the popular arts in the 1920s economy, and to the fact that the
secretary, like most other Americans, had come to see these arts as central
to the fabric of modern life.[45]

A popular humanitarian even before he joined the Harding cabinet in
1921, Hoover now became a celebrated promoter of consumer capitalism. As
a result, he became a tool of advertisers. His reputation as a prophet of
industrial abundance led publicists to use his words and likeness in a spate
of unauthorized ads for a wide variety of products. The Victor adding
machine thus was celebrated for "compl[ying] with the *Hoover* Standardiza-
tion Principle"; Hoover's supposed endorsement of heating oil over coal
became grist for ads for the Superior Automatic oil heater; his support of
free trade in agriculture was used to sell California figs; a New York clothing
company published an "open letter" to Hoover alongside a large portrait;
and the National Farm School pedaled an endorsement from Hoover on
ads emblazoned on the sides of city buses. His office at Commerce suppressed all but the last effort, which used an authentic Hoover quotation
from the 1910s that he could not retract.[46] More than the statue-like William
McKinley, the instinctively publicity-hungry Theodore Roosevelt, or the
public relations–savvy Woodrow Wilson and Calvin Coolidge, Hoover lived
the life of a potent symbol available for public consumption for years before
he was elected president. It was inevitable that Madison Avenue advertising
agencies played a large role in portraying Hoover as "the Great Engineer"
during the presidential campaign of 1928; even with his strong reputation,
he and his advisers felt that no opportunity for promotion or publicity
should be neglected. Nor was it a surprise, as we shall see, that President
Hoover nurtured an unprecedentedly close relationship with individuals in
the newly ascendant motion picture industry.

―――――

In the century and a half since George Washington's debut as the modern
Cincinnatus, American culture had overlaid new trappings of celebrity on its
presidents. Washington society made the chief executive and his First Lady
prime among the elites in the capital city beehive, while the political parties

turned presidents into safe and sane figureheads who existed mainly to unite splintered regional factions. Presidents sought a portion of the celebrity lime- light enjoyed by actors and other star performers, and occasionally they pon- dered the similarity of their role playing to that of the actors in the theater. As realism became a desired trademark in drama and other art forms, pragmatic attention to gritty social problems became the stock-in-trade for progressive politicians. Still, progressives such as Theodore Roosevelt and Woodrow Wil- son also betrayed an understanding of the need to use publicity techniques to build support for good-government initiatives.

The turbulence of World War I and the 1920s caused average people and elites to become more confused and more cynical, and more susceptible to the deployment and the reception of artful manipulation at the hands of public relations, advertising, and mass entertainment. Like entertainers, presidents were dependent upon public appearances and speeches and craved the approval of the masses. Equipped with an ambiguous set of constitu- tional powers and the vague trappings of republican royalty, presidents struggled to master the powerful techniques of persuasion that were sweep- ing through the culture. Those who held the office utilized its historical equipment and the new tools of public relations with varying degrees of effectiveness.

One new constant to the job after 1920 was the existence of Hollywood, a new industrial power in the US economy. Even in the face of the Great Depression and World War II, the movies' powerful projection of fantasies of social and individual desire and fulfillment reshaped—and threatened to obscure—the force of presidential leadership.

CHAPTER 2

THE STUDIOS' GOLDEN AGE AND THE WHITE HOUSE, 1929-1945

The presidency had deep roots in a culture of performance. Like entertainers, presidents (especially after 1900) exploited rapidly developing mass media to augment their presence in Americans' lives. Whether he was politically strong or weak, a twentieth-century president benefited from the status he enjoyed in Washington society; the perception of the power of the office around his person; public relations, advertising, mass periodicals, radio, and the other machinery of modern celebrity; and the innovative example of Theodore Roosevelt, who infused his time in office with dramatic gestures, theatrical oratory, and evocations of aggressive masculinity.

Into this context arrived motion pictures, the most powerful new force in celebrity creation to date. As a business, the movies replicated the production methods of the great industries, as well as the distribution mechanisms of retailers and theatrical performing circuits. Like the theater, the motion picture industry also came to market its leading performers—its "stars"—as commodities as fully as it sold its productions. The modern cult of personality, advanced by the theater and exploited by public figures such as Theodore Roosevelt, reached its apogee in Hollywood's crafting of its most charismatic leading actors and actresses. Much of the movies' power derived from what early Hollywood producers and directors were fond of calling their "verisimilitude"—their apparent, ultimate success at turning real sights and sounds into art, using real people and real locations—the ideal to which realist literature, painting, the phonograph, radio, and even photography had separately aspired but could never reach.

The movies, though, also exploited fantasy, creating exaggerated visions of space, time, and personality that often pulled the medium away from realism. Motion pictures' precarious straddling of both reality and escapism, interestingly enough, was roughly equivalent to Americans' highly conflicted feelings about politics: leaders and voters alike simultaneously struggled to confront ugly realities and to pursue seemingly fantastic goals of national unity and harmony, with the voters often putting their faith in politicians who made unrealistic promises and ran on platforms of utopian change.

As the United States struggled through the Great Depression and fought World War II, presidents and motion picture actors fulfilled similar cultural roles and increasingly crossed paths in both work and play. In the decade and a half after 1930, the movie star became both a commodity and a template of the American personality, broadly conceived. At the same time, Hollywood studios built themselves into corporate institutions that became central to American culture's self-identification. In those years, similarly, the president—particularly Franklin D. Roosevelt—became an active broker between the diverse and competing segments of US society, attempting to ease conflicts between interest groups. In the broadest sense, for their own political benefit presidents increasingly sought to take the pulse of American culture—to divine its evolution in rapidly changing times—and to serve as spokesmen for its values. As part of this pulse-taking, Roosevelt in particular paid increased attention to the content of motion pictures, and to the style and substance of the performances given by their leading players. Through his interaction with the movie world, Roosevelt especially absorbed lessons about performance and artifice that served him well on the political and international stages.

—————

The story of the motion picture industry's origins is a familiar one. Although he was not the first inventor in the field, Thomas Edison patented the first kinetoscope in 1893 and then, to profit from the device, he built the first moving picture studio, the "Black Maria," at his New Jersey laboratory. By the late 1890s Edison had competition, rival studios such as American Mutoscope in New York City, whom he also frequently faced in court over alleged patent infringements. Moving picture devices and production also spread across the world. In the United States, individuals first witnessed moving pictures through hand-cranked peep shows. Only after 1900 did film projectors become common, and over the succeeding decade the movie business made a full transition to showing its films on theater screens for groups of viewers. New York City's close-packed masses were the ideal audience for the expert retail merchants, mostly Jewish immigrants from Manhattan's Lower East Side, who began to blend film production and distribution into the studio–theater chain axis that would dominate the movie business for two generations.

As film historians have noted, the path from Union Square to Sunset Boulevard was filled with detours and tantalizing roads not taken. Until the late 1910s, for example, the majority of US theaters depended upon European suppliers for most of their moving pictures (especially films longer than one reel, including the first lavish historical epics). Gradually, though, Manhattan-based companies, filming pictures for the most part in studios on Long Island, acquired the necessary capital and mastered domestic distribution, thus achieving dominance in the US market. Yet within the American movie industry most individual companies remained financially insecure and vulnerable to hostile takeovers by competitors. It was these conditions which encouraged Carl Laemmle to take his Universal studio to Southern California in 1913, to escape meddling by rivals. Universal's success in a small agricultural suburb of Los Angeles called Hollywood quickly inspired other moving picture companies to make the journey west.

Takeovers and insolvency plagued the business for another decade, into the late 1920s, when the surviving studios largely made peace and formed a virtual cartel. The creation of the Academy of Motion Picture Arts and Sciences in 1927 led to a celebrated annual awards ceremony, but the main motivation behind the new organization was to preserve the new order— rule by the major studios—and to collude against potential union activism among the members' employees. Meanwhile, the culture of Hollywood took hold. Producers and financiers from eastern Jewish enclaves created an insular new community in the Hollywood hills—an affluent network of mansions, country clubs, and synagogues that both transplanted and gilded the culture of the Lower East Side.[1]

Simultaneously, techniques for marketing and distributing films became far more sophisticated. The nickelodeons or early theaters depended upon the efforts of company agents, much as music halls relied on the salesmanship of sheet-music company song pluggers, to advertise a panoply of short films and to fill orders for the next few weeks of exhibition. Movie marketing before 1915 (and long afterward in rural areas) was varied and colorful; it was a "barnburning" era of diverse and eccentric practices in film distribution, movie theater programming, and advertising. The motion picture as an art form coalesced in response to the aggregate demands of the market. While such films as the one-reel works directed by D. W. Griffith show a gradual movement toward the storytelling and genre conventions that would later guide Hollywood, well into the 1910s many other movies persisted in using amateur actors, slavishly adhering to one locale per scene (i.e., not cross-cutting between locales), and allowing performers to indulge in histrionic stage gestures. As David Bordwell and others have shown, the standard ways in which Hollywood would pace, light, compose, and enact scenes, and then weave those scenes into a coherent narrative lasting ninety minutes or even two hours or more, were adopted only after a period of trial and error that lasted well into the 1920s.[2]

It was in this era, for example, that studios settled upon the particular fictive nature of the average Hollywood feature film. The movies held the greatest mimetic visual potential yet seen among art forms; cameras could film anywhere in the real world, and adequate set dressing could create the illusion of a real place. As the psychologist Hugo Münsterberg noted in 1916, movies were the first art form to give audiences a sense of "omnipresence," of "the whole interplay" of life.[3] Still, for audiences, and even more for those who made films, this interplay had to be structured by a set of conventions. The challenge lay in creating a grammar of film, of telling stories in realistic settings in the most effective (and profitable) way. When it came to plotting, characterization, and scene construction, screenwriters persuaded themselves not to emulate the grittiness that characterized realist literature, painting, and photography. Audiences and producers told writers that while movies must resemble the real world cosmetically, they also had to distill that world into relatively predictable plots and characters. This early move toward cliché derived in part from the lack of sound in early movies, which was the equivalent of rendering theatrical plays into pantomime. It also resulted from the studios' and theaters' need to keep large, restless, and socially and educationally diverse audiences involved in the stories, to encourage them to advertise the films afterward by word of mouth, and of course to entice them back into the theaters week after week.

As a result, a lead character in a Hollywood movie was almost always driven by one clear motivation, and the movie's plot primarily showed the striving needed to achieve his or her goal. While the movie character might have worn clothing and existed in settings indistinguishable from those of the real world, he or she was curiously free of distractions, minor chores, doubts, and the rest of the typical clutter of real life. Individual scenes were ruthlessly economical. Every element of the characters' placement and mimed exchanges, as well as the framing of the cameras' various shots within the scene, was mounted for the sole purpose of advancing the story effectively. Plot devices such as a lost child or parent, or a displaced object or letter that, when found, would decisively alter the fate of a main character, were popular staples of early films, since they provided motivations for assertive, long-term action—such as a search or a journey—and the potential for dramatic plot twists.

Very few early Hollywood products violated these basic rules, and thus the movies' characterizations and plotting largely became far more primitive than the narrative structure found in most serious—and even some popular—literature. Exceptions proved the rule. D. W. Griffith's *Intolerance* (1916), a lavish and uniquely ambitious effort to weave together four separate tales of injustice across thousands of years, demonstrated the director's mastery of camerawork and plotting (although his crafting of many individual scenes looks primitive today). Yet *Intolerance* was a critical failure that taught Hollywood to shun Griffith's baroque multiplot structuring. Most telling was the Metro-Goldwyn-Mayer (MGM) studio's reaction to director Eric von Stroheim's *Greed* (1925), a unique attempt to film a modernistic novel (Frank Norris's *McTeague*) virtually paragraph by paragraph in a nine-hour-long movie, in the actual locales featured in the story. By 1925 storytelling conventions in Hollywood had solidified, and the studio executive Irving M. Thalberg felt fully justified in removing *Greed* from von Stroheim's control and excising three-quarters of the footage to prepare the version released to theaters.

From the very beginning, wild and escapist fantasy was popular in movies, and in Hollywood and abroad many "costume" efforts set in distant times and lands were produced. Nevertheless, the vast majority of Hollywood films were set in the present day and dealt with strata of society that were familiar to the average viewer. However, the portrayal of reality was carefully policed both within and outside studio walls. Virtually from the time of Edison's first productions, pressure from religious and social reform groups (as well as from local government movie-censorship boards) had caused filmmakers to set guidelines for content. This moral policing resembled that which controlled theatrical content, on Broadway and across America. Hollywood studios thus increasingly strove to avoid depictions of sexuality, alcohol and narcotics abuse, blasphemy, and violence that might incite unfavorable controversy. The studios' "Hays office," created in 1923, enforced the first Motion Picture Production Code, which expanded over the next decade into an elaborate list of forbidden topics for studio films. The definitive code that went into effect in 1932, and that held sway in Hollywood for the next three decades, severely limited the movies' claims to mimetic authority—to portraying the world as it really was. In Hollywood movies under the Production Code, for example, no murderer or adulterer went unpunished; no quantities of spilled blood or female navels were ever shown; characters never uttered profanities; and homosexuals, prostitutes, and bathroom toilets never appeared on screen nor were mentioned by the characters we did see.[4]

These prohibitions may seem ridiculous today, but this fact only underscores how fearful the movie business was of violating prevailing social mores, as well as how changes in the content of fiction films came only in the wake of revolutionary changes in those mores. Some studio executives encouraged creative, and even daring, storytellers to work for them as screenwriters, but they also stood ready to curtail wild imaginations in order to squelch potential controversy and maintain profit margins. Even at the peak of the studios' cultural influence in the late 1930s and early 1940s—after the business had righted itself from the Great Depression, and before television challenged the studios' role as a provider of daily entertainment—their masters feared boycotts, protests, scandals, and any other disruption that might enshroud their products in controversy. The growing antitrust investigations by the federal government only worsened their insecurity, even as filmmaking masters such as Frank Capra, David O. Selznick, and John Ford were helping to make the movies the world's most popular art form.

The prevalence of the movies in the pre-television era needs little restating here. By 1930 weekly national attendance in movie theaters exceeded seventy million, suggesting that the average resident of the United States took in at least one show a week. Theaters had evolved from the little nickelodeon storefront rooms in big cities of the 1900s to the lavish palaces of the 1910s and 1920s in those same cities, and by the 1930s theaters of varying size had risen in nearly every urban neighborhood and good-sized town in the country. By those years radio had also become a virtually universal medium, bringing entertainment and news directly into American homes. Clearly, though, despite the convenience of radio, Americans continued to invest their time and discretionary spending in trips to the theater every few days to catch the latest Hollywood releases (of which there were approximately six to seven hundred every year). Theater owners reported on the success or failure of particular new films, and trade journals published their reactions and those of audience members.

The presidencies of Herbert Hoover (1929–1933) and Franklin Delano Roosevelt (1933–1945) illustrate how the new cultural dominance of the movies affected the leisure activities of the chief executives, the business that came across their desks, and the evolving image of their office. Both men were inquisitive and alert students of their times, which brought economic distress and painful change to average Americans. Out of necessity, they looked to the movies for new tools and examples of leadership. For Roosevelt in particular, this new presidential interest in Hollywood grew out of profoundly personal, as well as political, motivations.

As a Californian and as the US Secretary of Commerce during the 1920s, just before he ascended to the White House, Herbert Hoover was well situated to witness the growth of the motion picture industry. Much of his perception of the industry was shaped by his close relationship with one of its most important early figures, Louis B. Mayer.

Mayer, like other founders of Hollywood, had traveled far in life. He left his native Ukraine in childhood, grew up in St. John, New Brunswick, and made an early living as a theater owner in Boston. In the 1920s, he was the head of production at Metro-Goldwyn-Mayer. MGM's very name illustrated the merger mania among studios in the 1920s—a dynamic business situation that was certain to attract the attention of the Commerce Department. Mayer and Secretary Hoover assiduously cultivated each other's loyalty. Mayer wrote Hoover in 1924 that he wished that all Americans "could know you intimately as you deserve to be known," while the secretary of commerce assured the producer "that I have you in mind many times a day."[5]

Mayer called on Hoover whenever he visited Washington, and Hoover reciprocated during his travels out west. During the 1928 campaign, Mayer sent MGM photographers up to Palo Alto, California, to take portraits of Hoover and his wife, Lou Henry Hoover, at their home. In the days before Hoover's election as president, one of his aides reported that Mayer, "unable to contain himself longer, called me up last night to 'bubble over.'" Ida R. Koverman was an intimate of both men who worked both in movies and in Southern California Republican politics. She knowingly characterized the insecurities of Mayer in the corridors of power. The production chief, Koverman wrote a Hoover aide soon after the 1928 election, "is another small boy" who would "strut around like a proud pigeon" if Hoover showed him attention, especially since the movie people "with whom he is intimately associated are inclined to sort of 'rub it in' that his efforts are now a thing of the past and he himself is more or less in the discard."[6]

In addition to tending to each others' egos, Hoover and Mayer worked together on issues that directly affected the latter's company and the industry as a whole. Mayer imposed on Hoover both before and after his election as president, seeking his help to fend off federal antitrust prosecution and to exploit the rising business of radio broadcasting. In the former case, MGM and other studios were facing the early stages of what would be a two-decade-long federal effort to expose monopolistic practices in the movie industry. Mayer was implicated briefly in one early federal antitrust lawsuit, and when his friend Hoover was serving in the White House, he succeeded in getting the Justice Department to arbitrate between Los Angeles prosecutors and the studios. Earlier, when still at Commerce, Hoover had played a more central role in assisting Mayer and the publisher William Randolph Hearst in gaining a desirable spot on the dial for Southern California's farthest-reaching radio station. He even cabled Mayer with news of the wavelength, although tellingly he informed the producer of the settlement months after his office had worked it out with Hearst, who was then more politically influential than Mayer. With Ida Koverman's assistance, Mayer became the leading activist for the Republican Party within the movie industry, persisting in that role even as the Great Depression severely damaged the fortunes of the party and forced Hoover from office.[7]

Studio executives found other ways to make their presence known in Washington. Beginning especially during the Hoover years, Hollywood distributors bombarded the White House with invitations to accept copies of their latest motion pictures for the First Family's viewing. A Washington newspaper reported early in Hoover's term that the president and his wife made movies their chief source of leisure. Two Movietone film projectors, similar to those used in the movie palaces, were wheeled twice a week into a White House reception room. On Monday and Thursday evenings at 8:30, the Hoovers greeted one or two dozen guests and treated them to a moving picture show. The president and the First Lady "invariably . . . sit thru [sic] to the end," and were fond of "seeing and listening to foreign celebrities in the news reels," dramas, and "the exceptional pictures" rather than the genre fare that made up most theatrical double features. The Hoovers saw films such as *Valiant,* a mystery, the epic Western *The Long Trail* (featuring John Wayne in his first role), and a documentary, *Round about the Hoover Home,* filmed at the couple's mansion under construction in Palo Alto.[8]

President Hoover's interactions with the motion picture industry signaled a new alignment of the movies with the presidency. Unlike the theater in earlier decades, Hollywood was an industry that attained the scale and scope of such Gilded Age manufacturing sectors as steel, meatpacking, and tobacco. In 1927 the producer Joseph P. Kennedy estimated that motion pictures were the third best capitalized industry in America. Because of their control of vast theater chains and the practice of "block-booking" their own products for extended runs in these venues, motion picture studios—like the oil refining and steel companies that preceded them—eventually ran afoul of federal antitrust laws. As suits were filed and settlements were explored in the Hoover years, studio heads and high federal officials managed their relationships cautiously. In response to the protests of independent theater managers and others about these relationships, Hoover's staff was compelled to state "that neither Mr. Mayer nor any other leader in the moving picture industry has made representations to the President in respect to their legal relations with the Government."[9]

This era also saw the introduction of what might be termed the "revolving door" between government and business, which led former public servants to lucrative new employment in the corporate world. The lobbying profession acquired its modern identity during the 1920s, due in large part to Herbert Hoover's dynamic networking as commerce secretary. In line with this new trend, Hollywood began to employ former Washington officials as lobbyists. Chief among them was Will H. Hays, Hoover's former cabinetmate in the Harding administration, who in 1922 began his long chairmanship of Hollywood's trade association, the Motion Picture Producers and Distributors of America (MPPDA). Hays's appointment came in the wake of two lurid scandals that had tarnished the movies' reputation just as they were becoming a major institution in American life: the comedian Roscoe "Fatty" Arbuckle's trials for manslaughter and the murder of the director William Desmond Taylor. For twenty years Hays presided over the MPPDA's celebrated self-censorship, embodied in the so-called Hays Code, and kept up a close and confidential relationship with Washington leaders from both parties. Herbert Hoover's connections with Hollywood helped to increase traffic through the revolving door. George Akerson, a member of the president's staff, left the White House to take a job with the Paramount studio, while the former assistant attorney general and Prohibition enforcer Mabel Walker Willebrandt became MGM's legal counsel.[10]

These structural connections helped to enhance the president's cultural debt to the movies as well. Even more than his immediate predecessor, Calvin Coolidge, Hoover found himself framed by the lens of the motion picture camera. As we have seen, during his years at Commerce Hoover's background as a celebrated humanitarian had already made his image an appealing (and often unauthorized) element in advertisements. His presidential campaign in 1928 represented a major leap forward in the use of public relations techniques in marketing a presidential candidate. The campaign was also the first to make significant use of movie technology as a promotional tool. Prints of a silent biographical film entitled *Master of Emergencies,* produced by Hoover's friend, the journalist Will Irwin, were made available for showings nationwide. "WHY WE SHOULD VOTE FOR HERBERT HOOVER TOLD IN TALKING MOTION PICTURES," proclaimed a billboard on the side of a truck that brought the film to towns across the Midwest.[11]

Calvin Coolidge had been the first president to make himself regularly available to newsreel services, the studios' quasi-journalistic subsidiaries. Hoover's White House aides were in regular contact with the newsreels, planning access to events featuring the president. They arranged, for example, to allow multiple newsreel services to cover Hoover's attendance at the Thomas Edison birthday celebration in Dearborn, Michigan, organized by the public relations pioneer Edward Bernays. On another occasion the newsreels covered the landing of an autogyro on the White House lawn. Various organizations wrote to the president asking him to film greetings for their conclaves. Others proposed starring roles for Hoover in nonjournalistic productions. One filmmaker requested his assistance in making a series of short films "that will glorify the United States President." White House aides declined almost all requests for the president's appearances in such filming, but they did agree to let Hoover appear in Paramount's inaugural newsreel, and in 1932 they allowed a filmmaker to plan a documentary about the president's daily routine (which apparently was never realized).[12]

––––––

In President Hoover's on-camera appearances, and in the assumptions about his celebrity that led filmmakers to record and pursue him, we can detect elements of the cult of movie stardom that had arisen by the late 1920s. The theater exhibitors' trade journals variously cited clever plots, lavish sets and costumes, and superior songs, humor, or dialogue as reasons why audiences might like a film, but these factors paled in significance to viewers' reaction to the lead actors. It was clear by the 1920s that stars were the dominant factor in the success of Hollywood motion pictures.

Although the special promotion of lead male and female actors—as well as use of the descriptive term "the star system"—had been prominent in the American theater for decades before 1900, it was years before the practice took root in the movies. In 1894 the boxer James J. Corbett signed an exclusive contract with the Edison Moving Picture Company—probably the first ever contract concerning an individual appearing on screen—and, like other real-life celebrities caught by the camera, he was identified by name in peepshow films. But Corbett did not play a fictional role until almost two decades after his debut in Edison shorts. Similarly, before 1910 stage actors believed that identification in film roles would cause them to lose theatrical work (which paid much better), while the movie companies themselves at first sought to built audience loyalty only to their own brands. Thus from 1907 to 1909 Florence Lawrence, a young Canadian actress, was presented in publicity materials only as "the Biograph Girl," and never credited by name in the films she made for that company.

Yet in 1910, when Lawrence's name was prominently featured in advertising and in the title cards for her films, screen stardom arrived. That year, as a result of a bitter battle among the Edison monopoly, the Motion Picture Patents Company, and independent producers, Carl Laemmle enticed Lawrence away from Biograph. She joined Laemmle's new Independent Moving Picture Company, and, in a deliberate slap at Edison, the latter featured her name in publicity. The marked success of her subsequent pictures led other studios to follow Laemmle's practice. Gilbert S. Anderson had been an insignificant player since his appearance in the first American fiction film, *The Great Train Robbery* (1903), even though he had co-founded and headed the studio, Essanay, for which he now made cowboy movies. Following Laemmle's and Lawrence's example, Anderson now advertised himself as "Broncho Billy" and became the first western movie star. Within a few years, the storied emergence of Mary Pickford, Charles Chaplin, and Douglas Fairbanks established the prototypical dynamics of movie stardom, in which the studio heavily promoted the looks and talents of the actor, mass audiences established an emotional attachment to him or her, and the attachment was strengthened by the release of subsequent films.

Almost all early film stars benefited from the recent triumph of naturalistic stage acting over the histrionic tradition that had prevailed during the nineteenth century. Exaggerated emoting, broad arm gestures, and contorted facial features—used by stage players to broadcast the plot to the most distant seats in the house—gave way, on both sides of the Atlantic, to underplaying and meticulous attention to detail. In Britain, Henry Irving was the acknowledged master of byplay—the use of small, true-to-life physical actions that marked his characters as real-seeming people (in concert with the realistic, often laconic dialogue written for Irving by contemporary playwrights). In America, the actor William Gillette championed what he called "the Illusion of the First Time," the impression held by the audience that a theatrical event involving performers had never occurred before, that it was a seemingly authentic new experience that bore no trace of earlier premeditation or rehearsal. Such innovations resembled the more systematic, intensive, and revolutionary method of realistic acting taught by the Russian Constantin Stanislavski, who would shape future generations of US stage and screen actors.[13]

David Wark Griffith, a strikingly inept actor himself in his first years of work in the movies, proved to be Gillette's most important disciple in films. During his time as a director of one-reel movies for Biograph before 1914, he had played an important role in shaping the understated and realistic style of film acting that became the hallmark of many stars in later years. For example, the refreshing naturalism of Dorothy Bernard as the telegraph operator–heroine of Griffith's *The Girl and Her Trust* (1912) compares favorably with the screen acting of our own time. Bernard's casual diligence at her desk, understated double-takes, and bemused reactions to an amorous co-worker are both realistic and endearing. The film's frantic chase scene obscures Bernard's subtlety, but Griffith had multiple artistic priorities, which he would realize on a grand scale in his later multireel epics. Mary Pickford, Lillian Gish, and Henry B. Walthall emerged from Griffith's Biograph years with a command of the new craft of screen acting. Their work beginning in 1915 tutored an entire generation of film actors in the power of carefully calibrated, understated, yet emotionally powerful screen artifice. Some stars, of course—especially comics such as Chaplin and action heroes such as Fairbanks—made their fortune by being larger than life, making broad facial and physical gestures and enacting remarkable physical stunts.

Lon Chaney, with the help of his precious makeup kit, threw himself into psychologically agonized and outsized performances which resembled those of German expressionist actors such as Max Schreck. Chaney, though, was the exception that proved the rule, as his style became the hallmark of horror films, which studios and critics alike would deem a minor, even juvenile, Hollywood genre. Calculated naturalism, creating the Illusion of the First Time within the carefully blocked space and carefully edited time of motion picture scenes, became the ether in which movie stardom glowed.

Screen actors were more or less conscious of how their craft evolved to best suit the technical challenges of moviemaking. There was novelty and oddity in shooting scenes out of sequence; working under often trying conditions outdoors and on location; and sweating under heavy studio lighting and in strange costumes that were optimized for camera lenses and black-and-white film. What they or their bosses could not anticipate, or easily react to, was the unprecedented power of certain varieties of movie acting. While most actors reduced their gestures and emoting to a naturalistic minimum, their faces and bodies were simultaneously being blown up to grand proportions on wall-sized screens. For the first time in performing arts history, the simple movement of a facial muscle could become a dramatic event, multiplying considerably the significance of byplay in the theater and bringing a new power to fleeting emotions. Griffith's pioneering perception of the impact of subtle acting on the large screen was shared by important silent film directors of the 1920s worldwide, such as von Stroheim, King Vidor, Carl Dreyer, and Josef von Sternberg. Even expressionist directors such as F. W. Murnau, Fritz Lang, and Douglas Sirk would seek subtlety, rather than histrionics, in many of their actors' performances. The most unexpected result of this trend was the emergence of wildly successful movie actors who had shown virtually no promise as stage performers.

The rise to fame of two archetypal film stars of the 1920s illustrated the new trend. Rodolpho d'Antonguolla was an Italian immigrant who played bit parts in 1910s movies and danced in cabarets, working his way into New York society. As Rudolph Valentino, he brought a new European male sexuality to the American cinema and became a major star of the early 1920s. Like his second wife, the tempestuous studio set designer Natacha Rambova (née Winifred Hudnut of Salt Lake City, Utah), Valentino was an American of modest origins who reinvented himself in Hollywood. Unlike most such individuals, though, Valentino's success became a cultural turning point— one in which the American mass audience saw a new way of behaving and of perceiving the world in the glances, gestures, and deeds of a screen performer. In particular, of course, Valentino vividly enacted an overt new mode of sexual self-presentation. Defying prevalent social mores, and even Hollywood's own self-censorship, the actor's gestures taught young viewers how to violate them. The term "idol" is often used lazily in reference to such performers, but it suggests the power of their social influence. As Buster Keaton illustrated in his comic masterpiece *Sherlock, Jr.* (1926), young people were taught by the movies how to court, how to embrace, and how to kiss. The celebrity of Valentino in particular stimulated the growth of fan magazines and clubs that further nurtured the cult of screen stardom. His death in 1926 at the age of thirty-one also revealed a macabre element of stardom. Although the response to it had been presaged somewhat by reactions to the deaths of earlier stage celebrities, Valentino's passing received unprecedented press and newsreel coverage, and famously inspired hysterical reactions by grieving female fans. The institution of the fallen young idol became a new part of motion picture celebrity culture.

Clara Bow, a native of Brooklyn, did not have to change her name, but her rise from obscurity offered a variation on Valentino's early career. In 1922 Bow won a talent contest intended to discover new movie actors, but for some time after she arrived in Hollywood she failed to win substantial roles. By 1925 Bow was finally getting those parts, and journalists and producers conspired to make her the cinematic embodiment of the "flapper," the liberated young white woman already publicized in print (particularly in the magazine illustrations of John Held Jr.). In 1927 she played the leading role in the comedy *It*. The screenwriter Elinor Glyn had remarked offhandedly one day that Bow had "it"—an elusive charisma—and a producer encouraged Glyn to develop the idea into a film vehicle for Bow. "It," Glyn wrote, was "that strange magnetism which attracts both sexes . . . full of self-confidence." The individual possessing this indefinable quality is "indifferent to the effect . . . she is producing and uninfluenced by others." "It" was the cinema's potent realization of the modern concept of charisma, which, as we have seen, was defined in the mass democratic age as the projection of a rare and exciting personality.

While the studios were happy to benefit from the wild success of films starring Bow, Valentino, and others, they remained as unaware as Glyn or anyone else how to define, harness, or cultivate "It." The strange but unmistakable impact made in 1927 by Greta Gustafsson, one of the countless young European actresses who came to Hollywood hoping for stardom, further illustrated the problem. Within a few years Gustafsson, as Greta Garbo, would embody screen stardom, even though her looks, gestures, accent, and bodily proportions did not fit established Hollywood norms. By contrast the career of Clara Bow, the paragon of mid-1920s screen womanhood, scarcely survived the introduction of movie sound. Newcomers such as Garbo had seemingly redefined "It" and made Bow culturally obsolete. Bow soon abandoned acting, married, and raised a family. (Her husband, the cowboy actor Rex Bell, later became one of the first movie performers to be elected to public office, serving as lieutenant governor of Nevada in the 1950s.)

Film stars shared a number of characteristics. First, almost all of them were youthful. The early kings of comedy such as Chaplin, Keaton, and Harold Lloyd, as well as the swashbuckler Fairbanks, owed their fame to their athletic vigor and acrobatic grace. Even a dramatic performer such as Lillian Gish established her celebrity in part through physical derring-do, like her leap across swift river ice floes in Griffith's *Way Down East*. Mary Pickford famously prolonged her onscreen adolescence well into her thirties, continuing to portray the teen heroines who had defined her career. Understated acting claimed preeminence in the late silent era, but in many other ways Hollywood movies remained committed to bold and frantic action. This occasionally was the result of accelerated playback on poorly synchronized projectors, but it mainly reflected the fact that the movies, above all, *moved.* Griffith, like Chaplin and Russia's Sergei Eisenstein, made the cinema the realization of Futurism in modern art, thus helping win allies for movies among modernist intellectuals. Surging crowds, bounding locomotives, spiraling aircraft, car chases, and roaring rapids were as central to the filmgoing experience as the subtle terrain of the star performer's face.

In Hollywood films in particular, action was heavily gendered. The western genre, largely defined by 1915, was a male preserve of horsemanship, gunplay, and struggle against the forces of nonwhite "savagery" and nature. The prevalence of wide-open spaces close to Hollywood—some studios were established on actual ranch sites—made cowboy films the most obvious outdoor genre, and in a culture that raised boys on the stories of Buffalo Bill Cody and dime novels, the films' success seemed preordained. Cody, Wyatt Earp, and other actual veterans of the celebrated old days came to Hollywood to work as actors and studio advisers. Just as Griffith codified the denigration of African Americans and mixed-raced southerners in *The Birth of a Nation*—using white actors in blackface—western movies created stereotypes of Native Americans that permeated the national culture. Thus, while mainstream dramas usually dealt apolitically with social and familial themes and only occasionally touched on class and socioeconomic conditions, western films (along with related action genres such as jungle adventures) explicitly depicted American ideologies of imperialism and racial hierarchy. Theodore Roosevelt's preferred self-image as the Man on Horseback and combatant "in the arena" received a vivid recapitulation in the standard celluloid cowboy hero, as embodied by Tom Mix, Buck Jones, Harry Carey Sr., William Boyd, and Gary Cooper. As TR hoped to do, these heroes displayed gallantry, chivalry, and other genteel courtesies—especially toward white women—proving that Anglo-Saxon civilization was heading west along the wagon trails.

Given the marginalization of women throughout most of Hollywood history, it is surprising to recall how many influential female producers, scenarists, and executives were active in the silent era. The ability of overtly sexual stars such as Clara Bow and Gloria Swanson to change the course of 1920s culture also testifies to the presence of women in the movies. Even young female newcomers to Hollywood generally exercised some control over their destinies; the evidence suggests that prostitution and the producer's casting couch snared only a minority of them. Nevertheless, sexism eroded the relative influence of women on both sides of the camera. Female directors such as Dorothy Arzner especially found their authority, and eventually the ability to make any movies at all, taken away from them by jealous male colleagues. The studios' relentless interest in youth proved especially damaging to actresses entering their thirties; only the most ambitious and thick-skinned performers, such as Joan Crawford and Bette Davis, could overcome their employers' persistent attempts to relegate them to comic and sexless character roles.

By 1930, the studios had developed elaborate machinery for creating stars. Its foundation was the contract system, designed to attach new actors to studios. They were educated in diction, dance, horseback riding, fencing, and other skills; had their looks, wardrobe, and names recast to suit them better to the camera and to studio publicity; and tested in a variety of small screen roles. Studio heads never could codify how a young bit player might be molded to become a guaranteed hit with audiences. The strange alchemy that made Greta Garbo a star, captivating directors and audiences alike, was repeated in dozens of surprising cases, while hordes of good-looking, talented, and ambitious young actors who seemed perfectly suited for stardom never achieved it. Stars' names went above the titles of their movies, and their appeal to audiences allowed films with poor scripts and production values to transcend their mediocrity. Producers, as Jeanine Basinger has put it, relied on stars "to weave gold out of straw."[14]

Weaving gold out of straw might also describe the task presented to presidents during the Great Depression. This complex chain of events seemed to curse the world's richest nation with unexplainable scarcity and poverty. Film historians have noted that the suffering caused by the Depression intensified Americans' craving for, and reliance upon, the emotional releases and escapes provided by the movies. Similar wish fulfillment emerged in politics. The letters written to Franklin Roosevelt in 1933 by thousands of jobless, shame-ridden victims of the economic slump revealed their need for rescue and refuge. As Robert McElvaine, Lawrence Levine, and Cornelia Levine have noted, the letters also expressed a reverence for the new president and a familiarity with him, bred of his straightforward Fireside Chats on the radio. Asking for jobs, clothing, or simple recognition of their plight, these citizens perceived the president as much more than a mere constitutional officer. He was both a provider and a beacon of hope.[15]

In these similarities between Americans' perceptions of screen stars and of FDR, we see a sharper definition and intensification of the presidency's relationship with mass celebrity. As if in realization of this fact, Roosevelt as president greatly enhanced social and political ties between Hollywood and the White House. At the outset of his term, given his family background, Franklin Roosevelt seemed as unlikely as his sixth cousin Theodore to develop personal relationships with motion picture executives and actors. However, just as the movies cast an unlikely spell on Herbert Hoover, they also captured the imagination of his successor in the White House. At the same time, the dramatic events of Roosevelt's twelve years in office helped to make him more of a mass-media celebrity and more of a vividly human presence to the electorate than any of his predecessors had been. The Great Depression and World War II intensified the escapist power of the movies and the voters' tendency to search for idealized, cinematic, heroic traits in their elected leaders.

Elsewhere in the world such escapism and idealization resulted in the poisonous politicizing of movies and the cult of charisma. The rise of Nazism in Germany was rooted in Adolf Hitler's magnetic appeal as a speaker, as well as in Joseph Goebbels' mastery of film and radio propaganda on his behalf. The desperate plight of German society during the Depression, as well as the wild and inchoate appeal to national greatness made by Hitler, attracted creative artists to Nazism. The French writers Céline and Robert Brasillach, among others, interpreted Nazi-style fascism as the political equivalent of Futurism, an ideology of movement and violence that they believed would bring both aesthetic and visceral satisfaction to a spent and weak continent. Many German film professionals (mostly non-Jews) were similarly drawn to the aesthetic lure of Nazism, including Thea von Harbou, whose screenplay for *Metropolis* (directed by her husband, Fritz Lang) was perhaps the pinnacle of German Expressionism. Portraying the eventual union of "the hands" and "the head" through "the heart" against the background of labor struggle in a kinetic future world, *Metropolis* was Europe's most lavish attempt to surmount Hollywood's silent spectacles. Yet under the Nazi regime the German cinema would be compelled to exalt Hitler and manipulate the nation into war and racial hatred. In America, by comparison, the machinations of the demagogic politician Huey Long (who appeared regularly in early 1930s newsreels) and the Hollywood studios that helped in 1934 to defeat Upton Sinclair, the socialist candidate for governor of California, were minuscule, but they also revealed the reactionary potential of film in desperate and politically volatile times.[16]

Within this context, it is striking how much more visible Hollywood became in the Roosevelt White House. Social contacts between movie makers and politicians increased considerably in the mid-1930s. Movie stars, familiar to Americans from their appearances on theater screens, began to show up regularly at the White House during the Roosevelt administration. The main impetus was an annual event on behalf of a charitable organization founded by the president, the National Foundation for Infantile Paralysis (which later renamed itself after one of its fundraising efforts, the March of Dimes). While the public never received a clear account from the press of the extent of Roosevelt's handicap, they were aware of his illness, and the novelty of having a president afflicted by polio intensified press coverage of the disease and efforts directed toward its prevention and cure.

As a result, in late January 1934 a small gathering of movie celebrities at a Washington hotel, hosted by the performer and humorist Will Rogers, celebrated Roosevelt's birthday for the purpose of raising money for polio research. Hollywood publicists then concocted a plan to transport a larger group of well-known movie performers to Washington every year, beginning in 1935, in conjunction with the president's birthday. The performers lunched at the White House with the First Lady and attended a variety of fundraising affairs around the capital. With the exception of young Ginger Rogers's invitation in 1936 to witness the delivery of a Fireside Chat in the Oval Office, none of the participating actors met the president himself. FDR instead attended annual birthday dinners, which were held the same evenings as the movie stars' lunches but were attended only by government officials. From 1935 to 1937, when Roosevelt was at the height of his popularity, the annual Washington birthday event inspired similar events on the same night in other cities, to raise money for the fight against polio.

The March of Dimes was formally created in 1938, and despite FDR's growing political problems and rising foreign concerns in the late 1930s, the Washington birthday events became more lavish. The film actors on the rosters became more prominent as the decade turned. In 1940 the birthday celebration attracted James Cagney, Tyrone Power, Olivia de Havilland, Edward G. Robinson, Dorothy Lamour, Mickey Rooney, Melvyn Douglas, Gene Autry, Elsa Lanchester, Red Skelton, Pat O'Brien, and many other well-known performers. On the other hand, some of the most illustrious stars invited by the White House—such as Clark Gable, Bette Davis, Norma Shearer, Claudette Colbert, and Spencer Tracy—sent their regrets. In 1941, newly inaugurated for an unprecedented third term, Roosevelt attended the movie stars' luncheon for the first time, sitting between Lana Turner and Maureen O'Hara and across the table from George Raft, Wallace Beery, Deanna Durbin, and Lauritz Melchior. In April 1942, with the United States now at war, perhaps the most dazzling constellation of all arrived at the White House in the form of the Hollywood Victory Canteen, featuring de Havilland, Cagney, Colbert, O'Brien, Tracy, Cary Grant, Bob Hope, Bing Crosby, Stan Laurel, Oliver Hardy, and many others. These actors attended a reception and tea at the executive mansion during the course of a multi-city tour designed to raise money for armed services entertainment.[17]

Owing to such Hollywood–White House contacts, Alan Schroeder argues, "it was Franklin Roosevelt who first perceived the power of association waiting to be harnessed in Hollywood stars."[18] This power of association was a deeply emotional bond connecting Roosevelt, his family, and more liberal members of his administration with their most fervent supporters in the movie industry. During Roosevelt's terms, the unwritten but long-standing American taboo that barred star performers from partisan activism was often breached. In two instances, famous radio performers were even elected to office. The conservative southern Democrats Wilbert "Pappy" O'Daniel and Jimmie Davis operated at a great geographical and ideological distance from FDR, but their electoral victories were notable first achievements by show people. O'Daniel, a native of Ohio, parlayed an advertising job in Fort Worth into ownership of a flour company and his own radio program. "Pass the biscuits, Pappy," his studio musicians, the Light Crust Doughboys, would call out between O'Daniel's ruminations on religion and the virtues of his Hillbilly Flour. O'Daniel was elected governor of Texas in 1938, and in 1941 he won a special Democratic primary for US senator, handing Lyndon B. Johnson the only election defeat of his career (amid allegations of voter fraud). Jimmie Davis was a popular radio performer who was credited as the composer of "You Are My Sunshine" and other hit songs. He had served in local government in his native Shreveport, Louisiana, before he was elected governor of the state in 1944. Davis pioneered the trick of starring in government and movies simultaneously, taking time off from his official duties to travel to Southern California to perform in low-budget singing-cowboy films.

More directly related to Roosevelt's political concerns was the growth and increasing visibility of Hollywood's committed liberal wing. The studios were politically diverse in the 1930s. Louis B. Mayer and most other executives were active and fervent Republicans, while at the other extreme, some actors and screenwriters dabbled in Communism. Hollywood contacts with the White House produced a visible and highly motivated liberal contingent, dedicated to FDR's New Deal. As Ronald Brownstein has shown, celebrity involvement in Roosevelt's reelection campaigns first became evident in 1940 and evolved into a full-fledged phalanx in 1944. Among Roosevelt's outspoken supporters were Humphrey Bogart, Fredric March, the director William Wyler, and the producer Walter Wanger. Their appearances on FDR's behalf on radio and before crowds associated the president in the public mind much more closely with the film industry.[19]

In the process, some denizens of Hollywood followed in the footsteps of Pappy O'Daniel and Jimmie Davis and became involved in politics, either by running for office themselves or by taking on occasional tasks for the Roosevelt administration. The stories of Helen Gahagan Douglas and Douglas Fairbanks Jr. illustrate this new trend. In 1922 Gahagan, an operatic ingénue, had become an overnight star in her first Broadway musical, and she found further success in other stage vehicles. In 1931 she married her co-star in one play, Melvyn Douglas, with whom she soon made the trek to Hollywood. In 1935 Gahagan Douglas played the titular African demi-goddess in the adventure saga *She,* but audiences and studio executives alike found her performance stiff and cold, and she never acted in movies again. She subsequently devoted her energies to raising two children and participating in liberal political causes. In 1944 Los Angeles labor officials asked Gahagan Douglas to challenge a conservative Democratic member of the city's House delegation, and to her surprise, she was victorious in the primary and general elections. (Her husband, conversely, achieved screen stardom but was stifled in his efforts to enter politics.) "Here I am a Congresswoman," she wrote to Eleanor Roosevelt; "it's really very ironic. Perhaps I can go around kicking Congressmen when they get o[r]nery."[20] In later years Gahagan Douglas made her most enduring mark on political history by los-

ing a race for the US Senate to a young opponent, Richard M. Nixon. Helen
and Melvyn Douglas moved back to New York soon afterward, and for the
next three decades she only occasionally involved herself in the theater and
in public affairs.

In contrast, Douglas Fairbanks Jr. descended from lofty Hollywood heights
to public service. The son of silent film's greatest action star, Fairbanks rarely
saw his father during his glory days; his parents had divorced in 1917 and he
was raised by his mother in New York City. Coming west as a young man,
he strengthened his relationship with his father, and in the early years of talking pictures he achieved stardom almost effortlessly. Along with his famous
name, young Fairbanks benefited from classically handsome looks and a talent
for light dramatic and comedic roles. On both coasts he cultivated elite social
connections. Only his brief first marriage to an ambitious actress of working-
class origins, Lucille "Billie" LeSueur—whom the MGM studio rechristened
Joan Crawford—diverted him somewhat from high society.

Despite appearing in successful films such as *The Prisoner of Zenda* and
Gunga Din, Fairbanks never attained the first rank of stardom. As he later
recalled, "I was repeatedly advised [in Hollywood] that I should concentrate
on an always recognizable set of mannerisms in the same way that Gary
Cooper, Jimmy Stewart, Clark Gable, and Jimmy Cagney did. . . . But I preferred variety—whether it was good business or not." Fairbanks happily
escaped Hollywood for frequent travel and socializing, and like Gahagan
Douglas he came to visualize a role for himself in the public sphere. By the
late 1930s, Fairbanks believed, "the whole business of entertainment, however good, seemed a trivial pursuit when compared to the grim realities
from which we all sought escape. . . . My interest in government, business,
and world affairs grew." He consulted tutors on real-world issues such as
the astronomer Edwin Hubble, the historians Will and Ariel Durant, and the
columnist Walter Lippmann.

In 1939 Fairbanks renewed his acquaintance with Franklin D. Roosevelt
Jr., "an old friend from my Central Park boyhood." After visiting the White
House to meet "Frank's" parents, Fairbanks was advised on public affairs by
Cordell Hull, Robert Sherwood, and other members of the Roosevelt admin-
istration. In the months before World War II, the actor became an articulate
and passionate advocate of military preparedness and a critic of isolationism.

In the homes of British appeasers, Fairbanks met and argued with Joachim von Ribbentrop and Count Galeazzo Ciano. The actor also played an important role in persuading the Roosevelt administration to invite George VI to visit the United States and encouraging the king to accept. George's visit, the first of its kind by a British monarch, was a rare and powerful expression of the two nations' affiliation in the months before the fall of France.[21]

In 1940 Fairbanks spoke widely on behalf of the Committee to Defend America by Aiding the Allies and in support of Roosevelt's reelection. The following January, after Fairbanks helped to host the president's inaugural festivities, the under secretary of state, Sumner Welles, recommended him for a diplomatic mission. Welles wanted the actor to counter what Welles called the "somewhat marked pro-Fascist tendency on the part of the younger generation of the well-to-do groups in Brazil and in Argentina." Fairbanks accepted the assignment and took a crash course in Spanish. His eleven-week tour of Brazil, Argentina, Uruguay, Chile, and Peru brought him numerous speaking engagements, including an appearance before fifty thousand workers in a football stadium in Montevideo and drawing-room soirees with Latin America's young elites. Fairbanks reported back to Welles in detail, despairing of the efficient pro-Nazi propaganda in the countries on the Atlantic coast and theorizing about the potential effectiveness of Hollywood films as countervailing Allied messages.

The remainder of 1941 found Fairbanks quickly making a final prewar film—*The Corsican Brothers,* perhaps the best of his career—and enlisting in the Naval Reserve. Hoping to serve in the State Department in a new propaganda effort he had envisioned, he instead was called up to serve on a supply ship making its way to Iceland—"despite Franklin's vain efforts to get me on *his* destroyer," he wrote in a note to Franklin's father, the president. After US entry into the war, Fairbanks became a leading naval attaché in London and the inventor of diversionary amphibious landings. His military and social activities in those years encouraged him largely to abandon his acting career after the war, but he also did not pursue further public service in those years.[22]

It is striking how contacts between movie personnel of all kinds—not just politically liberal actors—and the White House increased during the Roosevelt years. Perhaps owing to the fluidity in social relations caused by the turmoil of the Great Depression, motion picture executives and performers felt more comfortable moving frequently and easily in the corridors of political power.

The realms of Washington and Hollywood held a twin fascination for figures in business, who appreciated both the theatricality of politics and the potential for political communication inherent in motion pictures. The prototypical figure in this sense was perhaps William Randolph Hearst. The flamboyant newspaper publisher had striven for twenty years to get elected to office, running for Congress, the New York governorship, and the presidency. In the 1920s, though, Hearst abandoned running for office and entered film making, creating Cosmopolitan Studios and moving west to his native California (where he commenced the building of a palatial estate).[23]

Hearst's trajectory was emulated by Joseph Patrick Kennedy, the young Boston banker and wartime naval builder. In the 1920s Kennedy invested his accumulated earnings in the stock market and in Hollywood. Kennedy had already invested for years in a chain of New England movie houses, and his purchase in 1926 of the Film Booking Offices (based in Los Angeles) made him a major player in the business. Under Kennedy's management FBO evolved into an independent movie studio, producing silent films starring the cowboy actor Fred Thomson and the Hollywood star Gloria Swanson, whose career had recently been foundering. A generation younger than Hearst, the energetic Kennedy also came to the rescue of financially distraught minor studios, gaining de facto control of as many as four of them at once; he also owned Keith-Albee-Orpheum, the most important vaudeville touring company in the country. Like Hearst (who made the actress Marion Davies his mistress), Kennedy took a romantic interest in his favorite movie performer, producing four films for Swanson and resurrecting her personal finances. Unlike Hearst, though, Kennedy largely divested himself of movies and stocks in 1930, shrewdly sensing the imminence of economic difficulties, and turned his attention to politics.[24]

Kennedy and Hearst crossed paths at the most important moment in Franklin Roosevelt's political career. During the deadlocked balloting for president at the 1932 Democratic convention in Chicago, Kennedy, a fervent supporter of FDR who was in attendance, called Hearst and persuaded him to instruct California and Texas delegates under his control to vote for Roosevelt. Hearst made the move, and it guaranteed FDR the nomination. The indebted Roosevelt rewarded Kennedy with a series of prominent government jobs: the first chairmanship of the Securities and Exchange Commission, leadership of the US Maritime Commission, and the ambassadorship to the United Kingdom. In 1940—weeks before his outspoken isolationism provoked the disastrous end of his tenure in London and a bitter break with the president—Kennedy proclaimed, "there are only two pursuits that get in your blood—politics and the motion-picture business."[25]

Franklin Roosevelt might well have agreed. Even more than Hoover, he was a regular screener of Hollywood films in the White House, eschewing his predecessor's preference for newsreels and dramas in favor of Mickey Mouse cartoons and comedies. His favorite film actress was Myrna Loy, the star of light dramas and screwball comedies who also was the perennial top choice in movie magazine polls, and he long expressed the regret that he never was able to meet her.[26]

Family ties to Hollywood illustrated the Roosevelt family's deep affinity for the industry and its people. Three of Franklin and Eleanor's five children developed business connections with the movie industry, connections which derived in part from the appeal of the Hollywood lifestyle for privileged young people from the political world, but also from the studios' willingness to perform expedient favors for the president. Anna Roosevelt, Franklin and Eleanor's eldest child, married her second husband, the journalist John Boettiger, in 1935, soon after he left the anti–New Deal *Chicago Tribune* to begin work at the Motion Picture Producers and Distributors of America. Will Hays undoubtedly made Boettiger his assistant as a favor to the president; it was the first in a sequence of lucrative positions offered by Hollywood to the Roosevelt children. In 1936, however, John and Anna Boettiger were hired away by William Randolph Hearst, at lavish salaries, to edit one of his newspapers, the *Seattle Post-Intelligencer*. The publisher had a complex, almost indecipherable relationship with the president, dating back to their rivalry in New York Democratic politics. Hearst was a violent opponent of the New Deal and Roosevelt's internationalism, but he supported FDR when it suited his interests—as we have seen, he was probably responsible for his nomination in 1932—and he did not hesitate to curry favor. Will Hays, Louis B. Mayer, and other Republicans in Hollywood also pursued that strategy.

The president and the First Lady's two eldest sons were awarded jobs in Hollywood in part to rescue their parents from embarrassment. James Roosevelt had served as his father's assistant in the White House, but he created minor scandals by advocating in Washington for his friends' business concerns. In 1937, as a favor to the president, the independent producer Samuel Goldwyn hired James as an assistant and later helped him to establish his own small production company. Elliott, the second son, drifted from a stormy college career and failed first marriage into another arranged position in Los Angeles—this one again engineered for FDR by Hearst. Elliott Roosevelt spent the late 1930s based in Fort Worth, Texas, as a regional director for Hearst Radio. Emulating James, Elliott caused trouble for his father by seeking his assistance in securing investors for his bid to buy the southwestern stations from Hearst and create his own conglomerate.

Even graver allegations shadowed Elliott as a stateside Army officer during World War II, when he and his future third wife, the movie actress Faye Emerson, were implicated in Hughes Aircraft's expensive and rather garish campaign—involving ingénue actresses and nightclub visits—to persuade War Department contractors to commit themselves to Hughes. This scandal, which made headlines for years after the war, involved the Roosevelts tangentially with the aircraft magnate Howard Hughes, based in Los Angeles. Hughes, like Hearst and Kennedy, was obsessed variously by business, motion pictures, movie actresses, and politics. The president's third son, Franklin Delano Jr., as we have seen, more innocuously enjoyed a friendship with Douglas Fairbanks Jr., which helped to place the movie star in the thick of prewar diplomacy and wartime naval strategy.[27]

The allure of movies at the height of the studio era enticed some of Roosevelt's political opponents as well. Wendell Willkie admittedly was a very liberal Republican who had joined the party only two years before he opposed FDR in the election of 1940. After his defeat, Willkie provided Roosevelt with crucial bipartisan support for the Lend-Lease bill and the United Nations. Simultaneously, he became professionally active in Hollywood. Willkie served as legal counsel to the MPPDA, and in 1942 he was one of the hosts of the annual Academy Awards ceremony. In the first capacity he provided symbolic support for the movie industry in hearings held by a US Senate subcommittee in the months before the Pearl Harbor attack. In a desperate late move by the Senate's staunchest isolationists, Burton Wheeler (chair of the parent committee) and subcommittee member Gerald Nye, the hearings alleged a plot by the Hollywood studios to saturate American movie screens with pro-British propaganda. Editorial comment on these highly publicized hearings demonstrated how the coming of war had shuffled political allegiances, with one commentator perceiving them as an isolationist "plot to disorganize the movie business and deliver it into the control of William Randolph Hearst, with Joe Kennedy as his Will Hays." (While this charge was fanciful, it correctly noted the fervent isolationism of Hearst and Kennedy and their antipathy to FDR.) The demagogic Nye bungled his attacks badly by stressing the alleged disloyalty of the largely Jewish corps of film producers, "individuals . . . in the majority born abroad." By contrast, Darryl F. Zanuck, Twentieth Century Fox's chief of production, provided an eloquent defense before the subcommittee (undoubtedly refined by his screenwriters) of Hollywood's patriotism and deference to public opinion. "We have grown only because the people have let us," Zanuck claimed, adding in an aside that he had found "that when someone produces something that you do not like, you call it propaganda."[28]

The hearings were inconclusive and of little help to isolationists, but as Willkie's presence in the counsel's chair illustrated, they provided evidence of the new centrality of motion pictures in national public life. Roosevelt had adumbrated this view in 1938—echoing in part Hollywood's own self-promotional language—when he told movie producers in a written greeting that their "responsibility . . . may be measured by the possibilities of the motion picture as a force in our national culture," by means of "maintaining good entertainment and a high standard of artistic merit." Even Senator D. Worth Clark of Idaho, an isolationist member of the Nye subcommittee, echoed this claim at the movie hearings, telling Zanuck that "you and your associates are probably the greatest trustees of culture in this country."[29] In a comment on the hearings, the newspaper editor John McManus expressed in passing his assumption that it was Hollywood's "job" to "awak[en] America to the full meaning of Fascism, and why and how to fight it"—a "job" that McManus, ironically, felt that Hollywood was not doing well enough. Zanuck, fresh from producing the gritty, documentary-style film version of John Steinbeck's *The Grapes of Wrath,* provided in his testimony a strong endorse-

ment of Hollywood's ability to render real life in its productions. Speaking of
Nazis, he testified that "we have portrayed them no differently than they are
pictured daily in newspapers, magazines, books, and all other mediums of
expression. In fact we have merely portrayed them as they are." Most tellingly, the New York Herald-Tribune editorialized that public policy could be
best measured by the proclivities of "the millions who flock to . . . films. Is it
[Senator] Wheeler's notion that he knows these millions better than the men
who take in their dimes and quarters?" The isolationist Wheeler might have
been out of step with the times, but he was nevertheless a duly elected representative of the people of Montana, and the Herald-Tribune's demotion of
him to beneath the rank of movie makers was both startling and significant.
The sentiment displayed in the editorial suggested an increasingly central role
for Hollywood in American political culture.

This new role was also evident in the first significant depictions of US
presidents—fictional and real ones—in sound films. Not coincidentally,
these depictions first appeared during the depths of the Depression, at the
precise time the nation looked to Roosevelt for leadership. D. W. Griffith
presented Washington and Lincoln as supporting characters in his silent
historical epics, and his first talking film was a Lincoln biography, but before
1932 Hollywood avoided depicting real or imagined presidents; politics, in
the main, was not considered dramatic. The Depression steadily altered this
view in a number of the popular arts, as exemplified by the groundbreaking
musical comedy Of Thee I Sing (1931). In Hollywood it was, perhaps not
surprisingly, William Randolph Hearst who produced the first, fevered
cinematic portrayal of the presidency. Gabriel over the White House (1932)
has long fascinated critics and historians with its story about a weak president who is transformed by a blow to the head into a bold, quasi-dictatorial
leader. Walter Huston (who had portrayed Lincoln for Griffith two years
earlier) enacts Hearst's own thwarted fantasy of a populist leader unbound
by legalistic restrictions, free to confront the Great Depression and the threat
of organized crime with paramilitary squads and government by decree.[30]

As the Great Depression eased later in the decade, presidents in movies
were portrayed in a more sentimental fashion. The avalanche of Lincoln
lore, unleashed in the wake of Carl Sandburg's very popular biography,
epitomized the back-to-the-land sentimentality of the New Deal era. It was

manifested in Hollywood in the late 1930s films *Abe Lincoln in Illinois* (from the play by Robert E. Sherwood, soon to become FDR's speechwriter) and *Young Mr. Lincoln,* as well as Frank McGlynn Sr.'s supporting appearances as Lincoln in many films.[31] More generally, the leading director Frank Capra developed a passion for contrasting homespun, Lincolnesque American goodness with ruthless corporate power in a series of celebrated films. The most overtly political of Capra's films, *Mr. Smith Goes to Washington* (1939), was vaguely based on the story of Senator Burton Wheeler, who before his isolationist heyday had arrived in Washington from the Montana farmlands as progressive young crusader. Yet, as Michael Rogin and Kathleen Moran have shown, *Mr. Smith* muddled its political messages and obscured its ideology so completely that Capra—possibly by design—leaves the audience with only a vague yet powerful sense of pride in the little man. (Capra's last political film, *Meet John Doe* [1941], is more pessimistic but equally opaque in its political orientation.)[32]

Finally, there was FDR himself, whose representations in 1930s studio films still startle viewers today. The first FDR movie "appearance" occurred in the 1933 musical extravaganza *Footlight Parade,* in which the Broadway impresario James Cagney's closing stage show "Shanghai Lil" evolves unexpectedly into a patriotic celebration of the New Deal (and the National Recovery Administration in particular). An audience onstage holds up cards to produce a large image of the president's face, as martial band music explodes on the soundtrack. The scene is often considered an illustration of the fervent support of FDR by the brothers Warner, well known as the leading Democrats in Hollywood. Darryl Zanuck at Twentieth Century Fox was another Roosevelt supporter, as was the director John Ford, and it was undoubtedly these men who ensured that the resettlement camp director in California in *The Grapes of Wrath* (1940)—the virtual savior of the Joad family, welcoming them smilingly to the clean and friendly camp at the end of their cross-country ordeal—resembles an ambulant FDR, down to his grin and eyeglasses. In wartime, Warners and Cagney revisited Roosevelt in *Yankee Doodle Dandy* (1942), an award-winning biography of the entertainer George M. Cohan, which begins with Cohan (played by Cagney) visiting the Oval Office and receiving warm praise from President Roosevelt (portrayed once again by a lookalike, but only shown reverently from the back). Zanuck then gambled the Fox studio's assets on an expensive film biography of FDR's mentor Woodrow Wilson, which explicitly endorsed the internationalism at the heart of American policy during World War II. These films collectively represented the apex of Hollywood's favorable depiction of a sitting president and his goals.

———

Franklin Roosevelt's strong and varied relationship with Hollywood was woven out of political, economic, and social strands. In many ways, the relationship was the maturation of the connections between politics and show business that had been nurtured since the early 1800s. Like Fanny Elssler and General Tom Thumb before them, movie people came to call at the White House to lighten momentarily the chief executive's burdens and to integrate themselves into the reputable social circles to which he belonged by virtue of his office. Like Edwin Booth and Joseph Jefferson, 1930s movie figures consorted with the president and his family as approximate social peers, as people who understood equally the pressures of life in the public eye and who shared in the amenities of a privileged existence. Politicians and entertainers of the first rank now helped constitute a new leisure class. Franklin and Eleanor Roosevelt's children, raised in comfort but also often neglected by their busy parents, found kindred spirits in the spendthrift, restless, and often-married young people who populated much of the 1930s film community. By FDR's time in office, both actors and politicians similarly pursued the elusive approval of the mass public, employing professionals who engaged in the arcane practice of building their clients' popularity and public allegiance. Like Louis B. Mayer and other studio chiefs, FDR exploited new mass media to ensure the maximum distribution and effectiveness of his "product"—the New Deal, followed by the preparedness effort preceding World War II.

Nevertheless tensions existed between the two camps. Studio heads such as Mayer, Hearst, and Zanuck did not merely socialize with powerful officeholders; they also lobbied them. Like other industries before it, Hollywood beat a path to Washington to win support for favorable legislation, taxation, and a diminution of government regulation. The Justice Department's two-decade-long effort to divest studios of their theater chains on the basis of the

Sherman Anti-Trust Act formed the policy background against which the Roosevelt's social relationship with actors, actresses, and producers evolved. The issue came briefly to the foreground in the late 1930s, when a new anti-trust campaign led by the Justice official Thurman Arnold brought public attention to James Roosevelt's employment by Samuel Goldwyn. The producer was accused by Arnold of "block-booking" his movies in theaters to the detriment of smaller movie producers. War temporarily revived a more collegial tie between government and the movies. Washington's interest in movie making as a vehicle for wartime propaganda, first nurtured by George Creel during World War I, led to a full-blown effort to recruit Hollywood for the cause during its sequel. FDR's Office of War Information set up an office in Hollywood with a staff of one hundred, which collaborated in "close liaison with representatives of the motion picture industry" to produce dozens of "informational" short films, to be shown in theaters.[33]

It is equally true, though, that Franklin Delano Roosevelt's personal qualities and story helped to invest the diverse relationship between Hollywood and the White House with a special resonance. This resonance in particular would enhance the figure of the president in certain cinematic terms—in other words, in terms that reflected the publicizing of heroic male figures in mass culture. As the theater provided Lincoln with emotional and philosophical guides to leadership, movies provided FDR with a mirror in which he could perceive and evaluate the deeper meanings of his life and his presidency. The fundamental reason for this deep bond lay in Roosevelt's unprecedented employment of performance (as dramatic artists understood the word) in service to his presidency. While Lincoln mined Shakespeare to enrich the music and the tragic weight of his prose and pondered melodramas (as well as Shakespearean tragedy) to elucidate his career-long fascination with tyranny and its consequences, Roosevelt, in keeping with his times, strove for a lighter touch. Through his effective use of radio in the Fireside Chats, he built on his cousin Theodore's efforts to transform political speech from orotund Victorian practice to casual conversation suited to the age of mass media. He consciously confined the vocabulary of the Chats to about a thousand of the most common words, and always broadcast to a small group of guests in the Oval Office to create the feeling of an actual conversation. To be sure, Roosevelt proved equally effective, especially during election campaigns, at booming and occasionally portentous oratory before huge crowds, but here too he showed his mastery of the microphone, adjusting his voice to the space and its echo and providing a novel new variety of temperaments, extending to effective uses of humor. Through his skilled introduction of light and humorous speaking qualities to presidential oratory, as well as the general buoyancy of many of his public appearances, Roosevelt conveyed his appreciation for comic acting and monology, in the style of Will Rogers and similar performers of the time.

The president's most important performance by far was the deception with which he masked his physical disability. As biographers have increasingly stressed in the past few decades, while every citizen knew about Roosevelt's bout with polio, which afflicted him below the waist in 1921, almost none of them ever saw it literally paralyze him. In public the president walked, stood, smiled, and confidently led the nation. FDR was brazen enough in his first inaugural address to characterize fear as "nameless, unreasoning, unjustified terror, which paralyzes needed efforts to convert retreat into advance," apparently unworried that his passing reference to paralysis might diminish his own image at the very moment he was attaining power. As recent chronicles of his life especially attest, from the time he contracted polio FDR spent virtually waking hour of his life battling the image of the invalid, first to restart and to advance his political career and then, as president, to project the traditional image of the national leader—a Washington, Jackson, Lincoln, or Theodore Roosevelt "running" for office and "marching" the people forward. In the age of movies, this expectation was heightened. As the art historian Sally Stein has observed, "today's mass media intensifies the popular impulse to scrutinize the bodies of leaders and would-be leaders for signs of the[ir] abilities." Even in the electronic age, while "absolute monarchs may sit . . . politicians dependent on popular mandate are expected to demonstrate quite literally their 'good standing' by rising to present themselves to their constituents."[34]

For Roosevelt, confronting such expectations was an unyielding physical and psychological challenge. His campaign led him to acquire a spa in Warm Springs, Georgia; experiment with quack medical remedies; devise steel leg braces and paint them black so that they would not be detected against his socks; and feign walking, falling forward while a strong man grasped his arm.

He even assumed the traditional leader's pose by mounting a horse during his campaign in 1928 for the governorship of New York. Since his legs could not grip the horse's flanks, this was a dangerous stunt; a slight movement by the animal likely would have thrown him to the ground. These efforts were only part of his ordeal, though. As one biographer, H. W. Brands, has put it, FDR

> had determined, not long after contracting polio, that he would deny its effects on his life and dreams. The sheer physical effort of standing in his braces, of staggering forward, step by lurching step, of smiling through the sweat and the clenched hands gripping the lectern for dear life, would have exhausted anyone. But the emotional effort was at least as great. He couldn't show his anger at his lost athleticism, his vanished virility, his physical dependence on others. He couldn't be discouraged or despondent. . . . The result of all this was that the actor never left the stage.[35]

Even during times of relaxation such as his "children's hours"—afternoon cocktails usually in the company of his adoring female secretaries and cousins —FDR projected an air of insouciance and buoyancy, mixing drinks while seated behind the liquor cart. In the dark first days of his administration, as the financial system hung in the balance, his adviser Raymond Moley found him to be almost unreal, "unmoved" by turmoil as if he "had no nerves at all." Earlier, at the inaugural ceremony, the pioneering motion picture actress Lillian Gish—who was perhaps uniquely qualified to render evaluations of an individual's "star quality"—marveled at Roosevelt, exclaiming that the new president seemed "to have been dipped in phosphorus."[36]

Coupled with this, as Brands perceptively notes, was the fact that Roosevelt was by nature a devious and misleading personality. "He had been emotionally isolated since boyhood. His close relationships had always been with persons not his equal. He had no close friends as a boy or young man, no one at Groton or Harvard in whom he genuinely confided." Decades before he fell to polio, he enjoyed fooling people with verbal misdirection and his befogging brand of charm. Voters heard the young FDR boast about achievements that were entirely the work of others; election opponents, lulled into complacency by his genteel demeanor, learned only later of his ruthless campaign plotting and dealmaking; and he betrayed Eleanor by conducting an affair with Lucy Mercer, her own secretary. Eleanor's uncle Theodore, as

Booker T. Washington and many others noted, had seemed totally lacking in deviousness, possessing a "straightforward indiscretion, [a] frankness to the point of rudeness."[37] His cousin Franklin's demeanor could not have been more different. Part of the difference was due to changing times. In the decades after Theodore's death, the advertising and public relations industries asserted that individuals (as well as corporations) must wear a carefully constructed public face in order to succeed, and the motivational speaker Dale Carnegie sold millions of books advising ambitious young men to mask their mundane, everyday selves in job interviews or in business transactions. In an era that celebrated public deception for the benefit of advancement, FDR was a truly representative man. His Herculean efforts to mask his paralysis and his despair made him a virtuoso of deceptive public performance.

As president, manipulating allies and foes alike, Roosevelt kept the goals of the New Deal multiple and often contradictory, so that he might preserve maximum political flexibility. He admiringly called himself "the juggler," but some of his machinations also held a cruel edge. More than most presidents, as the biographer Conrad Black put it, "Roosevelt punished his enemies." Stung by the opposition to the New Deal of Moses Annenberg, publisher of the *Philadelphia Inquirer,* FDR led a relentless effort to convict Annenberg for income tax evasion and sentence him to maximum time. Roosevelt ignored petitions on Annenberg's behalf from Jack Warner, the movie comedian Eddie Cantor, and many others, and the publisher remained in federal prison until shortly before his death. Ambassador Joseph Kennedy had done FDR no favors by blatantly claiming that Great Britain—the country in which he was stationed—was doomed to fall to Hitler, but Roosevelt's bizarre and utterly insincere audiences with Kennedy during his visit home in November 1940, in which he lavished praise and sympathy on the diplomat, seemed designed only to make his imminent firing all the more brutal. As in Annenberg's case, the movie industry played a supporting role in Kennedy's fall. Speaking at a luncheon in Hollywood given in his honor by studio chiefs, the ambassador made his most strident isolationist comments to date, praising Hitler's regime in front of dozens of Jewish producers and directors. Douglas Fairbanks Jr. reported Kennedy's comments to the White House, and the president summoned Kennedy to his home in Hyde Park. Moments after he greeted the ambassador, FDR seethed to Eleanor, "I never want to see that son of a bitch again as long as I live!" brusquely ordering her to take him to the train station.[38]

Such deviousness and cruelty, of course, are not uncommon in the annals of politics and leadership, and more than most leaders, Franklin Roosevelt might be excused for utilizing such means to achieve noble ends. Nevertheless, if we observe his tactics in tandem with his campaign to hide his paralysis and with his sensitivity to the power of mass media, such as radio and motion pictures, we sense that FDR was building new connections among the presidential image, political tactics, and the growing cultural appetite for celebrity. It is particularly notable that while Roosevelt and his inner circle worked to hide his paralysis, they also relied upon his audiences—the press and the electorate—to willingly suspend their disbelief, to play along with the ruse that FDR really could walk and "stand for office" like any other strong leader. As Sally Stein notes, the public conspired with FDR to cover up his actual physical condition, engaging in "a collaborative process of dealing with the president's lack of conventional signs of mastery." In late 1932, when an article in *Time* magazine made a passing reference to the president-elect's "shriveled legs," hundreds of readers wrote indignant letters, and the magazine refrained from using such language again.[39] It is difficult to quantify the impact of the public's desire to protect Roosevelt's image and to help him maintain the illusion of conventional physical strength. Although he faced some of the most adverse political and social challenges in American history, across an unprecedented three full terms and four election campaigns, the illusion persisted.

Nevertheless, under the strain of managing the greatest war effort in history, Roosevelt's health gave way. As H. W. Brands has put it, "by the twelfth year in the presidential spotlight, the performer's constitution was breaking down."[40] On September 18, 1944, during meetings in Quebec with Winston Churchill, FDR treated the prime minister to an evening screening of *Wilson,* Darryl Zanuck's lavish new film biography of the last wartime president. The evening was a testament to the growing role of motion pictures in the formulation of the presidential image. The movie itself was both the apogee of presidential depictions during the FDR presidency and Zanuck's personal endorsement of the Wilsonian internationalism that Roosevelt and Churchill were promoting through the United Nations. Wendell Willkie—FDR's erstwhile opponent, the MPPDA's counsel, and a champion of international-ism—was one of the film's producers. Willkie's recent heart attacks (which led to his death weeks later) cast a pall over the screening, deepening every-one's concerns about Roosevelt's own declining health. Churchill in Quebec had been shocked by the president's appearance, and when the film drama-tized Wilson's stroke and failed battle for the League of Nations, the prime minister rose and retired for the evening. FDR exclaimed to the audience, "By God, that's not going to happen to me!" but after the movie ended and the guests left, a physician recorded a dangerously high blood pressure read-ing for the president.[41]

That fall, as FDR sought reelection for the last time, his purported ill health became the dominant campaign issue. The concerned president reached out to Hollywood for help in discounting the rumors. As a journal-ist reported in October, the film producer Walter Wanger, "friend and champion of the President, has sent his best lighting experts here to super-vise all still photographs of the Chief Executive, [the] result of a number of badly handled pictures recently." The photographs reproduced in the news stories eradicated few of the signs of overwork and failing health on FDR's face, but the symbolism of Wanger's gesture, at that point in the life of the most complex political performer and most dedicated friend of Hollywood in presidential history, was entirely apposite.[42]

———

In April 1945, two weeks after Roosevelt's death, the film critic James Agee remarked in *The Nation* that his view of the president had changed in the past two years. To him, "much that had seemed frivolous and even silly in Roo-sevelt" now appeared to be "the high-pitched nervousness of a vivid, sensitive intelligence . . . inextricable from an extraordinary gallantry." "Now, beyond any question, it seems to me," Agee wrote, "he was himself becoming a great man. . . . His face was becoming the face of a religious [man], even of a seer, without loss of its adroitness and worldly resourcefulness and its singular, tri-umphant, essential gaiety." FDR's "curiously light, shining, calm recklessness" gave Agee "hope of a kind it was impossible to feel in any other living man."

Agee, a film critic by profession, drew his impressions of Roosevelt from filmed images of the president made at the Big Three conferences at Teheran and Yalta. Never having met FDR, he evaluated his apparent significant evolution as an individual on the basis of the newsreel record. The month of Roosevelt's death and Agee's essay was one of the most dramatic in modern history; the vast movements of armies in Europe and the ghastly events in Berlin and Okinawa eclipsed the visions of even the most ambitious movie scenarists. If the events of preceding years had not yet persuaded Americans, April 1945 confirmed that real life provided drama far in excess of any fiction. In his ruminations Agee searched for the truth in FDR's movie face and claimed that he was convinced that these images provided evidence of the president's unique and profound character. The prose in this *Nation* piece was a transcendental (or perhaps merely grandiose) version of the language Agee typically used to evaluate actors' film performances. Agee even infuses Roosevelt's successor, Harry S. Truman, with an unlikely supernatural quality. Truman "is not very far, if far at all, from what we too contemptuously describe as mediocrity," but "the best that is in any ordinary man is illimitable; and now when that kind of faith is to be so severely tested, in the President and, just as acutely, in millions of others, I find it greatly fortified."[43]

As the apparent drama of national leadership took on portentous new dimensions in the atomic postwar era, and as the president became both increasingly powerful and more of a personification of America's global struggles, citizens, like Agee, adopted the perspectives and the critical language of the discerning moviegoer to make sense of presidents, their power, and their responsibilities.

CHAPTER 3

THE OLD MAN AND TV,
1945–1960

On February 10, 1945, Franklin Roosevelt's new vice president, Harry S. Truman, made an unannounced visit to the National Press Club in Washington, where a delegation from the Hollywood Canteen was entertaining troops, journalists, and bureaucrats. The names of participating movie celebrities had remained unannounced as well, to build anticipation and excitement among the crowd. A young studio contract player named Victor Mature appeared in one skit, but the heaviest applause greeted Lauren Bacall. Only twenty years old, Bacall was even greener than Mature as a screen actor, but her single role to date was a radiant one, a starring performance as Slim opposite Humphrey Bogart in *To Have and Have Not*. The movie had been released nationally on the same day that Truman became vice president, three weeks before the Canteen show in Washington. New and inexperienced, Bacall arrived late to the show, just as Truman, a skilled pianist, sat down at an upright to play an impromptu number. At the urging of a studio press agent, she climbed on top of the piano, stretching out her long legs. As eager photographers went to work, Bacall maintained the smoldering look she had developed for Slim while Truman, playing away, obligingly smiled for the cameras.[1]

These famous images—a handful of different shots of the occasion have competed for primacy—remain among the most arresting portraits of the conjunction of politics and motion pictures. In large measure they were the products of two converging cultural tendencies. Bacall's instant stardom, coming only months after she had been discovered by a studio agent while working as a Canteen hostess in New York, was a kind of apotheosis of Hollywood's now-celebrated star-making alchemy. For *To Have and Have Not*, the former Betty Joan Perske was given a stage name, coached to speak in a husky new voice, and restyled and dressed to resemble Nancy "Slim" Hawks, the wife of the film's director, Howard Hawks.[2] In the movie Bacall projected a novel, blunt femininity that captivated movie audiences (as well as her co-star, Humphrey Bogart, who became her husband months later). Truman's willingness to play along with the photo stunt, by contrast, was a by-product of the traditional lack of seriousness with which Americans regarded their vice presidents. Even though six vice presidents before him had ascended to the presidency on the deaths of their predecessors, nominees to the office continued to be chosen by the parties largely on the basis of their electoral appeal and were given virtually no meaningful work to do after they were elected.

The insouciance of the moment, as a representation of the spirit of the movies and of Truman's career, was fleeting. Although FDR's failing health was evident, the popular self-delusion about the vitality of the chief executive, who had been in office for twelve crisis-filled years, persisted until the end. His death on April 12, 1945, shocked the public, and the ascendancy to the Oval Office of Truman, a relative unknown, at a pivotal moment in national and world history made them uncertain and anxious. It was unthinkable for Truman, now president, to participate in photo opportunities as frivolous as the one at the National Press Club. Similarly, the "golden age" of the Hollywood studios, as popular historians have come to call it, was on the brink of coming to an end. As World War II wound down, labor pressures reshaped the industry and began to erode the contract player system; antitrust actions by the government finally stripped studios of their theater chains; and independent producers gained new power and took much filming away from Hollywood soundstages, and even out of the country altogether.

Later in the 1940s, as America eased into peacetime prosperity and assumed world leadership during the Cold War, television matured as a mass medium. To an extent, it began to take on some of the movies' function of transmitting images to the mass audience and thus began to drain away some of their prominence in the culture. TV also usurped much of radio's role as a mass medium that brought entertainment and news into the nation's living rooms. Television differed from movies in some important ways; above all, its tiny screens seemed to pose little challenge to their vast and glamorous movie-theater counterparts. Nevertheless, studio executives considered the arrival of television a threat to their livelihood. The first Cold War presidents—Truman and Dwight D. Eisenhower—did not smoothly master the challenge of tailoring their communication styles to the parameters of the small screen. Yet it was during the 1950s that TV came to replicate some of the cosmetic realism and star-making power that had made movies so potent. As a result, even the often ungainly early television appearances of Truman and Eisenhower helped to fix a cinematic image of the presidency more firmly in American culture. Despite the turmoil in the entertainment industry and other cultural changes in the fifteen years after World War II, the structural and imagistic connections between American politics and entertainment strengthened, and they helped to blend public figures and celebrity image making in the perceptions of citizen-moviegoers.

———

In the days and weeks after Truman became president, there were reminders of the close new familiarity that had developed between Hollywood and the White House during the Roosevelt years. The day after FDR's death, the producer David O. Selznick cabled the secretary of the navy, James Forrestal, with the suggestion that Truman film a greeting to the nation that might be shown in movie theaters. A few days later, Will Hays sent a telegram in which he conveyed his sympathies, along with those of "many outstanding members of the Film Industry," and took the opportunity to recommend Eleanor Roosevelt for some kind of government job. Later that month, during the week of Adolf Hitler's suicide, the studio head Harry Warner requested a meeting with Truman to discuss the possibility of using American movies to "re-educat[e] the present & future generations of Germany, so that a calamity such as we are now experiencing, will never happen again." (Soon after the Nazi surrender, Warner's brother Jack toured Germany and Italy for that purpose, and two years later Samuel Goldwyn explained to

Truman how his film *The Best Years of Our Lives* was being used "in re-educating the Germans.") Later that year, Truman telegraphed his thanks to the studios for their assistance in the sale of war bonds. The studios briefly kept the FDR birthday observations alive in Washington in support of the March of Dimes. In January 1946, what a presidential aide called "the usual movie stars' luncheon" took place at the White House for the last time, in conjunction with the unveiling of the new design for the dime, featuring Roosevelt's image.[3]

Like Herbert Hoover, but rather unlike FDR, Truman set a policy that strictly regulated the use of his image in movies, as well as in other mass media. White House aides refused to allow newsreel footage of the president to be used in commercial features and denied permission to various produc-ers who sought to have actors impersonate him in fiction films. These included Frank Capra's *It's a Wonderful Life*, which called for "Truman," shown from behind, to award George Bailey's brother the Congressional Medal of Honor, in a scene that was scripted but never filmed. In an excep-tion, MGM was permitted to inspect and then re-create White House interiors for its film on the first atomic bombs, *The Beginning or the End*, and the president was portrayed in a cameo by the actor Art Baker. (Baker and his mother wrote letters to Truman expressing their pride in this per-formance and received warm replies.) More generally, the War and Navy departments—later merged as the Department of Defense—continued to cooperate extensively with Hollywood, providing access to materiel, ships, and even bases for the production of military-themed movies. In 1946 the Navy even found propaganda value in a proposed film on the life of the Revolutionary War hero John Paul Jones and offered assistance to its pro-ducer, Samuel Bronston.[4]

In other ways the Truman presidency maintained cordial relations with motion picture professionals. General Harry Vaughn, the president's mili-tary aide, lobbied studio heads to cast his friend, the actor Phil Regan, in leading roles, while John R. Steelman, the White House's public relations specialist, wrote friendly notes to film stars such as James Stewart. Stewart, an Air Force Reserve officer, met Truman in the Oval Office with a group of his military colleagues, and Bob Hope also shook hands with the president there on the occasion of a Red Cross fundraising event. The 1948 campaign and the inauguration ceremony the following January brought Truman into his heaviest contact with well-known movie performers. Ronald Reagan, Humphrey Bogart, and George Jessel joined the president on the dais during a campaign event, while many other stars traveled to Washington for the inauguration. These festivities yielded a striking photograph in which the film actor Robert Preston strikes a conciliatory pose, standing between President Truman and his defeated rival, Thomas E. Dewey, as they shake hands.[5]

These contacts, though, were relatively few in number compared with the annual birthday celebrations of the FDR years. Their paucity may have reflected new tensions surrounding the movie industry, which in some cases were echoes of larger disputes within American and international politics and culture. First of all, postwar conditions led studio chiefs to be deeply uncertain about the future. Simmering conflicts between unions and management in Hollywood erupted in 1945 after V-E Day. Congresswoman Helen Gahagan Douglas cabled the president about the use of tear gas and "goon squads" to break up demonstrations in the bitter strike by the carpenters union against Warner Brothers; another eyewitness to this battle, the young film actor Ronald Reagan, was sufficiently shaken to deepen his involvement in industry politics. Wartime financing had also hobbled Hollywood. The British and Australian governments, among others, had impounded all US studios' profits held within their borders; the squabbles over these monies (which totaled hundreds of millions of dollars) persisted long after 1945. Settlements eventually forced the studios to spend their captive assets abroad, on location filming around the globe. This new trend put great influence (and capital) into the hands of the independent producers who spearheaded most of these overseas productions and who, by 1950, had begun to set up shop in Southern California as well. The monopoly of the major studios steadily weakened.[6]

Simultaneously, in 1948, the US Supreme Court, in the climax of twenty years of federal prosecution under the Sherman Antitrust Act, ruled in *United States v. Paramount Pictures, Inc.* against the studios' ownership of movie theater chains and control of booking across the nation. In another boon for independent producers, theater divestment sharply reduced the major companies' profits. Coupled with the rise of television, *United States v. Paramount* heralded the end of the studios' dominance of American movies.

President Truman occasionally turned his attention to these issues, such as in 1949, when the veteran producer and director Cecil B. DeMille wrote the president about his concerns over captive assets in Britain and declining studio profits. DeMille recommended that Truman speak with Reagan, now the president of the Screen Actors Guild, about these issues. Truman responded to DeMille later, reporting that "I had a very pleasant interview with Mr. Ronald Reagan and Mr. Ray Brewer in regard to some difficulties of the Picture industry."[7]

Hollywood's economic difficulties were matched by the profound moral dilemmas of the early Cold War era, as politicians' exploitation of the internal security issue gave rise to the hunt for suspected Communists in the movie industry. The efforts of the House Un-American Activities Committee (HUAC) to ferret out Communists and "fellow travelers" who had supported the prewar Popular Front, the United States' alliance with the USSR, and continued US-USSR cooperation after the war—resulting in the persecution of the Hollywood Ten and many others and in the studio blacklists—are all familiar chapters in modern US history. It is sufficient to note here that the legal morasses, the savage personal divisions, and the general pall over artistic freedom that the Red Scare inflicted on Hollywood helped to embroil motion pictures more fully in the ugliest national political conflicts.

Members of the community were compelled to take sides. While some were humiliated and rendered unemployed by accusations of Communist sympathies, others found a new public voice as advocates either for prosecution or for the defense of the accused. While Humphrey Bogart, Gene Kelly, Betsy Blair, Lauren Bacall, and others—who defended the rights of the accused—and Gary Cooper, Robert Taylor, Walt Disney, and John Wayne—who championed the exposure of Communists—continued to make movies and maintain their artistic and celebrity profiles, years of accusations, subpoenas, headlines, and highly publicized recriminations derailed friendships and fostered animosities that persisted for decades. In the process, what Hollywood did, and especially the content of the films it produced, became associated more closely with the bitter political and policy disputes of the early Cold War.

These tensions are for the most part curiously absent from the Truman White House's correspondence with movie people. An exception can be found in the exchange of letters between the presidential aide John Steelman and a broadcast professional in New York in 1951. In the exchange, Steelman and the executive discussed the Truman Administration's "plan to combat lies with history" through an anti-McCarthyite "White House Radio and TV concept" that would utilize "broadcasting and television facilities" for a "Campaign for Truth." These letters indicate that while White House relations with the movie industry had become rather tenuous, lacking in energy and a common purpose, relations with film's new sister medium, television, grew in importance every year.[8]

––––––

In 1939, President Franklin Roosevelt had been the first person ever to appear on an interstate television broadcast, relayed from Washington onto screens at the New York World's Fair. Yet World War II had curtailed the growth of TV. When Truman took office in 1945 virtually no one owned a television set, and only a handful of local stations had been established. Broadcasting was in its infancy. Cable television debuted prematurely in 1945, when service between New York and Washington was inaugurated through the coaxial telephone lines; in December of that year the Army-Navy football game was relayed this way to a few cities. A full year later, though, at the end of 1946, TV still was largely a local phenomenon, and even the White House contained not a single television set. Within four years, however, President Truman had "several television sets including one for color" at his disposal, and a year later his staff was producing its own television program.[9] Just as the years 1945–50 witnessed a dramatic growth in the United States' world leadership and Cold War belligerence, they also saw a revolution in presidential mass communication that was driven by the growth of television.

White House aides initially treated television in the same way their predecessors had movies and radio—as a new technology that was largely an annoyance and an intrusion. Responding in 1947 to a request that Truman address a conference in Boston via television, White House secretary Charles G. Ross insisted that "the President can't possibly take this on. He has been besieged with requests for stunts of this sort and has turned them all down." Every communications medium starts out as a novelty, and television, like the others, inspired odd experimentation in the years before society finally determined its most appropriate functions. Once Truman began speaking on television, a number of citizens sent the president photographs they had taken of him appearing on their consoles; "this is a new hobby I am trying to get started in Chicago with the television photo fans," one of them wrote. Naïve individuals wrote the president to ask him to evaluate a piano instruction program airing in Washington, D.C., and to appear on a New York show called *Bowling Headliners.* Television coverage of important events in the late 1940s was minimal. Even a major anticipated event such as Truman's victory speech in November 1948 to a crowd in Independence, Missouri, the day after his stunning upset of Thomas E. Dewey, was not captured by any television camera; one of his aides was left to speculate that the speech "may have been carried by a local radio station."[10]

Television emerged fitfully in the late 1940s, but with the establishment of broadcasting networks and improvements in technology, its presence grew steadily. In 1940 Harry Truman himself, then a senator, had foreseen the new medium becoming a tool for politicians and journalists, remarking that "television, no doubt, will be perfected very shortly and then I don't see where the newspapers will have a leg to stand on." TV was first used as an instrument of communication in the White House on October 5, 1947, when Truman taped an appearance in the Oval Office with an official from the Food Committee Program. Echoing his earlier statement, the president noted that with this event, "we certainly have reached a milestone in broadcasting and I am wondering how the old time orators are going to meet the situation. Since I am not an orator it doesn't affect me." By late 1947 the White House was stocked with TV consoles; Truman acquired the habit of watching broadcasts of his own filmed speeches, and he entered the good graces of reporters by "letting those in the press room use his television set [to watch] the World Series." The political conventions of 1948 were the first to be televised, and a makeup artist was made available to speakers at the Democratic gathering. The following January, in a sign of the changing times, Lowell Thomas spun his "live" description of Truman's inauguration on his radio program while watching the event on television. Later in 1949 Truman made occasional broadcasts, such as a partisan message he delivered on Democratic Women's Day.[11]

It was in that year, the first in which television broadcasting became a national fixture, that the earliest popular fascination with the president's appearances on the small screen can be detected. Correspondence coming to Truman's office illustrated how people's ideas about TV derived in part from preexisting concepts of motion pictures, particularly newsreels, and radio. Even before television became prominent, Truman had been urged by many letter writers to deliver his own series of Fireside Chats on the radio. The Korean War increased the sense of urgency with which these suggestions were made, and as the war had begun in 1950, they now usually recommended that the Chats take place on television. One letter writer urged Truman to create a television program called *Let's Pray with the President.*[12]

The White House did not act on this suggestion, but it did devise a show for TV, an informational series entitled *Battle Report: Washington,* produced in cooperation with NBC News. Airing from August 1950 to April 1953—after Truman left office—the program echoed both the stated intent and the eventual product of George Creel's Committee on Public Information during World War I. Ostensibly a neutral source for information on the Korean War, *Battle Report* was in fact the White House's "campaign for truth," "basically . . . a vehicle for presenting the Truman Administration's policies and views to the American public." Eighty-six episodes featured figures from the administration and the military, who described both the war effort and domestic policy from Truman's point of view. The host of the program was John R. Steelman, an economist and former New Deal official who had also worked in public relations, and who first served Truman during his battles in 1946 with the United Mine Workers and other striking unions.

Steelman directed the White House's Radio and Television Office, the first organized effort to shape the presidential message for the mass media. His primary assistant was Charles W. Jackson, a veteran advertising executive who had worked in the Office of War Information and had also concocted the National Forest Service's "Smokey the Bear" fire prevention campaign. Truman himself never appeared on the program, and since opinion polls indicated that his presidency remained highly unpopular from 1951 to 1953, its impact on public opinion was apparently negligible. Nevertheless, *Battle Report: Washington* was a harbinger of future efforts at presidential image making. Just as Calvin Coolidge was an unlikely but significant pioneer in the presidential exploitation of radio and photo opportunities, Harry Truman was responsible for important new public relations techniques that depended on television.[13]

The culture of motion picture stardom had encouraged the public to take an interest in the president's personal qualities as they came across in the mass media, in his manner and apparent personality. The origins of this interest in personality can probably be traced back to the Hoover presidency, when the chief executive first appeared in widely disseminated talking newsreels. Herbert Hoover was not an accomplished orator in any setting, and correspondents noted his particular shortcomings as a speaker on film. In the process, they anticipated the emphasis on personal authenticity and relaxed style that we tend to associate with the television age a generation later.

In 1931 a man named E. I. Kauffmann suggested in a telegram to Hoover that "for [the] purpose [of] restoring public confidence facts and figures are seldom understood by [the] masses[, but] nearly everyone understands and remembers all they see and hear at picture shows." Kauffmann proposed a US Department of Public Relations, "certain that foremost actors['] and actresses['] aid could be enlisted." "Possibly [the] entire motion picture industry will cooperate . . . pictures can do more than any other method." George Akerson, a former Hoover aide who now worked in Hollywood, endorsed Kaufmann's ideas and noted that studio heads had also been notified of his suggestion. Akerson added that behavioral psychologists such as John Watson had demonstrated the primacy of visual imagery in shaping the political perceptions of citizens. Kaufmann's proposed department was not created, but his sentiments were echoed in other letters to Hoover. Shelby O'Neal of Brooklyn lamented that Hoover took "a very unflattering talking picture . . . due I feel to the necessity of having to take his eyes from his audience to refer to his text." O'Neal suggested that Hoover use a primitive teleprompter, printing his speeches in large type on a roll of paper that would unspool behind and above the newsreel camera. This "would give a more definite impression to the audience that [Hoover] is talking to them and not reading his speech. It will also eliminate those side views which do not do him justice."[14]

Twenty years later, Harry Truman received very similar suggestions from citizens who were concerned that his oratorical limitations on television would weaken his effectiveness as president. A Harvard professor suggested in 1949 that aides project his speech behind the TV camera, again so that the president would not have to look down at the text, to "allow the vast audience to see a full-face picture instead of a bowed head." The next year a government employee made the same recommendation and also suggested "that you occupy a seat at a desk or in an easy chair to create a 'man-to-man' or 'homey' atmosphere and permit more effective gestures for emphasis." Another correspondent advised that Truman use a hearing aid through which an assistant might verbally relay his text, to "eliminate distracting shuffling of papers and the reading of notes wherein the speaker must concentrate on the printed material before him and not on his visual appearance which is of prime importance in the television medium." A public relations executive, Richard Krolik, delved further into the problem, noting that "the visual image and the auditory impression" in Truman's TV speeches "do not complement one another. . . . What the eye sees and what the ear hears must be skillfully blended to produce a single, unified impression, or the net result is confusion." Krolik uniquely recommended that Truman use flip charts, "Maps, Graphs, Movable Models, etc." to make his points.[15]

An entire subcategory of the correspondence dealt with the distracting glare that television lighting cast on Truman's eyeglasses. One suggestion (which was rejected by an aide) urged the use of the first generation of teleprompters "due to the thick glasses which the President must wear." Truman himself had earlier dismissed such a conclusion, telling an aide that the problem with one televised speech "was the angle and not the glasses." Nevertheless, broadcasting executives kept harping on the issue, and one from CBS even sent Truman's aides information about glare-proof lenses that he might use for these broadcasts. Interestingly, Truman himself had foreseen this interest in mass-media cosmetics. As we have seen, he had predicted in 1940 that television would supersede print journalism, and after his first screen appearance in late 1947 he predicted that traditional oratory would fade in the glare of TV lights. He also commented at that time that he "would like very much to see himself [on television] so that he could make corrections of errors of appearance. . . . [It] is going to be pretty hard on the old politicians to stand in front of the television and talk."[16] Increasingly in future years, presidents and other politicians would strive to perceive themselves as the masses of television viewers saw them.

As president during the early years of the Cold War, Harry Truman routinized the global power of his office and made permanent the national security state that Franklin Roosevelt had originated during World War II. As we have seen, such responsibilities encouraged Truman to foreswear casual public appearances such as his vice-presidential tête-à-tête with Lauren Bacall. FDR enjoyed the company of creative and somewhat flamboyant people such as those who had become successful in Hollywood; in addition, he befriended motion picture figures in the 1930s to help revive the industry and maintained those friendships in the 1940s to involve it in the war effort. During the Cold War, Truman's aides recruited the movies to disseminate policy propaganda, but the relationship between the president and his advisers and Hollywood was strained by the HUAC investigation, the studio blacklists, and the studios' forced divestment of their theater chains. Truman's personal aversion to consorting with film stars (or anyone else who flaunted wealth or social position) weakened the social bonds between the movies and the presidency that Roosevelt had nurtured. Yet the revolving door between Washington and Hollywood did persist after the war. Donald Nelson, FDR's head of war production, served as head of the independent producers' lobbying organization after 1945, and Eric Johnston, a businessman who served Roosevelt as both a bureaucrat and a diplomatic troubleshooter, succeeded Will Hays as head of the MPPDA (which under Johnston was renamed the Motion Picture Association of America, or MPAA).

Nevertheless, Truman as president had little time or patience to exploit his political connections with Hollywood. He struggled with world turmoil and with the public's increasing disapproval of his performance, especially in the last few years of his term. Truman was a dapper dresser, but he was also proudly plainspoken, resisting the kind of theatrical gestures and oratorical flourishes that Franklin Roosevelt had cultivated as a political leader. American voters' turning away from Truman toward Dwight D. Eisenhower in the early 1950s represented in part a search for a more appealing and inspiring national leader.

As some scholars have noted, this search also took the form of a new thirst among Americans in these years for wise and fatherly—or grandfatherly—leadership. The historian Kenneth Lynn, for example, has suggested that Ernest Hemingway's mediocre novella *The Old Man and the Sea* (1951) became a best-seller and cultural phenomenon because readers accepted its philosophical bromides as the aged protagonist's—and the aging writer's—hard-won pearls of wisdom. In movies of the moment, Lynn argues, the most celebrated elder paragon was sheriff Will Kane, portrayed by Gary Cooper in *High Noon* (1952). The weathered and stooped Kane famously grasped the horns of an imminent crisis as the seconds ticked away on the town clock, shouldering the burden of confronting a gang of outlaws when cowardly townspeople refused to assist him. (Alan Nadel finds further evidence of such a trend in the biggest box office hit of the 1950s, *The Ten Commandments,* which portrays the aging Moses struggling to preserve his authority over his band of wayward and rebellious Hebrew exiles.) In politics, Lynn notes, the wild public acclamation of General Douglas MacArthur upon his return from Korea, after his firing by Truman in 1951, epitomized Americans' yearning for political leadership from an "old soldier." MacArthur's own awkward steps into the political arena were eclipsed by the successful maneuvering of his counterpart from the other theater of World War II, Dwight Eisenhower. As president, the balding and avuncular Eisenhower embodied the sage leadership that Americans sought in the early 1950s.[17]

———

Eisenhower, unlike Truman, had rehearsed his self-presentation for years before he arrived on the presidential stage. Stationed in the Philippines before the war, Ike was fond of joking, "I studied theatrics under MacArthur for seven years," though his own special skills were honed at the typewriters and in the meeting rooms of the peacetime military bureaucracy. Administrative efficiency and an infectious smile were Eisenhower's main assets as he steadily rose in rank and stature. During the climactic final year of the European war, from D-Day to the German surrender, Eisenhower proved to be a willing and effective mass communicator, giving radio speeches at crucial junctures, narrating a newsreel feature, and introducing the Oscar-winning documentary film *The Final Glory*. David Levy, an advertising executive then serving in the Navy, provided Ike with advice on his radio presentations, and he would remain a confidant to Eisenhower into the next decade. After the war Eisenhower was the most popular man in the United States, an obvious beneficiary of the "man on horseback" syndrome in politics. For years he declined entreaties to run for president, but he also continued to develop his communication skills and keep up his contacts in the mass media.

In the first days of 1952, Eisenhower, then serving in Europe as commander of NATO, maintained a studied indecision about running for president. Nevertheless, a group of supporters led by Senator Henry Cabot Lodge Jr. of Massachusetts put the general's name on primary ballots, launching his campaign for the Republican nomination. This group, which stood outside Eisenhower's private circle of advisers, perceived him through the traditional lens of the military hero entering politics. In a memo from these early days, the president of the Young & Rubicam advertising agency, Sig Larmon, discussed prospective strategy through this soldierly lens. The theme of the campaign, Larmon argued, should be that "here is the only man who can literally save this nation." Larmon did not encourage the campaign to celebrate Eisenhower's character or personality, but to highlight his "outstanding administrative achievements as director of SHAEF." These achievements would receive their apotheosis in a motion picture presentation. Larmon placed great emphasis on a kickoff rally in New York's Madison Square Garden, in which the "smashing dramatic climax" would occur when "the Garden would slowly darken, a large movie-size screen would be lowered, and a television or newsreel film of Eisenhower making one of his historical speeches would be shown on the screen. . . . Its impact upon the audience could have a lasting effect."[18]

The rally at the Garden took place the night of February 8, 1952. No film footage of General Eisenhower was projected, but, tellingly, what Larmon had conceived of as a celebration of a hero was instead, in the words of the *New York Times,* "led by stage, screen, radio, and television stars." Larmon had advised in his memo the previous month that while Eisenhower was attractive in his own right, for the kickoff rally "there is no gainsaying the drawing power of top-notch talent." Ethel Merman belted out a song by Irving Berlin that featured appropriate new lyrics by the composer; Mary

Martin and Richard Rodgers contributed another number; Clark Gable gave a short speech; and Miss New Hampshire, "clad in a bathing suit," led a delegation from the first state to vote in a primary election that year. Eisenhower listened to the event in France via a live radio hookup, but while he remained on active duty he refused to become an active candidate. When he finally did enter the fray, and as he won the hotly contested Republican nomination and stood for the general election, his campaign developed the first television advertising strategy for a presidential candidate (although it was assisted by the Kudner agency, not by Larmon's Young & Rubicam).[19]

In 1952, motion picture actors first became prominent figures in a Republican presidential campaign. Eisenhower's fame and personal appeal encouraged his supporters in Hollywood to create a conservative version of the celebrity phalanx that had contributed to Roosevelt's campaign in 1944 and Truman's in 1948. The veteran film star and director Robert Montgomery, for example, gave hard-hitting speeches before Republican groups, attacking Truman's administration as a "power-drunk cabal of political adventurers" who, by means of the New Deal, were making "an open and notorious flirtation with Marxism."[20]

Also speaking for Eisenhower during the 1952 campaign was John Davis Lodge, the governor of Connecticut and the brother of Senator Henry Cabot Lodge Jr. Lodge, whose appeals for bipartisan support for Eisenhower (whom he portrayed as a moderate) were far less strident than Montgomery's rhetoric, remains a little-noticed but significant pioneer in bridging the movie and political worlds. He was, in fact, the first former Hollywood star ever to be elected a state governor. In the late 1920s Lodge had turned his back on his family's illustrious reputation for public service, his Harvard law degree, and his Wall Street legal practice and followed his wife Francesca, a professional dancer, onto the Broadway stage. In 1932 the couple traveled to Hollywood, where a Paramount executive invited the tall and handsome attorney to make a screen test. After a short apprenticeship, Lodge was given lead roles alongside Marlene Dietrich (in *The Scarlet Empress*), Katharine Hepburn (*Little Women*), and Shirley Temple (*The Little Colonel*), among other leading ladies, although he never achieved major stardom on his own. In the late 1930s the Lodges left California for Europe, where they appeared in films made by important directors. After war broke out there, Lodge returned briefly to Broadway before he entered military service.

Like Douglas Fairbanks Jr., John Lodge found that wartime upheavals made him feel (as his wife put it) that "mouthing the words of others did not seem very much of a challenge anymore."[21] Resettling in Fairfield County, Connecticut—a popular residential area for affluent Broadway show people —Lodge won election in 1946 as a US representative, succeeding the some-time playwright Clare Boothe Luce. Four years later he narrowly won the Connecticut governorship. In 1954 Lodge would be defeated for reelection by an even narrower margin, and he moved on to a series of ambassador-ships in Republican administrations. He reentered politics only once, in an unsuccessful run for the US Senate. Lodge never returned to acting, although his wife occasionally performed, and their daughter Lily became a respected stage performer and acting teacher.

A wartime friend of John Lodge's argued that his two careers were similar and complementary: "90 percent of politics is acting and a political life par-allels an actor's life. Both have to take it on the chin along with the applause." After his gubernatorial defeat, though, Lodge found no success in obtaining a high post in the Eisenhower administration, despite his brother's close ties to the president. An acquaintance of the Lodge brothers at Harvard observed caustically that "John was basically an actor through all his activities—a ham, a performer. . . . not very bright or original," while Henry Cabot Jr. "was intelligent and clever, . . . mean and cold-hearted. He only spoke to those who could aid his work." The contrast between the two brothers per-haps illustrates why show business acumen remained a limited political asset in the 1950s, and why behind-the-scenes calculation remained a more useful skill in public life.[22]

Both show business and cold calculation were amply evident in the most celebrated televised event of the 1952 presidential campaign. The enormously influential "Checkers" speech featured not Eisenhower, but his young run-ning mate, Senator Richard M. Nixon. Nixon's rapid rise in the six years since his first election to Congress was mostly due to his relentless ambition, aided by the support of a group of conservative Republican businessmen in Southern California. Despite his roots in the Los Angeles area, Nixon's relationship with the motion picture industry was largely antagonistic. He participated in the HUAC investigations of Hollywood (although his own focus was fixed on the US State Department and alleged Communists such as Alger Hiss) and, in 1950, won his Senate seat after a bitter fight with his Democratic opponent, Helen Gahagan Douglas, the congresswoman and former film actress who was fully supported by liberals in Hollywood. During the 1952 campaign, when the revelation of a secret businessmen's fund that paid Nixon's political expenses seemed to threaten his place on the national ticket, the senator improvised a hasty television appearance to defend his actions and to ask for fair treatment by the Republican Party.

Nixon's "Checkers" speech was a remarkable new episode in political performance. Attracting thirty million viewers, he spoke before the largest audience in history ever to watch a live political speech. From a mundane apartment set on the stage of Hollywood's El Capitan Theater (the origin of many television broadcasts), speaking from a few pages of scrawled notes, Nixon delivered a mostly improvised defense that had no precedent in American politics. The domestic props, along with the presence of his wife Pat onstage, sitting silently in an easy chair, underscored the fact that Nixon's speech was virtually bereft of policy content. The first third featured the senator's description of the fund and his defense of its use, while the last few moments consisted of his appeal to voters to send messages of support to the Republican National Committee (a highly successful tactic that preserved his place on the ticket). For much of the talk, though, Nixon delineated his family's modest finances and lifestyle. In a particularly maudlin passage, he defended the family's pet, a cocker spaniel named Checkers, who had been given to the family by an admirer. Nixon would later resent the dog's subsequent association with the speech, but Checkers's popularity reflected the senator's canniest rhetorical decision. The references to Checkers were a deliberate evocation of Franklin Roosevelt's celebrated, wry defense of his terrier, Fala, from Republican criticism during the 1944 campaign. In another borrowing from Roosevelt, who had noted Fala's feisty "Scotch" temperament, Nixon paid tribute to his wife's "Irish" fighting spirit.

Against all likelihood, this improvised, issue-free, and dramatically amateurish "performance" became the most startling political triumph of 1952. Above all, the Checkers speech illustrated how a passionate and determined public figure, no matter how ill scripted or ill served by his staging, might strike a golden chord of sympathy with viewers who could appreciate a good show when they saw one. Ironically, in later years Nixon would draw the wrong lessons from the improvised roughness of his Checkers triumph, as well as from his equally spontaneous star turn in the "kitchen debate" in Moscow with Soviet Premier Nikita Khrushchev in 1959. As a presidential candidate the following year he would underprepare for his first televised debate with John F. Kennedy and lose much of his advantage in the public opinion polls. As a defeated candidate for governor of California in 1962, Nixon impulsively gave an angry "last press conference" that inspired journalists to write his political obituary; immediately after he strode away from the microphones he acknowledged to an aide, Herbert Klein, that he should not have made the appearance.

Even in 1952, in the immediate wake of the Checkers speech, Nixon found himself the target of derision as well as sympathy. As always in politics, but especially in the dawning television era, audiences could not fail to detect an element of insincerity and make-believe—in short, the element of playacting—in leaders' public appearances. In the Checkers speech Nixon did not prepare a text, pay much attention to his dress or to the set, or even know, as he began speaking, where his talk might exactly lead. But the overwhelming verdict of Americans in subsequent years, as Nixon's career progressed, was that while the businessmen's fund was at worst a minor ethical offense, the speech Nixon delivered as an explanation committed a more egregious violation: it manipulated symbols and facts for political expediency at all costs. Democrats in particular felt that Nixon's evocations of his daughters, home, and pet, and his constant references to the wife at his side, poorly disguised his ruthless political behavior and craven ambition. The biographer Stephen Ambrose has gone further, arguing that the candidate concocted the entire crisis. Ambrose claims that the inexperienced Nixon overreacted to a few partisan headlines about the fund which could easily have been countered with references to similar financial arrangements made by Democratic politicians. "It was almost as if the whole thing was a drama in which Nixon had somehow contrived to be simultaneously the playwright, the leading actor, and the director."[23] In the short run, Nixon's appeal for support succeeded wildly, as thousands of viewers flooded the Republican

National Committee with pleas to keep him on the ticket. Eisenhower kept Nixon in suspense for a couple of days, shrewdly gauging the impact of his running mate's audacity and the speech's novelty on his November prospects. As Ambrose notes, for manifold political reasons Ike never seriously considered forcing Nixon off the ticket; but as reporters badgered him for a response in the days after the broadcast, the general was compelled against his will to be a supporting player in Nixon's little drama.

The overdetermined and possibly unnecessary theatrics of the Checkers speech foreshadowed the nature of politics in the television age for decades afterward. Hollywood studios had spent decades engaged in similar practices, employing Barnum- and Bernays-style ballyhoo to create countless representations, reflections, comments, pseudo-controversies, critical quarrels, and gossip about otherwise unremarkable new motion pictures. The noise that the trailers, the critical notices, the posters, and the gossip columns created, it was hoped, would sweep consumers up in the frenzy to purchase tickets and see the show. One of the first phone calls Nixon received after returning to his hotel room after delivering the Checkers speech was from Darryl F. Zanuck of Twentieth Century Fox, who congratulated him on "the most tremendous performance I've ever seen."[24] Given Zanuck's expertise in all phases of movie production and publicity, it is doubtful that he was simply praising Nixon's stage comportment. He was likely exulting in the totality of the candidate's calculations in appearing before a new kind of mass audience amid the domestic artifice provided by the set and by Pat Nixon, and in concocting a crisis that invited audience participation and superfluous reactions from the presidential candidate.

While watching Nixon's surprising performance, Eisenhower (who barely knew his running mate) both seethed and marveled at the impertinence of the younger man's self-defense. In the remaining six weeks of his successful campaign for the White House, and in the entire eight years of his presidency, Ike would never engage in a television performance as revealing or as audacious as the Checkers speech.

Still, as we have seen, Eisenhower came to the presidency with a greater appreciation for mass media performance, and for television, than any of his predecessors. His campaign staff in 1952 crafted the first widely broadcast presidential campaign TV commercials, many of them featuring Eisenhower himself. The general easily defeated Adlai Stevenson, his Democratic opponent. As president, Eisenhower pioneered the broadcasting of press conferences on a time-delayed basis, and his performance in this venue was widely praised. Ike seemed, to many, to be a new kind of mass media president, entirely comfortable under the glare of television lights. When Vice President Richard Nixon congratulated his boss on the success of his press conferences, Eisenhower's response was nonchalant: "I've faced cameras too long to mind them now."[25]

Nevertheless, the intensity of the mass gaze on the nation's television screens increased the level of scrutiny of the presidential image. Early complaints about the cosmetics of Eisenhower's TV appearances superficially resembled those directed at Truman, but since television sets were now increasingly common, the criticisms were far more numerous. An appearance soon after the inauguration caused a writer to be "annoyed by the man who flipped and filed the copy of the speech in the background of the television picture." An Eisenhower speech broadcast from New York City in May 1953 incited much criticism for background distractions, in the form of "two pompous . . . politicians" in the audience, "stupid, uncouth, untrained, lacking any semblance of culture," who could be viewed over the president's shoulder chewing on cigars, yawning, and drinking cocktails. Eisenhower received even more advice than Truman had about his eyeglass lenses and frames. An optometrist recommended nonglare lenses and complained that "his present dark frame dominates the picture and detracts from his pleasant expression." Citizens also asked him to speak more slowly than he did at his inauguration, and the editor of a speech magazine criticized Eisenhower's "falling inflection which makes our listening less pleasant."[26]

Eisenhower, though, made little use of television as president until, some months into his term, he became frustrated with his inability to persuade members of Congress to adopt his policies. In response, he made a groundbreaking experimental broadcast from the White House on Christmas Eve and prepared carefully for the televised State of the Union message from the Capitol the next month. Ike and his press secretary, the veteran journalist James Hagerty, anticipated that these appearances would be the first in a series of regular television events. As they had with Truman, citizens picked up on this news and recommended some kind of regular broadcast series. Weekly televised prayer with the president remained a popular request; "breakfast at the White House," as well as daily or weekly broadcasts that might replace traditional press conferences, were also suggested.[27]

Unlike Nixon's Checkers speech, President Eisenhower's TV presentations were carefully scripted, even though the latter disliked reading from prepared texts. He and his staff aspired to ensure a "presidential" dignity in his broadcasts. Harry Truman's often-criticized television appearances weighed heavily on his successor; as Craig Allen writes, Eisenhower's "major concern[s] were details 'beyond his control' that might reduce the impact of his communication."[28] The Christmas Eve 1953 broadcast, essentially a message of thanks for the Korean War armistice that Eisenhower had pushed through earlier that year, also marked the arrival of Hollywood expertise in the White House in the person of the actor Robert Montgomery. The tall, impeccably tailored Montgomery had volunteered his services as a troubleshooter for the president's television appearances, but he became a far more influential shaper of Eisenhower's media image, working on White House broadcasts for six years.

Montgomery had the diverse career experience to straddle the worlds of politics and show business. Drifting as a young man from playwriting to manual labor to acting, he eventually landed in Hollywood in the 1930s and quickly becoming a dependable leading man. Yet almost immediately after securing that status, Montgomery plunged into studio politics, getting himself elected president of the Screen Actors Guild during the turbulent war years (preceding Ronald Reagan in that post). During the war he briefly offered advice on radio delivery to Franklin Roosevelt. Simultaneously he tried his hand at directing, but the commercial failure of his innovative movies—such as *The Lady in the Lake,* which was filmed entirely from the protagonist's point of view—led him to become one of the earliest film stars to embrace television. In 1950 he began producing and serving as the host of a dramatic anthology series, *Robert Montgomery Presents,* which ran on the NBC network for seven years. Unlike Helen Gahagan Douglas or John Lodge, Montgomery never ran for public office. Like Douglas Fairbanks Jr., though, he developed a passion for current events. In 1952, as we have seen,

Montgomery gave forceful speeches before Republican gatherings, attacking the alleged corruption and softness toward Communism of the Truman administration. Tellingly, though, unlike Fairbanks, Montgomery kept a foot in the public sphere by lending a president his expertise in facing the complex image-making challenges posed by television.

The actor found a willing student in Eisenhower. The president's policies and words were the product of the now-standard large team of advisers and writers, but the mechanics of the video broadcast were the sole province of Montgomery, who flew from New York to Washington every Monday night after the live broadcast of his own program. For the 1954 State of the Union address, Montgomery inspected the lectern and lighting in the House chamber and raised the podium three inches, so that the president would face the camera more frequently and not reflect as much television lighting off his bald head. As the *New York Times* reported, Montgomery set up two teleprompters from which Eisenhower could read the text of his speech, to give "audiences the impression that he was talking informally and looking directly at them." The actor also "brought down one of the Columbia Broadcasting System's makeup girls from New York to dust the Presidential pate and face with pancake make-up." Montgomery apparently advised Eisenhower to make frequent use of his famous grin during the address, but according to the *Times,* "to some observers . . . the Eisenhower with the smile . . . was not so impressive as the one who unsmilingly" appeared before the United Nations some weeks before.[29]

Eisenhower enjoyed Montgomery's company and welcomed his professional advice. In March 1954 he wrote the actor a memo that detailed the suggestions of "a man" regarding television appearances. "He objects to any kind of a striped suit on me—from this angle he thought I looked very badly last evening"; "he thinks the lens of the television machine [teleprompter] is too high when I am sitting at the desk"; "he suggested a talk some day on physical fitness in America"; "he also believes that we should occasionally refer to some of the past 'false prosperity' as prefaced by the 'killing of American boys.'"[30] The memo reveals that Eisenhower discussed content as well as style with Montgomery. What it mainly shows, though, is that the chief executive was highly sensitive to the unseen hazards of television broadcasts, which might harm both the substance and the look of his appearances.

Montgomery was instrumental in improving the White House's primitive TV production facilities, located in the basement, and in setting the stage for the president's weekly press conferences, which were edited for broadcast later in the day. The actor's relationship with Eisenhower remained strong during the president's first term, but as early as 1954 Montgomery's tutelage was provoking controversy. The fact was that the actor, like everyone else in broadcasting, was experimenting in a new medium, in which the cosmetic and substantive results, as well as the public's reaction to them, were still difficult to predict. Little stir was caused by Montgomery's designing of a simplified office set, mainly consisting of a desk in front of curtains; but his more intrusive stage-managing of Eisenhower's gestures beginning in early 1954 generated considerable criticism.

Since Montgomery was a well-known figure, his participation in White House image making became a target for critics who mistrusted Hollywood's techniques and who condemned its commitment to artifice. William Klein, who ran a TV studio in Chicago, complained to Eisenhower that the "publicity you have been receiving in the newspapers relative to Robert Montgomery's coaching you on how to speak and face the cameras is doing you no good, and perhaps a great deal of harm." For Klein and many viewers outside the broadcasting profession, the danger lay in obscuring Eisenhower's authenticity. "A good speech [must] sound natural and . . . come from the heart, in which case it will serve its purpose. When the audience feels or notices that a speech is written in advance, or a heart-to-heart talk has been coached and rehearsed in advance, the speaker is at a distinct disadvantage." (Klein seemed to be advising Eisenhower to emulate Nixon's Checkers speech.) The acknowledgment in the press that techniques were at work led Klein to believe that Ike's authenticity was imperiled. "It is a mistake to let the audience 'look behind the scenes.'" Finally, Klein accused Montgomery of exploiting his service to Eisenhower, calling press reports on his work "a personal promotion for Mr. Montgomery rather than . . . constructive publicity for you and your distinguished office."[31]

Attacks on Hollywood artifice, Montgomery's alleged motives, and the cloaking of the "real" Eisenhower intensified after a speech televised on April 5, 1954. Dealing with the momentous issues of the day—the Cold War, the new hydrogen bomb, and McCarthyism—Eisenhower, coached by

Montgomery, adopted an unprecedented "casual" stance (as virtually every observer termed it), on the edge of his desk, often with his arms folded. The president, wearing no eyeglasses, read the speech's text off cue cards. Despite the serious content of the talk—or more likely because of it—viewers angrily protested the casual style of the presentation. Mrs. M. M. Robertson of Kansas City argued that "Ike doesn't need Robert Montgomery to 'stage' his TV appearances. He did better throughout the campaign without Montgomery. There was too much showmanship around FDR & HST. We would rather Ike would just be himself." Robertson knew where to identify the "real" Ike: "It is the look in his eyes we trust—not whether he sits at a desk & peers *over* horn-rimmed glasses or whether he sits *on* a desk & wears no glasses." She accused his adviser of molding the president in his own image. "Montgomery himself is hypersensitive on the subject of age and the use of glasses on his own TV show. Ike is our President—not an actor."[32]

A TV speech given by the president on August 23, 1954, while he was vacationing in Colorado, brought the criticism of Montgomery to a head. Calling the speech "a sorry exhibition, visually and audibly," the Detroit newspaper columnist Fred Tew repeated the charge that "Montgomery apparently is trying to cast Ike in his own image—the smooth, casual type." A letter writer agreed, claiming "there were times when it seemed as though we were looking at Robert Montgomery. . . . He crossed his hands in the approved Montgomery fashion. He put one hand in his coat pocket in the casual Montgomery manner. Like Montgomery, Ike forsook his glasses"—an error, since "Montgomery is television's most notorious fluffer of lines simply because he is too vain to wear glasses and too nearsighted to see without them." A correspondent from West Winfield, New York, alleged that his neighborhood rang with criticism: "'The president is not himself' . . . 'He has lost his own personality by being Montgomerized' . . . 'I had much rather Ike would walk before the TV audience with a May West [*sic*] jacket on or come in a jeep than sit on a table like RM for Ike is a *He-Man* and we don't want a matinee idol.' . . . 'For heaven's sake let's have the *Man* we elected and not a Pygmalion statue by Montgomery.'"[33]

The actor, critics wrote, erred in creating an inauthentic Eisenhower, supposedly untrue to the "real" military hero with whom they claimed to be familiar. A writer to a Wisconsin newspaper lamented "the histrionic touches, the studied gestures and the devices of a professional speaker" in the Denver speech. Montgomery, the writer felt, "is not doing a very good job of making an actor, a performer or whatever he is trying to make out of" the president. Fred Tew also listed things that he believed the president was not. "Mr. Eisenhower is not a politician in the usual sense of the word. He is not the tweedy, casual type. He is not an actor. He is not a smoothly articulate orator like Adlai Stevenson, for example." In a similar vein, E. C. Mills complained to the White House that "we did not elect an actor, or a punster, as President. Had that been what our people wanted, they'd have elected Stevenson."[34]

The critics of the speech drew their perceptions of the "real" Ike from exploits and imagery that predated television. Casualness, Fred Tew argued, "fits Mr. Eisenhower's personality not at all. The man is dynamic. He radiates energy. He speaks rapidly and forcefully. His military bearing adds to the appearance of decisiveness." Above all, Eisenhower "is sincere. And that sincerity has a magnetic quality that makes him a natural leader and turns all of his supposed handicaps into virtues. If the TV advisers and speech writers would just let him alone, his naturalness would 'project' very nicely." In short, Tew argued that Montgomery was thwarting the very goal he had professed, of eliminating obstacles in television broadcasting that would obscure the "real" Eisenhower. E. C. Mills agreed that the president should be presented "in his own natural and most preferred manner." The writer in Wisconsin also endorsed sincerity and authenticity: "there is nothing that projects more effectively on TV than a man simply being himself. . . . We much preferred the old Eisenhower to the No. 1 student of the Robert Montgomery School of Television Acting. We wish Robert Montgomery would leave our president alone."[35]

A White House policy forbade Montgomery and other aides from giving interviews about behind-the-scenes operations, but years later, in a brief book he wrote about television, Montgomery insisted that he had never attempted to turn Eisenhower into a performer. "What I did attempt to do was, in a sense, to educate him about the uses of television," the actor claimed; this included dispelling the president's apparent conviction that on TV one must remain immobile behind a desk or avoid saying "some things." Montgomery portrayed his task largely as a negative one, "to see to it that no technical nonsense or jargon would interfere with" Eisenhower's television appearances. Yet

Montgomery's own account (as well as the evidence presented earlier) contra-
dicts his claim to modesty—"as far as television, was concerned," he states,
"no authority [in the White House] was to supersede mine"—and his description of a 1958 broadcast with Secretary of State John Foster Dulles, in which
Montgomery instructs Eisenhower to feign interest, if necessary, in the secretary's remarks, seems to illustrate a form of performance coaching. That same
year, press secretary James Hagerty declared that it was "entirely up to Mr.
Montgomery . . . to say whether or not there will be any television addresses
by [the] President during [the] month of Oct[ober]."[36]

Montgomery's book, published in 1968, bristles with anger about the
newly strident and hegemonic role of television in public affairs, but it
fails to explore the contradictions inherent in his service to Eisenhower a
decade earlier. Through his attention to lighting, sets, body mannerisms, and
eyewear (or its absence), Montgomery was striving, perhaps unconsciously,
to present a "real" Eisenhower—presumably a civilian version of the military hero, or an idealized political version of Sheriff Will Kane or Hemingway's Old Man of the Sea. As the correspondence to the White House attests,
viewers could not easily disassociate any calculated presentation of the chief
executive on television from role playing, from the deceptiveness of the
theater so long regarded as a disreputable part of American culture. On the
other hand, virtually no one wrote in to criticize the weekly broadcasts of
the president's press conferences, presumably because (as Montgomery
claimed) they provided greater exposure of the "real" leader at work. However, Montgomery had also been responsible for managing the artifice of
those broadcasts, deleting footage that showed the president mangling his
syntax or mishandling an exchange. Citizens' often-expressed wishes to see
the "real" or "sincere" Ike reflected a major cultural shift. In the early twentieth century, Americans had been told to expect and to value the "masks"
developed for appearances in public and on the job—stylized deceptions
that were epitomized in the presidency by FDR's polio-masking artifice.
Now, after World War II, they were newly concerned with authenticity, a
desire to perceive their leader's "real" personality and character and to de-
bunk any traces of deception.

Eisenhower's tenure as president began with energetic efforts to end the
Korean War, recast the rivalry with the Soviet Union, and find a middle road

between laissez-faire and New Deal domestic policies, but as the 1950s progressed, his administration increasingly became reactive and passive, and even directionless. Much of this was the result of Eisenhower's declining health, especially after his heart attack in 1955 and surgery to eradicate ileitis the next year. For much of 1956 it seemed likely that Ike would retire after one term, but he recovered enough to seek reelection. His successful second campaign against Adlai Stevenson necessarily relied heavily on television. The president, weak and still recuperating, largely campaigned in front of the cameras instead of undertaking grueling speaking engagements.

As before, Robert Montgomery was the prime adviser for broadcast efforts in 1956. After his victory in November, Eisenhower sent Montgomery a campaign medallion and claimed "that I can in no way repay you for the time and talent that you expended—and this is a totally inadequate way of saying 'thank you.'" However, the Eisenhower-Dulles broadcast of 1958 drew heavy criticism and likely caused a chill to develop between the president and the actor. In that broadcast, the inexperienced and poorly coached Dulles unexpectedly spoke without pause for twenty minutes, forcing a bored Eisenhower to sit uncomfortably and nod awkwardly at the secretary's monologue. In the late 1950s Montgomery failed either to secure a desired subcabinet position in the administration or to produce a film biography of Eisenhower, in the wake of the cancellation of his TV series *Robert Montgomery Presents*.[37] For these reasons as well, Montgomery virtually ceased his work in the White House. Much of the common perception that the later Eisenhower years were aimless and unsuccessful probably resulted from the comparatively slack and unoriginal efforts to present the president on television during his second term. The innovations of 1954 had run their course.

———

The unprecedented turbulence of the 1930s and 1940s had provided Franklin Roosevelt and Harry Truman with the opportunity to expand the powers of the presidency and the federal government far beyond their previous scope. Dwight Eisenhower preserved and perpetuated this expansion of power in the following decade. The ways in which the public perceived these changes were dictated by their portrayal in the mass media. This was not a new dynamic in the presentation of the presidency, but the perceptions were now inevitably shaped by the nature of the newly dominant media. Radio, motion pictures, and television placed their stamp on the presidential image, but the president himself also worked to construct that image. Owing to physical necessity, FDR had become the master of such image manipulation, but Eisenhower, and even the relatively cautious Truman, also took care to craft successful appearances before broadcast microphones and cameras. Motion pictures, as the mass-disseminated heir to the theater, provided the dominant (fictional) physical and aural representations of masculinity and male leadership, and thus proved to be the most potent model for presidents seeking to present themselves effectively to the public. Radio and television had their own strengths and constraints, but personal presentation in each of these media (especially on TV) owed much to the compelling model found in motion pictures. Politicians' use of movie techniques of self-presentation grew along with their social and regulatory connections with the Hollywood studios, which in turn became a major component of America's economy and were, in various ways, linked to many of the major issues of the day, ranging from antitrust regulation to the hunt for Communists.

The presidents of this era, born in the late nineteenth century, were typical Americans of their generation, shaped by the most dramatic growth of mass communications and the entertainment media ever seen. Yet much of this growth had taken place during their mature years. For all of Roosevelt's and Eisenhower's effectiveness and experience as communicators, they still felt the need to consult professional actors such as Robert Montgomery for advice in broadcasting. However, younger generations of politicians—those "born in this century," as Joseph P. Kennedy's second son would memorably note—had absorbed the cultural impact of the movies as children, and motion pictures would be far more influential in shaping their views—as well as the voters' views—of what being a public figure meant. In the 1960s, even as the motion picture business continued to be buffeted by dramatic economic and technological change, and as domestic and international turbulence reshuffled the array of issues that challenged politicians, the centrality of movies in American political culture only deepened.

In the 1950s, while figures from the generation of elders continued to dominate US politics, Hollywood had undergone its first major purge of older executives. Some of the founders, such as Adolf Zukor of Paramount and the Schenck brothers—Nicholas of MGM and Joseph of Twentieth Century Fox—lingered on as semiretired chairmen of the board. Darryl Zanuck, the mastermind behind Fox's productions, battled with his corporate board over expenses and projects and detested McCarthyism; like many of the actors who were driven away from Hollywood by the blacklist, Zanuck moved to Europe in the 1950s, in his case to pursue a new career as an independent producer.

Louis B. Mayer's forced retirement as MGM's head of production in 1951 was the event that signaled the passing of the old regime. From 1937 to 1945 Mayer had been the highest-salaried individual in the country, earning more than a million dollars annually, and MGM—the studio of *Gone with the Wind* and *The Wizard of Oz*—had largely earned its self-proclaimed reputation as Hollywood's premier production company, with "more stars than there are in the heavens." But times were changing. Mayer's taste in films, rooted in star vehicles with literary credentials and lavish production values, seemed antiquated in the wake of Hiroshima and Auschwitz. In addition, his embrace of HUAC's search for Communists in Hollywood and support for the blacklists enraged younger executives at MGM, particularly Dore Schary, Mayer's titular second-in-command. Schary's political liberalism and endorsement of socially conscious movies in turn alienated the older man. It was Schary who replaced Mayer as head of production. In 1953 David O. Selznick, the independent producer and Mayer's erstwhile son-in-law, advised the former MGM chief to get out of movies and explore public service, noting that "Hoover, [Earl] Warren, [and] Eisenhower" were his "intimate friends."[38] Mayer died four years later, never having made a transition to government work.

That same year, 1957, MGM was on the brink of bankruptcy, having mismanaged the hazardous transition into the television age. Schary had maintained the strong musical production unit, which continued to churn out celebrated song-and-dance films, but under his aegis the studio also overinvested in substandard epics and failed to produce profitable or critically acclaimed lower-budget films. Like most other studios, MGM had made a tentative investment in television production, creating an anthology program of dramas based on the studio's archive of screenplays. Among the major companies, only Universal (actually then known as a "minor major") made an early and successful transition to production for TV. As Thomas Schatz has noted, after the 1948 *Paramount* decree the studios made a critical error. They assumed that since the studios could not legally own clusters of television stations, the new medium was an enemy that should not be courted.[39] Only after television became a ubiquitous fixture in American homes, and after it became clear that TV needed vaults full of old Hollywood films to fill up its endless hours of broadcast time, did a rapprochement occur. Younger executives largely managed the studios' transition to TV production, but they were joined by film actors such as Robert Montgomery, Loretta Young, and Lucille Ball, who had the foresight to realize that the new medium might extend their careers.

Generational transition and the coming of television, though, were only two of the convulsive forces that transformed Hollywood almost beyond recognition in the fifteen years after World War II. Even before the war, independent producers such as David O. Selznick and Samuel Goldwyn were working successfully outside the studio system, crafting their own films and engaging the major companies in bidding wars for distribution rights. Walt Disney, the visionary animator, showed that it was possible for an independent producer to create his own studio. A few major stars, notably Cary Grant, broke free from the contract system before World War II and became freelance performers. Moves toward independence were hastened by conditions during the conflict. In 1944 Olivia de Havilland won a pivotal court decision that allowed her to break her restrictive contract at Warner Brothers, enhancing the ability of other lead actors to become free agents. Some, like Bette Davis and Humphrey Bogart, broke loose after protracted struggles with their studios (Warner Brothers in the case of both Davis and Bogart), while others, such as Clark Gable at MGM, waited patiently until their long contracts expired. The studios' contract system nevertheless persisted into the 1950s, grooming a final batch of young new stars that included Rock Hudson, Kim Novak, and Clint Eastwood.

By then, the actors' agents had assumed a dynamic new role. By the 1950s middlemen such as Lew Wasserman of the Music Corporation of America (MCA) were creating their own film projects, bundling together their actor, writer, and director clients. The finished products then were presented to the studios for advertising and distribution. By 1960 the major companies were largely out of the movie making business, stamping their brands onto films produced elsewhere and overseeing the national and worldwide marketing campaigns that put them into theaters. Wasserman negotiated pathbreaking contracts for such clients as James Stewart, who foreswore salaries in return for the far more lucrative percentages of gross earnings that his movies brought in at the box office. By 1959 MCA was rich enough to buy the Universal studio, divesting itself of its original talent agency to conform to antitrust laws. Meanwhile, the old major studios sold off their soundstages, costumes, props—and even some of their own movies—in a feverish effort to keep themselves afloat. Most of these efforts would fail.

All the while, though, the studios, like MGM in the post-Mayer years, invested huge sums of money each year on a handful of prestige projects that might perpetuate their status as "majors." Epic widescreen movies were mostly produced overseas, to expend captive profits and to exploit cheap labor, and they increasingly featured European co-stars to enhance the films' international marketing appeal. Sometimes, as in the case of Twentieth Century Fox's *Cleopatra* (1963), a studio's reckless spending on a single potential hit pushed it to the brink of bankruptcy. By the late 1960s most studios had to be rescued by corporate buyers, conglomerates that used profits earned from petroleum products, farm crops, and best-selling books to subsidize the free-spending movie producers and directors they now employed.

A final development in the postwar era was highly representative of emerging trends in American culture. Small studios, Hollywood's so-called Poverty Row, had existed on the fringes of the movie business since the 1910s. Early in the era of the talkies, those still surviving on scanty overhead paid subsistence wages to actors and technicians and churned out the grade-B (or -C) westerns, detective stories, and science fiction and comic-book serials that filled out the programming on most movie screens. Unlike the major companies, these studios could not afford to provide elite or even middlebrow entertainment to the public. Veterans of Poverty Row such as the producers Samuel Z. Arkoff, Sam Katzman, and Albert Zugsmith professed little interest in the major studios' artistic aspirations and instead mastered the art of providing escapist, formulaic entertainment for juveniles, adolescents, and young adults. Such movies became the staple of young people's favorite new viewing venue, the drive-in outdoor theater. These studios survived the television era by staying frugal and closely following the thematic tastes of the mass public. Hollywood elites, as well as politicians across the nation, decried the influence of low-budget science fiction, crime, and exploitation films on America's youth—the cinematic equivalent of comic books—but the vitality and popularity of these movies spelled more long-term trouble for the big studios. As in the age of Andrew Jackson and P. T. Barnum, the less polite and more raucous preferences of average Americans were reasserting themselves, and the sheer energy and enterprise of grade-C entertainment upset the prevailing polite codes of production and behavior. Drive-in movies became the analogue to Elvis Presley's shaking up of 1950s popular music with the earthy sound of rock 'n' roll.

The greatest spiritual upheaval in mainstream Hollywood, though, was generated by the unprecedented political turmoil of the McCarthy era. As we have seen, HUAC and the blacklists made the movie industry a deeply unwilling locus of political controversy. Careers were shattered, and some cases deaths were hastened by the predations of the blacklists. Hundreds of victimized performers, writers, and directors—along with others merely disgusted with political conditions at home—fled to Europe to live and work. Henry Fonda, a leading star, left the movies for six years to act on the New York stage, allegedly after having a bitter falling-out with his old friend James Stewart, a conservative Republican, over the subject of HUAC. Those who remained in the movies in the 1950s became notably more politicized. The battle over loyalty in Hollywood encouraged Stanley Kramer to produce crusading, politically liberal movies on social issues, but it also led John Wayne to become an outspoken right-wing critic of Kramer and other overtly liberal filmmakers. (Wayne even became president of the Motion Picture Alliance for the Preservation of American Ideals, the movie industry's leading anti-Communist organization.) Until the present day, the political division in Hollywood precipitated by the blacklists has made the movie industry a peculiarly hot incubator of activist sentiment, encouraging actors and others to take up causes with the same flamboyance and thirst for publicity with which they promote their films. The genteel pre-HUAC political activity of John Davis Lodge or Melvyn Douglas, for example, had almost no influence on their film work. Now, in the late 1950s and early

1960s, film makers increasingly displayed their politics and passions in their movies.

All of these pressures encouraged the Motion Picture Association of America to loosen the strict administration of the Production Code. Eric Johnston, Will Hays's successor at the MPAA, struggled mightily to lessen the impact on studios of theater divestment, the blacklists, and television. Johnston was also an active supporter of the Republican party, and his time in the 1950s was in addition taken up with informal diplomatic assignments given to him by President Eisenhower. The harried Johnston adopted a policy of benign neglect toward independent directors and producers who were beginning to challenge the Production Code and the blacklists. The director Otto Preminger's provocative violations of the Code in his films *The Moon Is Blue* (1953), *The Man with the Golden Arm* (1955), and *Anatomy of a Murder* (1959) led the way for other filmmakers who sought to portray sexuality, violence, and morally ambiguous situations with greater frankness. The transition remained gradual for the next decade or so until the Code was abandoned in 1968 in favor of the movie ratings system that still exists today. Like widescreen formats and epic international productions, Code violations were in fact a deliberate gambit by the movies, to counter competition from television entertainment programming (which, like its radio counterpart, was heavily sanitized owing to the concerns of commercial advertisers and the Federal Communications Commission). Equally important was the fact that more American viewers, especially college-educated youth, were demanding movies that explored the ugly, erotic, and morally ambiguous aspects of contemporary life found in books such as *The Catcher in the Rye* and Alfred Kinsey's studies of sexual behavior and in other less-censored media.[40]

These dramatic changes in the culture of the movies inevitably transformed trends in film stardom. Prewar pretensions to upper-class manners and looks, evident in the popularity of such mustachioed wits as William Powell and Warren William and such well-behaved ladies as Jeanette MacDonald, largely vanished after 1945. Robert Montgomery's rather cold, patrician acting style fell out of favor and consigned him to television. Younger male stars such as James Stewart and Henry Fonda returned from military service to find that audiences now demanded that they portray more rugged and conflicted characters. Female roles were more melodramatic, and the studios' obsession with beauty (often at the expense of talent) persisted, but after the war there was a decided turn toward more emotionally rugged female stars, such as Barbara Stanwyck and Joan Crawford, who elbowed such ladylike actresses as Loretta Young and Irene Dunne off the screen. The crime cinema dubbed film noir, rich in moral ambiguity and male-female conflict, became the showcase for tough new postwar varieties of film acting, proffered by Sterling Hayden, Robert Mitchum, Robert Ryan, Jane Greer, Thelma Ritter, and others.

At the same time, though, the post–World War II obsession with marriage and childbirth—which led to the Baby Boom, as well as young white families' desire to seek security in suburbia—nurtured a new emphasis in Hollywood on beautiful, innocent young archetypes. As Tyrone Power, a precursor of this trend in the 1930s, entered premature middle age, studios promoted such "beautiful" young men as Montgomery Clift, John Derek, Farley Granger, and Tony Curtis in his stead. In the 1950s, social concern about the alleged threat of juvenile delinquency helped make a star out of James Dean, the tormented beautiful young man, and helped to valorize the "method" approach to acting. The Method was the heir to Stanislavski's ultra-realist school of performance, but it was also a new approach, replacing attention to surface detail with a grappling with inner motivations and the unconscious. With Marlon Brando as their paragon, young students of Stella Adler, Sanford Meisner, and Lee Strasberg brought to movie screens a representation of 1950s America's growing obsession with psychological themes and therapeutic solutions.

The cultural tumult was particularly evident in the case of actresses. Gender roles in the 1950s, of course, were highly restrictive, largely keeping women out of the professions and the corridors of power, demeaning their intellects, and relegating them to marriage and motherhood. Movie actresses of that era found less diversity in their roles than many of their 1930s predecessors had enjoyed; only those (such as Anne Bancroft and Julie Harris) who fled baby-doll roles for innovative theater productions, and then reemerged in provocative films, were able to break somewhat free from the dominant movie stereotypes. The unique and extreme example of Marilyn Monroe—whose entire early life directed her toward the sex-kitten starlet

career she ultimately achieved, and whose subsequent years found her craving a new identity defined by intellectualism, the Method, and a psychological
distance from Hollywood—remains the most potent artifact of this era.

———

Very few of these new trends, featuring youthful performers at the cusp of
the economic and cultural forces transforming Hollywood, would affect the
elderly chief executives of the immediate postwar era, Truman and Eisenhower. When former President Truman made a groundbreaking dramatic
appearance in 1959 on the TV situation comedy starring his friend Jack
Benny, playing himself, he conformed to standards of performance that had
been set by the stage and radio decades before. Still, as the presidents' experiences with television while in office especially indicated, the image of
the leader was part of the transforming culture of spectacle and stardom in
the postwar era. The image was being broadcast through new media and
was even being contested by viewers. In the process, the largely cinematic
image of the president that Franklin Roosevelt had constructed was altered
and partially absorbed by television. This process might have continued on
beyond 1960 in a fairly predictable fashion if Richard Nixon had been elected
that year to succeed Eisenhower. Instead, a man who identified to an unprecedented degree with cinematic imagery and its power in the public sphere
became the new president. Of the same generation as the new postwar film
stars, John F. Kennedy melded the cinematic and televised images of the
president, and through his personal qualities and experiences he wove the
psychological and social upheavals of postwar America more fully into those
images.

CHAPTER 4

CHARISMA'S HOUR, 1960–1969

After 1960, when Dwight Eisenhower's successor was elected, presidents made a bold return to the movies.

This shift was made manifest in several ways. The 1950s had offered virtually no Hollywood portrayals of real or fictional chief executives. The only exceptions were two portrayals of Andrew Jackson by the young Charlton Heston, adding a southern accent to his granitic Moses persona. *The President's Lady* was a low-budget throwback to the presidential biographical films of the 1930s and 1940s—in fact, its chronicle of the ill-fated Rachel Jackson (Susan Hayward) might be considered a prequel to *The Gorgeous Hussy* (1936), which depicted the widowed chief executive (here, Lionel Barrymore) defending the scandalous Peggy Eaton (Joan Crawford). Heston's second portrayal of Jackson was a cameo appearance in *The Buccaneer,* a movie delineating "Old Hickory's" victory in the Battle of New Orleans. *The Buccaneer* was a remake of a 1930s picture, so both films were echoes of Hollywood's prewar treatment of Andrew Jackson.

In the early 1960s, though, the number of presidential portrayals on film increased considerably, and for the first time since the early 1930s, these presidents were predominantly fictional. A rare exception was a brief and reverent portrayal of General Dwight Eisenhower by a lookalike actor, ordering the Normandy invasion in Darryl Zanuck's *The Longest Day* (1962). That same year, the fictional chief executive in *Advise and Consent* was portrayed by Franchot Tone (who had also appeared in *The Gorgeous Hussy* with Crawford, then his wife). In 1963 came *Kisses for My President,* a comedy featuring

Polly Bergen as the first female holder of the office and Fred MacMurray as her conflicted husband. That same year, Irving Berlin's musical comedy *Mr. President* first appeared on Broadway. In 1964 fictional presidents appeared in a cycle of films that allegorized real-life issues: Lee Tracy in *The Best Man,* Henry Fonda in *Fail-Safe,* and Fredric March in *Seven Days in May.* The cycle was parodied that same year in the best-remembered fictional portrayal from this era, Peter Sellers's turn as the bland, hapless President Merkin Muffley in *Dr. Strangelove.*

The efflorescence of movie excitement about the presidency reflected the sense of ferment and change that came with the ascension of John F. Kennedy to the office, succeeding Dwight Eisenhower. In fact, Hollywood's presidential film cycle included a movie about Kennedy himself, the first biographical picture ever produced about a sitting chief executive. A few years earlier Robert Montgomery had tried to mount a film biography of his friend Eisenhower, who was then in office, but he had failed, and instead went on to produce a picture about the World War II admiral William Halsey. However, the enhanced sympathy between Hollywood and Washington in the Kennedy years helped a studio to realize the kind of project that Montgomery had not even been able to begin.

PT 109 was released in June 1963, late in JFK's tragically shortened term. The story of Kennedy's World War II heroics, rescuing sailors under his command after their ship had been rammed and sunk by a Japanese destroyer, had been a vital component of the senator's campaign biography in 1960. It had given the youthful, wealthy, and relatively inexperienced candidate a wartime record that made him seem at least a plausible successor to Eisenhower as commander in chief. Robert Donovan's book *PT 109* appeared in 1961, and Warner Brothers quickly bought the film rights. The resulting movie was a moderate commercial success but a critical failure, and probably a keen disappointment to Kennedy and his political team. Given a grade-B treatment and filmed on Florida locations, *PT 109* ironically may have been the worst entry in the cycle of presidential Hollywood films of the early 1960s.

Although business contingencies at Warners ultimately defeated them, the president and his close aides had striven for two years to help make the movie a success. Kennedy, the son of the controversial former businessman and diplomat of the Franklin Roosevelt era, had partially grown up around the movie industry, and he knew it better than any man heretofore elected to the White House. According to Pierre Salinger, JFK's press secretary, Joseph P. Kennedy supervised the Warner Brothers production deal, ensuring that the studio paid handsome stipends to Donovan and to surviving members of the PT 109 crew. In addition, the contract "gave the White House final approval rights on the script and . . . on the actor to play Lieutenant Kennedy." Salinger recalled, however, that the president's goals were defeated by Bryan Foy, the film's producer, who viewed *PT 109* purely as "an exploitation picture." The wily Foy managed to veto Kennedy's initial choice for the leading role, a promising young actor named Warren Beatty, who had also declined to be involved. Foy also replaced the director, the veteran Lewis Milestone—whose credits included the classic 1930 antiwar movie *All Quiet on the Western Front*—with Leslie Martinson, a novice to feature films. Delays nearly doubled the film's cost to over $5 million, a rare sum for a grade-B production and one that yielded no perceptible improvement in the quality of the finished product.[1]

White House correspondence indicates that the public was intensely interested in the production of *PT 109*. Even before the film had been announced, Kennedy's wartime exploits had stimulated a vast array of letters from citizens, including reminiscences from Navy veterans, queries from children working on school projects, and even apologetic missives from crew members of the Japanese ship that sank Kennedy's craft. Women wrote in to recommend their sons or husbands for roles in the movie—ranging from the lead to bit parts—while others sent criticisms of the project. "The dignity of that office would not be enhanced by a film popularizing its present incumbent—even if that film were done well," one woman wrote. Salinger, who handled the bulk of this correspondence, was not above some misdirection about the White House's role. "The President is not participating in the selection of an actor to play his role in the movie of PT-109," he wrote a New Yorker in late 1961, a falsehood he repeated in many other letters. The movie actress Maureen O'Sullivan, unaware of Milestone's recent hiring, wrote to ask if the president could persuade the studio to give the directing job to her husband, John Farrow. Navy veterans wrote to Salinger requesting employment as technical advisers for the movie.[2]

The excitement and promise surrounding *PT 109* persisted for two years, despite its slow gestation and diminished status at Warner Brothers. President Kennedy was satisfied with the choice of actor Cliff Robertson as a replacement for Beatty. As the film's premiere approached in 1963, Salinger exulted to a California political contact that he "had discussions with Jack Warner about the possibility of using 'PT 109' for Democratic fund-raising and he is agreeable to the idea." Kennedy himself objected to using the film nationwide for fund raising, but Salinger "personally [did] not see any reason why it should not be used in California." The president attended the gala first showing in Washington, D.C., which was followed by an official premiere in Boston. Warners subsequently informed Salinger of its box office success in large urban theaters, and of premieres in cities such as Paris and Singapore.[3]

PT 109's troubled production and subsequent critical rejection, which rendered it a nearly forgotten curiosity in the years after Kennedy's death, should not deter us from appreciating it as a representative product of a powerful new cultural impulse. The persistent appeal of motion pictures into the 1960s, despite the industry's economic struggles, had helped to make each new generation of Americans more captivated by the emotional, sensuous, and epic possibilities of theatrical entertainment. Even television, long considered to be the movies' nemesis, had helped condition Americans to desire more mimetic and fantastic entertainment in their lives. During the decade, intellectuals such as Marshall McLuhan and Guy Debord discerned the emerging primacy of visual "reading" and acculturation, at the expense of the written word and argument.[4] In the movies and in the culture as a whole, by the 1960s Americans—especially young people—were influenced far more deeply by the sights (and sounds) of electronic media. However, in a decade of social upheaval, war, and radical protest, those sights and sounds also often evoked violence, discontinuity, and a crisis in the political order. By the end of the 1960s, a timid and derivative war movie such as *PT 109* seemed hopelessly outdated and phony.

The same, though, could not be said of the film's subject. As a president and as an individual, John F. Kennedy broke with tradition in ways that roughly resembled the general cultural change of the 1960s. Kennedy was not only younger and an advocate of a more vigorous federal government at home and abroad; he seemed representative of an energy in American society, often described as a youthful vigor, that had percolated in the culture but only now seemed to enter the halls of Washington. This perception was first given voice on the eve of Kennedy's election by the pugnacious novelist Norman Mailer. "Since the First World War," Mailer wrote in a celebrated article in *Esquire* magazine, "Americans have been leading a double life, and our history has moved on two rivers, one visible, the other underground; there has been the history of politics which is concrete, factual, practical and unbelievably dull if not for the consequences of the actions of some of these men; and there is a subterranean river of untapped, ferocious, lonely and romantic desires, that concentration of ecstasy and violence which is the dream life of the nation."[5]

Mailer argued that this subterranean culture of desire—emerging in speech and action through absurdist and cynical humor, sharp-edged dress and mannerisms, and sensual enjoyment—had been broadcast intermittently in the movies. "The film studios threw up their searchlights as the frontier was finally sealed, and the romantic possibilities of the old conquest of land turned into a vertical myth, trapped within the skull, of a new kind of heroic life, each choosing his own archetype of a neo-renaissance man."[6] Movie stars such as Barbara Stanwyck, Humphrey Bogart, James Dean, and Marilyn Monroe, among others, had excited moviegoers with glimpses of the skeptical, amused, fun-loving, and critical stance that would emerge as a full-blown sensibility among the rebellious classes of the 1960s. The emergence of this sensibility in the movies, of course, helped to erode the strictures of the Production Code in the 1950s. More than any other man destined for the White House in recent times, Kennedy was an aficionado of these subversive undercurrents of American culture, and he used his familiarity with them to his electoral advantage. A complex alchemy of character, family background, and experiences, including a social familiarity with Hollywood, encouraged JFK to adopt this unique sensibility. In the language of the day, Kennedy brought charisma—of the sort transferred in the modern era from religious leaders to popular performers—to the White House.

US politics would never be the same. Before 1960, motion pictures dealt only allusively with the violence and turbulent sexuality that helped to define life in America. Similarly, as we have seen, politics until that time largely conformed to the republican ideal of virtuous officeholders and disassociated their personal lives from their official duties. Culturally, of course, leaders had been defined by their apparent masculine virtues and by qualities such as military prowess—and the techniques of public performance, increasingly adopted by politicians, had stoked the public's interest in the personal qualities of their leaders. The illusion of intimacy afforded by television in the 1950s increased the scale and the breadth of this interest.

In the light of posthumous revelations about Kennedy, it is tempting to reduce his special appeal as a public figure, and the Kennedy phenomenon of the early 1960s, to a matter of sex. While information and rumors regarding his relentless womanizing did not become public until a decade after his death, it was plain even by the late 1950s that the basis of much of JFK's political appeal grew out of the sort of female adoration that was usually reserved for attractive male actors and musical performers. Charisma associated with youth and vigor was difficult to disassociate from sexual attractiveness. Kennedy's studied emulation of the image-building techniques used by Hollywood stars encouraged voters themselves to perceive a similarity between the wish-fulfillments found in the movies and those in JFK's campaign. As a result, a vague association of leadership with sexuality emerged in 1960s America. The general social upheaval of the decade, which led to a franker discussion of sex and wider experimentation, nurtured a new perception of sex in politics—although the political sphere was not one of the most radically transformed battlegrounds of the sexual revolution in those years.

John Kennedy's tenure in the White House was cut short, but partly due to his near-martyrdom in the half-decade after Dallas his example of charismatic cinematic leadership was widely emulated, especially by his followers in the Democratic Party. What might be called the liberal school of cinematic leadership, led at least honorifically by the president's younger brothers, thus became a major new stage in the evolution of the presidential image. As in the movies, images were, of course, deceiving. Even more than FDR, John Kennedy was a master of deception, especially when it came to disguising and lying about his serious health problems. In addition, JFK's complex motives as president, coupled with his dubious attachment to liberalism, make him in retrospect an imperfect patron saint of the liberal charismatic movement.

The movement itself became a casualty of the turmoil of the late 1960s. Lyndon Baines Johnson, the slain president's successor, possessed few of the overt qualities that made Kennedy such an attractive political figure (although their private sexual behavior was not dissimilar). While Johnson achieved liberal triumphs in civil rights and welfare legislation, his disastrous war in Vietnam shattered the liberal consensus that JFK had begun to knit together. LBJ enhanced the Democratic Party's financial and social ties to Hollywood, but as liberal politicians and progressive-minded filmmakers fell into parallel troughs of despair, their once-dazzling joint creation—the charismatic public mystique embodied by John Kennedy—lay virtually in ruins. Among the voters, disenchantment with Kennedy-style leaders became so great that by the late 1970s these politicians had lost any special influence they once might have had.

———

John Fitzgerald Kennedy was a complex individual. It is important to note that fact at the outset, because the impact of his celebrity was so intense that, even long after his death, many observers reduced him to a purely sensual or glamorous figure. Even his rivals for the Democratic nomination in 1960, as well as surrogates for Richard M. Nixon, his opponent in the general election, dismissed him as an attractive lightweight.

As recent biographers especially have shown, however, Kennedy's charismatic appeal supplemented more traditional strengths on his political résumé. His serious interest in foreign policy took wing in the late 1930s, while he studied current events at Harvard (writing a substantial senior thesis on Britain) and witnessed them first-hand while touring Europe. Kennedy took full advantage of the privileges of access granted to him as the son of the ambassador to the Court of St. James's. His covert opposition to his father's isolationism brought passion and tenacity to his thinking about America's responsibilities around the world. In addition, his long periods of recuperation from illnesses (digestive problems, back pain, and Addison's disease) gave him countless hours to read and reflect on political history and the lives of leaders. For young Kennedy, an interest in foreign policy competed for primacy of attention with his health struggles, obsessive sexual activity, and diverse family and social life. His focus on politics was sharpened considerably after the combat death of his elder brother Joseph Jr. in 1944 and during his campaign for a US House seat from Massachusetts in 1946.

Almost immediately after he arrived in Congress, JFK set a course for the White House. Standing aloof from regular legislative operations, he cultivated a broad mastery of the issues. A close-knit group of advisers, financed by his father and including his younger brother Robert, became dedicated to a persistent and occasionally ruthless struggle to advance "Johnnie's" political fortunes. The effort bore fruit when Kennedy defeated the incumbent Massachusetts senator Henry Cabot Lodge Jr. in 1952. The young senator continued to pull away from his father's isolationist past, endorsing vigorous prosecution of the Cold War, but he remained dependent on Joseph's funds for campaigns and on his influence to win a Pulitzer Prize for the book *Profiles in Courage.* Much later, in December 1961, the father's debilitating stroke sent the young president into considerable anguish—and into his most reckless months of sexual activity—but it also seemed to free him to develop more of his own personal identity.

Kennedy was a facile yet able student of politics, and his facility only grew in the White House. It was well publicized that he was a speed reader who could digest complex texts and issues with considerable ease. Kennedy delegated less substance and oversight than Eisenhower, resembling more Truman and FDR in his desire to channel all significant information and decision making through the Oval Office. During his term in office JFK was tested by an almost continuous series of crises. The Bay of Pigs fiasco, Nikita Khrushchev's belligerence at the 1961 Vienna summit, the Berlin Wall, the Cuban Missile Crisis, and the decay of South Vietnam—not to mention the bloody battle over civil rights at home—forced Kennedy to improvise crisis management, which in the secrecy behind White House walls sometimes verged on the chaotic. His long years of reflection on statecraft had not prepared him particularly well for the rapidly building and complex crises that were thrown at him. It helped, though, that he employed creative and resourceful aides, and that the United States—then at the height of its global prestige and power—had a wide array of tools at its disposal. Even though

Cuba and Vietnam remained dangerous irritants, Kennedy's persistence and attention to detail helped to keep these dangers manageable.

Similarly, on the home front, federal aid to education, creation of public old-age health insurance, a "war on poverty," and the expansion of black civil rights all attracted Kennedy's attention and support. But far more than in foreign policy, he delegated these domestic issues to his highly credentialed staff. His concerns as president, even overseas, never became crusades. In Richard Reeves's summation, JFK "was not a liberal moralist—he did not call himself any kind of liberal—but rather a managerial politician. An efficiency liberal, a man, at his best, looking for the most efficient means of attaining the greatest happiness for the greatest number." In his personal tastes, Kennedy was "a meat-and-potatoes guy, a middlebrow," who adhered to the common premises that the Cold War was real and that the United States should win it, and that a big military, an expanding suburbia, and reduced taxes were good things. His everyday preferences tended to be commonplace as well. Jacqueline Kennedy noted that her husband's "tastes are distressingly normal—plain food—children's food."[7]

In another sense, though, it is probably ludicrous to call Kennedy a meat-and-potatoes guy or a managerial politician. Beyond primacy in the Cold War, there was a vagueness to his goals that was almost certainly intentional. As the historian David Kaiser has stated, with reference to the "G.I. generation" emerging from World War II, "In many ways Kennedy was an archetypal GI—quick, eager to do great things, self-confident, cheerful, but relatively unemotional and hardly introspective." Making a cinematic allusion, Kaiser finds Kennedy calling for civil rights or support for South Vietnam "almost diffidently, in a manner similar to that of his fellow GI Henry Fonda in *Mr. Roberts* or *Twelve Angry Men*." As president, "his objective was rarely anything so concrete as a legislative program or a victorious war, but rather the more elusive goal of maintaining his effectiveness as President. . . . he would seldom move very far in advance of public opinion, or take any firm decision before he absolutely had to."[8]

This effort to maintain a vague effectiveness indicated Kennedy's fluid conception of leadership and his understanding of the cultural roots of authority. A president obtained power not just from Article II of the Constitution and from statutes, but by keeping his hold on the public's imagination. As Mailer so floridly put it in his 1960 article on Kennedy, "Superman Comes to the Supermarket," the typical Democratic politician "is not happy about the secrets of [Kennedy's] appeal, not so far as he divines these secrets; they seem to have too little to do with politics and all too much to do with the private madnesses of the nation. . . . Yes, this candidate for all his record; his good, sound, conventional liberal record has a patina of that other life, the second American life, the long electric night with the fires of neon leading down the highway to the murmur of jazz."[9]

When Mailer evoked madness, jazz, and the movies' "vertical myths" he was of course being a highly subjective observer and not presenting quantifiable historical data. This approach typified the "new journalism" of the 1960s that his very article helped to launch—a school of writing which challenged the pretenses to empirical objectivity found in traditional reporting. The subjective perceptions of new journalists, though, have become reliable data on the cultural life of the era. For example, by observing Kennedy, Mailer divined his intense affinity for Hollywood-style self-presentation and self-promotion. Beginning very early, Jack Kennedy (as his Hollywood friends especially called him) cultivated a film-star look that disdained the middle-aged, Everyman persona affected by the typical politician. In 1948, as a young congressman, Kennedy was written up in a woman's magazine as "America's most eligible bachelor."

At Joseph Kennedy's urging, *Life* kept a regular watch on JFK and his doings, and beginning with his engagement to Jacqueline Bouvier in 1953, the magazine devoted covers and photographic essays to the senator. A 1959 *Life* article was a standard puff piece: "when women meet him they give off the kind of glow usually reserved for movie stars. In Milwaukee a starry-eyed waitress who got his autograph whispered admiringly, 'He's got sort of an all-American, wholesome face.' . . . Students of Beloit College hung on every word, followed him outdoors as if he were the Pied Piper, then stood in an ogling semicircle until he drove away." "Kennedy's campaign," the article continued, "is more a personality display than a crusade. There are no burning issues. Instead the crowds get an image of a vigorous, intelligent and immensely attractive young man." That same season, Joseph Kennedy indicated in an interview that such copy was exactly what the family's effort was hoping to produce: "Jack is the greatest attraction in the country today. I'll tell you how to sell more copies of a book. Put his picture on the cover. Why is it that when his picture is on the cover of *Life* or *Redbook* that they sell a record number of copies? . . . He can draw more people to a fund-raising dinner than Cary Grant or Jimmy Stewart. Why is that? He has more universal appeal."[10]

Kennedy cooperated fully with his father's image making campaign. His marriage to Jacqueline Bouvier was timed to coincide with the early stages of his national self-promotion as a senator, and the birth of their daughter Caroline in 1957 came fortuitously just as his presidential explorations were beginning. It was also apparent by that year that, with the assistance of sympathetic reporters, Kennedy could hide his suffering from Addison's disease and severe back pain. Surgery on his back in 1955 had worsened the problem and even threatened to kill him, although in an indication of both his fierce determination and his attention to image, Kennedy used his recuperation to work on *Profiles in Courage* with his ghost writer, Theodore Sorensen.

As a candidate, Kennedy took an unprecedented interest in his self-portrayal. A well-known story from the 1960 campaign told of his role in choosing the photographic portrait that would appear on most posters and banners. The choice ended up being between a "mature" and a "young-looking" Kennedy portrait. JFK studied both pictures for a long time before announcing, "OK, let's go with the young one." In the White House, photographers nicknamed the president "Jack the Back" for his practice of keeping turned away from them until he had groomed and composed himself for their cameras.[11] Kennedy was appropriating for presidential candidates the tradition of cosmetic preparation that had long been associated with First Ladies—careful selection of hairstyling, clothing, and words with an eye toward their impact on the most discerning and influential social circles and press coverage. While JFK spoke of the "missile gap" and made reference to his wartime Navy career, he also regularly dyed the gray out of his hair, and he showered and changed his shirts and tailored suits several times a day. Thanks to Kennedy, American male politicians acquired what had been a traditionally feminine concern for fashion and cosmetic appearance.

Kennedy's self-promotion grated against the sensibilities of older politicians who were used to more traditional modes of presentation. This became especially apparent during the 1956 Democratic convention, when the

senator, barely out of recuperation from back surgery, narrated a polished
introductory film about the party's history and philosophy, produced by
MGM chief Dore Schary. The next day he mounted a last-minute and nearly
successful campaign for the vice-presidential nomination. Senator Clinton
Anderson, a veteran of Harry Truman's cabinet, felt at the time "that it was
too much of a jump for this young boy to get to be vice president or anything
else on the basis of that film. . . . A film had been made at a cost of what I
understood was $250,000, and this was paid for completely by Kennedy's
father. . . . Many people thought that John Kennedy was wrong in narrating
the film if he were going to be a candidate for vice president in 1956. He was
advanced to a very prominent role by the film and then later on he nominated [Adlai] Stevenson. Most of us felt that his money had brought him too
much prominence." Anderson, like others, came to respect Kennedy's intelligence and leadership skills, but these had initially been overshadowed
by his youth and showmanship. Younger people also were startled by Kennedy's daring, but in contrast to Anderson, they often found it exhilarating.
The journalist Gloria Emerson marveled at Kennedy's "tremendous self-
assurance. . . . I've never met anyone like that again. It was the audacious-
ness, the intensity, the impatience, the brusqueness. Here was a man who
wasn't going to wait; he was going to get what he wanted. . . . It was quite
thrilling."[12]

Kennedy's style of campaigning, and the obsession with image it displayed,
became a general issue for discussion in 1960. Norman Mailer, as we have
seen, made some prescient observations about the subversive nature of JFK's
presence on the political scene, but on occasion even his critical analysis
went soft, most notably when he wrote, "if elected he would be not only the
youngest President ever to be chosen by voters, he would be the most conventionally attractive young man ever to sit in the White House, and his
wife—some would claim it—might be the most beautiful First Lady in our
history."[13] The senator had, in fact, flattered and partially won over Mailer
in a few short meetings during the presidential campaign, using the techniques for captivating journalists he had honed for years.

Joseph Kennedy's press agentry was accompanied by JFK's own willingness to engage personally with reporters. Benjamin C. Bradlee of *Newsweek*,
a neighbor of the Kennedys in Georgetown, was convinced that the senator

genuinely liked reporters, in part because Kennedy had once contemplated becoming a journalist himself. Bradlee was led to believe that he was an intimate of JFK's, although the latter kept much from the reporter (including his extended affair with Bradlee's sister-in-law, Mary Pinchot Meyer). Kennedy's quasi-seduction of journalists also reaped the benefit of winning over Theodore H. White, who was granted unprecedented access to the campaign staff and repaid the favor in his best-selling account, *The Making of the President, 1960.* White's book was the first to make harried, hardworking aides into virtual celebrities, detailing their biographies, thoughts, and work on the campaign. This narrative approach had the effect of reflecting some of the candidate's glamour onto the operatives behind the scenes. Hugh Sidey of *Time* magazine similarly became a smitten conquest of the dashing president-elect. In the White House Kennedy fretted constantly about the influential reporters and columnists he could not easily win over, but his rate of success in gaining journalistic acolytes was high.[14]

Americans were hardly innocent of the dynamics at work here. During the 1950s, a critique of the techniques of salesmanship and audience manipulation, especially in the mass media, had been percolating in academe, and it was finding a receptive mass audience. The year Kennedy was inaugurated the historian Daniel J. Boorstin published *The Image,* a witty and erudite polemic that lamented the triumph of style over substance in contemporary journalism, politics, and mass media. Particularly devastating was Boorstin's critique of the insular world shared by politicians and the newspaper reporters who covered them—a world in which entire cycles of front-page stories dealt with non-events such as reporters' and officials' misattributions of each other. Kennedy clearly took it for granted that he was operating in this political-journalistic continuum. Yet *The Image* errs in its general assumption that, back in the days before Madison Avenue and television, a golden age existed in which the printed news was always substantial and reported objectively. Leo Braudy has shown that for millennia rulers have hoodwinked their subjects by mounting pseudo-events and circulating twisted autobiographies and other misinformation, and as we have seen in this study, presidents since Washington have manipulated their public images for political gain. Presidents, as well as other politicians, have fabricated images of their power and position that were fundamentally misleading. In *The Image,* the indignity of Boorstin the citizen tended to trump the perspective of Boorstin the historian.[15]

However, Boorstin and other critics were accurate in perceiving that a new continuum of media, centered on television, provided powerful and influential opportunities for mischief for those who shunned old republican ideals of clear and honest communication. In the case of President Kennedy, it became the task of every interested citizen to try to disassociate the real merit of the man and his administration from the manipulative efforts that were undertaken on their behalf. Leftist intellectuals—as well as those, such as Boorstin, who had named names to HUAC and who were now former leftists—never trusted Kennedy's values and never were satisfied by his cautious advocacy of black civil rights and social welfare programs.[16]

Kennedy's administration placed great hope in his televised press conferences. Sixty-four of them aired, and unlike Eisenhower's, they were broadcast live. These unrehearsed events showed off JFK at his most attractive: he was well informed and humorous, and he usually seemed to enjoy his cordial dueling with journalists. Some college-educated viewers—and scholars following in their wake, viewing videotapes—appreciated Kennedy's performances, but many in this group were at work during the broadcasts and missed them. In general, as the political scientist Andrew Hacker observed in 1962, "very few Americans bother to tune in on these conferences and it is hard to understand why the White House has concluded that they are useful in gathering public support." Hacker wondered why Kennedy did not make more of his eloquent speeches to mobilize the public. The reason was that his presidency was largely reactive, improvising in the face of oncoming crises. Furthermore, as Hacker noted, Kennedy had no electoral mandate for bold action, and he also faced opposition on welfare issues and civil rights from the southern wing of his own party. The president's legislative proposals thus never received more than a bare majority of approval in opinion polls, and he did little to try to rally support and raise those numbers.[17]

Still, Kennedy's personal popularity remained high. In a partial confirmation of Boorstin's fears and Mailer's musings, the young president seemed to benefit from a cult of personality that exempted him from his policies' struggles in the polls. The *Life* magazine strategy conceived by his father thus bore rich fruit. More surprising—not least to Kennedy himself—was how the celebrity of his wife Jacqueline scaled dizzying new heights. Jackie Kennedy was an aggrieved, often neglected wife who suffered numerous miscarriages and resisted the stereotypical role of the loyal political spouse. Unhappy in the White House, she fiercely protected the privacy of her two young children, spent excessively on clothes and interior decorating, and often fled to the family farm in Virginia to ride horses. Yet out of this crucible was created a new plateau of fame for a First Lady. Whether by accident or by design, Mrs. Kennedy's appearances in lavish gowns at the inaugural balls and on visits to France and India, as well her televised tour of the redecorated White House, made her perhaps the most celebrated First Lady to date. Taken by surprise, President Kennedy increasingly took to complimenting his wife in public.[18]

Even more than before, their marriage became a partnership in virtuoso image making, as every photograph and clothing decision helped to define Mr. and Mrs. Kennedy as the common American's aristocrats, an ideal type of the white suburban middle class. Tension between them emerged, though, when the president brought photographers into private White House rooms to snap pictures of the children, Caroline and John Jr., when his wife was out of town. Mrs. Kennedy did not want to include the kids in the political tableau—although she gave in at a crucial moment, during the funeral procession in November 1963, when she whispered into her three-year-old son's ear and encouraged him to step forward and salute his father's coffin. Instinctively Jacqueline Kennedy realized that John Jr.'s gesture—like the other solemn symbolic touches in the official ceremonies of mourning that she had requested—was an unforgettable opportunity that could not be missed.[19]

Kennedy's surprise at his wife's extraordinary hold on the public attention reveals that his perception of his father's picture-magazine strategy was limited by conventional gender prejudices. He may not have realized that this strategy tended to feminize both his image and that of the presidency. By paying close attention to the photographic impact of his hair styling, clothing, physique, and tanned skin, JFK embarked on a strategy that had been associated for over a century with the beauty culture of white American women.[20] More specifically, at least since the days of Julia Tyler, First Ladies had defined their public role by serving as arbiters of female fashion and as decorators of the executive mansion. Jacqueline Kennedy's flamboyant French gowns and Impressionistic redecoration of the White House revived traditionally feminine styles that had gone into eclipse during the practical years of Eleanor Roosevelt and Bess Truman and the eccentric fashion regime of Mamie Eisenhower.

While Mrs. Kennedy's fashionableness fit the long-standing practice among First Ladies, her husband's similar tendencies represented a real innovation in presidential behavior. Some earlier presidents had closely followed changes in men's fashion, although only Chester A. Arthur might have been considered a sartorial innovator at the "cutting edge" of taste (to use one of JFK's own favorite phrases). The Broadway-happy mayor of 1920s New York City, Jimmy Walker, served as a fashion-conscious link in American politics between Arthur and Kennedy. Walker's dandyish concern with fashion, however, ran the risk of being coded by observers as homosexual in nature. Kennedy was a sexual adventurer with some exposure to gay culture—Tennessee Williams complimented JFK on his "great ass" when they met in the late 1950s—but he bristled at the notion that his vanity denoted a sexually ambiguous aesthetic. The best-known anecdote describes Kennedy exploding in anger at Hugh Sidey when the latter suggested that the president had been photographed for the cover of *Gentleman's Quarterly,* a magazine reputed to be a favorite of gay men.[21]

In tandem, John and Jacqueline Kennedy may be said to have played the same kind of game as FDR and Eisenhower, who had been highly aware of the political value of their warm smiles and cordial personalities. Bolstered by Joseph Kennedy's fortune and promotional zeal, the couple took the process further than had those two presidents, but their basic effort and goals were similar. What had changed most vividly by 1960 was that the American public was now more comfortable with the marketing of a president's personality and private life. By 1960, thanks to radio, television, and the movies, citizens sought to become more familiar with the personalities of their leaders, searching for authenticity in their speech, manner, and actions and finding an apparent solace upon its discovery. This tendency aided Kennedy's rise to the White House, and his awareness of it made his tortuous path to power somewhat smoother. It was in the 1950s and 1960s, in short, that Americans blatantly adopted *charisma* as a necessary quality for leadership.

For millennia, charisma—from the Greek phrase meaning "gift from God"—had been a specialized term used in religious treatises. Charisma was a gift that permitted an individual to infuse others with spirituality. In the early twentieth century, the German sociologist Max Weber declared that charismatic political leadership was one of the three major sources of ruling authority in modern societies. The others, of course, were traditional and bureaucratic leadership—rule through traditional, usually monarchical, rights or through highly organized government structures and rules. While Weber's main concern was the seeming triumph of bureaucracy in the early 1900s, and how they might even "rationalize" or codify the wild appeal of the charismatic leader, his tripartite classification really gained currency in the West in the 1930s, as observers struggled to understand the rise of totalitarian dictators. Hitler and Mussolini had bent both tradition and bureaucracy to their charismatic wills, and intellectuals looked to Weber's taxonomy for answers.[22]

The authoritarianism inherent in the general concept of charisma has led some scholars to deem it alien to traditional US politics. The sociologist Barry Schwartz, for example, concluded that the 1700s "Whig" version of hero worship associated with George Washington, founded on the leader's perceived virtue, was "the very antithesis of Max Weber's formulation of charismatic leadership." A team of political scientists led by Robert J. House has countered Schwartz with the observation that, "over time, this ideal of the restrained statesman weakened" and has "facilitated the emergence of charismatic leaders and behavior." In the view of House and his associates, the mass media have allowed presidents increasingly "to influence subordinates and masses through their actual or presumed charismatic behavior," and since 1945 the United States has confronted crises more frequently— a common precondition to a charismatic leader-follower relationship. As a result, House writes, "as the presidency has aged as an institution, the charisma of the president has increased."[23]

A generation earlier, during the beginning of the Cold War, some intellectuals had accepted Weber's model as a guide to the new reality. Weber's essay had been popularized in 1946 through its inclusion in an influential collection of his writings that was co-edited by the Columbia University sociologist C. Wright Mills.[24] Mills, one of the best-selling and best-known scholars in his discipline, spent much of the 1950s exploring bureaucracies and their deleterious effects on society, and he rarely explored the concept of charisma. By 1960, though, he had become enamored with the peasant revolution in Cuba. Fidel Castro became the sociologist's paragon of a charismatic leader who might bring new meaning and excitement to the stultifying Cold War world. While his rapid conversion to charisma studies was cut short by his death in 1962, Mills's emotional response to Castro and other Maoist peasant leaders was shared by left-wing student activists and many older liberals. Mills thus helped to shape the radical vanguards of the 1960s. Some intellectuals did not join Mills in embracing charismatic rebels. His colleague at Columbia, the historian Richard Hofstadter, had spent a decade dissecting the danger posed by charismatic, anti-intellectual leadership in American politics, finding its apotheosis in Joseph McCarthy and warning against its threat to the strength of liberty and a free society.[25]

Others also gradually adopted Weber's concept. If the *New York Times'* current historical search engine is accurate, the word "charisma" had appeared in America's newspaper of record only five times from 1851 to 1960. None of these uses were made in a political context, reflecting the *Times'* apparent slow recognition of the Weber renaissance in US social science. Yet political scientists had begun to adopt the concept. In 1954 James C. Davies explored "charisma in the 1952 campaign," arguing that both Dwight Eisenhower and Adlai Stevenson gained support primarily through the magnetic force of their personalities. Charisma, in Davies's formulation, arose as political currency in response to crises in which traditional and bureaucratic authority seemed impotent. Voter surveys, Davies claimed, showed that "unlike Truman and Dewey in 1948, Stevenson and [especially] Eisenhower were dramatic candidates, both expressing a sense of destiny and both successful—as the size of the vote indicates—in evoking widespread and enthusiastic support." Social scientists applied the concept of charisma more frequently as the decade progressed, to explore the nature of successful leadership both in US institutions (such as labor union locals) and in newly independent former imperial colonies in Asia and Africa.[26]

The 1960 campaign brought the language of charisma into the main-stream. The startling advantage Kennedy possessed in demeanor, clothing, posture, and poise in his first TV debate with Richard Nixon (who looked ill and tired) sharpened discussion in the press about Kennedy's advantage in image, and what it might tell about his potential as a president. On the eve of the election, the *New York Times* columnist C. L. Sulzberger placed a remarkable amount of faith in charisma in a short opinion piece that amounted to a personal endorsement of Kennedy. (The paper had already formally endorsed the senator.) Arguing that in foreign policy, "it's charisma that counts in the end," Sulzberger wrote that "only Kennedy has in any sense seemed to emit a charismatic aura of popular leadership"—an "aura" that decided the choice between him and Nixon, who essentially shared the same foreign policy goals. While Sulzberger also put faith in Kennedy's hiring of "a team of brilliant men," regardless of their party affiliation, he also expected him, if elected, to "stimulat[e] the nation to awareness that we are in a desperate race with Russia. . . . His charisma is linked to a mass craving for assertive leadership in precisely this quest."[27]

The man and the times were thus made for each other. While President Kennedy was a vehement enemy of Fidel Castro, Ho Chi Minh, and other charismatic leaders of peasant revolutions and was indifferent to the student instigators of the black civil rights movement, he shared in their good fortune in finding a receptive audience for vigorous innovation, for a break with the slow pace and the complacent assumptions of older generations. The Peace Corps, the promotion of the arts in the White House, and his interventions against Jim Crow segregation showed Kennedy reluctantly adopting initiatives and stances for which he held little enthusiasm, but which the times seemed to demand. Meanwhile, he exploited ripe opportunities that appealed more strongly to him, such as when he charged NASA with planning a voyage to the moon and angled himself into photo opportunities with Mercury astronauts. Equally exciting was his speaking appearance in June 1963 in West Berlin, where a million cheering Germans astonished even Kennedy. Neither Joseph Kennedy in his prime nor *Life* magazine, with its finger on the popular pulse, could have conceived of such favorable settings for the charismatic young politician. Poses with John Glenn and the West Berlin speech could not be considered examples of what Daniel Boorstin called "pseudo-events"—occasions that possessed no meaning beyond their own spectacle. Beginning with Kennedy, presidents and their staffs coveted photo opportunities that aligned the chief executive with authentic heroism, public adoration, and other rare and favorable circumstances that might emerge on the public stage. Such moments, it was hoped, would enhance the president's political viability and allow him to gain some mastery over the chaotic stream of events with which he had to deal.

———

Motion pictures lent both style and substance to John F. Kennedy's ascent to the presidency. His political advancement in the 1950s coincided exactly with the studios' decline and their effort to come to terms with the impact of television. Kennedy revealingly paid very little attention to TV in the 1950s. In his first extended television appearance, in tandem with his wife on Edward R. Murrow's *Person to Person* in 1953, JFK is remarkably (and winningly) awkward and hesitant. In 1960 he scored great advantages over Nixon in the televised debates, but he seemed almost surprised by the medium's impact. After his election he said of TV, "we wouldn't have had a prayer without that gadget."[28] As president Kennedy was highly effective in the televised news conferences, but he also retained an interest in newspapers' coverage of his administration that, in retrospect, seems antiquated. After the *New York Herald-Tribune,* a leading Republican paper, criticized Kennedy once too often, he angrily canceled all White House subscriptions —but the *Herald-Tribune* was already dying because of evaporating advertising revenues, and it would close down in 1966.

The movies had been Kennedy's formative guide to political imagery. As a child his idol was the silent western star Tom Mix; JFK's father, then in Hollywood, brought home Mix's movies and miniature cowboy wardrobes for his son's tenth birthday party. As a sickly teenager, Kennedy spent hours watching movies, and he modeled his hair, clothing, and mannerisms on those of the leading men. In 1939, when Ambassador Kennedy visited Hollywood to give the disastrous pro-appeasement speech that was to cost him his job, his second-eldest son followed him there. His family name opened doors and got him into elite parties, where he met such luminaries as Spencer Tracy, Lana Turner, and Clark Gable. According to biographer

Nigel Hamilton, stars became JFK's lifetime models. "His narcissistic personality craved success—social, sexual, professional. Deprived of early mater-
nal warmth, he wanted attention, adulation, affection." With a famous
father who had lavishly publicized his first book, *Why England Slept*, Kennedy "was lionized" at Hollywood parties, as a college friend recalled. "The
stars would come over and speak to him: 'Oh, Jack, darling, I just loved your
book.'" Kennedy "*put up* with these people, but he saw through them. . . .
He was fascinated by the stars and the glamour, sure—but not to take too
much of his time." As with his lust for women, his pursuit of fame and
glamour would be ravenous and persistent, but firmly compartmentalized.
In the 1940s, after the end of his relationship with the journalist Inga Arvad
—possibly the only real love of Kennedy's life—wrenching wartime service,
and the death of his elder brother, "his time" would be increasingly dominated by politics.[29]

Kennedy nevertheless continued to expand his contacts with Hollywood
and to pursue the immaculately groomed and pampered young actresses
that the studios still kept under contract. Joining him on one trip was his
former Harvard roommate, Torbert Macdonald. Macdonald dated the movie
actress Phyllis Brooks, and they later would marry; some years later Macdonald followed JFK into Congress as a representative from Massachusetts.
Interrupting his congressional campaign in the summer of 1946, Kennedy
headed once again to California and enjoyed trysts with Peggy Cummins,
Sonja Henie, Gene Tierney, and other movie actresses. Visiting his PT boat
crewmate Paul Fay in northern California a few days later, Kennedy astonished and offended Fay and his family by leaving in the middle of a dinner
party given in his honor to attend a picture show.[30] In the 1950s Kennedy,
now a senator, frequently socialized with his brother-in-law, the movie actor
Peter Lawford. The two married men enjoyed regular rounds of parties and
starlets' favors in Hollywood and in Las Vegas, sometimes in the company
of Lawford's famous friends Frank Sinatra, Dean Martin, Sammy Davis Jr.,
and Joey Bishop.

The story of JFK's relationship with the movies contains many unusual
subplots. What, for example, should we make of the fact that on the evening
of the crucial West Virginia primary in 1960, John and Jackie Kennedy,
along with Benjamin and Antoinette Bradlee, slipped into a theater in Wash-

ington to watch a salacious B movie called *Private Property?* They did so, Bradlee notes, because *Suddenly, Last Summer,* the grade-A production playing in the theater across the street, was sold out. While JFK was barely attentive to *Private Property* (about a young wife kept in a form of bondage), ducking out every few minutes to receive the latest primary results on a pay telephone, the anecdote provides a glimpse into the adventurousness and casual curiosity of both Kennedys, and of his reliance on freewheeling leisure in times of stress. Promoters of the low-budget film *Poor White Trash* might have inferred this aspect of the president's character when they decided to feature him on posters as a supposed fan of the movie, until a communication from the White House forced them to desist.[31]

After his election, as difficulties immediately began piling up, Kennedy increasingly sought refuge with Lawford, who arranged numerous liaisons with women. The movie actress Angie Dickinson was allegedly "available" to JFK during the entire evening before his inauguration, when they traveled in the same entourage to a series of gala events. Kennedy's contact with Judith Campbell, the ex-wife of a television actor and the girlfriend of the Chicago gangster Sam Giancana, both provoked the ire of FBI director J. Edgar Hoover and illustrated the administration's shadowy dealings with organized crime figures (who, JFK and others hoped, might help topple Fidel Castro from power). In 1962 Lawford arranged liaisons for Kennedy while he stayed at Bing Crosby's home in Palm Springs; during this time he supposedly introduced the president to the charms of Marilyn Monroe. The famed Madison Square Garden birthday salute, featuring Monroe crooning "Happy Birthday" and "Thanks for the Memories," took place the following month. Only time will tell if evidence of relationships between John and Robert Kennedy and Monroe, during the last three months of her life, will emerge. Meanwhile, Kennedy's extramarital sexual activity reached a fever pitch, with his long-suffering wife alternately serving as an enabler for some liaisons and protesting his callous neglect.

If testimony given decades afterward is to be credited, these bedroom antics exposed Kennedy's virtually juvenile infatuation with Hollywood-style glamour. He pursued female celebrities far below his social standing, such as Monroe, Jayne Mansfield, and Blaze Starr, and well above his own age, such as Marlene Dietrich. Allegations by Seymour Hersh and others about the president's involvement in drug use, sadomasochism, and group sex, if true, showed him exploring psychic territory that even the boldest film directors of the early 1960s (except for low-budget auteurs who churned out movies such as *Private Property*) had yet to explore.[32]

It is more certain that the deep involvement of Kennedy and his intimates with Hollywood, as well as their obsessive concern with the administration's public image, ensured that the movies would gain an unusually high profile in the White House. The making of *PT 109* was only one aspect of the close and constant relationship between Washington and Hollywood in the early 1960s. In these years, for example, the administration gave Hollywood directors their first opportunities to film on the grounds of the White House. This permission was granted to Otto Preminger's *Advise and Consent,* which was filmed in Washington during a long location shoot that provided movie makers and politicians with many opportunities to mix. The film adapted the former journalist Alan Drury's best-selling novel, which fictionalized actual Washington sex scandals that reporters had largely kept out of print. Peter Lawford portrayed a womanizing senator that Drury had based on John Kennedy. The crews filming *Kisses for My President* and *Bridge to the Sun* (a biographical movie set during FDR's years in office) were also permitted to shoot at the White House. However, the White House refused to allow a crew for a proposed television series to film the actor Arthur Kennedy (who was not related to the president) stepping off a helicopter on the South Lawn.[33]

The Kennedy years coincided with the peak of influence of the independent producer. Like JFK in Air Force One, self-employed filmmakers such as Darryl Zanuck, Samuel Bronston, and Sam Spiegel jetted around the world, securing funding, stars, armies of cheap labor and extras, and far-flung locations for their films, which tended to be lengthy wide-screen epics. To an even greater extent than in the studio era, megalomania came quite easily to these producers, as did other fabled excesses. Spiegel, in the fashion of the ex-producer Joseph Kennedy and his offspring, was a notorious exploiter of actresses, on and away from the casting couch.

John Kennedy's tastes in movies matched almost exactly the aesthetics of these producers. Their epics were historical in nature and sweeping in scope and in emotion, and they tended to feature heroes who confronted brutality and unfairness with a mixture of idealism, cynical humor, and hard-nosed combat. On his second weekend as president, JFK traveled with friends to a Washington movie theater to see *Spartacus*, a prime example of this kind of film, produced by and starring Kennedy's acquaintance and supporter Kirk Douglas. Like many big films of the era, *Spartacus* depicted a rebellion against dictatorial tyranny (in this case, by slaves in ancient Rome), but it also took the time to explore the workings of the malevolent empire; through such films, American screenwriters and filmgoers pondered their own country's dual role in the Cold War as both a champion of freedom and a hegemonic power. *Spartacus*, not incidentally, was itself the subject of controversy. Douglas had openly hired Dalton Trumbo, one of the Hollywood Ten, to write a script based the novel by Howard Fast, a former Communist. This move caused John Wayne to launch a campaign against the film and to contrast it publicly with his own rival production, *The Alamo*, a traditional paean to patriotism. Meanwhile, the Cold War itself was also being filmed to the president's liking. In the last months of his life JFK enjoyed the first James Bond movies, produced by Harry Saltzman and Albert R. Broccoli, which were based on spy novels by Ian Fleming that were among Kennedy's favorite books. Ben Bradlee joined the president for a screening of *From Russia with Love* and noted later that "Kennedy seemed to enjoy the cool and the sex and the brutality."[34]

The stark realities of the Cold War intruded on the Kennedy White House's interaction with movies in many ways. Right-wing groups such as the John Birch Society took up John Wayne's call and launched a letter-writing campaign to Kennedy, condemning *Spartacus* and praising *The Alamo*. Much correspondence and internal memo writing concerned *Operation Abolition*, which was not a Hollywood production at all but a short "documentary" film produced at the behest of the House Un-American Activities Committee. The film sought to expose the Communist instigation behind student protests that had disrupted HUAC hearings in San Francisco, and the image-conscious Kennedy administration spent much time worrying about the implications of this government-produced film. (*Operation Abolition* quickly faded from memory in the 1960s, except as a target of ridicule by the left.) The executive branch's own filmmaking clearinghouse, the United States Information Agency (USIA), was led by the broadcaster

Edward R. Murrow and George Stevens Jr., the son of a leading Hollywood producer-director. Murrow and Stevens oversaw the production of official propaganda films but also ruled on the usefulness of various Hollywood movies to the international PR effort. The USIA, for example, refused to endorse the diplomatic thriller *The Ugly American,* which criticized United States actions in Southeast Asia, but avidly supported the filming of *PT 109* and other flag-waving films.[35]

Especially in the wake of the Cuban Missile Crisis, Kennedy sought to redefine United States–Soviet relations along the lines of détente. One independent movie producer pursued the same goal through cultural means. Lester Cowan had been active in Hollywood since the 1920s, when he was hired out of college by the new Academy of Motion Picture Arts and Sciences to create its annual awards ceremony. Cowan's subsequent career as a producer was uneven, and by 1962 he had failed to release a film in fifteen years. Now, though, in the spirit of détente, he strove to arrange the first joint US-Soviet movie production. *Meeting at a Far Meridian,* adapted by Mitchell Wilson from his novel, told of an American scientist who falls in love with a Russian colleague; both get caught up in global intrigue. Cowan obtained the support of the US ambassador to Moscow, Llewellyn E. Thompson, and after much shuttling between America and Russia, he was able to persuade Nikita Khrushchev to sign a memorandum of agreement to make the film. Gregory Peck, a leading Kennedy supporter among film stars, met with Cowan and Thompson in Washington and agreed to play the male lead. The British intellectual C. P. Snow was also recruited to promote the project. In November 1962 Cowan wrote to Pierre Salinger about an "acceleration of interest" in Moscow concerning the film in the wake of the missile crisis. Problems with the script dragged on into 1963, and at the time of JFK's death no production date had yet been set. Cowan spent another three fruitless years on *Meeting at a Far Meridian* before abandoning the project. (In the meantime, he planned another ambitious film, *The White House,* to be scripted by the former Kennedy aide Arthur Schlesinger Jr. and directed by John Ford. That film also was never realized.)[36]

In his letter to Salinger in November 1962, Cowan had complimented Kennedy's team on its resolution of the missile crisis. "As a fellow professional, may I add a word of praise and admiration for the skill and technique with which the whole Cuban business was handled and for brilliant timing."[37] The film producer's choice of words tells us much about the role of motion pictures in the Kennedy administration. Students of the Cuban Missile Crisis give Kennedy high marks for resisting military commanders' calls for air strikes and for avoiding an escalation of arms that might have triggered World War III. However, some of them also criticize the president for turning the missile issue into such a dangerous crisis in the first place. While the Soviet installations might have been patiently negotiated off the island, Kennedy instead chose to force them off in a quick démarche that humiliated Khrushchev, eventually driving him from power, and that led the USSR to launch a massive nuclear arms buildup. Appearances and drama, in other words, were of prime importance in the crisis, and despite Cowan's approving words, historians generally agree that Kennedy was very lucky that no tripwire confrontation erupted before Khrushchev agreed to rough terms for removing the missiles. Cuba, in any event, would remain a vexing burden for JFK for the remainder of his term.

The missile crisis would encourage future presidents to play up emergencies for their perceived political benefit (and perhaps to gain a bolder reputation in the history books), with far less justification than Kennedy had enjoyed. The cinematic attraction of such crisis leadership was already evident to Hollywood producers, who in late 1962 were preparing a fictional tale of nuclear crisis, *Fail-Safe*, with the administration's approval (and with yet another Kennedy supporter, Henry Fonda, starring as the president).

Kennedy's posturing during the Cuban Missile Crisis was the most portentous episode in his career as a presidential performer, a chief executive who perceived his job as involving a great deal of artifice on the national and international stage. As many studies have noted, both the swagger and the glamour of these White House years were used by Kennedy and his closest aides, David Powers and Kenneth O'Donnell, to mask less attractive aspects of his private life. Thick layers of security and a compliant press hid his many extramarital affairs, and his serious health problems were effaced by his aides' and physicians' lies and deceptions. Such practices set an ominous precedent for future chief executives who lacked the compassion, good humor, and political flexibility that helped make John F. Kennedy, against the odds, a successful and popular president. His two immediate successors proved that point all too well.

———

Kennedy's assassination in Dallas, of course, had an impact on Americans that dwarfed the emotive content of even the most potent cinematic image making. Nevertheless, mass media delivered the news and the images and shaped how citizens perceived the event. The uninterrupted network coverage of the series of grim events—four days that told of the president's death, the return of his body to Washington, the suspected assassin's murder at the Dallas police station, and the funeral in the capital—was a landmark event that caused Americans to rely more on television as their portal to the world. It gave notice to politicians that they could be "covered" electronically, given regular exposure to a mass public, and broadcast around the world. (Telstar satellites had begun to transmit signals in 1962, though by November 1963 their operation was still fitful.)

Such expansive coverage, however, still lay in the near future. And, although the killing had been captured on Abraham Zapruder's home movie camera and frames from the film would soon be published in *Life* magazine, the moving image itself—blurred, low in resolution, and almost impossible to enhance with the technical tools of the day—was not broadcast on television until 1975. While the assassination tied Americans more closely to their TVs, it also compelled them to embrace more traditional rituals of coping and mourning. Religious services and canceled school and work days predominated, and Jacqueline Kennedy's rapid advocacy for a Victorian-style funeral in Washington, draping the city in black, and for a monumental gravesite in Arlington Cemetery drew heavily on precedents such as the funeral procession for Abraham Lincoln.[38]

In 1963 as in 1865, the shock of sympathetic Americans was existential and spiritual; artists, like everyone else, could only absorb the shock and try to articulate its meaning well after the fact. During the rest of the decade, filmmakers would take up that task, using the tools of their trade to dramatize and evoke the dread, the paranoia, and the sense of social fragility that the

Kennedy assassination had exposed with such force. In 1967 Warren Beatty, the young actor JFK had initially selected to play him in *PT 109*, produced and starred in one of Hollywood's most potent new depictions of violence, *Bonnie and Clyde*. In the climax of the movie, which coincidentally was filmed in Texas, the 1930s bank robbers are killed in slow motion, spurting blood from numerous wounds caused by a hail of gunfire. It was probably the most shocking and cathartic depiction of gun violence in a cinematic era filled with such portrayals. "When a piece of Clyde's head is blown away by a bullet," Peter Biskind notes, the filmmakers "wanted it to remind audiences of the Kennedy assassination." Beatty's life, meanwhile, took a trajectory that seemed roughly analogous to that of the late president. He, like Kennedy, was an ardent womanizer, pursuing almost every attractive actress in his path ("I get slapped a lot, but I get fucked a lot, too," he reputedly claimed). Beatty also became a committed liberal activist, working for eighteen months on George McGovern's 1972 presidential campaign. When he resumed making movies, he appeared in a film about political assassinations, *The Parallax View,* and in another, *Shampoo,* that juxtaposed tawdry public sex with television coverage of Richard Nixon's triumph on election night, 1968.[39]

Despite the agony and turmoil that Dallas unleashed for the rest of the decade, political successors to JFK sought to re-create his apparent delicate balance of compassion and aggression, family values and sex appeal, youthful vigor and world-weary experience. For the first time, a large number of former White House staff members sought public office on their own. Over the next decade, Kennedy aides Pierre Salinger, Theodore Sorensen, Kenneth O'Donnell, Sargent Shriver, and Arthur Goldberg all ran for public office— and all of them lost. The journalist Donald Smith wrote that "one might have predicted a brighter future for those who had shared a proximity to power and grandeur matched by few other men. . . . But evidently their political skill and effectiveness were dependent on the master craftsmanship of Kennedy himself. All seemed to lack the ability to run their own campaigns."[40]

First among JFK's successors, of course, were his two younger brothers, but their careers were uneven as well. Before 1963 Robert had experienced nothing similar to Jack's wartime trauma or health crises, and he largely served as his brother's hard-nosed adviser and advocate; but the

Dallas assassination—as well as his delving into existentialism and Catholic philosophy—allowed him to enact a complex leadership role of his own. The wild swings of his final months in 1968, punctuated by the frenzy of his supporters, the assassination of Martin Luther King Jr., and Robert's own death, exaggerated the excitement and danger that Norman Mailer had perceived in Jack's ride to the White House in 1960. The term "Kennedy-esque" appeared in the *New York Times* for the first time in early April 1968, in the early days of Robert's campaign, in reference to Canada's young new prime minister, Pierre Elliott Trudeau.[41] The shock of brown hair and the rolled-up shirtsleeves—the last a particular innovation of RFK's—became signifiers of charismatic political activism in the late 1960s. As soon as he was old enough to take office, Edward Kennedy had been steered into a US Senate seat by its former occupant, the president, but he struggled awkwardly to live up to his brothers' examples. Lacking their skills at self-presentation and their dedication to public service, "Teddy" drank too much, womanized clumsily, and nearly consigned his family's reputation to oblivion by wrecking his car on Chappaquiddick Island in 1969 and causing the death by drowning of Mary Jo Kopechne.

Outside the family, a variety of young liberal politicians tried to rerun the JFK movie to attain high political office and provide America with glimmers of idealistic leadership. A 1972 cover article in *Esquire* magazine, "The Ghost of Charisma Past," provided something of a postmortem on the phenomenon. New York City's mayor John V. Lindsay, who had switched from Republican to Democrat only to fail to capture the latter party's presidential nomination that year, was still considered by *Esquire* to be "another JFK." The Michigan representative Donald Riegle, another party-switcher, whose book *O Congress* critiqued traditional politics, "talks a lot about the Kennedys." Georgia governor Jimmy Carter was said to look "eerily like JFK from certain angles," while California congressman Paul N. McCloskey, a liberal Republican, was "often compared to his political idol John F. Kennedy." ("I'd say you're even more handsome than Kennedy," a New Hampshire woman told McCloskey during his quixotic 1972 primary campaign against President Richard Nixon.) Finally, *Esquire* noted, "out of Massachusetts has come a new JFK," the Vietnam War veteran John F. Kerry, bursting "with 'charisma' and political aspirations."[42]

Perhaps the most illustrative member of this group was John Varick Tunney. Now a forgotten figure, in 1973 Tunney, a US senator from California, struck many observers as the most promising of all the JFK emulators. Tunney, like Kennedy, was raised by a celebrated and domineering Irish Catholic father, the former heavyweight boxing champion Gene Tunney. After retiring from the ring, Tunney had become a wealthy corporate director; he mixed a love of poetry with pugilism, and, like Joseph Kennedy, he had four sons whom he drove mercilessly to succeed. Varick, as the second son was called, happened to attend law school with Edward Kennedy, who became his closest friend. In 1959 their drunken escapades in Pamplona, Spain, during the annual running of the bulls led them to destroy hotel property, causing a diplomatic incident that the US ambassador—the former movie actor John Davis Lodge—had to defuse. Tunney moved to Riverside, California, with his Dutch-born wife Mieke, an aspiring singer, and in 1964 won a seat in Congress. From then on his fate was bound up with that of the Kennedy mystique and Hollywood.

Also in 1964, the former movie song-and-dance man George Murphy, a conservative veteran of the studio blacklist campaign, won a US Senate seat in California, defeating Democrat Pierre Salinger, who had been appointed to the seat some months earlier. (JFK's former press secretary then briefly took up a position in the film industry.) As the musical satirist Tom Lehrer observed in a cabaret song that year,

> Hollywood's often tried to mix show business with politics,
> From Helen Gahagan to . . . Ronald Reagan?
> But Mister Murphy is the star who's done the best by far.
> Oh, gee, it's great—
> At last we've got a senator who can really sing and dance!
> We can't expect America to win against its foes
> With no one in the Senate who can really tap his toes![43]

Murphy, however, was an ineffectual member of Congress, and his continuing presence on the payroll of the Technicolor Corporation made him vulnerable in his 1970 reelection campaign. He was defeated by John Tunney. The latter also ran well ahead of another Republican and former actor, Ronald Reagan, who won his second term as governor that night. The *New*

York Times noted Tunney's "Kennedyesque, prize-fighter glamour" and "Kennedy-like accent and mannerisms" and labeled him "a swinger who wears his hair styled like a tight, furry helmet." During the campaign his image had been played up in an influential television commercial produced by the advertising executive David Garth, which showed Tunney walking on the beach with his three young children, suit jacket slung over his shoulder.[44]

Yet the *Times* also noted the senator's "surprising difficulty in communicating sincerity. . . . He seems to be testing each phrase just before he speaks it." As the leading Democrat in the most populous state, Tunney should have been a national leader in the making, but instead he seemed mired in indecision about both the issues and his own future. This quality was exploited by the screenwriter Jeremy Larner, a former speechwriter for Democratic politicians, who fictionalized Tunney's story in the script for the 1972 movie *The Candidate*. Robert Redford's devastating portrayal of a well-meaning but aimless young politician—preyed upon by his domineering father (played by the veteran Hollywood liberal Melvyn Douglas), unfaithful to his wife, and utterly perplexed on election night by the meaning of his victory—suggested the imminent demise of the JFK model of political image making and leadership. The real-life Senator Tunney underwent a divorce and struggled to win renomination in 1976, when the former 1960s student activist Tom Hayden challenged him in the Democratic primary. Jane Fonda, then Hayden's wife, dismissed Tunney as "a playboy dilettante who dates teenage girls." Tunney managed to defeat Hayden, but he lost in November to his seventy-year-old Republican opponent, S. I. Hayakawa, a former university president who had never before run for public office. Tunney's public career came to an end.[45]

———

With the eclipse of the "new generation" of idealistic and vigorous leaders John Kennedy had heralded in his inaugural address, it fell to an older—and far less idealistic and glamorous—politician, succeeding constitutionally to Kennedy's chair, to complete his term and take the presidency into the late 1960s. Lyndon B. Johnson proved to be a departure from JFK in many ways, not the least of which was his almost complete refutation of the latter's cinematic concept of charismatic political leadership.

With respect to exposure to Hollywood, it seems difficult to imagine an early life less similar to John Kennedy's than that of his vice president and successor. Lyndon Johnson's father was not a studio mogul but a state legislator from Texas's isolated Hill Country, a man reduced in later years to a menial state government job and near-poverty. One resident of Johnson City, the family's home town, recalled that "there were no movie houses then, no nothing. . . . no form of paid entertainment whatsoever." "There wasn't anything in the community except the three churches and the court-house," another resident recalled. "Lyndon was more interested in what happened in the courthouse." Strict Texas Protestantism, of the sort that once banned theaters in the thirteen colonies, helped to dictate this relatively bleak cultural landscape. Karl Hoblitzelle, the first movie theater magnate in Texas, recalled that during the silent era "it was a heart breaking job to con-vince the good people of Texas in those early days that we were presenting only clean, wholesome entertainment." As a young congressman in Wash-ington in the 1930s, LBJ rarely took his wife Lady Bird to a movie, and they never attended a play. Unlike Kennedy, Johnson was a president who, in David Kaiser's words, "almost literally never relaxed," who drove his assis-tants to work even on Sunday afternoons. The twentieth-century culture of dreamy spectatorship in darkened movie theaters passed Lyndon Johnson by completely.[46]

Yet Johnson seemed to conform to a particular type out of the movies—that of the dominating Western hero. White Texans endorsed an ideal type of male leadership that had predated Hollywood by almost a century—a type exemplified by a relentless drive to tame a huge and hostile land, with little regard for unnecessary cultural pretenses or for the racial minorities and natural obstacles that might stand in the way. Movie actors such as Harry Carey Sr. (of New York City) and John Wayne (of Iowa and Los Angeles) provided only superficial imitations of that type, but their cowboy portrayals became a staple of Hollywood westerns and other pre-1960s films.[47] Lyndon Johnson grew up fearing the mystique of the white male Texan—he always avoided fights, and his playmates chided him for his physical cowardice—but he exploited his own great height and blunt atti-tude to the fullest, to get what he wanted. To Texans and non-Texans alike, Johnson throughout his career seemed to exemplify the domineering white

male of the Lone Star State. His colleagues and staff members, in Congress
and in the White House, found him to be a tall, somewhat ugly, vulgar, and
abusive taskmaster.

In some ways Johnson resembled Kennedy. Like many politicians, both
were ruthlessly ambitious. While the latter patterned his career on those of
great leaders he encountered through books and his father's connections,
the young Johnson ingratiated himself with Franklin Roosevelt and modeled
his career on the president's. "FDR—LBJ, FDR—LBJ," he would tell an aide.
"Don't you get it? What I want is for them to start thinking of me in terms
of initials." Johnson, like Kennedy, visited Hollywood in 1942. The congressman and his aide John Connally, who now were also commissioned Navy
officers, had been ordered to tour Pacific shipyards. Mixing business with
pleasure, Johnson and Connally lunched with film stars in the Paramount
commissary and posed in tailor-made uniforms in a session with a studio
photographer. Allowing for regional and class differences, Johnson shared
Kennedy's obsession with tailored suits, hair styling, and grooming.[48] (They
of course also "shared" Connally, who remained Johnson's disciple, was
later elected governor of Texas, and was wounded sitting in front of Kennedy in the limousine in Dallas.)

LBJ and JFK each exhibited an enormous intelligence, a relentless impulse
to womanize, and a compassion for the disadvantaged. Otherwise, though,
Johnson's background and manner differed completely from Kennedy's.
Johnson's 1942 Hollywood visit was a fairly isolated event in his life, compared with the long relationship with the movies that was central to JFK's
life. Johnson lacked Kennedy's urbane charm, conquering women with a
form of the domineering persistence he inflicted on everyone. (Among his
more frequent lovers was the congresswoman Helen Gahagan Douglas, the
married former actress.) Political rivals, Johnson and the Kennedys also held
little personal affection for each other.

After he became president, Johnson used his legislative acumen, combined with his desire to memorialize his slain predecessor, to drive Congress
to pass a raft of major laws. His "Great Society" numbered among its achievements civil rights legislation, the end of public segregation, voting rights,
immigration reform, Medicare, student loans, and the War on Poverty.
Simultaneously, Johnson's simplistic view of the Cold War and of colonial

struggles for independence led him to escalate the conflict in Vietnam into a costly, bloody, and ultimately hopeless war that ruined his prestige as president and caused painful national divisions. As a result, as the journalist Tim Wicker later recalled, "it is difficult today to remember, much less . . . to understand, the extent to which 'the President'—any President— was . . . revered, respected, feared" as he had been before Johnson's prosecution of the Vietnam War.[49]

It would be naïve to claim that John Kennedy's mastery of image and the equanimity with which he maintained his effectiveness, based in part on his familiarity with Hollywood, would have allowed him to avoid disaster in Vietnam and the social fragmentation at home that the unattractive and graceless LBJ was powerless to stop. Despite his sophisticated background in foreign policy, JFK committed his share of blunders, especially in Southeast Asia, and his smooth style did not yield a fraction of the domestic legislation that Johnson achieved. It is unquestionable, though, as Wicker's comment suggests, that Johnson substantially destroyed the illusion of mastery, command, and personal competence that the cinematic image of leadership honed by Kennedy had created.

One aspect of Johnson's difficulties resulted from his disinterest in performing on television. His years of behind-the-scenes work as the Senate majority leader and vice president had afforded him little opportunity or motivation to acquire the presentation skills that Kennedy carefully nurtured. In 1964 Johnson insisted that he would not debate his Republican opponent, Senator Barry Goldwater. Nervous, cautious, and grimacing, LBJ could never feel comfortable staring into a television camera lens or imagining the "space" that actors use to achieve the illusion of intimacy. "Television was not his friend, it was his enemy," Lady Bird Johnson famously remarked.[50] He made a game effort to continue JFK's practice of holding regular televised press conferences, which undoubtedly helped him to maintain a very high public approval rating into 1965. But in direct proportion to the escalation of US involvement in the Vietnam conflict that year, Johnson's question-and-answer appearances declined. His Hill Country background and profoundly tactile approach to politics—which, in its essence, consisted of looking into the eyes of the people in front of him to persuade them to do his bidding—simply did not prepare him for the abstract, cool, and calculated world of political leadership through television.

This did not mean that Johnson was not a performer, or that he was cut off from the entertainment profession. LBJ loved to dance. He would dance for hours, quite skillfully, during White House functions, especially enjoying the opportunity it gave him to consort with a variety of female partners. As Alan Schroeder notes, when Johnson feigned mock horror at a function at a series of jokes told by Bob Hope at his expense, the president showed a surprising gift for light repartee. Moreover, LBJ exceeded even JFK and his idol FDR in his willingness to invite film celebrities to the White House. Johnson and his staff began the practice, followed since by every president, of including a healthy quota of Hollywood figures on the guest list to every state dinner. The net was cast broadly enough to bring Woody Allen—a thirty-year-old comic who was just entering the movies—to the White House in 1965, and the African-American cabaret singer Eartha Kitt three years later. (Kitt's emphatic criticism of persistent black poverty on that occasion caused a wave of headlines, and she insisted that Lady Bird Johnson's subsequent disapproval destroyed her career for years afterward.) Johnson was also the first president to invite a large number of jazz musicians to the White House.[51]

It was characteristic of Johnson that his relationships with Hollywood figures were mostly behind the scenes, motivated by the unglamorous demands of politics and governing, and that they were rewards for individuals' loyalty to him at a time when many former supporters, including movie people, were turning against him. In January 1967, Paul Newman, speaking to an antiwar group at Columbia University, almost certainly became the first movie star to recommend in public that a president be impeached. Johnson and J. Edgar Hoover, a longtime friend and former Washington, D.C., neighbor, placed surveillance on both Newman and the campus organization to which he spoke. By contrast, the president showered praise and attention on Gregory Peck. A strikingly handsome movie icon, like Newman, but with an extra decade of experience in Hollywood's upper echelon, Peck befriended Johnson early in his term by narrating a USIA film about his life. LBJ showed an even greater interest than Kennedy in such films, for both foreign and domestic political consumption. It also helped that Peck's public persona was shaped by his performances in roles of great rectitude, such as his Oscar-winning turn as Atticus Finch in *To Kill a Mockingbird;* Newman, in contrast, had personified the disillusioned antihero in movies of the early 1960s. Peck offered public defenses of Johnson during difficult times, and the grateful president invited him to stay at his ranch in Texas, encouraged him to run for the US Senate, and offered to make him ambassador to Ireland. (The actor declined both the Senate candidacy and the ambassadorship.) On his last day in office, LBJ awarded Peck the Presidential Medal of Freedom, making him the first screen actor ever to receive the nation's highest civilian honor.[52]

In the larger context of the Johnson administration, though, this relationship was overshadowed by the president's careful cultivation of two leading Hollywood executives, mostly for the purpose of raising funds for his campaign and his party. Johnson's relationship with Arthur Krim had its beginnings during the Kennedy years. Krim had been one of the masterminds behind the revival of the United Artists studio in the aftermath of founder Charles Chaplin's political troubles during the blacklist era. UA went on to become the principal midwife of the prepackaged Hollywood deal, allowing creative agents to bundle scripts, stars, and producers together and to make their films free of executive interference. Producing *The Apartment, West Side Story,* and *Tom Jones*—all Oscar winners for best picture—Krim and his partner Robert Benjamin made UA the heir to MGM as the new standard of quality in Hollywood. It was Krim who devised the 1962 birthday salute to President Kennedy at Madison Square Garden and hosted the intimate party for the president held afterward (both of which were dominated by the presence of Marilyn Monroe). The salute launched the President's Club, a White House initiative to enlist wealthy people to contribute to a fund that would pay off debts from the 1960 campaign and directly finance JFK's anticipated bid for reelection. Krim attracted numerous New York volunteers, each of whom paid $1,000 for membership. The birthday salute thus launched the modern era of presidential campaign fundraising. Paying tribute and treasure to the individual in office, the President's Club bypassed the traditional funding source—the political party—and reinforced the new focus on the personality of the candidate that Kennedy's image making had emphasized.[53]

After Johnson became president, Krim continued his fundraising efforts without pause. His extraordinary abilities impressed LBJ, who had appreciated the importance of money in politics since his first race in Texas. A discreet man, Krim became one of Johnson's most intimate and least visible confidants. During 1968, the troubled final year of LBJ's term, Krim was consoling and advising the president almost constantly. He and his wife often stayed overnight in the White House.

Krim also helped to solidify Johnson's important relationship with Lew Wasserman, the head of MCA, the parent company of the Universal studio. In the 1950s Wasserman had been the agent most responsible for the revolutionary new package deals that had allowed Krim's UA to prosper. After MCA purchased Universal, Wasserman became the most influential man in Hollywood. While no longer an agent, he knew everyone and could assist in the closing of big deals at any studio. Wasserman was instrumental in maintaining a constant flow of credit to the always cash-strapped studios, even if that meant arranging shady deals with representatives of organized crime, such as the Hollywood attorney Sidney Korshak. (Neither Wasserman nor Korshak would ever be indicted for their dealings.) Wasserman, a Democrat, had proven his fundraising acumen by arranging a lucrative event for Kennedy in Hollywood in June 1963, and in the months to come Krim enlisted Wasserman to launch the West Coast branch of the President's Club. During the Johnson years, Wasserman and Krim made Hollywood into the largest and most dependable source of Democratic campaign funds after organized labor. Through persuasion and socializing—but never compulsion—they cajoled wealthy executives, actors, and investors to become part of a permanent Democratic fundraising enterprise. The millions that were raised were crucial in underwriting the significant new costs of campaign advertising on television. This income machine outlived Johnson's time in office and still operates today.[54]

Wasserman's other major effect on Johnson's term was his recruitment of Jack Valenti, one of the president's closest aides, to become the new head of the Motion Picture Association of America. In 1963 the MPAA's president

Eric Johnston died suddenly of a heart attack, and after three years of drift during a tumultuous time for the industry, Wasserman concluded that Valenti would be a perfect replacement for Johnston. Hollywood needed an advocate who had the ear of powerful regulators in a time of studio takeovers by conglomerates, expansion of outlets for movie exhibition (such as network and cable television), and controversy about uncensored content in films. Valenti was lured to the job by its high salary and base in Washington, and Wasserman succeeded in the formidable task of persuading Johnson to let Valenti go. As Eric Johnston had done for Eisenhower, Jack Valenti continued to perform tasks for the White House while also serving as the go-between for figures in movies, finance, and politics. He would remain at the intersection of those worlds for thirty-five years. The aura of sex and fast times that had characterized John Kennedy's interaction with the likes of Peter Lawford, Frank Sinatra, and Angie Dickinson less than a decade before was now largely gone, replaced by a more sedate tone and a middle-aged Hollywood political network that operated primarily to raise money and keep the industry represented in the halls of power.[55]

————

The definitive era of the liberal cinematic model of presidential leadership lasted little longer than John F. Kennedy's thousand days in office. More than any other episode in the story told in this book—save FDR's and perhaps Ronald Reagan's presidencies—this intersection between the White House and the movies reflected the strong and influential personal qualities of the man in the Oval Office. While Kennedy's legislative record was sparse, his contribution as president to the United States' sense of well-being and in building its confidence in the present and the future showed that his mastery of style could produce true substance. Like movies, a politician who propagates an illusion of mastery and progress can help citizens perceive their own strengths, as well as positive possibilities in the materials and circumstances of their lives. It was this intangible benefit that Americans came to miss the most when Kennedy died and his successor proved quite unable to revive his charismatic brand of leadership.

While Lyndon Johnson used his formidable skills to ensure Hollywood's financial support for the Democratic party, his intervention in Vietnam led to a military quagmire and his Great Society programs fell victim to convulsive urban rioting. LBJ's political downfall was severe enough to wound liberalism and diminish John Kennedy's concept of the liberal leading man. By 1968 many Americans could no longer perceive the president as an advocate for the people who blended grace, compassion, and toughness and made government work for them. Out of the liberal disaster of the late 1960s emerged a presidential prospect who was familiar, but who also seemed likely to return the nation to right-wing Republican leadership. Richard M. Nixon was conservative and controversial, and no one could accuse him of possessing excessive charisma. But through sheer labor and nerve, Nixon began to build a reactionary cinematic model of presidential leadership, which eclipsed the Kennedy-Johnson tradition in 1968 and remains to this day a significant feature of American politics.

CHAPTER 5

ENTER STAGE RIGHT, 1969–1989

As a young man, a future Republican president of the United States was a magnetic stage performer. He appeared in every theater production at his small private college, twice playing the lead. Long after the young man became a famous politician, his drama director recalled that "he was one of our first successful actors. . . . I wouldn't have been surprised if, after college, he had gone on to New York or Hollywood looking for a job as an actor." The director recalled that in one play the student portrayed a sixty-five-year-old man and was able to summon up copious tears for the poignant climax. "Buckets of tears. I was amazed at his perfection." A few years later, acting in amateur theatricals, the young man received more qualified praise from another director. "I wouldn't have put any money on his becoming a successful actor, unless he had gone into the movies. He was very handsome." At tryouts for the troupe's next play, the young man met a young woman who had worked in Hollywood movies as an onscreen extra. She became his wife, and decades later, as First Lady, she would be the first former professional movie actor ever to reside in the White House.[1]

Readers with some background in presidential biography might guess what I will say now. The young man in question who became a Republican president of the United States was not Ronald Reagan, who, as everyone knows, is the only movie star to date to ascend to the presidency. The young man was, rather, Richard M. Nixon. Even today, Americans rarely associate Nixon with any of the appealing attributes found in the traditional movie star persona. Nixon, like his immediate successor Lyndon Johnson, has gone down in history as one of the great presidential failures—a corrupt, divisive, scowling schemer whose prolongation of the Vietnam War strained American politics almost to the breaking point, and whose dirty tricks in his campaign for reelection in 1972 ultimately forced his resignation.

Biographers, whom Nixon has attracted by the legion, have added much nuance to this general portrait. Especially since 1990, they note regularly that the gloomy conspirator in the Oval Office was also an innovative foreign policy thinker, a probing critic of the welfare state, a moderate on civil rights and the environment, and even a significant advocate of federal funding for the arts. Even these positives, though, contain qualifiers that repeatedly reference his penchant for ruthless political calculation. Nixon pushed détente, biographers write, to victimize socialist governments such as Salvador Allende's in Chile and to help crush North Vietnam; he expanded welfare at the same time he weakened federal commitments to its enforcement; he desegregated public schools and, in his next breath, demonized African Americans to win the urban white vote; and he enlarged the National Endowment for the Arts to strike a blow against the liberal, New York–based arts establishment. A lonely man in the backslapping world of politics, a cold personality who nevertheless won the loyalty of his wife and the love of his daughters, a hated warmonger who achieved one of the great reelection landslides in U.S. history—Nixon and his paradoxes continue to fascinate and perplex us. Stephen Ambrose, as able a biographer as Nixon has ever had, writes amid hundreds of lucid pages, "I confess that I do not understand this complex man." Ambrose marvels at "Nixon's inability to take pleasure in living" and concludes that "it must have been a terrible thing to be Richard Nixon."[2]

In this chapter I do not delve too far into the murky complexity of the Nixon phenomenon. We return to it only to explore the implications of the opening point—that Nixon, as much as John Kennedy and Ronald Reagan, was a child of the golden age of motion pictures, who at least in part responded to the terrors of real life and the perils of politics by playacting. (As we have seen, Lyndon Johnson, only a few years older, had been deprived by his rural upbringing of an acculturation to movies, and he did not share the other three presidents' starstruck attitudes.) Nixon's acting background emerged during his famous early "crisis," as he called it: the funds scandal of 1952, which he confronted by delivering the "Checkers" speech (which we examined in chapter 3). His passion for self-presentation grew, especially in the wake of his defeat in the presidential election of 1960, as a bitter response to John F. Kennedy's liberal cinematic imagery. Having lost to Kennedy by a razor-thin and possibly manufactured margin, Nixon labored for the next eight years to win the prize on his second try. The former vice president obsessively re-tailored his "image," the landscape of looks and gestures and catch phrases, caught by TV cameras and featured in magazine spreads, which he believed JFK had ridden to the White House. David Greenberg has summarized it well: "Nixon was the first president to make the presentation of his image his dominant goal; his papers brim with notes on tailoring his public persona, strategic memos on projecting that persona, and directives on handling compliant or hostile journalists. He created the White House office of communications and a White House office for dealing with television. He was the first president to hire what he called a 'full-time PR director,' advertising executive Jeb Magruder."[3]

Nixon's obsessive crafting of a self-image of maturity, calmness, and wisdom—one that often blatantly misrepresented his petulance, anger, and shortsightedness in the White House—was a rejection of the glamorous Kennedy model and a canny response to the cultural turmoil of the late 1960s. To the extent that it was successful, Nixon's image crafting became the template for what might be called the conservative cinematic presidential image. This image evoked the stolid competence of the "silent majority" much as that population had been imagined in Hollywood's many portrayals of traditional, Anglo-Saxon Protestant small-town values. Many of Nixon's image making assistants, coming from advertising agencies and television production teams, became key designers of Republican Party campaigns for the next few decades. Their work formed a creative counterpoint to liberal efforts in Hollywood, upon which Democratic candidates relied for campaign money, celebrity endorsements, and occasional new ideas.

In the late 1960s, even as Nixon was polishing his new image and plotting his comeback, the astonishing political debut of Ronald Reagan as the newly elected governor of California (and instant contender for the 1968 Republican presidential nomination) posed both a contrast and a challenge. In the next decade, as Nixon's presidency crumbled, Reagan's heretofore stymied

The young Theodore Roosevelt was a pioneer in mass media self-promotion. In Dakota Territory in 1885 he restaged a real incident for the camera, standing guard over "boat thieves" (impersonated by ranch hands). The image was sent to newspapers to advance TR's political career. *Theodore Roosevelt Collection, Houghton Library, Harvard University.*

Actors John Drew (left) and Al Jolson (right) pose with First Lady Grace Coolidge and President Calvin Coolidge during a visit to the White House by a delegation from Broadway on October 17, 1924. The event, organized by Edward Bernays, helped to ally entertainers with politicians in popular culture. *Prints and Photographs Division, Library of Congress.*

Herbert Hoover's presidential campaign in 1928 was the first to make intensive use of moving pictures. *Herbert Hoover Presidential Library, National Archives.*

Franklin D. Roosevelt significantly increased social and political ties between Hollywood and the White House. In 1935 movie studios initiated annual celebrations of FDR's birthday in Washington, to benefit polio research. Actress Jean Harlow poses with a cake during the 1937 event. *Photofest.*

Lauren Bacall makes an impromptu appearance atop the piano played by
Vice President Harry Truman at the Washington Press Club, February 10, 1945.
Photofest.

Movie and television actor Robert Montgomery became the first presidential TV adviser, assisting Dwight D. Eisenhower from 1953 to 1959. *Photofest.*

President John F. Kennedy exuded Hollywood-style star power. Amazed passers-by joined the president in the surf at Santa Monica Beach on August 19, 1962. *Photograph by Bill Beebe, Los Angeles Times, reprinted by permission.*

President Kennedy captivated leading Hollywood figures as well. Princess Grace of Monaco, the former Grace Kelly, gazes intently at JFK during a state visit to the White House, May 24, 1961. *Photofest.*

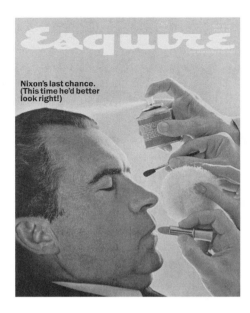

Presidential candidate Richard M. Nixon was satirized by George Lois for a 1968 *Esquire* magazine cover. Among presidents, Nixon displayed the greatest obsession with shaping his mass media image. *Reprinted by permission of art director George Lois.*

Nixon's last chance. (This time he'd better look right!)

For conservative voters, Michael Evans's spontaneous photo portrait of Ronald Reagan at his ranch on August 2, 1975—five years before he was elected president—would sum up the essence of his appeal. Reagan's Western movie roles and self-presentation as a politician became indivisible. *Wikimedia Commons.*

President Bill Clinton possessed a Baby Boomer's fascination with movies, and during his term the Hollywood-Washington connection grew more intimate. The president and First Lady Hillary Rodham Clinton appear with (left to right) actors Djimon Hounsou, Matthew McConaughey, and Anthony Hopkins, director-producer Steven Spielberg, actress-producer Debbie Allen, and actor Morgan Freeman at the Washington premiere of their film *Amistad*. *Photograph by Dave Allocca, Time & Life Pictures; Getty Images.*

President George W. Bush poses with sailors aboard the USS *Abraham Lincoln* after landing on the carrier in a Navy jet, May 1, 2003. Bush's Hollywood-style arrival and premature declaration of "Mission Accomplished" in Iraq generated criticism of the cinematic presidential image. *George W. Bush Presidential Library, National Archives.*

In the White House Situation Room President Barack Obama, Vice President Joseph Biden, Secretary of State Hillary Rodham Clinton, and others view drone images and listen to audio feeds of the raid by a US Navy SEAL team on the compound of Osama bin Laden in Abbottabad, Pakistan, May 1, 2011. One of those present likened the experience to "watching a movie." *Photograph by Pete Souza, White House, public domain.*

bid for the White House gained steadily in momentum and culminated in his victory over President Jimmy Carter in 1980. While Carter and Gerald Ford—the presidents between Nixon and Reagan, both turned out of office by the voters—had halfheartedly borrowed cinematic techniques from both the liberal and the conservative schools, Reagan brought his own idiosyncratic mastery of film acting and stardom to bear on presidential politics.

Reagan's campaigns and his presidency represented both an apotheosis and a synthesis of earlier cinematic trends. As commentators never tired of noting, decades of experience in Hollywood had taught Reagan, even in old age, how to offer his own effortless version of the smooth male screen idol. Stricken by an assailant's bullet and weakened by various ailments, Reagan in office also mimicked FDR's deceptions to appear a sufficiently healthy leader. While critics dismissed him as being the "performer in chief," an ex-actor who repeated old movie lines and seemed inattentive when not before the camera, Reagan also grounded his presidency on a sturdy, albeit controversial, ideological foundation. His expressed convictions—in favor of smaller government, lower taxes, and a holy war against Communism—provided the substance for policies that significantly transformed the nation. Reagan's style helped to make these policies palatable to a majority of Americans. His skill at self-presentation produced a polished and steady model of conservative cinematic leadership that contrasted with the unsteady, and often unconvincing, self-image that Nixon concocted to obscure his anger and resentments. Today, decades later, these contrasting and complementary presidential public images strongly contribute to American conservatives' concepts of how their leaders should appear and sound.

––––––

Acting was one weapon in an arsenal of skills that helped Richard Nixon, from his youth onward, to compensate for his unhappy family origins and modest means. Dramatics allowed him to bring some flair to his public appearances, in which his skills at debating, orating, and arranging (critics would call it manipulating) facts into arguments were also on display. The downward thrust of the fist, the shake of the jowls, and the melodramatic drop of a few tones in the course of making an accusation became Nixon speaking trademarks, in league with such forensic tics as the springing of a disturbing "fact," the opening of a harsh attack with a mild disclaimer, and the insistence that he, not his opponent, was the victim of the most personal and unfair criticism.

Beginning in 1946, when a group of Orange County, California, business-men recruited the thirty-three-year-old attorney and Navy officer to run for Congress, Nixon honed these skills to construct his public face. Privately, shutting out anyone who might offer him comradeship or advice, he studied endlessly and mulled over the angles of his arguments, the multiple sides of the issues, and the vectors of alternative campaign strategies. In the context of the Republicans' desperate desire to regain control of Congress after six-teen years as an abject minority, and the rising fear of the Soviet Union, Nixon's youthful good looks both mitigated and complemented his snarling attacks on his Democratic opponent, Representative Jerry Voorhis. The head of the businessmen's "Committee of 100," Roy Day, exulted about his find: "This man is salable merchandise!"[4] Conservative voters sent Nixon thousands of letters of support, bordering on fan mail, and helped him defeat Voorhis in November.

Nixon's wife, the former Pat Ryan, had climbed out of an equally humble Southern California background by means of hard work. In the early 1930s she gained employment as a movie extra, appearing onscreen in films such as *Becky Sharp* (the first Technicolor feature) and the Oscar winner *The Great Ziegfeld*. By 1936—the year before Ronald Reagan came to Hollywood—Ryan, disliking the dull routine endured by extras, had left the movies and become a schoolteacher. She remained in amateur theatricals long enough to meet her future husband, who labored for two years to overcome her reluctance to marry him. In later years Pat Nixon reminisced fondly about playacting episodes early in their marriage: "Dick was always the highlight of the party because he has a wonderful sense of humor. . . . In those days we were all very young, and we had to do home entertainment rather than go out and spend money. We used to put on funny shows. It was all good, clean fun, and we had loads of laughs." Once her husband and some other male friends delivered an impromptu "Beauty and the Beast": "Dick was the Beast, and one of the other men dressed up like Beauty."[5] After Nixon's election to Congress, Pat left theatrics behind, concentrating on raising her two daugh-ters. As Dick became consumed by ambition, their marriage became strained.

Within the confines of his modest Quaker background and desk lawyer's sobriety, Nixon located his showman's instinct and applied it to his political advancement. As he hunted Alger Hiss as a member of HUAC, Nixon originated a dynamic approach to the normally drab duties of congressional committee investigations, and his speeches were peppered with dark hyperbole about the imminent Communist threat. His 1950 US Senate contest against fellow representative Helen Gahagan Douglas—the former stage and film actress, wife of Melvyn Douglas, and mistress of Lyndon Johnson—was one of the bitterest, and most theatrical, political contests of its era. The congresswoman labeled her opponent "Tricky Dick," a moniker so apt that Nixon never was able to shake it off. Gahagan Douglas, though, was no match for Nixon's unstoppable ambition and willingness to say and do almost anything to win; tarring her as "the Pink Lady," he won the Senate seat and positioned himself to become Dwight Eisenhower's running mate two years later.[6]

Nixon's staging and impromptu recitation of the 1952 Checkers speech, as we have seen, was a landmark in the application of theatrical values in politics. Fighting for his political life, Nixon came up with a performance that revolutionized politicians' use of television. It also brought him a new avalanche of fan mail. Nixon's eight years as vice president were both constructive and trying. He became the Republicans' most indefatigable campaigner, and he traveled the world to learn about foreign policy, but Eisenhower shut him out of every major decision.

Running against Kennedy in 1960, Nixon unwisely attempted to manage the campaign himself—as he had always done—and had the bad luck to injure his knee and repeatedly fall ill. He appeared gaunt and sweaty during his first televised debate with Kennedy, and he struggled to channel his thoughts into words. As Norman Mailer described it, in his only mention of Nixon in his 1960 article on Kennedy, "the words [came] very slowly from the tired brain, somber, modest, sober, slow, slow enough so that one could touch emphatically the cautions behind each word."[7] For the first time in his life, Nixon failed utterly to rise to a performing opportunity. Losing the election by a hair, he began to brood over the failure, now perceiving Kennedy and his family as enemies and the press as their accomplices in his political destruction. His second disastrous television appearance two years

later, the morning after his ill-advised campaign for the California governorship ended in defeat, found Nixon evoking the self-pity he first displayed in
the Checkers speech. This time, however, he was scowling and unrestrained,
lashing out at reporters, who he alleged had distorted his statements during
the campaign.

For his family Nixon went through the motions of retirement to private
life, becoming an attorney in Manhattan. Behind closed doors, though, he
plotted a political comeback. He now realized the absolute necessity of
expert guidance in how he should present himself in public. The trappings
of the Checkers speech seemed almost vaudevillian by the 1960s, outshone
by the slick self-presentation and cool persona John Kennedy had brought
to presidential politics. Marshall McLuhan's theory that television was a
"cool" medium that responded poorly to old-fashioned, "hot" stage or
movie histrionics was now all the rage, and in Nixon McLuhan found a
receptive student. In March 1963, a few months after his "last press conference" and alleged retirement from politics, Nixon wrote the Texas oilman
H. L. Hunt about the latter's proposed effort to recruit Republican candidates and market them on television. "Too many of the public relations
firms who handle political campaigns," Nixon argued, "are concerned only
with buying television time for the candidate from which they receive a
percentage as a fee and too little interested in putting enough of the campaign funds into television production, technical advice, etc., for which they
do not receive a fee." Such micromanagement of imagery now appealed to
Nixon, more than it had to any other presidential candidate to date. "It is
vital," he wrote Hunt, "that the production personnel be selected by the
candidate and controlled by him rather than the station. . . . It is essential
that the director, the producer, the lighting man and the make-up man be
selected by the candidate or his manager and be absolutely loyal to him."[8]

Loyalty and control were Nixon's supreme priorities as he planned ahead
for a presidential run in 1968. Stung by his defeats, vulnerable to political
vitriol despite his professed toughness, Nixon demanded loyalty above all
else from his aides. (Not that Nixon himself was loyal to them: Herbert
Klein, a longtime adviser, noted that there were a "great number of loyal
people [who] rose quickly and fell out of favor just as rapidly.") Years later,
as president-elect, Nixon's demand for loyalty only became more intense,

such as when he set forth his criteria for a proposed historian of his admin-istration: "the man . . . must be not only a good writer (many will fill that bill) but above everything else, loyal to RN."[9]

Even before he became a manic chief executive—endlessly scrutinizing the loyalty of his staff through phone wiretaps and other means, and firing off memos to micromanage West Wing operations—Nixon resembled a type of director that had been familiar in Hollywood during the height of the studios. Thin-skinned, boastful, prevaricating, in search of yes-men, and seemingly more concerned about his current status and career trajectory than the end products of his labors (in his case, public policy), Nixon echoed the self-mythologizing of John Ford, the petty tyranny of Michael Curtiz, the brusqueness of Otto Preminger, and the outsized self-pity and reliance on toadies typical of many studio executives. Such personality flaws were evi-dent in white male executives in many fields in the mid-twentieth century—denoting, perhaps, a pathology in this generation of American men—but Nixon's actions and attitudes aligned themselves especially with the trans-parent egotism of Hollywood's studio era.

Moreover, his goal of producing imagery that dramatized his personality and leadership for mass consumption closely resembled Hollywood's own efforts. In 1969 Garry Wills called Nixon "the plastic man," "the least 'authen-tic' man alive," and "the tester of responses," allying him with the adver-tising industry. More specifically, Nixon might be called a theatrical (or cinematic) huckster, selling a prefabricated personality on a carefully pre-pared and strongly lit political stage. At a basic psychological level, Nixon seems to have lacked a core identity, and like some actors, only felt at home in his public role. In the 1950s he once told Dr. Arnold Hutschnecker, a psychiatrist who became his confidant, that when he looked into a mirror "it was as if there were nobody there." Unfortunately for Nixon, he rose to prominence during the very years when Americans began to expect personal authenticity from their leaders. This allowed Adlai Stevenson, among other Democratic opponents, to taunt Nixon for his indistinctness: "This is a man of many masks, but who can say they have seen his real face?"[10] Unlike the fabricated "authenticity" of Joseph Kennedy's promotion of his son, Nixon's own effort was protean and unstable, due likely to the discontinuity between the private man and the public persona he wished to display. JFK's attractive

public image was, in part, a reflection of his socially adept and sexually prof-
ligate private behavior; Nixon, by contrast, strove to camouflage his awkward and introspective nature.

Some of Nixon's advisers in 1968 (all of them male, except his secretary, Rose Mary Woods) had worked for him for years, even since the vice-
presidential era, but the young men who managed his mass media image all
signed up soon before that election year. None proved more colorful, or more
politically conservative, than a young editorial writer from St. Louis named
Patrick J. Buchanan. In 1967, working late in his office across the street from
Nixon's law firm, Buchanan wrote a rambling memo about how his boss
might use television. His basic advice was that Nixon should make non-
political appearances: "there is no sense showing you are a *sophistica[ted] pro*
to a lot of people who think politics is a dirty business." Instead, "RN ought
to get on shows where he can kid himself, where he can talk about family,
where he can crack jokes about past foibles." Appear "on Cronkite telling a
joke," Buchanan advised. "If a guy doesn't know if RN can handle Vietnam,
that minute [on Walter Cronkite's *CBS Evening News*] won't convince him.
But a guy who thinks RN is a humorless S.O.B. might be stunned and convinced by a grinning RN telling about his 'getting stoned in Caracas.'"[11]

In 1968, not surprisingly, neither Nixon nor his campaign image making
staff remade the candidate quite as puckishly or casually as Buchanan recommended. Nixon did try clumsily to connect with 1960s youth by using
phrases like "getting stoned" and by appearing on the network comedy show
Rowan and Martin's Laugh-In, but he was too insecure to engage in true
self-deprecation. But what the staff did accomplish may have been good
enough to get Nixon elected. Journalist Joe McGinniss's highly publicized
book *The Selling of the President 1968,* published a year after the election,
made precisely that argument. In McGinniss's view, Nixon's image makers
succeeded in concealing the candidate's awkwardness and past controversies, and their work made him the winner on Election Day. The 1968 Nixon
media campaign—concocted by the advertising executive Harry Treleaven,
journalist Ray Price, television producers Frank Shakespeare and Roger
Ailes, attorney Leonard Garment, and school teacher William Gavin—thus
was a milestone in the history of political image manipulation.

Ray Price, like Patrick Buchanan, wrote Nixon a memo in November 1967. This document is probably the main evidence for McGinniss's theory that the Nixon men held the voters' intellect in contempt and were eager to manipulate them with emotional messages. Price agreed with Buchanan that the "received impression" of Nixon had to be altered. In his fundamental assumptions about the electorate, Price drew in part upon the thoughts of Marshall McLuhan, whose work circulated among Nixon staffers in 1967, but he also dusted off prejudices against the irrational, impressionable American voter that dated back to the era of Andrew Jackson. "Politics is much more emotional than rational. . . . We should be concentrating on building a *received* image of RN as the kind of man proud parents would ideally want their sons to grow up to be. . . . That's what being a 'winner' means, in Presidential terms." The presidency, Price argued, was a blur to most people: "what we have to deal with now is not the facts of history, but an image of history," voters' vague notion that the president is "a combination of leading man, God, father, hero, pope, king, and just a touch of the avenging Furies thrown in." Price disdained the use of trite and obvious "slick gimmicks and phony merchandising" which were "repugnant to RN." He hoped instead that television might somehow encourage voters to perceive Nixon at a fundamentally mythical level, in a spirit of deference that predated—and counteracted—the era of democracy. Nixon, Price argued, should seem "larger than life, a living legend, and yet quintessentially human; someone to be held up to their children as a model; someone to be cherished by themselves as a revered member of the family, in somewhat the same way in which peasant families pray to the icon in the corner."[12]

Price's emphasis on emotion over reason was echoed by an unsolicited memo from William Gavin, a high school English teacher, whose musings earned him a job on Nixon's television staff. Gavin argued that "voters are basically lazy" because "reason pushes the viewer back, it assaults him, it demands that he agree or disagree," while "impression can envelop him, invite him in, without making an intellectual demand." Impressions of the past two presidents arose from the unconscious: JFK's "king bit," "clean, handsome, witty, articulate, rich, sure, pacesetter, stylesetter, elan, verve, guts," and "LBJ's strong-man, big-man, tough-man, colossus." Presidents

might be perceived not as popes, as Price claimed, but as Christ or as sha-
mans. "There's a tactile quality here, somewhere, in a transubstantiated way,
the lord's supper, that gory feast; the mystical communion—cannibalistic."
Like the medieval king, modern leaders might seem to followers to inhabit
their own and the state's body, and use their touch to heal. Gavin noted a
powerful "aural, tactile, suffusing" desire among 1960s youth, which in
politics resulted in adulation for Robert Kennedy. "[T]housands of little
girls . . . want him to be president so they can have him on the tv screen and
run their fingers through the image of his hair."

The right candidate could convey this irrational appeal to Americans of
all ages. To the Nixon camp's likely distress, Gavin identified California's
new Republican governor, Ronald Reagan, as such a candidate. Reagan, he
wrote, "manages to appeal to [all] at the same time; he's the tv candidate,
who instinctively reaches the aural-tactile; he speaks with a linear logic, and
his quick simplicisms appeal to children old and young."[13] Gavin did not
have to add that Nixon, by contrast, was among the least tactile men on
Earth. His reference to Reagan made plain what he and Price had inferred:
if the president of the United States had become in the public mind a wish-
fulfillment figure, an amalgam of male authority figures from history, religion, and storybooks, who better to fill the role than a professional actor,
trained to impersonate such figures?

Reagan's quick rise in national politics had startled Nixon and his advisers. Until the eve of the 1968 Republican convention the former vice president feared that Reagan might win over the most conservative southern state
delegations and deny him the nomination. Reagan had risen from moderate
movie stardom in the early 1940s to the presidency of the Screen Actors
Guild, which whetted his interest in public affairs. As a spokesman for General Electric in the 1950s, Reagan perfected what observers came to call "the
Speech," his signature attack on the welfare state and defense of the free
market. Millions saw the actor deliver it in October 1964 in a presidential-
style setting before a TV studio audience. Square-shouldered, lacquer-
haired, squinting through his contact lenses, Reagan peppered his talk with
tax statistics (some of questionable accuracy), sarcastic references to Democrats, and high-flown rhetoric about the crisis for western civilization posed
by communism. Two years later, Reagan's strong appeal among white Cali-

fornia voters allowed him to dispatch bland, moderate rivals in the Republican primary and in the general election.

As governor, and as an almost immediate prospective candidate for the 1968 Republican presidential nomination, Reagan blended a smooth and amiable television speaking style with often ferocious conservative rhetoric. He ridiculed liberals by identifying them with the hippie counterculture then breaking out in San Francisco's Haight-Ashbury district and in communes in Big Sur, and he tore into the University of California's tolerance of anti–Vietnam War student activists. Even more than Nixon would in later years, Reagan practiced cultural politics: demonizing hairstyles, dress, and attitudes—and their depiction in mass culture—as indicators of the depravity and bankruptcy of his opponents' political ideas. Before conservative audiences, Reagan raised the specter of antiwar groups raising funds at parties that featured "the smell of marijuana . . . thick throughout the hall," movies showing "the nude torsos of men and women . . . in suggestive positions and movements," "three rock bands," and "other happenings which cannot be mentioned." Drawing on old movie imagery, he quipped that the average hippie "dresses like Tarzan, has hair like Jane, and smells like Cheetah."[14]

Audience members greeted Reagan's wisecracks with roars of approval that Nixon, with his less polished theatrics, could never elicit. On the one hand, Reagan seemed far more amiable and authentic than Nixon, even when he delivered vitriolic and scornful rhetoric. On the other, Nixon's words often were less conservative than Reagan's. He calibrated his positions in the hope of retaining the support of political and cultural moderates, even on occasion appealing to liberals with current slang and references to new lifestyle trends. Nixon's rhetoric became more conservative during the general election campaign, in response to the surprising popularity of George C. Wallace's raucous and reactionary independent presidential bid, but many right-wingers continued to distrust Nixon and consider him an ideological chameleon.

Joe McGinniss's account of the 1968 Nixon advertising campaign introduced readers to a group of broadcast professionals who, in future decades, would be among the main marketers of conservative politicians. The most significant of them was Roger Ailes, a television producer at *The Mike Douglas Show* who took on the role for Nixon that Robert Montgomery had performed for Eisenhower. Ailes would go on to become the most influential image maker in conservative politics, dominating his field for more than forty years. Only twenty-eight in 1968, Ailes devised a series of talk show–style forums for Nixon, airing in different cities across the nation. He and Frank Shakespeare also worked with the candidate to create a series of unscripted commercials, in which Nixon simply looked into the camera and delivered a position on an issue, often tailored for a specific television market or audience segment. (McGinniss begins his book with a memorable account of an evening of Nixon commercial shoots.)[15] As we have seen, Buchanan, Price, and the others considered Nixon a problematic product; he was no longer the new "salable merchandise" that had flown off the shelf in 1946. They attempted, never quite successfully, to place Nixon in spontaneous-looking situations that would demonstrate his casual humor and help to erase his abrasive "loser" image.

The Nixon camp's strategy in some ways was typical of all campaign promotion in these years. In a preface to his book written twenty years later, McGinniss recalled overhearing in 1968 an advertising man on the Democratic campaign staff saying that "he'd be selling Hubert Humphrey [Nixon's opponent] like so much toothpaste or detergent." When McGinniss had requested access to Humphrey's television strategists he was turned away; Nixon's advisers welcomed him. Only the latter candidate, as a result, could be depicted in the book as a mass-media manipulator.[16] Even so, the Nixon effort differed significantly from Humphrey's in scope and substance. Nixon spent three times as much as Humphrey on television advertising. Even more important, though the Republican often grumbled about having to accede to the demands of television, his aides' strategy appealed to the performer in Nixon. By contrast Humphrey, a farm boy from the Upper Midwest, was cast in the pre-electronic mold of the old-time, stump-speaking politician. His trademark ebullience often came across on television as querulous verbosity: as a performer, Humphrey was "hot," not "cool." By happenstance, McGinniss was banned from the media campaign of the weaker performer and permitted to study the strategy of the candidate who was most determined to make innovative use of television.

The Selling of the President 1968 has been criticized for its narrow focus and polemical tone, but it vividly illustrates the emergence of new techniques in the mass presentation of political personality. Ailes and the others sought to avoid the clichés of contemporary television spots and utilize cutting-edge communications and marketing concepts to promote their problematic candidate. Their mistrust of voters' rational choices, efforts to make the candidate a regular fellow and to inject casual humor into his appearances, and pursuit of "cool" television message delivery deeply influenced future presidential campaigns. If Joe McGinniss had been able to interview Nixon himself, he might have discovered that the candidate shared the image makers' obsession with mass media imagery. Out of public view, as Leonard Garment later recalled, Nixon "mused and muttered, fussing with details, calling here and there, soaking up information, reacting to events, doubling back, breaking away occasionally for a foreign trip or business meeting, ceaselessly tinkering, bobbing, weaving, and maneuvering at his disciplined chess player's pace toward the 1968 endgame. This time, Nixon must have said to himself, over and over, there must be no screw-up." Policy details were grist for what Herbert Klein called Nixon's "meat-grinder of a mind," but so were the elements of image making that he prized so highly.[17]

Nixon's campaign in 1968 never actually proclaimed (as it was later alleged) that the candidate was "tanned, rested, and ready" for the presidency. The phrase, though, effectively summed up the cosmetic rhetoric of the campaign. As early as 1965 the New York Times described Nixon as "tanned, fit, [and] relaxed." During the campaign three years later the candidate said of his vacations in Florida, "that's how I keep up the tan." A new regimen of massages helped him stay rested. Before each televised forum, Nixon wrote an aide, he required "1/2 to 3/4 of an hour for massage and [two hours] for preparation." Nixon's exhaustion before the first debate in 1960 would not be repeated—nor, in fact, would there be any debates at all, since Nixon refused to appear. (Nixon declined Humphrey's challenge to debate him, saying that LBJ had been wise to do the same four years earlier.) After winning in 1968, Nixon had his official presidential photograph retouched: the smile was widened, the teeth were bleached, and the tan was deepened. Only John Kennedy had surpassed Nixon's embrace of Hollywood-style techniques. The famous 1968 Esquire magazine cover illustration, depicting Nixon being touched up by a slew of makeup artists, encapsulated the situation, as did the heading "Nixon's last chance. (This time he'd better look right!)."[18]

McGinniss overlooked one important new impulse behind the campaign staff's obsession with television appearances: their fear of an attack on Nixon's life. More than in any other year, American politics in 1968 seemed on the brink of devolving into violent mayhem. H. R. "Bob" Haldeman, Nixon's chief aide, expressed his concerns in an uncharacteristically emotional memo written two days after the shooting of Robert Kennedy. "There is a clear and present personal physical danger to any man campaigning for the office of the Presidency whenever he presents himself to an unrestricted large crowd," Haldeman argued. Such appearances are probably "irresponsible"; it was advisable that "candidates . . . not present themselves to large masses of people in person. They [should], instead, utilize the mass communications media to carry their messages to the voters." Limiting Nixon to "telethons, televised press conferences, televised coffee hours with small groups of representative voters, televised interviews of all kinds, documentary-type presentations" was justified on the grounds of personal safety. "Eliminated would be all rallies, large public functions, press-the-flesh campaign techniques, plunging through crowds, whistle-and-prop-stops." "Other than tradition," Haldeman concluded, "there is no sound reason for putting a man considered to be of presidential timber through the physical strain and personal danger of the old-time format."[19] These fears subsided somewhat, but their persistence would only help feed the socially awkward Nixon's desire to present himself at an electronic remove from the voters. His preference helped make the president more of a figment on videotape—a figment (as Haldeman failed to note) that could easily be manipulated.

At the end of the 1968 campaign, Nixon was probably saved from another humiliating close defeat by South Vietnamese President Nguyen Van Thieu's refusal to send a delegation to Paris, where Lyndon Johnson had finally begun peace talks with North Vietnam. The move deflated Johnson's and Humphrey's claims that the war was coming to an end, and in the last two days of the campaign it probably provided Nixon with his winning margin. The Republican's use of surrogates to dissuade Thieu—likely the most brazen manipulation of public policy by a presidential challenger in US history—was revealed immediately in the press, but on election eve Nixon and his media advisers effectively "spun" the story their way. The fact that Johnson, behind the scenes, had refused to aid his own vice president by not halting the bombing of North Vietnam until it was too late to help Humphrey, apparently in the hope of encouraging Nixon's victory and the continuation of his own policies, only heightened the Republican president-elect's cynicism about the manipulations he practiced.[20]

It would take Hollywood years to catch up with the speed and audacity of the political double-dealing of 1968. By that year, basic social fractures along the fault lines of sex and violence had been revealed in a few powerful mainstream films, notably *Who's Afraid of Virginia Woolf?*, *The Graduate*, and *Bonnie and Clyde*; a group of movie brats led by Peter Fonda and Dennis Hopper were filming *Easy Rider*, an anarchic story about itinerant motorcyclists; and *In the Heat of the Night* offered a pioneering, if lukewarm, indictment of southern race relations. Otherwise, American movies had little purchase on the violent and corrosive politics that guided American leadership for the next four years. Instead, the studios, inspired by the huge success of *The Sound of Music* in 1965, made disastrous investments in expensive family musicals that few Americans wanted to see. In the wake of *Doctor Dolittle*, *Star!*, and *Goodbye, Mr. Chips*, motion picture attendance fell to its lowest level in history. Fewer than 10 percent of Americans regularly bought tickets at theaters.

Some moviemakers caught up with the depravity of presidential politics during Nixon's time in office. In 1971 films such as *Joe*, *The Hospital*, and *M*A*S*H* dramatized many Americans' deepening mistrust of all figures of authority. As president, Nixon first aspired to build up his image—and his image making machinery—by combining a version of Eisenhower's model of strong and respected leadership with more vigorous and youthful touches, borrowed from Hollywood and the Kennedys. He was, in effect, betting that while the values and aesthetics represented by *The Sound of Music* were waning at the box office, they might still prove potent at the ballot box. Nixon's showmen Ailes and Shakespeare thus produced such milestones in the history of presidential razzle-dazzle as the televised phone call to Neil Armstrong and Buzz Aldrin on the moon and the 1972 Nixon arrival ceremonies in Beijing and Moscow. Inexorably, though, the cynicism and cross purposes of the president's political maneuvering and official policies ground down the public's acceptance of White House show business initiatives. The outlandish political crimes that Nixon and his aides committed during his reelection campaign in 1972 (leading to Watergate), along with the tensions growing out of the Cambodian incursion, the Kent State killings, and the Christmas bombing of North Vietnam, led many—perhaps most—Americans to doubt that he had ever intended to live up to his manufactured image as a unifier and a peacemaker.

———

Despite its pretenses to novelty, the Nixon administration's mass media strategy followed the same general trajectory of those created by its predecessors. Since at least 1929, when Herbert Hoover took office, newly elected presidents had begun their terms eagerly tackling the public relations challenge. (Truman and Johnson entered office in the wake of their predecessors' deaths and thus lacked the optimistic fresh start the others enjoyed.) Brimming with ideas, newly installed White House aides would adopt plans for keeping their man in the limelight and gaining an advantage over Congress, the bureaucracy, and the general chaos of events, seeking to impose something resembling a widely broadcast cult of personality. Each of these initiatives waned with time. Efforts by Hoover (midwifed by Madison Avenue and Louis B. Mayer), Roosevelt, Eisenhower (aided by Robert Montgomery), and Kennedy started boldly, but all of them either were snuffed out by political disaster or simply trailed off owing to inattention, fatigue, or turnovers in staffing. FDR's nurturing of liberal Hollywood in his later terms, and Truman's bolder use of television after 1948, were perhaps exceptions to this rule. (The bracing effects of the New Deal and the Cold War, respectively, helped energize these midpresidency PR initiatives.) All presidents, though, found that mass imagery at best only modestly alleviated their political burdens. After the first or second year in office, White House aides' media strategies tended to become inchoate and ad hoc, as the moment for instituting new, charismatic mass leadership passed and the public set its sights on the horse race leading to the next presidential election.

Nixon, with his outsized insecurities, devious plotting, and perception of constant and enveloping crisis, created a grander and often feverish variation of the typical new administration's public relations initiative. Aided by a cadre of television producers and ad men who professed a cutting-edge level of sophistication, Nixon went about creating what Rick Pearlstein calls "a remarkably successful public relations campaign selling the new presidency as a magnanimous respite from a cacophonous era of division." Even before the inauguration, image trumped substance in at least one key instance. Nixon was forced to assemble his cabinet hastily because he had agreed to Frank Shakespeare's idea of revealing the entire team in a dramatic, made-for-television press conference on December 11, 1969, just over a month after the election. (In a double irony, Nixon, despite his haste, assembled a strong cabinet—but then undermined it by personally usurping many of its powers.) Nixon sprung on-camera surprises in other hiring announcements, such as in the Roger Ailes–produced unveiling of Warren E. Burger (the next chief justice) in 1969 and the introduction of Gerald R. Ford (Nixon's second vice president) in 1973.[21]

Nixon "was obsessed with television," his longtime aide Herbert Klein wrote, "frequently to the detriment of newspapers, magazines, and radio." A fear of hostile journalists animated him. Incredibly, Nixon professed in his memoirs that "the media are far more powerful than the President in creating public awareness and shaping public opinion." One month into the presidency, aide Jim Keogh happily reported that "media treatment of the President is almost uniformly excellent," only to be reprimanded by Nixon: "You don't understand, they are waiting to destroy us."[22]

Nixon used television to neutralize criticism, particularly from the liberals who allegedly ruled the print media. In his first year and a half in office, he gave nationally televised addresses more often than his three predecessors combined. The president fired off memos demanding that messages, such as "great public approval of RN's handling of foreign policy," be broadcast in the media. Lacking a PT 109–type incident in his war record, Nixon hoped to strike a hero's pose in a manufactured way: "Not concerned by Press, TV, or personal style. . . . Zest for job. . . . Strong in-charge President. *Aggressive.*" White House PR campaigns, he wrote, should illustrate "hard work, dignity, staff treatment (compared with Johnson), boldness in offering new programs, world leader restoring respect for United States and the world, RN family, and others that may come to mind." "RN's effectiveness in using the television medium is remarkable," RN himself noted. "RN has ignored them and has talked directly to the country by TV whenever possible. He has used the press and not let the press use him. . . . This is a remarkable achievement."

Biographers have revealed that Nixon, in fact, was not a particularly hard worker, wasting time and energy fretting over "enemies" in the press and the TV networks, and that he was often ineffective in unscripted television appearances. Klein commented devastatingly in his memoirs that "people had said that they wanted to see a human, genuinely emotional side of Nixon; however, when they saw it [such as in the 1962 "last press conference"], it was personally disastrous." Yet until the final days of his administration Nixon clung to the hope that image would trump everything else.[23]

Nixon often seemed to reverse behavior purely for the sake of variety or to spring a surprise. In 1972, for example, after the wounding of George Wallace in an assassination attempt, Nixon decided to greet startled people waiting to tour the White House, supposedly to demonstrate that leading politicians were still free to move about anywhere safely. Haldeman felt that "it worked out great," possibly because Nixon never left the mansion's security. The gesture, though, was publicized on the evening news and made the president look like he was recklessly daring would-be assassins to restrict his freedom of movement. Characteristically, behind the scenes Nixon resorted to scheming, ordering Democratic Party literature to be planted in the gunman Arthur Bremer's apartment and giving Edward Kennedy Secret Service protection to help encourage Democrats to nominate him. As Rick Pearlstein has noted, "the Wallace shooting . . . spiraled the political situation . . . beyond control, and Nixon was stricken with a rage to control."[24]

Nixon was highly idiosyncratic, but his fixation on image and obsession with the mass media also reflected the times. Some of his image making innovations became enduring White House institutions. One of these was the White House Office of Communications, created in 1969 and first headed by Herbert G. Klein. A Southern California newspaper editor who had befriended Nixon in 1946, just after both men had resigned their naval commissions, Klein typified the moderate Republican who was attracted to Nixon's more intellectual and nuanced side. In the White House, Klein upgraded television operations across the cabinet departments but also eagerly kept in touch with leading magazines and newspapers. His moderate politics and willingness to consort with print editors eventually led him to clash with more conservative White House figures such as H. R. Haldeman, the powerful chief of staff, and speechwriter Patrick Buchanan. Nixon kept Klein on, but fretted continually about the effectiveness of his public relations effort on behalf of the administration. Almost a year into his term Nixon wrote to Klein, "I have reached the conclusion that we simply have to have that full-time PR Director, who will have no other assignments except to bulldog these three or four major issues we may select each week."[25]

Klein's influence with Nixon, along with that of other moderate advisers such as Robert Finch and Leonard Garment, was eroded by the right-wing ideologues in the White House who fed the president's sense of isolation and persecution. Nixon's prolonging of the war in Vietnam and exploitation of generational, cultural, and racial divisions at home had already poisoned the political well, but his true-believer advisers encouraged even more polarization. Gradually they took over the White House communications effort. Haldeman, who considered Klein a "very inadequate" image maker, applied his own advertising experience to Nixon's PR. On one occasion he spent thousands of dollars to landscape a spot at the Honolulu airport where Nixon briefly appeared during a refueling stop. Patrick Buchanan kept putting right-wing rhetoric into speeches, and the former adman Jeb Stuart Magruder, ostensibly Herb Klein's subordinate, steered the communications office into the orbit of the 1972 reelection effort. Meanwhile, Charles Colson set up a new public relations effort in the West Wing that involved itself in campaign "dirty tricks," including illegal break-ins and money laundering. Nixon himself also helped to undercut the image of positive and optimistic leadership he professed to seek. Early in his term he muttered to Haldeman about the need to remain "aloof, inaccessible, mysterious," like his idol Charles de Gaulle, in an effort "to establish the mystique of the presidency."[26] Despite these trends, Klein soldiered on until 1973, attempting to highlight the president's accomplishments in nurturing détente, fighting inflation, and revamping the welfare state.

In a significant early decision, Nixon as president-elect had passed over Klein for the post of press secretary, choosing instead for the position the twenty-eight-year-old Ron Ziegler. The inexperienced Ziegler famously earned reporters' contempt by repeatedly dodging questions at press conferences. Partially in response their criticism, Ziegler hid behind the jargon he had learned at the J. Walter Thompson advertising agency, where he had worked with Haldeman. Ziegler's adman lingo—"stonewalling," "operational phrases," "bottom line"—was ridiculed at first, but in the years after Watergate it caught on with the American public. For better or worse, despite their disgust with Nixon's lies and manipulations citizens found use for the artifice and distancing tactics that the language of PR image making typified. The post–World War II search for authenticity—in leaders, in movies, and in life—was being supplanted by a fascination with surface effects and their contribution to the "bottom line" figure on the financial balance sheet. Ziegler also popularized the phrase "photo opportunity" in reference to a non-event that showed off the president to the best pictorial advantage.[27] At least since Theodore Roosevelt's time, presidents and other politicians had manipulated journalists and others into creating photo opportunities, but Nixon and Ziegler institutionalized the concept. The president was increasingly perceived primarily as a figurehead appearing in photographs and moving images, and the substance of what he did or said receded in importance.

Movies—especially the example of their impact on the Kennedy administration—played an elusive yet central role in Nixon's concept of presidential PR. Nixon's contempt for the Kennedys derived from his lifelong hatred of northeastern elites and his more recent conviction that the press was ignoring the family's scandalous and illegal behavior. He had nevertheless been somewhat friendly with JFK during their time together in Congress, and he always envied his smooth public image making. "The Kennedy influence on Nixon was not one of organization but of style," Herbert Klein recalled. "He never admitted it publicly, but even in matters such as working with Pat Nixon to redecorate the White House, the image of the Kennedys was on his mind."[28] Characteristically, Nixon as president boasted about working all the time, but in reality, like JFK, he was a movie fan whose "staff time" listed in the appointment books often involved viewings in the White House theater.

Perhaps out of appreciation for his own acting talents—honed first in amateur theatricals, and then for decades on the political stage—Nixon never modeled his public persona on a specific actor. Rather, he fervently embraced movies that evoked the mixture of traditionalism, aggressiveness, and paranoia that guided his thinking. Early in his term, Nixon viewed *Doctor Zhivago* at the Camp David retreat, prompting Haldeman to note in his diary that, as college campus opposition to the Vietnam War was intensifying, the film's depiction of the Russian Revolution seemed oddly relevant. In August 1970, during a speech on law enforcement in Denver, Nixon digressed into an examination of *Chisum,* a John Wayne western that he had recently screened. Watching the film, which he judged both "just basically another Western" and "better than average Westerns," Nixon "wondered why it is that the Westerns survive year after year . . . one of the reasons is, perhaps, and this may be a square observation, the good guys come out ahead in the Westerns, the bad guys lose." The message of the film, in his view, was that the frontier lacked law and order, "and the law was important from the standpoint of not only prosecuting the guilty, but also seeing that those who were guilty had a proper trial."[29] The speech became controversial for what Nixon said next, calling the cult leader Charles Manson "guilty" days before his trial for mass murder in Hollywood was to begin. Yet his digression on *Chisum* was significant as perhaps the first important occasion on which a president used a Hollywood film to draw an analogy to a current public issue.

Patton, the Oscar winner for best picture of 1970, provided Nixon with his most visceral and revealing viewing experience. Producer Frank McCarthy, working with Darryl and Richard Zanuck at Twentieth Century Fox, portrayed the World War II general ambiguously, in an effort to attract both older traditionalists and disaffected youth. Two writers, the Hollywood veteran Edmund H. North and the young rebel Francis Ford Coppola, took turns concocting *Patton*'s screenplay without ever meeting in person. As portrayed in the film by George C. Scott, the archconservative, authoritarian general is also a meditative believer in reincarnation, a *M*A*S*H*-style pain in the neck to his superiors, and a gleeful trickster on the battlefield. (The original title for the film was *Patton: Salute to a Rebel.*) Nixon loved the movie, watching it repeatedly at the White House and at Camp David. He identified deeply with Scott's Patton, a profane yet patriotic leader who infuriated the bureaucrats in the Allied brass—especially the unseen Dwight Eisenhower, Nixon's own erstwhile superior—and alienated himself from mainstream journalists. "I will be allowed to fulfill my destiny!" Scott rages at a high point in the film. *Patton*'s relevance to Vietnam was inescapable, especially when the general vows that "America has never lost and will never lose a war."[30] The intentionally artificial opening scene, posing Scott in full military regalia on a stage in front of a huge American flag, where he intones a medley of lines taken from various Patton speeches, became something of a template for stagers of presidential orations, beginning with Nixon's own team.

As the Watergate scandal grew, the Nixon administration's attempts at image management began to founder and fail. Even the president's serious health problems during his last year in office did not generate public sympathy for him. His last great performance, Nigel Hamilton has claimed, came in the weeks after his resignation from office in August 1974, when the ex-president (now living in San Clemente, California) feigned feebleness and even dementia to win sympathy from a White House emissary and a pardon from the new president, Gerald R. Ford.[31] That successful effort begat Nixon's long and slow campaign to rehabilitate his image as an "elder statesman," writing books on foreign policy and advising Republican politicians behind the scenes. Like his earlier campaigns, this one blended substance with self-serving rhetoric and a great deal of showmanship. More than any of his predecessors, Nixon strove to turn his presidential library into a public relations site, dominated by promotional exhibits that marketed his greatness as a leader (while the library itself remained empty for decades, since the National Archives denied his claim that he owned his White House papers).

─────

Nixon's extensive and deeply cynical image making in office eclipsed the far more limited efforts of his two immediate successors, Gerald Ford and Jimmy Carter. Ford's public persona was defined almost exclusively from without, by journalists and entertainers in the mass media. The White House communications office was left leaderless for almost two years after the Nixon resignation, and Ford's staff considered eliminating it entirely.[32] An unassuming man who never forgot the highly accidental nature of his presidency, Ford nevertheless became the first sitting chief executive to appear on a network entertainment program. He was shown on videotape whimsically introducing his press secretary, Ron Nessen, as the host of an episode of NBC's *Saturday Night Live*.

During the 1976 campaign, Jimmy Carter presented himself to the public as the antithesis of Nixon. A scientist and farmer by training, Carter turned his rather mild public manner and lack of conventional charisma into advantages. Nevertheless, Carter's long relationship with the Atlanta publicist Gerald Rafshoon, who shaped the former Georgia governor's improbable rise to the White House in 1976 and who became director of White House communications two years later, roughly resembled the efforts of Herbert Klein for Nixon. Rafshoon was dismissive of Klein's operation, calling it responsible for the "stroking of news people . . . to get support for the bombing of Haiphong Harbor and going into Cambodia" and noting that it "ultimately . . . became the office of apology for Watergate." Rafshoon denied any credit for crafting Carter's persona. "You can't make a person's image. I mean, he's the President of the United States. He is what he is. All I do is try to define what he is; to sharpen, to clarify." Rafshoon thus advocated turning back the clock, returning to a more modest form of presidential image making. However, Ford's and Carter's political failures—both were voted out of office—did not recommend old-fashioned methods to contemporary politicians. Rafshoon left the White House after only one year. He had once worked as a publicist for Twentieth Century Fox, and upon leaving the communications office he expressed a desire to produce movies—"where the public's mind was," in his view—and a television miniseries dramatizing the career of Robert E. Lee.[33]

———

Biographers in recent years have tended to emphasize common themes in the lives and careers of Richard Nixon and Ronald Reagan. Nigel Hamilton, for example, observes that while Nixon was born in California and Reagan in Illinois, both men were raised by midwestern parents. Each had a profane and weak father and a mother who was the devout pillar of the family. Dick and "Dutch" struggled as high school athletes and were drawn to amateur theatricals, where each of them courted their leading ladies. Both men launched their careers in Southern California and hitched their political fortunes to the Cold War struggle against communism. Until recently Americans viewed Nixon and Reagan disparately, seeing the former as a disgraced chief executive tarred by Vietnam and Watergate and the latter as a highly popular president who ended the Cold War. Since 2000, though, historians have tended to depict the two men as major figures in the continuum of modern conservatism, the dominant political force in America for the past thirty years.[34] Revelations about Nixon's highly valued service to Reagan as a behind-the-scenes adviser during the latter's presidency especially help to elide their two careers.

At the same time, though, biographers have noted that the relationship between the two men was complex, and that the conventional wisdom of the 1970s—that they were fierce rivals who didn't like each other—also still remains valid. Nixon never forgave Reagan (who had been governor of California for only a year) for his aggressive "non-candidacy" in 1968, which prevented Nixon from clinching the GOP nomination until the eve of the convention. Conversely, the journalist Lou Cannon, who knew Reagan very well, has argued that while the latter "greatly admir[ed]" Nixon "as a president and politician," he "was contemptuous of [his] skills as a performer and thought him lacking in manners."[35]

In these biographical intricacies, we sense both the continuity and the innovation that Reagan provided to the new conservative brand of cinematic leadership, which Nixon and his image makers had launched in the wake of the liberal disasters of the 1960s. Unavoidably, the fact that Reagan was the first professional movie actor to become president made a deep impression on the cinematic presidency, in ways that reshaped the chief executive's daily scheduling, public appearances, and regular approach to television. In many other ways, though, Reagan's cinematic leadership was an outgrowth of established trends in both Hollywood and Washington, which presidents such as Nixon had already subsumed into their thinking. Ironically, the fact that Reagan attained office late in his life meant that during his two terms, younger Americans—even those who voted for him—often perceived him and his dominant image as old-fashioned. Young Republicans often admired Reagan in spite of his 1940s-film-star persona, not because of it. Despite his antiquated manner, though, President Reagan solidified the right-wing obsession with PR and imagery that had taken root in the Nixon White House. His administration's basic approach to packaging the presidency remains central to the conservative cinematic political style to this day.

It is difficult to overstate how fully Ronald Reagan fused movie acting with political ambition during the four and a half decades that preceded his arrival at the White House. Similarly, it is hard to imagine another candidate whose election might have fixed cinematic leadership more firmly in the presidency, or embodied more fully the synthesis between politics and entertainment. Reagan's adult self-image had largely been crafted by Hollywood. After Warner Brothers signed the twenty-six-year-old to a contract in 1937, it jettisoned "Dutch," the nickname by which everyone had called him since he was a child, and billed him as Ronald Reagan (a given name he had never liked). Warners restyled his hair, bought him contact lenses, and tailored his shirts to make his neck look longer. The gossip columnist Louella Parsons, who hailed from the same Illinois town as Reagan, assisted the studio by promoting the actor's courtship and eventual marriage to the actress Jane Wyman. Beyond acting, Reagan took an interest in all aspects of moviemaking, especially direction and the crafting of screenplays (although he never took credits in those fields). He was enamored with the storytelling power of films and absorbed the cadences of good script language and the pacing of effective scenes.[36]

Reagan was also keenly aware of the movies as a big business. The studio labor upheavals of the 1940s—especially the violence of the 1945 carpenters' strike, which Reagan witnessed first-hand—turned him into an active corporate citizen. He had been groomed for leadership of the Screen Actors Guild (SAG) by two past Guild presidents and conservative Republicans, Robert Montgomery and George Murphy (who had played Reagan's father in *This Is the Army*). Succeeding Montgomery as the head of SAG in 1946, Reagan plunged into the issues that were transforming the movie business, such as the federal antitrust suit against the studios' ownership of theater chains and the rise of independent production. SAG's work became heavily politicized owing to labor strikes and the crusade against "disloyal" Americans. Horrified by the Communist presence in Hollywood unions, Reagan quietly aided the blacklists and became an FBI informant. The high point of his Democratic political activism came in 1948, when he met and campaigned for Harry Truman. That year Reagan paid a price for his activism when Jane Wyman, who hated politics, sued him for divorce.

Reagan's film career was also in decline, but his agent, Lew Wasserman, continued to negotiate shrewd deals. Decades before he became the Demo-

crats' leading Hollywood fundraiser, Wasserman had set the party's future
nemesis on the path to financial security. In 1942, as Reagan entered the
army, Wasserman negotiated with Warner Brothers what he called the first
"million dollar contract" (to be earned over seven years) ever offered to a
film actor. (Wasserman later also pioneered the lucrative back-end gross
earnings contract for James Stewart, another conservative movie star.) More
than a decade later, Wasserman and Reagan bent SAG's rules to help each
other out. During his second stint as the union's president, Reagan granted
Wasserman exemptions as an agent that allowed him to buy studio properties and film titles, while Wasserman overcame a ban on SAG members
becoming producers to permit Reagan to own a share of the profitable TV
series *G.E. Theater,* in which he appeared.[37] Remarriage to the actress Nancy
Davis brought Reagan under the political tutelage of Dr. Loyal Davis, her
archconservative stepfather. Speechmaking for General Electric shaped Reagan into a performer on the public stage (although GE would let him go in
1964, when his involvement in Barry Goldwater's campaign made him too
partisan for the company's taste).

Reagan's long apprenticeship in overlapping realms of art, business, and
politics made him the most seasoned actor-politician yet to come out of
Hollywood. He had possessed a lifelong ambition to become president of the
United States—a schoolboy's pipe dream—that John Davis Lodge, Douglas
Fairbanks Jr., Helen Gahagan Douglas, Robert Montgomery, and others
had not shared. Among Hollywood actors, only George Murphy's political
ascent resembled Reagan's. Early in life, the amiable Murphy had benefited
from social connections that the young John F. Kennedy might have envied.
Murphy's father was a legendary Ivy League and Olympic track and field
coach and a friend of Theodore Roosevelt; his connections allowed his son
to attend Yale. Murphy applied his own athletic gifts to dancing, and in the
1920s he became a Broadway star who socialized with New York City's leading entertainers and politicians. He repeated his success in Hollywood, winning over studio heads and local Republican leaders. Murphy headed the
party's state committee and arranged Dwight Eisenhower's inaugural festivities. He then won a US Senate seat in California in 1964, defeating the
incumbent Pierre Salinger, JFK's former press secretary. After he was elected
governor two years later, Reagan rather immodestly called Murphy "my
John the Baptist."[38]

It was an odd fact of Reagan's political career that steps in his seemingly inexorable rise often resulted out of happenstance or desperation. In 1965, an unemployed actor worried about his financial future, Reagan was rescued by a coterie of conservative Los Angeles businessmen who recruited him to run for governor, a position they considered a mere steppingstone to the White House. Nixon blocked Reagan's first attempt at securing the Republican presidential nomination in 1968, forcing the governor to be patient. In Sacramento he quarreled with Democrats in the legislature and attacked the academic counterculture, while compiling countless bits of data in support of the unwavering conservative vision he presented in speeches. When he ran for president a second time in 1976, Gerald Ford again blocked his ascent. Then Reagan became extraordinarily lucky. When Democrats and moderate Republicans lost their way amid the economic distress of the 1970s, Reagan was ready, and in 1980 he easily won the GOP presidential nomination. Like Nixon in 1968, though, Reagan resorted to dirty tricks to defeat his opponent, President Jimmy Carter: he used the latter's stolen foreign policy briefing book, prepared for their sole televised debate, to anticipate Carter's arguments.

The mendacity, personal corruption, and bilious and extreme ideology of many of Reagan's team members—some of them, not surprisingly, veterans of the Nixon administration—lent his presidency more than its share of scandals and political disasters. And Reagan, a septuagenarian set in his beliefs and habits, encouraged many of them in their ways. In general, though, biographers have come to understand how Reagan, despite these deficiencies, as well as his advanced age and frequent inattentiveness to his duties, managed to be an effective leader. Drawing upon his accumulated store of statistics and other data to craft compelling speeches in favor of smaller government, lower taxes, stronger defense, and a triumph over communism, Reagan left the daily minutiae of governing to his staff. In the words of James Baker III, a leading aide, members of the Reagan administration—moderate or conservative, corrupt or ethically pure—were treated by the president "all the same, as hired help."[39]

Reagan's past affiliation with the Screen Actors Guild reemerged to make news during his presidency. SAG was no longer the conservative bastion it had been when Reagan had led it. Liberal activists now largely controlled the Guild, and its current president, the television actor Edward Asner, relished the chance to clash with his illustrious predecessor on political grounds. Asner led a clumsy attempt to oppose Reagan's aid to the authoritarian government of El Salvador, unwisely involving SAG in his personal protest, and he also failed in his attempt to expand the union's clout by absorbing the film extras' organization. The Guild under Asner strove to strip President Reagan of his membership after he fired thousands of striking, federally employed air traffic controllers; when this effort foundered, the leadership revoked an award that had been planned for the president before the firings took place. Reagan did not involve himself in these SAG dramas, but he did reward his main defender in Hollywood, the film star Charlton Heston, with high-profile government assignments in the arts.[40] The president also intervened on behalf of his friends in film production, ordering the Federal Communications Commission in 1983 to stop an effort, led by Jack Valenti of the MPAA, to increase residual payments to actors and crew members for rebroadcasts of old films and TV shows. (SAG had gone on strike over the same issue in 1960, when Reagan was its leader, and members had criticized him then for being too amenable to the producers' position.)[41]

The president's involvement in 1980s Hollywood politics underscored how centrally his experience in the film community defined his performance in the White House. In Reagan's case, "performance" is a particularly apt word to apply to public service. Lou Cannon, a journalist long acquainted with Reagan and one of his best biographers, called him "the acting President." In Cannon's view, Ronald Reagan perceived his service mainly as a sequence of public appearances, in which he applied his professional actor's skills to achieve the maximum political effect. Unlike leaders such as Theodore Roosevelt or Charles de Gaulle, who were merely "theatrical," Reagan "had practiced acting as a vocation and allowed it to become his principal mode of behavior." Reagan enumerated for Cannon the ways in which his acting career had assisted him in politics. Acting, he claimed, had helped him to become sensitive to "the feelings and motivations of others" and able to handle bad reviews and "undeserved criticism"; prepared him for onslaughts by the press; and, "most important," enabled him to master "perform[ing] on the spot at public gatherings." "His life as an actor," Cannon concluded, "prepared him for new roles, new challenges and new performances in the world outside Hollywood."[42] The contrast with Nixon, the community playhouse actor, is telling. The thirty-seventh president's obsession with public relations led him to become absorbed in elaborate strategizing and political scheming, but he often fumbled his public attempts at self-presentation. Nixon, unlike Reagan, suffered from an amateur performer's mistakes. He was insensitive to his audience; was emotionally vulnerable to criticism, especially in his press notices; and lacked the skills to handle impromptu situations well.

Yet the daily production of the Ronald Reagan presidential movie owed much to the ideas and practices that Nixon's image making team had established in 1968. Roger Ailes, Patrick Buchanan, Harry Treleaven, and Ray Price had emphasized photo opportunities, humorous tag lines, and a relaxed speaking style, among other tactics, and Reagan's communications staff borrowed this strategy in full. With their boss's help, they realized the goals of the strategy far more effectively than Nixon's team ever could. As a result, in the 1980s new concepts of political mass communications became dominant. These included the idea of staying "on message" in public; conveying desired "sound bites" to the microphones; "spinning" issues in favorable ways at every opportunity; and foregrounding the president every day in a single favorable setting, so that one issue, one spoken line, and one facial expression dominated the national TV news broadcasts every evening.

Such presidential "performance" was correctly criticized as manipulation, but it also reflected White House aides' almost desperate striving to gain some control of the chaotic, never-ending stream of national and world news. In the 1980s alone, Reagan's rather simple agenda for renewing America faced steady competition in the headlines from an assassination attempt, labor strikes, revolutions, guerrilla wars, terrorist bombings and kidnappings, a killer epidemic, urban violence and decay, and scandals domestic and foreign. In this context, perhaps, one can best appreciate a favorite observation of Reagan's: "There have been times in this office when I've wondered how you could do the job if you hadn't been an actor."[43]

For better or for worse, the daily sound bite–stage managing of the presidency proved amenable to both Reagan and the majority of voters. Perhaps surprisingly, some communications staffers had been veterans of the hapless public relations effort of the Nixon-Ford administration of 1973–77. David Gergen, a young Ivy League–educated lawyer, had written speeches for Nixon and served as Ford's communications director (reviving the position two years after it had been tarnished by Watergate). Gergen held the same job during Reagan's first term, and he was succeeded in 1985 by Nixon's original firebrand speechwriter, Patrick Buchanan. Gergen's specialty was to keep the entire administration "on message"; he wrote brief "talking points" about current issues and conditioned advisers and cabinet members to voice them repeatedly to the press. Buchanan, by contrast, championed hard-line conservative rhetoric, which from 1985 to 1987 exacerbated the political difficulties caused by Chief of Staff Donald Regan's mismanagement of the administration's agenda. In the view of biographers such as Lou Cannon, Reagan was served far better by his communications and policy staffs in his first term than in his second.[44]

The effectiveness of Reagan's public persona during his first term is often credited to Michael Deaver, a political operative who had some PR experience. In the 1970s Deaver had essentially been Reagan's communications director, and he also became personally close to Nancy Reagan, who mistrusted many other advisers and was fiercely protective of her husband. Deaver's communications strategy grew out of his intimate understanding of Reagan's abilities more than from any standard PR wisdom. In 1981 he became deputy White House chief of staff, specializing in the crafting of the president's public appearances. Deaver recalled that he "had grown up stargazing in Southern California" and "could pick out an actor when I saw one," and he never shed his admiration for Reagan's sheer presence. On public occasions, Deaver recalled, Reagan "did more than star. He glowed."[45] Deaver did inspired advance work for the most memorable appearances of Reagan's first term: the dramatic first speeches before Congress; the address to the British Parliament; the commemoration of D-Day in 1984 on the Normandy beach; the stroll through his ancestral Irish village (which mimicked John Kennedy's similar pilgrimage as president); and the opening of the Los Angeles Olympics. Deaver's one failed advance effort, in 1985, at the cemetery at Bitburg, West Germany, filled with the graves of SS officers—which he said had been covered with snow when he visited previously—resulted in the most harmful PR controversy of the entire Reagan administration. Deaver submitted his resignation from the White House soon afterward.

The sunny optimism of Deaver's most successful Reagan appearances belied their roots in the pessimistic soil of the 1968 Nixon campaign. His convictions illustrated the persistence of conservatives' denigration of the mentality of American voters. Deaver shared Ray Price's and Roger Ailes's dismissive view of the electorate, regarding it as apathetic and in the mood for entertainment, not political content. His reminiscence of the 1980 campaign, given nine years later, was as blunt an announcement of the cinematic presidency as one could hope (or dread) to find. "If I had tried to do what I thought was . . . the right way to go about it, we would have lost the campaign. People would have been bored to tears. In a democracy interested in where their leaders are going to stand, what they're going to do on the issues, that would have been the right thing to do. But the country isn't interested in it. They want feel-good and fuzz and not be upset by all of this. They just want to sit in their living rooms and be entertained. And no, I don't feel good about that at all."[46]

It is tempting to conclude, as Reagan's critics often did, that the president himself shared Deaver's contempt for the average voter. Ronald and Nancy Reagan's flaunting of their friendships with very wealthy people, enjoyment of expensive clothes and lavish entertainment, and endorsement of reduced taxation for the rich and welfare programs for the poor indicated elitist attitudes. Nevertheless, Reagan was able to maintain high levels of support among the majority of middle-class white voters, although his policies caused a relative decline in their income and his advisers maintained their cynicism about voters' civic engagement. Perhaps these voters participated just enough in the uneven but real economic growth that began after 1983 to become optimistic, or they were mollified by the obvious fact that "Reaganomics" hurt nonwhites and the poor much more than it hurt them.

Despite his elitism and his other faults (including a tolerance for scandal and high deficit spending), Reagan benefited politically from economic prosperity, as well as from the polished, cinematic brand of leadership that he and his advisers concocted. America in the 1980s became more acclimated to the view that presidents were figures who lived within the mass media, whose effectiveness was to be judged in relationship not only to the impact of their policies on real life but also to their perceived standing among other celebrities. As Ray Price sensed back in 1967, people were increasingly viewing the president as a mythic figure to be judged in the company of quasi-fictional cultural points of reference. Even in the television age, male motion picture archetypes continued to provide many of the mythical reference points that helped to define mass perceptions of the president. The presence of a former movie actor in the position, during a decade when movies made a successful effort to reclaim some of the mythic overtones they had sounded before the rebellious 1970s, hastened this conjunction between the image of the president and the power of movie stardom.

Reagan had a strong grasp of movie mythology, but by 1980 it was an old-fashioned mythology. His success in carrying the Man on Horseback myth, originated in the modern presidency by Theodore Roosevelt, into a decade populated culturally by Michael Jackson and Madonna (among others) was a testament both to his image making skills and to the persistence of conservative tastes among many white middle-class voters. Ronald Reagan had tried repeatedly to become a star of western movies in the 1940s and 1950s. Warner Brothers cast him in a few such films, but always in supporting roles, and after he returned from military service in World War II his freelance roles in horse operas were even less heroic. As in the comedies and other movies he made after 1945, Reagan often played weak, amusing, or even doomed characters; he rarely appeared in the final shot of his movies, in the embrace of the leading lady, to the accompaniment of swelling music. He gained heroic western roles on television in the anthology series *G.E. Theater* and *Death Valley Days* largely because he also hosted and co-produced these series. In the 1950s, in order to pay his bills, Reagan also had to take such jobs as hosting the TV broadcast of Disneyland's opening and appearing in a Las Vegas nightclub act.

In real life and in politics, Reagan was better able to realize his horseback ambitions. Aided by Hollywood friends, he bought rural acreage in Southern California at very favorable prices, and in his fifties he was able to ride horses and enact the cowboy's life at his leisure. In 1975 the *Time* magazine photographer Michael Evans shot a close-up image of Reagan at his ranch, smiling broadly under a cowboy hat, at the end of a day of chores which Evans had also chronicled. In an off-hand manner that would have impressed John Kennedy and that undoubtedly infuriated the hapless Richard

Nixon, Reagan created a portrait that put him on horseback and established his personal warmth. Michael Deaver bought rights to the photograph and made it a staple of campaign literature, and in 1981 Evans was hired as Reagan's personal photographer.[47] The print and broadcast media adopted the image as an apotheosis of Reagan's electoral appeal; the former actor's western credentials were now secure. After his presidency the photograph remained an icon of American conservatism.

In other ways, as startled reporters and aides often noted, Ronald Reagan recycled elements of his film career and of Hollywood mythology in his own thinking about his presidency and the world of the 1980s. Beyond the practical skills taught by acting that Reagan listed for Lou Cannon, a career in Hollywood had shaped him in more fundamental ways as well. As early as the 1940s Reagan formed the habit of perceiving the world through the narrative and pictorial lenses of the film culture in which he lived and worked. The fact that voters did not punish him for this habit, but rather tended to indulge it and even reward him for it, helps to define the historical significance of Reagan's cinematic worldview. It was a peculiar worldview for a president to have, and it was rooted in a "golden age" of Hollywood studios that younger Americans had never known, but it fit a new culture of perceiving reality through the lens of fiction that took shape, independently of Reagan, in the late 1970s and early 1980s. The daydreaming president and the movie-obsessed culture of the 1980s reinforced and promoted each other, and the cinematic concept of the presidency reached a new prominence.[48]

Like earlier presidents, Reagan made film viewing one of his favorite pastimes. The records of his presidential library indicate that there were 345 screenings of films at Camp David—virtually every evening he and Nancy Reagan spent at the retreat—and 21 in the White House.[49] The movies were mostly new releases supplied by the studios, but they also included a substantial minority of older films, including some of Reagan's own. (One of them, *Hellcats of the Navy,* also starred the future First Lady.) While some of the new films were challenging or adult-themed, such as David Lynch's *Dune* or Bernardo Bertolucci's *The Last Emperor,* most were mainstream dramas or family-oriented movies.

Only a few of the screenings have been memorialized by participants. Warren Beatty—JFK's favorite to play himself some twenty years earlier—

brought a print of *Reds* to the White House in December 1981. *Reds* was an epic about the American communist John Reed, played by Beatty, who also produced, co-wrote, and directed the film. Beatty's co-star and current companion, Diane Keaton, also attended the screening. "I could tell that Diane was really surprised and really liking" Reagan, Beatty later recalled, but the two were mystified when the president commented in an unusual manner on the Russian Revolution, which was depicted in the film. "What's really wrong with the Russians is this," Reagan began, lapsing into a favorite story about a US pilot in World War II, in a dogfight with the Germans, who stayed with his injured gunner as their crippled plane went down. "I kept looking at Diane and she kept looking at me and we kept waiting for the punch line."[50]

The incident illustrated some aspects of Reagan's thought and behavior. He kept his opinion of the movie private, probably out of a combination of politeness and a lack of intellectual engagement. Movies to him were entertainment, not texts to pick apart. Second, despite spending hours in the dark seated next to two of Hollywood's most intriguing current stars (and leading liberal Democrats), Reagan kept up an impenetrable façade, disarming them with charm while also deflecting any personal contact with an irrelevant war story. Many anecdotes attest to the fact that almost everyone, from the "hired help" to distinguished guests, received this treatment from President Reagan. Third, the story he told was a famous example of Reagan's occasional confusion of real and reel history. Reagan insisted that the story of the doomed World War II aircraft was true, but journalists' research revealed it to have been a stirring scene from the 1944 film *A Wing and a Prayer* (though it may also have derived from a fictional tale that had appeared in *Reader's Digest*, Reagan's favorite magazine).When Reagan mentioned the story to Beatty and Keaton, he perplexed them because he did not supply his usual punch line, which claimed that while that the United States supposedly awarded the flyer the Congressional Medal of Honor, the USSR gave the Order of Stalin to Trotsky's assassin: "That explains the difference between our two societies." Reagan, in short, was a polite and charming man who excluded almost everyone from his confidence and his inner thoughts, and who tended to mix movie legends with fact and process cinematic content in ways that even fellow film actors could not fathom.[51]

Reagan famously had movies on his mind in the course of his official duties as well. During the first day of the 1983 G7 summit in Williamsburg, Virginia, the president shocked James Baker by claiming to have ignored his briefing papers the evening before because *The Sound of Music* was being broadcast on NBC. The next month, Reagan startled a group of congressmen in the White House by diverting a discussion of arms control into his critique of the recent adolescent thriller *War Games,* in which a high school student infiltrates the computers of the North American Aerospace Defense Command. "I don't understand these computers very well, but this young man obviously did," Reagan beamed, as aides squirmed visibly. His commitment to the Strategic Defense Initiative, a multibillion-dollar planned missile defense system made up of laser weapons in outer space, stalled nuclear weapons reduction talks for years. In one of Reagan's first films, *Murder in the Air* (1940), his character, Secret Service agent Brass Bancroft, keeps would-be saboteurs away from a secret antimissile weapon that the government is testing abroad an airship. Worried observers asked if this early screen role had planted the embryonic idea of SDI in the president's mind, four decades before he proposed it.[52]

Reagan's reference in presidential speeches to particular movie scenes, and his occasional confusion of those scenes with real life, generated much speculation and concern. The political scientist James David Barber claimed at the start of his presidency that "Reagan has a propensity to be more interested in theatrical truth than in empirical truth." In 1987, in the midst of the Iran-Contra scandal, journalist Tom Wicker lamented that Reagan seemed "to think the American people are either such gullible fools, or so trusting of those in power, or both, that they will believe anything—no matter how contradictory or implausible. Call it the Hollywood touch."[53]

Garry Wills located Reagan's confusion in his lifelong supplanting of his boyhood evangelical upbringing—in his mother's Disciples of Christ faith —with lessons from his career, which turned memorable movie scenes into parables and line readings into sermons. The political scientist Michael Rogin, applying psychoanalysis to the case, argued that Reagan had projected his insecurities and fantasies of overcoming them into a public persona (what Rogin calls "Ronald Reagan, the Movie"). Reagan's 1965 autobiography, *Where's the Rest of Me?,* related his search for "completion" in politics after being dissatisfied with his career in show business. The title came from the agonized cry of Reagan's character, Drake McHugh, in the 1941 film melodrama *Kings Row,* at the moment he discovers that a villainous doctor has amputated his legs. In Rogin's reading, Reagan "regained his legs" by marrying Nancy Davis and by demonizing alleged subversives in SAG and on California's university campuses—legs that eventually carried him into the Oval Office. In his second term, when Reagan seemed increasingly detached from his official duties and occasionally dozed off during public functions, critics claimed that the president was descending further into an inner, movie-dominated dream world. Some have speculated that this behavior represented an early stage of the Alzheimer's disease that would cripple his mind in the 1990s.[54]

In the context of the history of presidential image making, Ronald Reagan's peculiar mentality serves as a kind of exclamation point rather than a divergence from previous trends. His advisers refined and enhanced the Nixon team's techniques for marketing the president and the innovations of Robert Montgomery (for Eisenhower) and the Kennedy and Nixon teams in shaping television coverage. The real changes lay in the public response to the president. By the 1980s, television viewing was central to American life, and—thanks to the success of blockbusters such as *The Godfather* (1972), *Jaws* (1975), and *Star Wars* (1977) and new wide-release practices (discussed further in the next chapter)—the movies had rebounded from their earlier slump and had regained a mass audience. Videocassette recorders and cable TV now allowed people to view movies repeatedly at home—a revolution that exponentially increased Americans' contact with feature films.

The 1980s also witnessed a new cult of celebrity. Americans' widespread rejection of experts and lofty public goals and their retreat into searches for individual fulfillment—emblems of the "Me Decade" of the 1970s—had the effect of intensifying their interest in glamorous individual success stories. This new trend seems in retrospect to have helped doom Jimmy Carter's call for mundane collective sacrifices and enhanced the appeal of Reagan's celebration of individual achievement and fame. Within this general cultural change, the time-honored trades of show business publicity and celebrity making gained greater and more celebrated national prominence. Thus Time-

Life began to publish *People* magazine, and show business news programs such as *Entertainment Tonight* won high ratings on television.

The most twisted and striking example of the impact of this new cult of celebrity was the attempt on Ronald Reagan's life on March 30, 1981, two months into his presidency. Stepping out of the Washington Hilton after addressing an AFL-CIO luncheon, Reagan was met with a round of bullets fired at close range by a delusional university student. Press secretary James Brady was critically injured, and a police officer and a Secret Service agent also lay wounded. Reagan was hit by a ricocheting bullet which pierced his lung. The president coughed up blood in his limousine; he was able to stride into the hospital emergency room minutes later, but he then collapsed. Reagan came close to death, but the emergency room staff revived him with a breathing tube and massive blood transfusions. After his condition stabilized, surgeons removed the flattened bullet. Reagan spent the next two weeks in the hospital, but for months after his return to the White House he remained drawn and weak. In the opinion of physicians and of those close to the president—including his youngest son—the injury caused a serious and irreversible decline in his physical and mental health, which became more evident during his second term in office.[55]

Fact first merged with fiction when officials suppressed the truth about the president's dire initial condition. Physicians and spokesmen lied to the public by claiming that Reagan was never in serious danger. Then, as information about the gunman, John Hinckley Jr., emerged in the hours after his arrest, it became evident that delusions about fame and motion pictures had inspired him. A strange, nine-year historical progression had brought Hinckley to the Hilton that day. In 1972, a twenty-two-year-old sociopath from Wisconsin named Arthur Bremer recorded delusions in his diary about achieving fame by killing President Nixon. Bremer fantasized about his name and face appearing on TV news programs and in newspaper headlines. His path did not cross Nixon's, but he did encounter George Wallace, who was campaigning for the Democratic presidential nomination. At a rally in Maryland, Bremer fired four bullets into Wallace; one hit his spine and paralyzed him.

Bremer's twisted tale, as well as the two assassination attempts against President Ford in 1975, inspired a young screenwriter in Hollywood, Paul

Schrader, to craft a scenario about an alienated Vietnam veteran who trolls the streets of New York City in his taxicab and happens on the chance to assassinate a presidential candidate. *Taxi Driver* (1976), directed by Martin Scorsese, was one of the most visceral and violent films of Hollywood's most rebellious decade, in which the heroic and brightly lit tropes of studios' golden age were vehemently rejected and deconstructed. Travis Bickle, the taxi driver, fails in his pursuit of the candidate—and in his inept amorous pursuit of a campaign worker—and settles for mounting a vendetta against a pimp. In the bloodbath climax of the film, he acts as protector to his new supposed love interest, an adolescent prostitute named Iris. Hinckley was infatuated with the actress in the latter role, Jodie Foster, and he decided to win her attention by shooting President Reagan. "I cannot wait any longer to impress you," Hinckley wrote in the last of his many letters to Foster before March 30, 1981.[56]

Life imitated art imitating life—and then art, in the form of the motion picture industry, offered the next few iterations of the theme. In an apparent coincidence, Hinckley had shot Reagan on the day of the Academy Awards ceremony, the motion picture studios' biggest annual publicity event, which regularly attracted one of the year's largest television audiences. It was the event most viewed by US women—advertisers called it "the female Super Bowl"—although the show's usual extreme length, hollow pretensions, and dullness were often met with ridicule and scathing reviews. President Reagan, the recently inaugurated ex-actor, was to appear at the beginning of the broadcast in a taped segment that proclaimed the evening's theme, "Film Is Forever." In the wake of the Hinckley shooting, as it had in 1968 after Martin Luther King Jr.'s assassination, the Academy decided to postpone the program, in this case by one night. The most unusual moment in the broadcast came when the Best Actor Oscar was awarded to Robert De Niro for his role in Martin Scorsese's *Raging Bull.* De Niro, who had played Travis Bickle in *Taxi Driver,* accepted the award with the plea, "I love everyone."[57] Possibly shaken by these events, Scorsese and De Niro collaborated next on a strange farce, *The King of Comedy,* in which the latter portrayed a Hinckley-like sociopath who kidnaps a leading TV performer in an effort to win mass fame. In the meantime, in August 1981, Ronald and Nancy Reagan screened the thriller *The Fan*—about a psychopath who stalks a Broadway star—at

Camp David, and in a rare move for them, watched the movie a second time in the White House a week later. The nature of their particular interest in this film was not recorded.[58]

It would have been understandable if Americans had been perplexed by the lurches between reality and fantasy that took place throughout the 1980s. As Hinckley's story, *The King of Comedy,* and *The Fan* indicated, modern celebrity culture had nurtured a sociopathic tendency for obscure, resentful people to identify excessively with well-known performers. Politicians, as Bremer's story and *Taxi Driver* showed, also became targets of this pathology by virtue of acquiring their own celebrity status in the mass media. This new attachment of celebrity to politics—"show business for ugly people"— had been woven out of many strands in American culture, stretching back to the era of Abraham Lincoln and John Wilkes Booth and the foundational stages of the cinematic presidential image. Violence against presidents seemed yoked to an era of general violence at home and abroad, which now was disseminated in graphic detail through color photography and graphic video representations in movies and television. In the hands of skilled filmmakers such as Scorsese, motion pictures gave these pathologies of violence and celebrity obsession their most powerful narrative statements. Ronald Reagan himself would probably not have been surprised by this development.

———

Taken together, the highly contrasting Nixon and Reagan eras contained important similarities. Continuities of policy helped to make their administrations the foundations of the new conservatism in America, a conservatism dedicated to the reduction of the welfare state, the restoration of "traditional" moral values, the resurgence of the armed forces, and a diplomacy driven by the assumption of American exceptionalism. As the historian Gil Troy has put it, "Reagan's conservatism galvanized the country, shifting American attitudes and triggering a decades-long debate about the role of government, the strengths of capitalism, the meaning of morality, and the limits of individual compassion and charity." Sean Wilentz has labeled the era from Watergate to our own time as "the Age of Reagan," but he also notes that Reagan was the heir to Nixon, who had created the "revamped center-right coalition and the southern strategy" of attracting conservative white voters that would form the basis of right-wing political power into the twenty-first century.[59]

To an extent, there was also continuity in presidential image making from Nixon to Reagan. The temperaments and the leadership styles of the two men varied considerably, but they were both performers who considered public relations and television appearances central to the effectiveness of the chief executive. Through their various strategies, the power of the presidential speech or photo opportunity was co-opted from the charismatic liberal tradition launched by John F. Kennedy and enlisted in the support of conservative goals. Through their evocations of westerns and war movies, Nixon and Reagan also enlisted reactionary narratives from Hollywood's studio era to provide their policy pronouncements with emotion and style.

And both of them sought to place themselves in the spotlight. Nixon schemed, usually in frustration, to present himself heroically on television, while Reagan tended simply to apply his vast broadcasting and acting experience to a carefully selected series of public events. Both men's efforts helped to engrave the sensibility of Hollywood movies and publicity onto the everyday actions and perceptions of the presidency. At the same time, the movies' economic revival helped to make motion pictures once again central to the nation's popular culture. As the 1980s turned, the vivid "high concepts" of movies such as *Top Gun* and *Pretty Woman* provided acting stars with bigger and bolder public personas. Political campaigns and presidential appearances took on a similarly bold and simplistic cast. The Age of Reagan (and Nixon) thus helped to establish an even more cinematic political culture in the decades that followed.

CHAPTER 6

HOLLYWOOD
WAGS THE DOG,
1990–2000

August 20, 1998: President William Jefferson Clinton emerged from the site
of his summer vacation on Martha's Vineyard, Massachusetts, to announce
that the United States had just bombed a suspected terrorist training camp
in Khost, Afghanistan, and a nerve gas manufacturing facility in North
Khartoum, Sudan. Seventy-five Cruise missiles launched from US Navy
ships in the Red and Arabian seas found their targets hundreds of miles
away. The CIA suspected that the camp and the factory were parts of a terrorist organization, headed by the wealthy Saudi Arabian Islamic funda-
mentalist Osama bin Laden, which was responsible for the bombing of two
US embassies in Africa earlier that month. After making his short speech,
Clinton boarded a helicopter and headed back to Washington, interrupting
his planned two-week vacation.

This American military action was the first of its kind in two years.
Although it did not eliminate Bin Laden or his operation, the strike displayed the awesome might and reach of US missile hardware, as well as the
scope of the growing intelligence-gathering operation on the ground in the
Middle East. As Clinton's earlier initiatives in Somalia, Haiti, Iraq, and Bos-
nia had also indicated, in the decade after the collapse of the Soviet empire
and the end of the Cold War, America's new military mission was highly
diverse, responding to a host of smaller but deadly apparent threats to
domestic and world security. No one could then know that Bin Laden's

survival of the rocket attacks that day, to terrorize again, would change American history within only a few years.

The immediate public reaction to Clinton's announcement reflected the mentality of the era that preceded the 9/11 attacks and the war on terror. In their reactions, citizens slighted the grave threats and weighty foreign policy implications with which the president had justified his action. Instead they almost impulsively pulled out of their medium-range memories a Hollywood movie—not a blockbuster, but a moderately successful, critically praised film that had finished its run in the theaters a few months earlier.

"*Wag the Dog*. . . . Everybody at the office was talking about it," Valerie David, a Manhattan advertising copy editor for Avon Products, told the *New York Times*—"how ironic it was that life was imitating art. We all noticed it." "My brother called me to tell me what had happened," banking analyst Brian Cooper recalled, "and I said, 'Doesn't this remind you of *Wag the Dog?*'" Roger DeWitt, an actor working in his agent's office on Broadway, noted that he and his co-workers mentioned the movie immediately after hearing Clinton's announcement. At his briefing at the Pentagon on the air strikes, Defense Secretary William Cohen was asked by a reporter if he had seen *Wag the Dog;* Cohen did not answer the question, stressing instead that the United States had acting purely on the basis of strong intelligence from the region. In Little Rock, Arkansas, US special prosecutor Kenneth Starr, investigating the president's finances and personal life, was asked if he had seen film. "Yes, I have seen it," Starr responded. "Other than that, I'm not going to comment." At the Capitol, Representative Bob Ney, Democrat of Ohio, told a journalist, "I don't think the President would be foolish enough to do a *Wag the Dog*." The next day, a quickly completed national poll showed that "by a 2-to-1 margin [respondents] believed Mr. Clinton had acted out of genuine military concerns, rather than executing a so-called 'Wag the Dog' strategy to shift public attention away from his troubles." The people interviewed by the journalist Frank Bruni suspected that the bombings were "wholly justified" and doubted that Clinton would be "dumb enough to try bombing to change the subject." But some suggested that "the timing of the bombings, coming so fast on the heels of his televised confession to the country on Monday night, felt a little too tidy, a little too cinematic."[1]

Wag the Dog had opened nationally eight months earlier, on January 9, 1998. That same week, depositions were begun in the sexual harassment lawsuit filed by Paula Corbin Jones, a former employee of the Arkansas state government, against President Clinton. As governor of Arkansas in 1991, Jones alleged, Clinton had cornered her in a Little Rock hotel room, solicited sexual relations, exposed himself, and groped her. Failing for years to win the public apology she sought, Jones was now championed by a right-wing legal foundation that financed her new bid for a guilty verdict against Clinton, or at least a lucrative settlement out of court.

Wag the Dog was based on the 1992 novel *American Hero* by Larry Beinhart, a fantasy about Clinton's real-life predecessor, President George H. W. Bush. Beinhart satirized the Bush administration's manipulation of news coverage of the real-life Persian Gulf War in 1991. The movie that came out of the novel inspired its own lawsuit, in which the original screenwriter, Hilary Henkin, sued the studio to delete the credit given to a later reviser, the playwright David Mamet. A settlement awarded Henkin and Mamet co-screenwriting credit, and the two antagonists later shared an Oscar nomination. Mamet and the director, Barry Levinson, fictionalized the war, setting it in Albania (ironically a site of the CIA's real-life intelligence gathering on Bin Laden before the 1998 air strikes). The film's unnamed and largely unseen president shares Bill Clinton's well-known propensity for shadowy extramarital behavior. After the chief executive is shown on video fondling an underage female in the Oval Office, panicked advisers devise a distraction—a tail, so to speak, to "wag the dog" that is American public opinion. A political operative (played by an avuncular Robert De Niro, a generation after his turn in *Taxi Driver*) enlists a Hollywood producer (Dustin Hoffman) to film a fake US intervention in Albania. In the "war," an actor playing a US pilot saves an apple-cheeked peasant girl from danger, to the tune of patriotic country-western songs. Released to television networks as news footage, the war movie succeeds in gulling the media-crazed American public. White House advisers, though, leave nothing to chance; to tie up loose ends, they hire an assassin, who drowns the producer in the swimming pool behind his Beverly Hills estate.

Coincidental with the first weeks of the movie's release, depositions in Paula Jones's lawsuit yielded an explosive new revelation about Clinton's private life. Monica Lewinsky, a former White House intern in her mid-twenties, had testified in her deposition that she had engaged in sexual activity with the fifty-year-old president in 1995 and 1996. Lewinsky also claimed that Clinton had ordered his close friend, the Washington attorney Vernon Jordan Jr., to find her a job in New York City to buy her silence. Clinton immediately denied the relationship, as well as any bribery by Jordan or perjury in his Jones deposition, but his strangely qualified denials caused citizens to be puzzled and skeptical, and stoked his Republican opponents' demand for possible impeachment. Three days later the president declared, with an air of finality, that he "did not have sexual relations with that woman, Ms. Lewinsky." Nevertheless, Lewinsky's testimony, as well as the admission of her semen-stained dress into evidence, compelled the highly partisan Starr investigation to probe Clinton's likely perjury in his Jones deposition (in which he also denied an affair with Lewinsky). Months of legal and political maneuvering led to a fateful deposition of Clinton by Starr's lawyers on August 18, in which the president admitted to a relationship with Lewinsky that stopped short of sexual intercourse. His angry, brief confession that evening on national television inspired disappointment and resentment in most Americans, and set the stage for the peculiar *Wag the Dog*-inflected reaction forty-eight hours later, in the wake of the air strikes in Sudan and Afghanistan.

Nothing quite like this had ever happened before. Coincidences between movies and contemporary presidential events had occurred in the past— *The Manchurian Candidate*'s foreshadowing of President Kennedy's assassination a year later, for example—but the division between the two realms seemed substantial. Even though JFK had helped to cast and script *PT 109*, a movie about his wartime exploits, only a few Democratic Party leaders seemed to have thought that the film would have an impact on Kennedy's popularity. Nevertheless, the history of interactions of Hollywood and the White House up to 1998 had conditioned Americans to perceive immediately an association between Clinton's bombings and *Wag the Dog*. A cultural evolution had been taking place in America for decades. Nixon had deepened the association between fiction film and politics by placing public relations—however ineffectively—at the front of his administration's concerns. Reagan's professionalism in realizing his own PR program conformed to Americans' increased appreciation in the 1980s of well-produced mass-media content. Now, in 1998, further cultural transformation had inspired Americans to turn reflexively to motion picture storytelling to comprehend —or at least to create some order out of—unusual and even nonsensical news.

This intensified blurring of fiction and reality owing to the growing cultural influence of the mass media received much attention from contemporary critics. In the same year as *Wag the Dog*'s encounter with Bin Laden, for example, the historian Neal Gabler claimed in his book *Life, the Movie* that "entertainment" had "conquered reality." The communication scholars Shawn and Trevor Parry-Giles perceive the Clinton years as the first presidency to enter a media-created "hyperreality." Other commentators argue that *Wag the Dog* fostered a "postmodern" development, of the kind which erased the materialistic certainty of earlier "modernist" generations, their dedication to hard facts as the basis of consciousness and action. Depending on the definition one embraced, postmodernism could encompass indistinctiveness, amorality, hybrid styles and thought, and a dedication to manipulation of surface effects at the expense of rooted values and qualities. In movies, the *New York Times* critic Caryn James noted in 1990, postmodernism "rejuvenate[d] old genres—westerns, adventure serials, and musicals— by being them and mocking them at the same time." In the best postmodern films, such as director David Lynch's *Blue Velvet* (1986), James argues, "audiences hardly notice how deftly satire and seriousness are blended, how shrewdly the film maker has it both ways."[2]

James's funneling of a highly diffuse philosophical notion into a "being and mocking" formula of postmodern filmmaking is a useful tool for analyzing the 1998 *Wag the Dog* phenomenon. When citizens made reference to the film, they sensed the indefinite, postmodern boundary between their perception of the Clinton scandal and the movie—the middle ground on which the two mixed, the terrain that Gabler labeled "Life, the Movie." One might attribute a postmodern playfulness to Americans who associated *Wag the Dog* with Clinton, as well as to media outlets such as the *Times* and CNN that broadcast and echoed their sentiments. The August 1998 episode, as it happened, was only one of numerous apparent movie/politics conjunctions in mass public thinking. Two months after the Lewinsky revelations and the premiere of *Wag the Dog,* for example, came a second new film, *Primary Colors,* a thinly veiled fictional treatment (based on a best-selling novel) of Bill Clinton's first campaign for president in 1992. What 1990s journalists liked to call "the buzz" about that film also produced a postmodern effect. In print, especially, commentators asked: Was the fiction as relevant to real life as the fact? Should people study the movie as a guide to real-life politics? Would the movie significantly influence future political life? *Primary Colors'* cultural and political impact turned out to be slight, but the habit of speculation it inspired seemed to be a persistent and powerful new element in American culture. It was as if American citizens had adopted en masse Ronald Reagan's presidential habit of misrepresenting movie scenes as history and exploiting real events as opportunities to recycle potent movie phrases.

As an episode in the history of the cinematic presidential image, the Clinton era highlights both the apparent impact of postmodern realities in 1990s culture and the resulting public discussion about those realities. Inevitably, research into the workings of presidential image making in that decade identifies more discrete and concrete machinery at work, changing and enhancing the cinematic concept of the president. Some of it was technological, encompassing the rise of cable television, the twenty-four-hour news cycle, and the Internet. It was also begotten by commercial trends, such as the growing presence of multinational journalistic conglomerates typified by Rupert Murdoch's News Corporation (whose expansion into diverse media markets was assisted by the Clinton administration).

Above all, though, 1990s presidential image making was driven by a strong sense of generational change. Clinton's biographer Nigel Hamilton begins to capture it in his own definition of postmodernism, which on its face seems narrow. "Virtually all the traditional tenets and approaches of Western social hierarchy and thinking had come under fire [from] a new youth culture" in the 1960s, Hamilton writes; "along with the great political protest movements . . . against racial segregation and the war in Vietnam had come more relaxed political and social views about sex and sexual orientation." From this perspective, "Bill Clinton was the quintessential Postmodern Man. . . . If [Clinton, as governor in the 1980s] appeared on the same platform as a colleague who suspected him of cheating with his wife and the colleague was prepared to live with that—rather than challenge him to a duel, as in Arkansas's early days—then American politics, for all the claims of Reaganism, was surely also becoming postmodern."[3]

It is beyond the scope of this chapter to attempt to verify grand claims such as this one, about either Clinton or postmodernism. Rather, it will argue that the impact of cultural turbulence in the 1960s and 1970s on Clinton's generation (the celebrated Baby Boomers), through specific developments, enlarged and intensified the cinematic concept of the presidency. Hollywood movies changed to suit younger Americans' heavy usage of and familiarity with mass media, especially television, and employed new distribution strategies to maximize the Baby Boomers' investment in entertainment. In part to realize these goals, screenwriters reshaped film genres to exploit the rough outlines of classical mythology and drama—story arcs that have helped to guide presidential image making since George Washington's time. One result, in the 1990s, was the emergence of fictional US presidents as movie heroes, to a degree never before seen in Hollywood history. The naïve idealism expressed in these characters was echoed in the image making effort for Bill Clinton, who struggled throughout the decade against scandal rumors and a vitriolic Republican opposition. Clinton exhibited probably the strongest personal devotion of any chief executive to movies and movie stars, but as a political necessity he also persuaded Hollywood to contribute unprecedented levels of funding to Democratic campaigns.

In terms of politics and image making, Hollywood and Washington thus became more structurally similar and interdependent than ever before—and people more often perceived them as such. The particular content of Baby Boomers' lives in the 1990s also helped to dictate both the content of mass entertainment and the issues of national politics. The concerns of women were newly central. Contemporary feminism had put a political focus on issues affecting average women's lives. What P. David Marshall calls the "feminization of the news" highlighted these issues, but it also brought human interest stories about celebrities to the forefront.[4] Similarly, as Nigel Hamilton suggested, the freer sexuality generated by 1960s youth culture, as well as the opening of new career paths to women, increased attention to the social impact of relations between the sexes. In their explorations of sexuality, movies and other mass media in the 1990s particularly fixated on the phenomenon of workplace harassment—the imposition of sexuality by a superior or a colleague (usually a male) on another employee (usually an unwilling or hesitant female). Clinton's continuing sexual aggressiveness as president, coupled with his wife's apparent tolerance of some of this behavior, seemed to write the narrative of his presidency—in a time when consultants, copying Hollywood, embraced the power of "narrative" in presidential politics. His adultery outraged his conservative opponents, who used his possible perjury in the Jones case as the basis for an impeachment trial in the US Senate. Clinton was acquitted and served out his second term. However, Americans would be left to sort through the bewildering new influences of celebrity charisma, openly discussed sexuality, and politically themed movies on the image of the US president. In the 1960s, the saying went, the personal became political; thirty years later, perhaps, the political had become personal.

––––

Movie fans saved Hollywood from oblivion. Sophisticated young viewers in the 1950s and early 1960s imbibed innovative new works by French directors, who had channeled their admiration for the US studios' auteur directors to create their own "New Wave" cinema. Visionaries from other nations such as Fellini, Kurosawa, and Bergman also enlarged and stimulated American moviegoers' sensibilities. While Hollywood studios financed inert spectacles with bloated budgets and sold themselves to corporate conglomerates, insurgents from magazine writing staffs (Robert Benton, David Newman), grade-B studios (Robert Towne, Jack Nicholson), television (Robert Altman, William Friedkin), film repertory houses (Peter Bogdanovich), Broadway (Mike Nichols), and even movie brats' hangouts in Malibu and Beverly Hills (Peter Fonda, Warren Beatty) concocted the "New Hollywood" movie. *Bonnie and Clyde* applied the New Wave aesthetic to the bank robber genre; *The Graduate* violated traditional studio prohibitions on sexuality; *Easy Rider* sprouted out of, and exemplified, the hippie counterculture; and *M*A*S*H* insulted the military and flouted most of the conventions of movie plotting. People who helped to make *Easy Rider* and *M*A*S*H* insisted they used recreational drugs heavily while at work. When ticket lines at the theaters showing these movies began to stretch around blocks and the films made profits that studios hadn't enjoyed in decades, it was apparent that the counterculture had helped to revive Hollywood.[5]

This revival continued into the early 1970s, when young film-school graduates contributed their own personal, disruptive moviemaking. Martin Scorsese's *Mean Streets* and *Taxi Driver* and Francis Ford Coppola's *The Godfather Parts I and II* and *The Conversation* powerfully evoked the urban decay, social anomie, and official corruption of the Nixon era, while George Lucas's *American Graffiti* expressed a keen nostalgia for the 1950s. As in the 1960s, traditional Hollywood genres were deconstructed and critiqued. Other 1970s cinema seemed to be cultural dead weight. The western movie, so central to presidential imagery from Jackson to TR to Reagan, declined drastically in an age of urban and suburban sprawl, although its basic good-versus-evil plot was transplanted to urban cop and vigilante thrillers. For a time it seemed that parodies of the old movie genres, either gentle or biting—from directors such as Mel Brooks and Robert Altman—dominated, but the trend proved short lived. The most expensive studio projects in the early 1970s were "disaster" movies such as *Earthquake* and *The Towering Inferno,* which in their own way replicated the slow pacing and leaden creativity of the big 1960s musicals.

The young film school graduates then reinvented the blockbuster movie, at the cost of partially snuffing out much of Hollywood's rebellious and countercultural spirit. *The Godfather* (1972) was a long and bitter meditation on the corruption of the American dream, but since it also was recognizably a gangster movie based on a best-selling book, Paramount promoted it heavily on television and gave it a wide national release. The film opened the same night in hundreds of theaters, and the studio was pleasantly stunned when its moody Mafia picture earned back nearly half of its budget in the first weekend of release. Still broader release pushed *The Godfather* to the top of the all-time earnings list. Subsequently *The Sting* and *The Exorcist* opened even more widely and out-earned *The Godfather.* Those movies were surmounted in turn by *Jaws*, a 1975 thriller directed by the young film school dropout Steven Spielberg. *Jaws'* pre-release advertising and simultaneous national release were unprecedented in size, and so were its earnings for Lew Wasserman's MCA-Universal, which eventually totaled $250 million.

By 1977, when George Lucas's space opera *Star Wars* soared far past the heights scaled by *Jaws*, Hollywood clearly had arrived at a new plateau of financial success. The earnings of blockbusters helped to finance cheap teen comedies, musicals, and horror films—such as *National Lampoon's Animal House, Grease*, and *Halloween*—which became profitable pillars of the business in their own right. Sales of videocassettes and cable TV airing rights now guaranteed that virtually every movie would turn a profit. The big money, though, lay in the large-budget, technically showy movies that attracted the broadest audience and the most repeat viewers. *Star Wars* especially encouraged the studios to revisit the simplistic and bold themes of B-movie genres such as science fiction, adventure, and fantasy. In the late 1970s Hollywood coined the term "action film" to summarize this new trend, exemplified perhaps by Spielberg and Lucas's 1981 hit *Raiders of the Lost Ark*. "Steven and I come from the visceral generation," Lucas noted; "we enjoyed the emotional highs we got from movies and realized that you could crank up the adrenaline to a level way beyond what people were doing." Some were troubled by the rise of these brash, and now impossibly wealthy, young filmmakers. The critic David Denby imagined that if Lucas had made *The Wizard of Oz* he would have flattened out its emotions and plotting, in the end giving "the scarecrow his brain, the tin woodsman his heart, and the lion his courage." Lucas, sounding much like Reagan's image maker Michael Deaver, defended himself: "Why do people go see these popcorn pictures when they're not good? Why is the public so stupid? That's not my fault. I just understood what people like to go see, and Steven has too, and we go for that."[6] The old studios' aspirations to elevate public taste, as well as the New Wave's critical perspective, were now pushed aside by big, loud movies that seemed to be tooled primarily to earn the highest box office grosses.

These action-based "tent-pole" studio films became even more financially dominant in the 1980s and 1990s. To critics, they signified the dumbing-down of both movies and the US filmgoing public. (Since Hollywood now exported its products more widely and rapidly, these criticisms were directed at the worldwide audience as well.) The film historian Thomas Schatz lamented that movies now were "increasingly plot-driven," "visceral, kinetic, and fast-paced," "reliant on special effects," "'fantastic' (and thus apolitical), and increasingly targeted at younger audiences." The studios' alleged reliance on the "high concept" faced much blame, as stories circulated of $50 million movies that were financed on the basis of plot summaries that might have been written on cocktail napkins. Steven Spielberg himself claimed that "if a person can tell me his idea in 25 words or less, it's going to make a pretty good movie. I like ideas, especially movie ideas, that you can hold in your hand." The influential hit action movie *Die Hard* (1988) was allegedly born from the high concept "Wild West shootout in a glass building." Characterization, personal development, thoughtful dialogue, and variations in pacing, lighting, and mood were said to be thrown out in favor of nonstop, cacophonous action, much of it explicitly violent. As many critics pointed out, such post–*Star Wars* films often seemed to exist as "amusement park rides" designed to spin off broader merchandising campaigns. "The supposed 'identity' of the filmic text," one groused, "comes increasingly under the dissolving pressures of its various revenue streams." Critics also attacked the more frequent and more gruesome violence of movies, especially those with the R rating and in the renascent horror film genre. These in turn led to strong campaigns to protect younger viewers and in 1984 resulted in the MPAA's new PG-13 rating.[7]

Yet these jeremiads were not without their flaws. Romanticizing Hollywood's past, critics often forgot that most films from the "golden age" were formulaic affairs that rarely rewarded thoughtful viewing. In addition, some film scholars argue that newer movies maintained the studio's best storytelling traditions, updating "classical" narrative techniques. Kristin Thompson notes that the "high concept" in fact dated as far back as Hollywood in the 1930s, when abbreviated plot summaries were nicknamed "wienies." David Bordwell argues that in today's mainstream movies, as in the past, characters are guided by singular motivations; scenes work to reinforce the symbols and messages of earlier moments and to foreshadow later plot developments; and master, medium, and close-up shots are intercut to blend continuity, interaction, and inner states, respectively, within scenes.[8]

However, Bordwell detects some significant changes since the 1960s. Editing has accelerated to the point that the average shot length (ASL) in Hollywood films has fallen from about seven seconds to three or four seconds. Directors rely more heavily on close-ups, he argues, giving actors less chance to express themselves with their bodies. Proliferating screenwriting manuals have prescribed a "hero's journey" plot archetype, which has tended to dilute dialogue and plotting and allow for the casting of muscle-bound leads who exhibit little nuance as actors. Bordwell also identifies an "intensified continuity" in movies since the 1980s: a more baroque mixing of shots within scenes and transitional tricks between scenes which, in league with shorter ASLs (and more elaborate special effects), have made many films more "flashy." Similarly, directors such as Quentin Tarantino and Christopher Nolan jumble the timeline, moving between past and present. Bordwell notes, though, that time-bending occurs in some early studio films, and that the recent examples (such as Nolan's *Memento*) have highly redundant scene structure or other features that make them accessible to a general audience. This redundancy differentiates commercial movies from more challenging "art" films, which receive limited theatrical releases and usually earn little money.[9]

Nevertheless, it has been argued that billion-dollar grosses, eight-figure star salaries, enhanced sex and violence, intensified plot continuity, sophisticated special effects, high concepts, hero's journeys, and jumbled timelines have all cut newer films and younger audiences off from the Hollywood tradition. Critics maintain that the new blockbusters illustrated the greed of the studios' conglomerate owners and typified a decadent new culture of valueless, "postmodern" exploitation. Classically styled films such as *Wag the Dog* and *Primary Colors,* made by directors (Barry Levinson and Mike Nichols) who revere traditional storytelling, were the exception, not the rule. The overbearing qualities of blockbuster movies, critics say, obscured more modest films and defined the current public perception of movies and their cultural impact. Moreover, the deficiencies in movies reflected shortcomings in the culture as a whole. In the 1980s, enormous Hollywood grosses and paychecks were considered by some to be symbols of Reaganomics, which benefited entrepreneurs at the expense of small wage earners. Muscular movie heroes and heroines, abetted by steroids and plastic surgery, symbolized the egocentricity and narcissism of the "Me Generation." Above all, movie stardom was the epitome of America's unprecedented infatuation with celebrity.

Paralleling this cultural manifestation of free-market conservatism was mainstream journalism's increased appetite for scandal and intimate details of its subjects' private lives. At the same time that the Reagan administration deregulated the FCC's oversight of television news content, American viewers came to favor more "soft news"—information and stories about their favorite celebrities. New magazines that satisfied this urge included *People* and the revived *Vanity Fair,* published by Time-Life and Condé Nast. Television programs such as CBS's short-lived *Who's Who* and the more successful syndicated *Lifestyles of the Rich and Famous* followed suit. Observers perceived a re-gendering of journalism at work. The literary scholar Frederic Jameson noted the demise of "masculine" journalism—"factual, analytic, organized, and impersonal"—and the rise of a new "effeminate style of political communication . . . personal, excessive, disorganized, and unduly ornamental." Similarly, the communications scholar P. David Marshall described "celebrity coverage" as "an intricate feminization of the news, where soft news becomes more central to the news experience and new social and political issues emerge from its often scandalous content."[10]

In 1979 the historian Christopher Lasch argued that average Americans' retreat into celebrity worship had resulted from their new powerlessness, their loss of control of their lives and futures. The celebration of personal authenticity peaked in the 1960s, but with the failure of liberal politics and the counterculture, self-actualization and socially relevant struggle seemed difficult to effect. In desperation Americans revived the 1930s ethos of Dale Carnegie, in which personal artifice and the appearance of success were conflated with success itself. By the late 1970s, Lasch argues, "men seek the kind of approval that applauds not their actions but their personal attributes. . . . They crave not fame but the glamour and excitement of celebrity. . . . Most Americans would still define success as riches, fame, and power, but their actions show that they have little interest in the substance of these attainments. What a man does matters less than the fact that he has 'made it.'"[11] As Americans felt a loss of political relevance, a lack of control over their society and their future, and a feeling of hopelessness, they compensated by admiring and aping the trappings of a small, successful celebrity elite.

Cultural trends in the 1980s and 1990s often bore out Lasch's perceptions. New middle-class homes mimicked such mansion design elements as two-story staircases, cathedral ceilings, and "great rooms," and an underground economy put undocumented immigrants to work (on a cash basis, unreported to the IRS) as an affordable new servant class of maids, nannies, and landscapers. Emulation of the rich and famous drove a new culture of consumption which cut across party lines and geographical divisions. It was endorsed most heartily, though, by political conservatives, who championed "trickle-down" economics and low taxes on the wealthy and played upon Americans' vague hopes that they, too, might enjoy luxuries and high incomes one day.[12]

As cable television, home theaters, the Internet, on-demand viewing, and cell phones emerged as platforms for viewing films, the movie theater at first appeared to be an antiquated venue. Indeed, in the 1990s, many multiplexes with small viewing halls, as well as numerous drive-in theaters, went out of business. At the same time, though, "luxury" multiplexes with high-tech sound and video, stadium seating, and other amenities caught on with the public, and massive attendance at theaters for highly anticipated new movies became the norm. Big movie theaters made economic sense in the 1990s, and they made cultural sense as well. In its grandiose way, the big screen displayed better than any other media platform the outsized fantasies of the age of celebrity worship and emulation of the wealthy. The light given off by such screens—more dazzling and dripping with more lucre than ever before—would illuminate Bill Clinton's presidential trajectory in important ways.

———

The 1992 race was decided like no other presidential election. Public opinion polls leading up to the Democratic Convention in New York City were inconclusive. Ross Perot, the billionaire independent candidate, had just quit the race, claiming that his two opponents were now taking seriously his favorite issue, the spiraling federal debt. President George H. W. Bush maintained a modest lead over Bill Clinton in most surveys. The convention that nominated Clinton, though, caused a startling and unique reversal of these polls. Leaving New York, the Arkansas governor saw his lead in the polls rocket up by an average of twenty-five percentage points; he would maintain the advantage (albeit with a somewhat diminished margin) until his victory in November.

Clinton's nomination acceptance speech was not particularly stirring. Like many of his addresses, it was a long and hastily assembled montage of various speechwriters' drafts, and partly ad-libbed on the spot. Instead, in the view of many observers, his candidacy was boosted most effectively by the work of a Hollywood producer. Harry Thomason orchestrated an unusual stunt after Clinton won the nomination. He marched the candidate down a tunnel that connected Macy's department store with Madison Square Garden, to appear in person at the convention to thank the delegates. "Tomorrow night [formally accepting the nomination] . . . I'll really be the comeback kid," Clinton said—echoing a line Thomason had supplied him after he had avoided possible elimination in the New Hampshire primary months earlier. Clinton's acceptance speech was preceded by a fourteen-minute film, *The Man from Hope,* produced by Thomason. Millions saw the film, which many remembered as the message that persuaded them to support the young and still little-known new candidate.

The film's careful crafting is evident especially in what it leaves out. Clinton's academic achievements, even his Rhodes scholarship, are omitted entirely, as is virtually his entire career in elective politics. His twelve years as Arkansas governor are only mentioned once in passing. The Vietnam War—a pivotal event in Clinton's life, and the source of controversy over his draft status—is ignored. The Republican opposition is mentioned vaguely only once, and the key issues of 1992—health care, education, the federal deficit, the economic recession—are encapsulated in a general reference to tough times. *The Man from Hope* begins, fittingly, with Clinton's birth in Hope, Arkansas, and ends with his vague "hope" for America's future. In between, against a mellow musical soundtrack, Clinton is enveloped in the embrace of the women in his family. His mother, Virginia Kelley, recalls that the day before she gave birth to her son, she went to the movies and saw a feature with a portentous title: *Tomorrow Is Forever.* She relates Bill's love for his grandparents, their modest home, and his struggles with his alcoholic stepfather (whom Clinton calls "a good man" who "didn't think enough of himself"). The fact that well before her remarriage Kelley had moved her son from Hope to nearby Hot Springs—then a notorious center for drinking, gambling, and prostitution—is not mentioned; instead, the film covers the inspiration Bill gained from Arkansas's gospel

music and the shame that motivated him to improve its weak public education system.

In the film's best-known moment, grainy footage from the National
Archives shows the sixteen-year-old Bill Clinton shaking hands with President Kennedy at the White House during a reception for Boys' Nation, at
which Clinton represented his state. Clinton's disapproval of segregation
and his deep respect for the civil rights movement constitute the next motif.
The last long section relates his marriage and fatherhood. An amusing
device borrowed from Hollywood romantic comedies intercuts Bill and
Hillary Clinton's nearly identical descriptions of their first meeting as law
students at Yale. His joy at the birth of his daughter, along with brief testimony from twelve-year-old Chelsea Clinton and footage of them playing
ball, is succeeded by a complex, yet brief and deft, epilogue. Looking past
the side of the camera, Clinton states (as he had in past interviews) that
although he had caused "problems in our marriage," he and Hillary had
stayed together. These problems, in his view, paled next to those faced by
Americans struggling in the current economy. Clinton's lifelong compassion and concern are well-established by the end of the film, when he vows
that he "still believes in a place called Hope."

The man behind *The Man from Hope,* Harry Thomason, was a native
Arkansan who had become a successful television producer in Hollywood.
His wife and collaborator, Linda Bloodworth Thomason, met the Clintons
in the 1980s, and the Thomasons were among the "Friends of Bill" who
worked for a decade to help elect him president. (The Hollywood actress
Mary Steenburgen, also from Arkansas, was an active "FOB" as well.) In 1992
Harry Thomason took weeks off from work to travel with Clinton; he was
his closest friend in the campaign. The Thomasons' later frequent stays in
the White House, their role in the firing of the staff of the presidential travel
office, and their advice to the First Couple during the Lewinsky scandal
would make them somewhat controversial.

In 1992, though, it was Thomason's storytelling skills in *The Man from
Hope*—and Clinton's resultant dramatic and decisive rise in the polls—that
impressed many Americans. Television now dominated national political
campaigns. In the aftermath of the Democratic convention, Republican media
consultants commented with anger and admiration on the slick made-for-

television nature of the entire proceeding—which mimicked their own innovative work at the GOP gatherings in 1984 and 1988. Until recently, conventions had been relics of the old republican era of American politics, featuring colorful fights over platform planks and delegate seating, nominating speeches, and demonstrations that often pushed the proceedings into the early hours of the morning. Now they became televised showcases for the parties' rising and established stars and for their campaign messages. Wealthy sponsors (especially lobbyists) underwrote most convention expenses and threw private off-camera parties; these became the locus for the spontaneous human interactions that now were banished from the convention floor. Election years also featured ubiquitous, often harshly negative, advertisements that flooded television screens—expensive campaigns whose cost forced candidates to search relentlessly for millions of dollars in donations. (One of Clinton's strengths as a candidate, others noted, was that he was never reluctant to press donors for money.) Roger Ailes's and Harry Treleaven's then-revolutionary blueprint for a television-driven campaign for Nixon in 1968 had now become the norm in American politics.

Short films at conventions had been increasingly prominent since John F. Kennedy had narrated a feature for the Democrats in 1956, but *The Man from Hope* was particularly canny and effective. Bill Clinton was inexperienced in foreign policy, relatively unknown to the public, and plagued by stories of his Vietnam draft status and extramarital affairs. Like his appearance with his wife the preceding January on the news program *60 Minutes* immediately after the Super Bowl broadcast—in which they both denied Gennifer Flowers' allegations of a long affair with the governor—*The Man from Hope* was almost perfectly calibrated to remove doubts from voters' minds about Clinton's character and morality *as a leader*. To the surprise of many of his staffers—such as the moralistic former seminarian George Stephanopoulos and the profane, worldly campaign manager James Carville —Clinton eased the fears of millions, who seemed willing to overlook what likely would have been insurmountable liabilities for other candidates. A Bush administration official had warned Clinton earlier that "if you get into this race, we will do everything we can to destroy you personally," but the governor—abetted by his brilliant and ambitious wife—did not flinch. Clinton's refusal to buckle in the face of harsh GOP attacks during the fall

campaign—earning him the movie-inspired nickname "Robo-Candidate"
—represented a unique triumph of an individual politician's charisma over
his debilitating personal failings.[13]

The blame for current economic woes that fell on Clinton's incumbent
opponent, George H. W. Bush, also aided the Democratic candidate, but
Bush suffered from deeper flaws in 1992. In retrospect, his political ascent
and fall is a cautionary tale in the history of the cinematic presidential image.
Throughout his political career, Bush largely resisted the image making
lessons taught by FDR, Kennedy, and Reagan and promulgated by media
consultants beginning in 1968. Like Gilded Age presidents, Bush sought to
embody the virtues of education, good manners, discipline, and success that
were expected of Protestant American males, and like Theodore Roosevelt
he portrayed himself as a child of privilege who was rendering a service to
his country. Bush may have been the most exemplary war hero ever to run
for president: the youngest naval aviator in World War II, he flew numerous
combat missions and barely survived when the Japanese shot down his plane
over the Pacific. Characteristically, though, Bush refused almost completely
to exploit his war record in the cinematic manner voters had come to expect.
Instead he stressed the duty of "service," of noblesse oblige, in his career.

Bush had also been shaped by the personality-driven, back-room nature
of politics in Texas, his adopted state. Midland, the oil town where the young
veteran had moved to make his fortune, was as removed as Lyndon Johnson's Hill Country from mainstream American movie attendance and film-
star adulation. In the view of Texans such as Bush and LBJ, money, connections, and professions of religious faith—not cinematic self-presentation
—won elective office. Despite his adherence to this credo, Bush lost more
early elections in Texas than he won, and he ultimately took an alternate
route to the White House through a series of appointed positions in Republican administrations.

As Reagan's vice president, seeking in 1988 to succeed his popular boss,
Bush's approach to presidential politics was so antiquated that it threatened
to sabotage what should have been an easy promotion. Bush did benefit
from a traditionalist trend in 1980s American politics, an amorphous post-
Watergate emphasis on ensuring that political leaders were of superior
"character" and on promoting the correct "virtues" in public life. The "vir-

tuecrats" spanned political boundaries to include such notables as the left-leaning sociologist Amitai Etzioni and William Bennett, Reagan's secretary of education, while the promoters of "character" ranged from the conservative academic Shelby Steele to the liberal journalist Gail Sheehy. They helped to influence the climate that doomed the 1988 presidential campaign of Senator Gary Hart, a married Democrat who dared reporters to investigate his private life and was soon caught cavorting with a mistress. George Bush, unsurprisingly, presented himself as a paragon of public and private character. Class perceptions, though, seriously harmed the vice president's image. Journalists ridiculed Bush's wealthy Connecticut family background, crudely stereotyping him as a spoiled "wimp" who likely was unable to step into Reagan's weathered cowboy boots. (Bush, strangely, gave Reagan a stool with booted legs as a going-away present at the end of his term.)[14] To gain an advantage, the Bush campaign struck back—doing everything possible to destroy the image of the eventual Democratic nominee, Massachusetts governor Michael Dukakis.

This effort, in Kathleen Hall Jamieson's words, created "the nastiest campaign [to date] in the history of television." The grand design of the effort was shaped by the veteran Roger Ailes, Bush's communications director, while the tone of its toughest ads was the toxic creation of a young strategist from South Carolina named Lee Atwater. Dukakis (as would Clinton, four years later) emerged from his convention far above Bush in the polls, but Atwater pledged to "strip the bark off of the little bastard" through relentlessly negative advertising. The most potent ads—accusing Dukakis of running a state prison furlough program that permitted one inmate, a glowering African American named Willie Horton, to commit rape and murder—stoked the latent racism of many white voters and crystallized their old fears that liberal policies threatened to erode law and order. Funded by political action committees outside the formal campaign, the initial Horton ad grew into a series of spots that put his victims on camera. Spinoff literature described the "Dukakis/Willie Horton team" and claimed that "Michael Dukakis is the killer's best friend."[15]

The governor's belated and tepid rebuttals of these smears virtually doomed his campaign. Hard-hitting response ads were vetoed by his senior staff, but more generally, Dukakis made the error of debating subjects that had been chosen by the Bush team. The governor's ill-conceived photo opportunity in a rolling Army tank—showing a meek, waving candidate, his face obscured by a helmet and body engulfed in the vehicle's parapet—did not reverse the damage; instead, Ailes gleefully used the film as a backdrop for ads attacking Dukakis's stance on defense. According to polls and focus groups of voters organized by his staff, Bush's own popularity remained weak, but his demonization of Dukakis turned enough voters against the Democrat to ensure his defeat on Election Day 1988—amid the lowest turn-out in a presidential contest in sixty-four years.

The negative advertising of 1988 and succeeding years was devastating to American political discourse. It seemed to realize the most cynical prognos-tications about voter attention spans and intelligence made by Ray Price, Michael Deaver, and other campaign consultants. In addition, it brought a new element of demonization into mainstream politics. As the Cold War was ending, the political class (especially on the right) became obsessed with finding a necessary and worthy new enemy—a focus of American fears and machinations that might replace the failed Communist monolith.

This quest for demonization of opponents in politics was a manifestation of a larger trend in American culture, which found a vivid analogue in mass entertainment. By the late 1980s movie villainy was becoming baroque and outlandish. Sometimes sporting sinister European accents, sometimes not, the new villains exuded smug superiority and contempt for their adversaries, who tended to be average Americans of working- or middle-class origins. (Sylvester Stallone and Bruce Willis best epitomized this heroic persona, although Arnold Schwarzenegger overcame his thick Austrian accent to join their ranks—in part by marrying John F. Kennedy's niece and campaigning for George Bush.) Action-movie villains were sadistic and always killed many more innocent bystanders than they needed to. Increasingly, the bad guys were also unkillable, rising bloodily from apparent death to mount final attacks before the heroes finally finished them off.

Another telling archetype of this era was the psychotic villain-hero, best exemplified by Jack Nicholson's Joker in *Batman* (1989) and Anthony Hop-kins's Hannibal Lecter in *The Silence of the Lambs* (1991). Nicholson and Hopkins were sensitive actors, and *The Silence of the Lambs* contained a probing indictment of violence, but the grotesque comic-book villain and

the mass-murdering cannibal they respectively portrayed were often celebrated in a mean-spirited, misogynistic way, particularly by a young male
segment of the audience. (Although young black and white men approached
it from differing perspectives, "gangsta" rap music held a similar appeal for
the same population segment in these years.) Earlier Hollywood films (such
as Alfred Hitchcock's *Psycho* and *The Birds*) had recognized and toyed with
the audience's latent sadistic tendencies, but just as the 1960s mainstream
brought latent aggression and sexuality to the fore, post-1970s movies enlisted viewers in the temporary torment of characters who might have been
their neighbors or co-workers. Moviegoers' simultaneous search for new
villains and sadistic pleasure in viewing villains' infliction of violence formed
a striking analogue to the destructive impulses behind the new negative
campaigning. Hannibal Lecter, like Lee Atwater, gleefully stripped the bark
off of the little bastards. Many Americans complained about the sadism and
violence of these films and launched censorship crusades, but the movies'
large profits demonstrated their appeal and their hold on Hollywood.[16]

As Kathleen Jamieson had noted a few years after the 1988 campaign,
"taken together the [negative Bush] ads created a coherent *narrative*." The
power of narrative in campaigns, which gained special notice in the early
1990s in Jamieson's book *Packaging the Presidency* and elsewhere, became an
article of faith in American politics. Borrowed from story templates found
in movies, as well as other media, the idea of the political narrative also grew
out of prejudices held by image makers such as Ray Price and Michael
Deaver, who deprecated the voters' powers of abstraction and analysis. More
generally, though, the ascendancy of narrative illustrated the convenience of
applying the power of storytelling to real life. Movie narratives usually cut
out multiple protagonists, competing motivations, extraneous incidents and
developments, and even the bulk of everyday speech; advice books for
would-be screenwriters often compare screenwriting to haiku. Decades of
moviemaking experience—not to mention centuries of oral and written
storytelling—had validated the power and the appeal of narrative, which did
not necessarily rely on the exalted pseudo-mythologizing or stringent three-
act structure mandated by screenwriting manuals. By about 1992, largely due
to recent experience with devastatingly successful (and negative) political
advertising campaigns, the long American gestation of a cinematic notion of

politics was concluded. Old republican notions of issues, deliberation, and rational debate were weakened at the hands of visually oriented, mass-media storytelling.[17]

Nor was the omnipotence of narrative confined to political campaigns. In many segments of American mass culture in the 1990s, the need to confine reality to easy-to-discern storytelling molds became evident. As Neal Gabler notes, journalism in particular was affected by this impulse. The 1990s witnessed the rise of fictional narrative techniques in newspaper stories and TV news magazines, warping real topics into familiar dramatic genres.[18] Academia was not immune from this trend. Historical scholars also noted a "revival of narrative" in the late 1970s, a move away from the highly civic-minded yet stultifying quantitative analyses that had typified academic history writing in preceding decades.[19]

———

In 1992, despite facing an electorate filled with cynicism and antagonism, and primed for corrosive negative tales, Bill Clinton remarkably harnessed the power of narrative and rode it in a newly optimistic and positive direction. As in the case of Lyndon Johnson and some other predecessors, a combination of nature and nurture had bestowed on him unusual political gifts. One of these was his pure physical presence, which was difficult for people who saw him only on television to appreciate fully. Those who met Clinton commented that he seemed even bigger in person than he looked in photographs and videos. As a Yale law student, in the words of the biographer Nigel Hamilton, Clinton was "a friendly giant of a boy . . . with a big smile, a bear hug, and an almost evangelical love of life. His energy and intelligence were formidable: you never needed to tell him anything twice, and his memory for names and faces was phenomenal."[20] Or, as his classmate and future wife Hillary Rodham put it in *The Man from Hope,* "He was great-looking, he was fun, someone who challenged and made you happy all the time. I just had never met anyone like Bill."

Psychologizing about Clinton soon became a popular pastime, as observers speculated how his father's accidental death before his birth, his doting mother, and his alcoholic and abusive stepfather had instilled in him a boundless need for approval. Hamilton elaborates: "in many ways he was the personification of the best of the sixties." Owing to his working-class origins "he believed in equality of opportunity"; his stepfather's addiction led him to advocate "personal empowerment"; his attachment to his mother "made him comfortable with women . . . a natural supporter of feminism"; her ostracism in Hope "caused him to believe in a society that would be more tolerant . . . society as community." At Oxford as a Rhodes Scholar, Clinton also picked up the libertine qualities of the 1960s, learning how "to drink alcohol, . . . smoke pot and hash"—both "in moderation, owing to his allergies"—and to seduce women.[21] By 1992, years of policy-making and campaign minutiae had not obscured Clinton's tactile, sentimental, and sensuous approach to life and relationships with other people.

He was a character in search of a narrative, and in *The Man from Hope*, Harry and Linda Thomason provided him with one. The short convention film was a classic example of Hollywood storytelling, hammering home the protagonist's single motivation—in this case, his hope to improve America's future, a hope nurtured by his family's love and his passion for racial justice and educational attainment. Like mainstream studio films, *The Man from Hope* is apolitical, paying only the scantest attention to the white-hot campaign for which it was made and the powerful elective office that was its object. Instead, in true Hollywood fashion, it tells a simple, character-driven narrative. The problem with *The Man from Hope*, like all films, was that its fourteen blissful minutes excluded or ignored all of the problematic extra stuff of real life, in this case the messy realities of Clinton's character and biography. The Clintons and the Thomasons gave each other advice about how to romanticize Arkansas life on film; Hillary Clinton had suggested the title of her friends' new television comedy series, *Evening Shade*. Some Arkansans who knew Clinton from his first years in politics, though, wrote a different narrative about him—defining him, as Hamilton puts it, as "a sexually active, strapping wannabe; a predator; moreover, a figure who was potentially subversive in southern electors' eyes since he'd failed to serve in the military, was no athlete, did not fish or hunt—and was too liberal and clever for his own good."[22]

The friendship with the Thomasons would be a central influence on the style, substance—and scandal—of the Clinton White House. The eventual election victory in the autumn of 1992 was unexpectedly easy, despite the anticipated onslaught of Republican attacks on Clinton's youth and private life. The Democrat benefited from the premature death of Lee Atwater, the Republicans' most feared negative campaign strategist, and from the reentry of Ross Perot into the race. Perot mostly drew voters away from the Republican ticket, and he became Bush's second critic in the presidential debates. By 1992 these debates, like the party conventions, had become heavily scripted pseudo-events used by the candidates to advertise themselves, in the manner of a televised trade show. Bush's impatience with the debates' show business was evident at every turn, most harmfully when the camera caught him glancing at his wristwatch during the "town hall" meeting with citizens. Clinton, by contrast, looked compassionate and enthusiastic. After the debates, as he had done for months, he rode out further fierce attacks to claim victory on Election Day.

Harry Thomason staged a traditional rally that night at the Arkansas State House and then devised a week-long series of events building up to the inauguration on January 20, 1993. Clinton, vice president–elect Al Gore, and their wives took a symbolic bus trip from Thomas Jefferson's Monticello to Washington, where the couples were feted by a day of celebrations and concerts on the eve of the swearing-in. The made-for-television evening gala performance brought out some of the biggest stars in popular music. These included Michael Jackson (the biggest-selling artist of the past decade) and Barbra Streisand, a major star both in recordings and in Hollywood for a quarter century, who quickly became an intimate friend of the Clintons. Thomason, and to a lesser extent Streisand, assumed the somewhat sycophantic roles that had been played by George Murphy for Eisenhower and by Frank Sinatra (switching his party affiliation in midstream) for Kennedy and Reagan, as organizers of inaugural festivities and go-betweens for the President and movie and recording stars.

Clinton's identity as a Baby Boomer, shaped in part by the counterculture, helped to determine the style of his new administration. As president-elect, he procrastinated in choosing top cabinet officers and other officials and indulged in long and inconclusive seminars about economics, health care, and other important issues which resulted in no clear plan of action. Clinton resisted regimentation and chose a childhood friend with no Washington experience as the White House chief of staff. Clinton's has been called "the worst [presidential] transition in all American history."[23] The new chief executive craved creativity, discussion, and a horizontal (or non-existent) hierarchy, and he totally rejected the military-style White House command model of Republican administrations, led by such strong chiefs of staff as Sherman Adams, H. R. Haldeman, and James Baker III. (This in part reflected party history, since before Clinton no Democratic president had begun his term with a White House chief of staff.) George Stephan-opoulos was the new communications director—the heir to Herbert Klein and Patrick Buchanan—but in reality he "held a relatively amorphous job of political troubleshooter, public-relations adviser, policy expert, and crisis manager."[24] Stephanopoulos also became the de facto press secretary, usurping for a time the nominal holder of that position, Dee Dee Myers.

The result was a disastrous first few months in office, in which minor issues caused unnecessary controversy, big initiatives (to revive the economy and put in place a system of universal health care) were poorly thought out and executed, and quick, unwise decisions caused negative press to rain down on the president. Critics both within and beyond the Washington Beltway placed much of the blame on the First Lady. Hillary Rodham Clinton, as fervent a devotee of 1960s social reform as her husband, fought for a role as a virtual co-president, but she faced virulent criticism for bucking two centuries of tradition, which had confined the president's wife to domestic duties and social occasions. Caught in the interpretive crosshairs of the media and the political class, Clinton came to appreciate the value of a clearer master narrative.

Some of the gaffes during those early months could be attributed, at least in part, to the meddling of Harry Thomason. Thomson played a central role in Hillary Clinton's decision to fire the White House travel office staff and in the stopping of plane traffic for two hours at Los Angeles International Airport so that the president might get his hair cut by a high-priced Beverly Hills stylist. Five years later, when the Paula Jones and Monica Lewinsky scandals endangered the administration, Thomason was still at the president's side. He advised Clinton to issue his finger-wagging denial of sexual relations with Lewinsky, and weeks later he and Linda Thomason were White House guests during a lonely weekend for the president, when the three shared a Valentine's Day dinner. Six months later, Thomason helped

Clinton draft the short address he gave after testifying to Kenneth Starr, in which he admitted a relationship with Lewinsky. Thomason himself, as the columnist Maureen Dowd noted, was required "to explain his 'Wag the Dog' role to the grand jury [in] help[ing to] produce the President's rebuttal to designing women." Long after Clinton left the White House, Thomason was still trying to help his friend, in 2004 producing a documentary entitled *The Hunting of the President.*[25]

Thomason was far from being the only Hollywood influence on Bill Clinton. While in the White House, Clinton acquainted himself with the largest array of Hollywood personalities ever sought out by a sitting president. In the first three months of his term, the star-struck chief executive had sat down to dinner with Paul Newman and Joanne Woodward; welcomed Judy Collins and Barbra Streisand for overnight stays in the White House; met with a group of stars during a break in the summit with Russia's president in Vancouver, Canada; and attended a party fundraiser with a larger contingent of movie actors in New York City. Meanwhile, another delegation of actors (including Billy Crystal, Christopher Reeve, Lindsay Wagner, and Sam Waterston) visited the West Wing to discuss environmental policy. The White House sleepovers contributed to one of the many controversies that dogged Clinton, since Hollywood figures were among the wealthy people who seemed to trade large campaign contributions for their nights in the Lincoln Bedroom. As Alan Schroeder has noted, the interaction with stars kept up—and kept generating criticism—until "the waning days of the Clinton Administration," when "the first couple accepted numerous last-minute farewell gifts," some of them valued in the thousands of dollars.[26]

While Ronald Reagan had relived his Hollywood days with movie screenings and occasional entertainment galas, Clinton initiated relationships with show business figures through an array of screenings, meetings, and dinners in and out of the White House. To an extent this activity, like the Lincoln Bedroom initiative, reflected his ramping-up of the Democratic Party's fundraising efforts in Hollywood. Lew Wasserman, the chief money gatherer in the industry for Democrats, expressed his own appreciation for Clinton after the attempted impeachment of the president: "He outdoes JFK. . . . He works the crowd here, and they see him as friends. They genuinely like him. . . . So he made a mistake. He said he was sorry. What else can you do?" Clinton's strong narcissism, craving for acceptance, and need for consensual female intimacy also made him a sympathetic fit with Hollywood actors, who for generations had been driven by similar personal traits. "There's a tinge of show business about Clinton, and people here recognize that," noted the screenwriter Larry Gelbart.

Hollywood also related well to Bill Clinton's tactile, sensuous nature. The producer Marshall Herskovitz noted that show people understood the president's failings: "Clinton is a set of contradictions and many of those contradictions work quite well within the moral structure of Hollywood. . . . In Hollywood marriage is often not seen as a monolithic simple entity." Female celebrities were far more vocal about their attraction to the president than they had been in John F. Kennedy's day. The actress Sharon Stone was known to toy with reporters, playing up her screen image as a femme fatale, but she may also have responded honestly when she was asked if she would have an affair with the president: "Are you kidding? Like white on rice." The novelist Judith Krantz volunteered that "shaking hands with Bill Clinton is, in and of itself, a full-body sexual experience, I promise you."[27]

Clinton's close ties to Hollywood reflected his lifelong attachment to the movies. Kennedy had primarily been socially active in Hollywood, and Reagan had built his career there, but Clinton above all was an awestruck fan. From early boyhood his favorite film was *High Noon,* his favorite actor Gary Cooper. This paragon of elder leadership, so potent on the cultural scene in the year Eisenhower won the presidency, spoke to a quality of Clinton's that had irritated his friends in the 1960s: his deference to older people. Sheriff Will Kane's example seemed to provide him on occasion with a stronger backbone. In 1995, when his battle with the Republican-controlled Congress over the federal budget led to the shutting down of the government, Clinton told his aide Paul Begala that he perceived the need for "Gary Cooper–style leadership." In the Oval Office, Begala recalled, Clinton glowered at his opponent, Speaker of the House Newt Gingrich, and told him "that if he wanted someone to sign those [budget] cuts into law, he'd have to get someone else to sit behind that desk." As president, Clinton often told people that the screening room was his favorite room in the White House.[28]

Hollywood repaid Clinton's interest with a degree of adulation for the US presidency that was unprecedented in its history. Perhaps it was inevitable—

in an age of quasi-mythological plots, featuring streamlined quests by heroes relying on high technology and American global reach—that the high concept would exploit the mystique of high office. In the 1970s and 1980s, presidents had often been portrayed, usually with reverence, in historically themed television movies and miniseries, but theatrical releases contained very few chief executives, either real or fictitious. Oliver Stone's *JFK* (1991) dealt largely with the Kennedy assassination and its aftermath and gave no lines of dialogue to the president himself, who is seen only briefly in Dealey Plaza in the assassin's crosshairs. Yet *JFK* helped initiate a cycle of presidential dramas and comedies which tended to portray chief executives in a warm or heroic light. Even Stone's own *Nixon* (1995), a relative anomaly in this cycle (and an expensive box-office failure), cast this disreputable president in a glamorously tragic mold, presenting Anthony Hopkins's portrayal in a florid context that drew upon *Citizen Kane* and *King Lear.*

Fictional presidents were represented in a number of genres in the 1990s. In science fiction, the president in *Mars Attacks!* served as the straight man and foil for a variety of more absurd characters. In an echo of Peter Sellers in *Dr. Strangelove,* Jack Nicholson (a White House guest of Bill Clinton's) played both the president and a sleazy gambler. *Independence Day,* an alien invasion picture sober and silly enough to possibly be intended as a parody of action films, featured a young president, played by Bill Pullman, whose experience as a fighter pilot comes in handy in war against the intergalactic marauders. (The film also gave the White House an impressive cameo, in a scene in which it is vaporized by alien death rays. This nightmare reversal of Ronald Reagan's SDI dream was concocted by a special effects team with the help of a detailed architectural miniature, blasting caps, and slow-motion camerawork.) A more realistic and self-important portrayal, *Air Force One,* arrived in 1997, the year after *Independence Day.* Harrison Ford, at the time Hollywood's leading action film star, plays another former war hero turned president, who regains control of his aircraft when renegade Russians hijack it in midflight. Many scenes show the president sneaking around in cargo bays, in the manner of the heroic cop pursuing terrorists in a skyscraper in *Die Hard.* Ford's film came toward the end of the lone-hero-shadowing-villains cycle of action movies, but like *Independence Day* it acquired a vague prestige through its appropriation of the presidency. The film basks in the afterglow of America's Cold War triumph, stacking the deck against the stock enemies and making the scrappy chief executive the inevitable victor.

This same tone of reassurance had been evident in a 1994 comedy, *Dave*, which labored hard to bring a screwball style into the White House (although its premise seems to have been lifted from Akira Kurosawa's drama *Kagemusha*). In this film, the rigid and cold president vaguely resembles George Bush, but he is brought low by a Clinton-style bout of Oval Office philandering which induces a stroke. The sweet, funny, small-town fellow who is recruited by scheming aides to impersonate the secretly incapacitated president charms the country and even the real First Lady, who is almost persuaded that her husband has gained a pleasant new personality. *Dave* strove to seem credible by recruiting many real politicians and TV commentators to appear as themselves. The movie likely featured the largest number of cameo appearances ever seen in a film about the presidency, serving as an apotheosis of the notion that politics had become show business for ugly people.

Thanks especially to the powerful effect of Ronald Reagan and his image makers, the presidency had rebounded somewhat from the slough of corruption and mistrust into which it had fallen during the Vietnam War and Watergate. Influenced by the tropes of the mass media, especially movies, supporters of a new man in the office especially were apt to perceive him through the scrim of old-fashioned kingly honor. Bill Clinton burrowed his way into citizens' subconscious, as the 1994 book *Dreams of Bill* (a digest of the president's appearances during their sleep), seemed to indicate.[29] *Independence Day*, *Air Force One*, and *Dave* collectively suggest that despite Clinton's early woes in office, Hollywood was eager to help Americans celebrate the presidency as an office which might still elevate a flawed occupant to a position of official glory and goodness. Clinton's improving fortunes beginning in 1995 only intensified the good feelings. A long economic expansion and some success in foreign policy showed him growing more competent; his approval ratings in polls rose, and they remained high until he left office, despite the calamity of the Lewinsky scandal and impeachment. In a reflection of his popularity, the cycle of sex-scandal movies that exploited Clinton's problems, including *Wag the Dog*, *Primary Colors*, and *The Contender*, generated discussion and critical praise, but they sold relatively few tickets.

The most revealing, detailed, and admiring cinematic portraits of fictional presidents in the 1990s also made them deeply empathetic, vulnerable, and emotional men. The movie *The American President* and the television series *The West Wing* were both conceived by Aaron Sorkin, a young writer whose first success, the play *A Few Good Men,* had folded a Frank Capra–like search for human goodness into a military courtroom drama. *The American President* (1995) is a romantic comedy depicting a widowed father and Democratic Baby Boomer in the office, an intelligent and thoughtful man who falls in love with a single environmental lobbyist. The president soon confronts sniping Beltway gossip and a conflict between his girlfriend's liberal views and his administration's moderate agenda, both of which endanger his reelection. Sorkin confessed that he wrote the movie to boost the public image of the real-life office and its current occupant. "This was a way of starting to restore public confidence in public officials. And partly, it had to do with this President, who I happen to think is getting a lot of bad raps."

Borrowing the basic concept of a long-unproduced screenplay entitled *The President Elopes,* Sorkin and director Rob Reiner (in the words of the *New York Times*) made the story "less screwballish and more Presidential, not to say Clintonian." Reiner and Sorkin were granted access to the West Wing for two days and observed President Clinton at work. Clinton aides such as George Stephanopoulos are portrayed in thin fictional disguises. As played by Michael Douglas, the movie's president is virtually faultless, the embodiment of the competence and empathy that characterized Clinton at his best. He is tender toward his school-age daughter (as Clinton was said to be) and shows obvious emotional and sexual attraction to his new love interest, played by Annette Bening. (The film's lead actors echoed past presidential glamour; Douglas was the son of Kirk Douglas, a Hollywood intimate of President Kennedy, while Bening was married to JFK's preferred cinematic alter ego, Warren Beatty.) The president's attempts to resolve his problems are thoughtful and display malice toward none. In short, Sorkin and Reiner's film idealizes the kind of White House that the Clintons had hoped to create but could not, a "dorm" of idealistic conversation and exploration in which the pleasures of the flesh were at least partially accommodated. Released the same week that the Gingrich-Clinton dispute had led to the temporary shutting down of the federal government, *The American*

President coincided with and certainly abetted Bill Clinton's political recovery, which resulted in his triumphant reelection in 1996.[30]

Sorkin expanded his portrayal of the presidency in the network TV series *The West Wing,* which premiered in 1999. (A full season of scripts had been ready to shoot a year earlier, but NBC had delayed the show out of a fear that the Lewinsky scandal might weaken the public's appetite for a series about the presidency.) Sorkin had first intended to focus on the president's staff, to which he had given short shrift in *The American President* owing to the narrative constraints of feature films. *The West Wing* gave ample attention to the chief of staff, press secretary, communications director, and other figures, who again were drawn from real-life figures in the Clinton White House. Sorkin once more presented a kind of civic pep talk, as the *New York Times* put it, "yearning to depict a group of mostly smart people in their 20's and 30's who opted to work for the Government" for low salaries. The president initially was to be a supporting player, but almost inevitably Sorkin moved him to center stage. As in *The American President,* Sorkin's chief executive "may be too good to be true": a Nobel Prize–winning economist, moderate Democrat, loving family man, and kindly boss. Martin Sheen, the actor playing President Josiah Bartlet, had long had a complex public persona, as a fierce activist for the homeless and a symbol of the Vietnam War's heavy legacy (owing to his starring role in the film *Apocalypse Now*). Sheen could also draw on his raft of previous White House portrayals: Robert F. Kennedy in the TV film *The Missiles of October,* JFK himself in the miniseries *Kennedy,* and the chief of staff in *The American President.* Somewhat older and more personally settled than Michael Douglas's character in the film, Sheen's Bartlet nevertheless is a conflicted figure who is often torn between the requirements of politics and the human needs of his family and staff. The series was a hit and continued until 2006, long after Bill Clinton had left office.[31]

In these 1990s films and series the president becomes a full-blown male lead character, working through personal and emotional problems as well as political and governmental challenges. In accord with the legacy of the 1960s, the personal had become political (and vice versa) for the Baby Boomers in both the real and the fictional White House. Men and women of that cohort had questioned their parents' yearning for fixed values and

commitment to frugality and sacrifice, and they had come to consider personal relationships, sexuality, and popular culture as a continuum along
which new behavior and values were developed and explored. This post-
1960s continuum was the focus of "Liberties," the journalist Maureen
Dowd's regular column in the *New York Times,* which began appearing in
1995. Dowd's chatty conversance with the latest popular culture, the Washington rumor mill, and the cultural unease that seemed (especially to liberals) to settle over both realms during the Clinton era proved highly popular
with *Times* readers. It is perhaps too easy for any observer to perceive significance in Dowd's private behavior, but it remains interesting to note that
she entered into relationships with Michael Douglas, Aaron Sorkin's idealized movie president, and then with Sorkin himself. Dowd and Sorkin
especially seemed to share a central and passionate interest in the common
allures of politics and movies, an interest shared by others in Clinton's orbit.
After leaving the White House, George Stephanopoulos, the president's early
image maker, overcame his personal conflicts about that work to begin a
new career in broadcast journalism, and he also married a television actress.

The most highly publicized intersection of politics and entertainment in
the mid-1990s took place not in Washington but in New York City, involving a highly publicized new magazine. The notoriety surrounding *George*
derived entirely from the identity of its publisher: John F. Kennedy Jr. After
the death of his mother in 1994, Kennedy—a nonpracticing lawyer and
squire of countless female companions (including Hollywood actresses)
who was widely considered to be an aimless celebrity—dedicated himself to
the most passionate endeavor of his life. Working with two partners with
publishing experience, Kennedy served as the glamorous public face of
George. Named whimsically after the first president, the magazine aimed to
survey politics with the same breezy flair that *Premiere* and *Entertainment
Weekly* displayed in covering movies, television, and popular music. Kennedy conducted interviews with George Wallace and other figures, and he
lured well-paying and persistent advertisers to the magazine's pages.

Becoming chief editor in 1996, Kennedy proclaimed that his generation
viewed politics as "another aspect of cultural life, not all that different from
sports and music and art." He added that "it's not as emotional a connection
for us as the connection people who are older than we are have," emphasiz-

ing the cool pleasure principle to which the youngest Baby Boomers (born, like Kennedy, after the 1950s) might have subscribed. Despite Kennedy's distance from the more passionate perspective of Dowd and Sorkin, he shared their effortless conflation of politics with the style and content of popular culture.[32] *George* remained popular for about two years; subscriptions and advertising revenue far surpassed expectations, and the magazine exemplified the particular intersection of politics and entertainment in the 1990s. Much of its success, though, derived from its association with young Kennedy's public presence, which many sensed would lead to his first campaign for office. Around the time of the Lewinsky scandal, though, *George's* sales and revenue plateaued. Kennedy, now married, lost some interest in the magazine. In 1999, in a ghastly denouement, the glamorous editor in chief was killed in the aircraft he was piloting, along with his wife and sister-in-law. *George* staggered on without Kennedy for a few more months before it ceased publication.

Whether the public's investment in a pop-culture presidential image in the 1990s was cartoonish (as in *Mars Attacks!* or *Dave*), impassioned (as in Aaron Sorkin's work), or cool (as in Kennedy's *George*), it was a phenomenon that the real president could appreciate fully, and that he tried to exploit. For his part, Bill Clinton occasionally angled to feed the public's desire for a caring, personal, emotive, and emotional president. This effort was folded into his administration's "permanent campaign," reminiscent of Nixon's, in which Clinton's political team strove constantly to build their candidate's political advantages, even when no election was in sight. The team sought to polish the presidential image in cinematic terms in the months preceding November 1996. This initiative was led virtually in secret by the president's chief consultant, a Republican operative named Dick Morris, who had assisted Clinton during crises in his governorship. While Morris plotted the grand strategy of "triangulating" the president's positions to attract moderate voters, the campaign gauged people's preferences for nearly everything they might see Clinton do. Most famously, it commissioned a poll which concluded that Jackson Hole, Wyoming, struck respondents as the most appealing vacation spot from a list of such places. During the following summer, the First Family dutifully spent time off there. As the image makers had hoped, the Clintons looked very appealing against the backdrop of stunning mountain peaks and handsome lodge architecture.

Clinton himself also drew on his movie fan's knowledge to structure his public displays of emotion, which he shrewdly kept to a minimum. His frequent rages were almost never visible in public. Instead, he saved emotional display for the most politically beneficial moments. A horrendous tragedy gave him his best opportunity. Attending a memorial service for the 180 victims of the terrorist bombing of the Federal Building in Oklahoma City, Clinton famously adopted the role of "mourner in chief," consoling numerous relatives and friends of the dead with kind words, hugs, and pats on the back. His sentiments were genuine: few people were more eager than Clinton to connect emotionally with a room of strangers and engage in tactile familiarity. But the effectiveness with which television broadcast Clinton's caring became the main cultural result. Despite the ridicule critics heaped upon the term, other Americans were persuaded that the president "felt their pain." At the crossroads of Oklahoma City, at last, a highly motivated chief executive, an omnivorous and opinionated news media, and a public primed for emotional contact with leaders conspired to create a crucial cinematic presidential moment. The memorial service immediately reversed Clinton's low poll numbers and moved him well past the popularity of the caustic Republican leadership that had taken over Congress the previous November.

It was Clinton's publicized sexual antics, though, that put the final, definitive personal imprimatur on the emotional and sensuous presidential image of the 1990s. The sex scandal film cycle of the late 1990s gave evidence of its resonance, but as already mentioned, *Wag the Dog, Primary Colors,* and *The Contender* were not hits. Americans' deep fascination with sexual politics in the political realm had peaked earlier in the decade. Around 1991, Hollywood and Washington both fell into an intense fascination with sexuality in the workplace. Such stories made good drama, humanized politicians (as well as other office workers), and revealed a real social phenomenon that emerged as the first large coterie of female professionals achieved equal rank with male colleagues. Americans were fascinated by both fictional and real-life depictions of sexual harassment and gamesmanship between genders on the job. As the success of Maureen Dowd's column in the mid-1990s indicated, stories of sex mixed with politics, broadly defined, had a powerful resonance in the culture.

The first cycle of Washington sexual harassment stories had emerged in the 1970s, as the Women's Movement first began to shape public consciousness. The extramarital antics of the powerful congressmen Wayne Hays and Wilbur Mills evoked elements of old-fashioned sex comedies, such as leering old bosses, unskilled "kept" secretaries, and striptease dancers. Fifteen years later, much had changed; Baby Boomers had grown up under feminism, and young women had achieved positions of power and influence. Sexual harassment now shed light on the tensions that affected the working lives of millions of Americans.[33] The first explosive Washington harassment story arrived in 1991, when the former government attorney Anita Hill argued that the US Supreme Court nominee Clarence Thomas had made crude sexual advances to her and had possibly endangered her employment. Appearing before the Senate's hearings on Thomas's nomination, Hill appeared vulnerable and alone. The Republican senators who questioned her character and veracity were widely ridiculed for repeating traditional prejudices against female accusers in harassment cases.

In the public mind, the Hill-Thomas confrontation spun off two videotaped courtroom sequels. Senator Edward Kennedy, a member of the Judiciary Committee examining Thomas, was compelled some months later to give embarrassing testimony in the trial for rape of his nephew, William Kennedy Smith, held in Florida. Kennedy had joined Smith for a night of drinking in Palm Beach bars, which led to a surfside encounter between Smith and a woman and the latter's accusations of rape. The sixty-year-old senator's televised recollections of the night, dim as they were, revived the long-running popular narrative of the decline of the Kennedy family since its heyday in the 1960s (although Kennedy, then divorced, soon remarried and apparently mended his ways). Smith was acquitted of the charges.

In addition to bringing harassment to the fore, Hill-Thomas had also dramatized changes in race relations, squaring off two members of the new, African-American professional elite against each other. The confrontation thus presaged the decade's most lurid and sensational story of sexual harassment: the O. J. Simpson trial of 1995, which was amplified by the defendant's celebrity, the interracial identity of the couple, and the violent murder of the woman, Simpson's former wife. Broadcast live for months on cable television, the trial made celebrities of witnesses, DNA experts, attorneys, the judge, and nearly every close confidant of Simpson's. In some senses, the image-producing dynamics of the Simpson trial differed little from those of the sensational Lindbergh kidnapping trial sixty years earlier, but television brought a cinematic quality to the proceedings and transformed the players into characters in a potent drama. The bloody triggering event occurred off camera; the defendant protested his innocence while the state insisted on his guilt; and the public feasted on the personalities and the plot twists while the wheels of official inquiry slowly ground on. In the end the jury declared the celebrity not guilty, having concluded that the prosecution's complex, scientific DNA evidence of his guilt was "garbage in, garbage out."[34]

Coincidental with the early national Clinton scandals, during and after the 1992 campaign, the longtime US Senator Bob Packwood, a divorced Republican, became the focus of a sustained sexual harassment scandal. In 1992, while the Oregonian ran for reelection, published complaints from female lobbyists and members of his own staff alleged that Packwood had made repeated, unwanted sexual advances. The senator minimized the stories enough to win another term, but afterward a fully researched account of the allegations appeared in the *Washington Post,* and the Senate itself began to investigate his actions. Packwood fought back for two years, even plotting to expose fellow senators who he claimed were guilty of similar actions. In 1995, facing likely expulsion from his seat, Packwood resigned. In those same months, thanks to the activism of conservative opponents of Bill Clinton, Americans learned of Paula Corbin Jones's accusations.

Hollywood, simultaneously, had been exploring sexual harassment in its own way. Such topics had been exploited by low-budget and genre films for decades. With the demise of the Production Code in the 1960s, sexual tension in many contexts was explored frankly in the movies, even in grade-A productions. The proliferation of harassment scandals beginning in 1991 caught Hollywood's attention. The most prominent example of the cycle was *Disclosure* (1994), which posited the counter-phenomenon of female-on-male office intimidation. In this sense Michael Crichton's story fed off another Hollywood plot trend—that of the predatory woman, exemplified by the protagonist in *Fatal Attraction* (1987)—but it also mainly exploited the he-said, she-said dynamics of harassment charges and their impact on the office climate. (*Disclosure* also demonstrated that sexual harassment, and the need to regulate it, was as much of a concern for private companies as it was for government.) The film starred Michael Douglas—also the victim in *Fatal Attraction,* and soon to be target of milder female advances in *The American President*—and was directed by Barry Levinson, who later made *Wag the Dog.* Paced and plotted as a thriller and using the new medium of e-mail to channel story twists, *Disclosure* was a popular success. Less profitable was *Absolute Power* (1997), Clint Eastwood's adaptation of a best-selling novel about a sexually sadistic president who covers up the death of his mistress. Until *Wag the Dog* and *Primary Colors* returned to the topic with a political focus in 1998, sexual harassment was mainly exploited luridly in grade-B and television features. Indeed, the proliferation of explicit sexual content on cable, the Internet, and popular music helped to diffuse sober debate about office ethics and personal restraint.

We are "choking on lust," Maureen Dowd concluded in the *New York Times* in 1999. "In a society that is saturated with sex, the threshold of shock keeps dropping. . . . D.C. races against L.A. to see which capital can be more outrageously unexpurgated. . . . [*Esquire*] magazine ponders whether breasts might be 'a symbol of the new culture of falseness that pervades the corridors of power.'" "The reason Bill Clinton's scandal did not shock America," Dowd concludes, "is because it was coherent with the culture. The President merely attached the Oval Office to the rest of the country, and brought it down to the level of all the less revered venues where people are thinking and talking about sex all the time."[35] There were other reasons as well. Even in the alleged encounter with Paula Jones, Clinton—unlike Packwood and other well-known figures—had demonstrated an ability to pull back when his advances were rejected. ("Well, I don't want to make you do something you don't want to do," Clinton said, according to Jones's testimony.)[36] His likely misuse of Arkansas state troopers and US Secret Service agents in these encounters did not become grounds for impeachment.

Beyond the suspicion of perjury driving Kenneth Starr's investigation, for his conservative opponents Clinton's sin was to flaunt the tolerant sexuality of the post-1960s era. They were enraged that, like some well-known backsliding pastors in the fold, Clinton had adapted his Southern Baptist upbringing to an over-tolerant, amoral, secular age. Conservatives' attack on the president echoed their crusade on explicit sexuality in Hollywood movies. A leader of this attack was in fact not a Baptist but a Jewish man, Michael Medved, an author, film critic, and radio broadcaster (and coincidentally a former Yale law school classmate of the Clintons). In Medved's writings, the "Hollywood" at war with "American" values was clearly in league with liberal Baby Boomer politicians, led by the president himself.

In 1998, though, many Americans came to perceive the conservative attack on Clinton's sins as hypocritical and damaging to the country. In his report on the Lewinsky investigation, Kenneth Starr included gratuitous details about oral sex and vaginal penetration, and he provoked ridicule when he claimed to be "horrified" at the public release of the report. The moral failings of some right-wing leaders were soon reported as well. The extramarital affairs of Clinton's prime nemesis, Speaker Newt Gingrich, and his designated successor, Bob Livingston, caused both of them to give up the speakership and led Gingrich to resign from the House. The conservatives' overweening zeal itself became a political issue almost equal in importance to Clinton's alleged high crimes and misdemeanors. Starr was pilloried as an expensive snoop and an inadvertent smut peddler, because of his salacious digest of Lewinsky's testimony, and reporters gleefully exposed the marital indiscretions of such Clinton enemies as Congressmen Henry Hyde and Dan Burton. Culturally, the contemporary empathic and emotional cinematic image of the president helped ease the public's disapproval of Clinton and encouraged many to consider his impeachment trial a shabby political coup attempt.

The weak box office take of *Primary Colors* and other movie meditations on Clinton's foibles also indicated that by 1998 the Lewinsky affair and the impeachment trial had diminished the power of both the sexual harassment narrative and the liberal cinematic presidential image. Whether citizens simply had tired of perceiving the president as a flawed and emotive private person or now sought other central qualities in their leaders, by 1999 the sexual and narrative synergy that had allied Washington and Hollywood during the decade seemed largely spent. Clinton's acquittal by the Senate was a relief, but also a signal that America was now somewhat adrift, deprived of a guiding narrative about the interaction of leadership, values, and male-female interaction. As Maureen Dowd wrote, "we're stuck with a quarrelsome, raunchy, blurry period where we constantly scramble to figure

out what the rules are."[37] Warren Beatty began a highly public exploration
·of a run for the Democratic presidential nomination in 2000. Beatty's connections with JFK, *PT 109,* the rise of the New Hollywood, and the sexual
revolution were in the past now; the actor was now married with children,
and his political explorations were driven by liberals' desire for a strong
candidate. Still, characteristically, Beatty began his inquiry by directing and
co-writing a politically themed movie, *Bulworth,* in which he also starred as
a disillusioned US senator who evolves into a truth-telling rap singer. In the
real world, after months of publicly mulling over a possible candidacy in
enigmatic speeches and opinion pieces, Beatty decided not to pursue the
nomination.

   Bill Clinton, meanwhile, found refuge from political warfare in the film
world. During the impeachment trial there was considerable speculation
that he might join the board of directors of DreamWorks, a new movie
studio, after leaving the White House. He continued to attend celebrity-
studded events, such as the celebration of *Time* magazine's seventy-fifth
anniversary at New York's Radio City Music Hall. Clinton arrived late to the
function, which was also attended by Steven Spielberg, Sharon Stone, Sophia
Loren, Norman Mailer, Raquel Welch, and Tom Cruise; public figures such
as Louis Farrakhan, Mikhail Gorbachev, and Betty Friedan; newsmakers
such as Dr. Jack Kevorkian; and, representing the religious right, the Reverend Jerry Falwell. The 1,200 illustrious guests ate caviar and chatted as a
band played "I Feel like Being a Sex Machine."[38]

   In June 2000, six months from the end of his time in office, the president
finally got to act on the big screen. Bill Clinton had actually appeared in a
cameo in the Oval Office, as himself, in the TV movie *A Child's Wish,* which
was filmed in 1996, well before the Lewinsky scandal. Now he displayed his
acting skills in a six-minute film shown during the traditionally light-
hearted speaking period of the annual White House Correspondents' Dinner. Directed by the TV comedy show creator Phil Rosenthal, the film
depicted Clinton as bored and unoccupied during the waning days of his
administration. He does the laundry, clips hedges, makes his busy wife's
lunch, surfs the Internet, and of course enjoys a movie (*101 Dalmatians*) with
his dog, Buddy, in the White House screening room. Near the end, he cra-
dles an Oscar and delivers an acceptance speech before the bedroom mirror,

until the actual recipient of the statuette, the actor Kevin Spacey, retrieves it in mock disgust. The film is entitled *The Final Days,* in a joking reference to Bob Woodward and Carl Bernstein's chronicle of the tormented end of the Nixon presidency. (In another reference to Watergate, Clinton's remarks at the dinner included the laugh line, "it's the cover-up that'll kill you.")

———

This polished little film served as a bookend to 1992's *The Man from Hope.* It reasserted how central the cinematic construction of Bill Clinton had been to his success in national politics, in the face of repeated personal and political disasters and a vehement opposition. *The Final Days* also revealed how that success derived from his deep attachment to, and his uncanny understanding of, the centrality of movie imagery in Americans' concepts of a fully socialized citizen and a competent and caring leader. The sexual harassment narrative had run its course by 2000, but under Clinton, a cinematically defined presidential image had persisted and grown. It is a legacy that, for better and worse, helped to guide American politics into the new century.

CHAPTER 7

THE TWIN TOWERS,
2001–2009

The presidential cinematic image achieved its definitive form during Bill
Clinton's presidency. It was an image that had been woven out of many
strands. The marketing of individuals as political commodities through carefully calibrated public relations campaigns began in the Coolidge era and
flourished in the 1960s, through the efforts of Kennedy and Nixon. Models
from the movies helped to define the contours of those commodities. JFK and
his charismatic emulators in the Democratic Party modeled their public personas on male types prevalent on the motion picture screen. Ronald Reagan
did this as well, drawing upon a repertoire of models and techniques from
his long first career in Hollywood. His administration applied PR techniques
on a daily basis, shaping the president's duties to suit television news coverage. Through these means, Reagan constructed the modern conservative
brand of cinematic charisma for the office. Bill Clinton, by contrast, proved
most adept as a fan of the movies, bonding with his fellow Baby Boomers
by absorbing and emulating the tolerance and playful sexuality of post-1960s
Hollywood. Clinton also perfected the massive Democratic Party fundraising
apparatus, based in Hollywood and founded by Lyndon Johnson, Arthur
Krim, and Lew Wasserman. Pre-cinematic archetypes of the US president—
as military hero, pillar of republican virtue, passive figurehead, and bourgeois
role model—were variously adapted, discarded, and transformed in the age
of instant communication and pervasive mass entertainment.

The electorate, though, was bored. During the presidential election that
closed out the twentieth century, at a time of relative peace and prosperity,

Americans evinced considerable ennui about the office and the men contending for it. In the year 2000, the excitement that had occasionally been produced by image makers in previous elections and administrations seemed to be in short supply. The Democratic presidential nomination was sought by two serious, low-key public servants who were infatuated by the minutiae of policy. Bill Bradley rarely exploited his glamorous past as a star basketball player, emphasizing instead his three terms in the US Senate and his deep understanding of economic issues. According to a strong contemporary measure of public interest—the number of references to candidates in late-night television comic monologues—Bradley rated poorly. As Jay Leno, host of the top-rated *The Tonight Show*, argued, "politics in America is a lot like auto racing; Americans don't really like racing . . . they just like car crashes. So when you get a thoughtful, intelligent candidate like Bill Bradley, oh, my God! It's impossible [to joke about him]. . . . here's a man who's a genuine thinker and to me, alas, came to politics almost as a philosopher would."[1] Vice President Al Gore's stolid manner and slow, monotonous way of speaking had made him a comedian's punch line—Billy Crystal, hosting an Academy Awards ceremony, likened him to the Oscar statuette—but otherwise he generated very little cultural discussion. His earnest crusade to clean up the natural environment was met with skepticism by progressives and derision by conservatives, and in 2000 Gore's indistinct and vaguely unfavorable public persona became a liability in his quest for the presidency. The vice president paid a small army of consultants to advise him on how to enliven his speaking style and wardrobe during the primary campaign, but his eventual victory over Bradley still came after a struggle.

On the Republican side, a more colorful mix of candidates—propelled by conservatives' zeal to replace Clinton after eight years—generated more voter interest. However, the early front-runner, Governor George W. Bush of Texas, struck many Republicans (and others) as a lightweight who owed his prominence to his father, former President George H. W. Bush, and his positions on the issues to briefings from the latter's advisers. On the eve of the New Hampshire primary, the conservative *Manchester Union-Leader* dismissed Bush as "Governor Smirk" and "an empty suit," and the governor lost the primary in a landslide to Senator John McCain of Arizona.[2] Bush fought back and won the nomination, but his reputation as a dilettante turned him into a punch line in late-night television monologues, and many voters continued to doubt that he had the intelligence and experience to be president.

Skepticism and ennui persisted during the autumn campaign. The television comedian Bill Maher dismissed the two candidates as "Bore and Gush."[3] David Plotz complained in the *New York Times* that both candidates and parties, as in campaigns past, were playing it too safe: for most Americans, "the campaign isn't too hard [to follow]. It's too dull." Gore, Plotz argued, "can't stop being dull," while "Bush willfully suppresses his charisma in order to seem serious." The problem, then, was that both men had resisted the lessons of the cinematic tradition. "Aversion to stardom and celebrity isn't just impractical; it's downright un-American." Beginning with the scripted nominating conventions, both parties' campaigns "are eerily devoid of direct conflict." Both sides ensure that the presidential debates, for example, are not debates at all, but parallel news conferences, in which time for answers is limited to allow the candidates to recite memorized responses. While party surrogates might occasionally voice strong criticisms of the other side, "the candidates themselves don't squabble or wrestle."

In Plotz's view, the two leading campaigns in 2000 erred by failing to tell movie-style narratives about their candidates. Since the Bush and Gore teams resolutely squelched conflict and uncertainty—two of the "three fundamental requirements of drama"—the third element, "a shapely narrative . . . becomes crucial. Any tale that you care about arcs from beginning to middle to end." Gore violated this requirement by giving speeches on different policy issues day after day; "wash, rinse, repeat till November. . . . this is not a story." Plotz, like other cultural critics at the turn of the millennium, endorsed the theory that in American culture, life had become a movie, and that politics ought to be part of the show. "The Safety First campaign will win Gore or Bush the election, but at a cost. The nation lives by the agenda of sports and entertainment. A president who can't understand that risks irrelevance. He won't know how to speak to his constituents, and we won't take the trouble to listen. Maybe it's time for another movie star in the White House."[4]

Election night, though, astonished Americans. Instead of ending the dull campaign season with a predictable result, in which one lackluster candidate was duly elected, the night—and the morning after—brought a deadlock. Voters with only the vaguest notions about the workings of the Electoral College were suddenly compelled to brush up on the nation's presidential selection mechanism, crafted in 1788. The candidates retreated into isolation while the recount in the crucial state of Florida, where the popular vote was tied, pitted two well-paid legal teams and colorful camps of emotional voters against each other. After five weeks of heated battles in county election offices and state courts, the Republicans' one-vote majority on the US Supreme Court decided the issue in favor of Bush. Al Gore and his supporters, who had outpolled Bush's nationwide by half a million, reluctantly accepted the defeat, nursing the hope that the victor might assume the office with humility and in a spirit of conciliation.

This hope was dashed. The Florida recount instead was a prelude to a decade of political trauma, worsened by the impact of a terrorist attack on America and two resulting wars. In the 1990s the US victory in the Cold War had seemed to promise a peace dividend, in terms of lower federal spending and taxation and a reduction in the social and political tensions generated by America's global commitments. The Cold War had largely defined the presidency in the late twentieth century, but in 1992 Bill Clinton became the first nonveteran in sixty years to be elected; that fact, in addition to Clinton's efforts to avoid the draft during the Vietnam War, made him an unacceptable commander in chief in the eyes of many voters. The turmoil surrounding the Florida recount indicated that the political vitriol of the Clinton era would persist. Bush, directed by his strong-willed vice president, Dick Cheney, and his ambitious political director, Karl Rove, shunned compromise with Democrats and pursued a strong conservative agenda. Then, on September 11, 2001, Osama bin Laden's Al Qaeda—the virtually unknown terrorist group that Bill Clinton had targeted in the *Wag the Dog* attack of August 1998—hijacked airliners and crashed them into the World Trade Center and the Pentagon. In the midst of continuing political bickering, America was returned to a vigilant and often paranoid war footing.

During the decade since 9/11 the cinematic presidential image seems to have reached a point of crisis. George W. Bush produced a thesis, as it were, of how the presidency must cope with deep political divisions and the threat of terrorism at home and abroad. His policies were rooted to a great extent in the bureaucratic skills of his top advisers, who had served in his father's administration and in the 1991 Persian Gulf War. They were also shaped by the zeal of neoconservatives from right-wing think tanks, who were eager to battle Islamic fundamentalism, and from the rising evangelical Christian segment within the Republican Party (of which Bush himself was a member), who sought a return to "traditional" social values. The aggressive promotion of these policies, though, was fashioned by Karl Rove, who gained unprecedented power by blending image making and policy formulation in his West Wing office. Rove, it might be argued, created the definitive conservative version of the presidential cinematic image, in which Bush's presence as a heroic and decisive leader was constructed systematically and unceasingly, out of elements from past image making efforts. Despite the failure of Bush's policies in the disastrous war in Iraq, the calamitous response to Hurricane Katrina, and the collapse of Wall Street, Rove solidified the loyalty and passions of right-wing voters behind the president and his agenda.

Yet in 2008 the electorate at large rejected Bush and his administration, decisively choosing Democrat Barack Obama as his successor. Obama's cinematic presence offered a liberal antithesis to Bush's. He differed from his predecessor as much as was possible in mainstream US politics, in terms of ideology, style, language, manner—and race. Obama in 2008 was as wildly popular among liberals—"blue state America"—as Bush was among the conservatives of the "red" states. Unlike Bush, though, Obama did not rely on a Karl Rove to construct a mass media image. Advisers helped with the details, but Obama's image was overwhelmingly the candidate's own handiwork—an amazing act of autobiographical narrative that transformed a little-known young politician from Chicago into the world's most powerful officeholder.

These two dramatic political stories from opposite ends of the spectrum were culminations of the Hollywood effect on the White House. By the 2000s candidates, staffs, and voters took for granted image making and the rootedness of political perceptions in mass entertainment, and Bush and Obama each played his role with unprecedented care and polish. Such showmanship, however, did not unite the country. The two presidential showmen played to two culturally polarized halves of the electorate. At no time since the traumatic weeks after September 11, 2001, have the compelling theatrics of the White House stage effectively overcome real political divisions. The eventual impotence of this imagery might serve notice that the effectiveness of the cinematic presidential image in American culture is on the wane.

———

In his early years, George W. Bush possessed all of the advantages a future presidential prospect could want. He came from a wealthy, politically ambitious, and accomplished family; he was tall and handsome; and he had earned an Ivy League education. The younger Bush nevertheless was highly ambivalent about pursuing elective office. Fun-loving, swaggering, rarely interested in public policy, Bush resembled other diffident presidential offspring (such as James and Elliott Roosevelt and John F. Kennedy Jr.) who largely drifted through their early adulthoods. Bush was intelligent, always able to pass his classes at Yale University and Harvard Business School, but he was unfocused and did not apply himself. As he himself put it in his memoirs, "nobody was asking me to match Dad's record, and I didn't need to try. . . . When I left the [Texas Air National] Guard in my late twenties, I had no serious responsibilities. I was spontaneous and curious, searching for adventure." He was also notoriously silly, given to tormenting acquaintances with practical jokes and saddling them with absurd nicknames.[5]

Politics proved a passing adventure in 1978, when George W. Bush ran for a US House seat in Texas and narrowly lost, but his father's ascent to the vice presidency and the presidency involved him repeatedly in campaigns. Republicans and journalists inevitably mentioned Bush as the political heir to his grandfather (a US Senator from Connecticut) and father, but for nearly two decades he dodged that mantle. (His younger brother Jeb, by contrast, prepared diligently for a political career.) Family life, the oil business, "playing hard" in bars and at resorts, and eventual co-ownership of the Texas Rangers baseball franchise kept Bush's focus off politics. It is worth noting, though, that he assiduously built up contacts in business and in politics, embraced evangelical Christianity to give up alcohol, and (unlike any other president before him) gained experience as an executive in the entertainment industry (of which major league baseball was a part). While at the Rangers Bush gave countless speeches in central Texas, developing a skill at "conveying a clear message," and he played a central role in launching the team's new stadium.[6] His decision to run for governor of Texas in 1994 surprised some, but it was a logical product of his privileged background and diverse prior experiences.

Bush's victory in the governor's race, upsetting the incumbent Democrat, Ann Richards, sealed his relationship with Karl Rove, the innovative and controversial Texas Republican political consultant. Rove had endured an unhappy early life in Utah, raised by a stepfather who claimed biological paternity and a mother who later committed suicide. Bookish and determined, Rove threw himself into Republican politics, dropping out of college to organize campaigns. His most famous early campaign was his own, a stormy effort in 1974 to win control of the national College Republicans, which led to accusations that Rove committed vote fraud. He was awarded the group's presidency by the party's national chairman, George H. W. Bush. As a designer of campaigns, Rove was driven by data and issues, not by cosmetic imagery, but even he could be shaken by the presence of an individual with rare personal magnetism. The bespectacled, thin, overworked Karl Rove fell hard for the young George W. Bush, five years his senior. Rove first encountered Bush in 1973, "walk[ing] through the front door . . . exuding more charm and charisma than is allowed by law. He had on his Air National Guard flight jacket, jeans, and boots." A circle in the back pocket of his jeans showed where he carried his "tin of snuff . . . in Texas you see [that] a lot." "He was . . . *cool*."[7]

For years the smitten Rove had no opportunity to manage Bush as a candidate, but in the meantime he moved to Texas and established the state's most effective political consulting group. Tutored by Lee Atwater and other ruthless professionals but also inspired by his own heavy reading in political history, Rove shaped clients' efforts through meticulous research and planning. As he described it later, his campaigns were "driven by historical data" and "the use of sophisticated modeling to identify potential supporters and match them with issues that will persuade them and turn them out." Consumer trends, educational attainment, church attendance, and many other social and cultural indicators became grist for Rove's computations. "It's the relationship between all kinds of data points that can be revealing. . . . the modeling is complex and difficult to do, but it can make a huge impact by allowing a campaign to focus its energies on voters who are truly up for grabs and on those who need extra encouragement to turn out."[8]

On the other hand, Rove also gained fame in Texas as an obsessive and emotional man who would harangue his fellow political professionals— Democrat or Republican—and who might do anything to advance himself and his candidates. According to one popular story, in 1986 Rove had a hidden microphone installed in his own office to create a controversy for the Democratic governor, who was running for reelection against Rove's client. The story further claimed that Rove had gotten the idea from a recent Hollywood movie, *Power,* about a campaign manager whose office phone is bugged. Rove denied the anecdote, insisting that no one had ever determined who had planted the device and that he viewed *Power* after the 1986 election (in which his candidate won).[9] In general, it is fairly clear that Rove (like most of his competitors in Texas political consulting) seemed to share the disinterest in movies and in mass-market imagery that characterized the Lone Star State in the days of Lyndon B. Johnson. The backroom deal, the personal touch, evangelical Christian rhetoric, and, above all, money still seemed to animate Texas politics, even in the age of heavy TV campaign advertising. (For his part, Rove was an agnostic Episcopalian who deferred to Texas's dominant religious culture.)

Bush's election as governor in 1994 virtually announced the Republican Party's takeover of Texas politics, and more than any professional, Karl Rove could—and did—take credit for the triumph. In 1990 he had run a slate of victorious GOP candidates for state office, and he installed his candidate in the US Senate three years later. Like Ronald Reagan's early boosters in California, Rove set his sights early on the top prize. By 1990 he was telling friends that "George can be president." Now at the top of his profession, Rove created an operation which melded his meticulous research and planning with a new focus on mass media image making. Even in Texas, a conservative brand of cinematic candidate molding was required to mount a successful television advertising effort. As Nicholas Lemann has put it, "the Rove operation, at its peak, was like an old-fashioned Hollywood studio, with Rove as the mogul. Rove and his aides, the people behind the camera, were smart, geeky, ruthless, and workaholic; the candidate-clients were handsome, forthright, vigorous, friendly, and easy, with firm jaws and great hair. After they made it through the auditioning process, they'd be sent around the studio lot for buffing and polishing—a stop in Message, a stop in Fund-Raising—before they were given their public debut." Rove later claimed that one of his clients in 1990, Rick Perry, then a candidate for agriculture commissioner, was victorious in part "because of his marquee good looks."[10]

Rove's clients gained control of the Democrats' last bastion, the Texas Supreme Court, in 1998, just in time for Governor Bush's anticipated bid for the White House. As Rove began to chart the course, Bush and his wife Laura purchased a small "ranch"—more accurately, a house with acreage—in the remote town of Crawford, Texas, to conform to the cowboy presidential image that had gained currency among Republicans since the Reagan years. Bush also enlisted the image making skills of Karen Hughes, a former television news reporter who became a close adviser.

In Texas George W. Bush inhabited a notoriously weak governorship, exploiting his personal charm but accomplishing little by way of legislation. Conservatives from both parties largely enacted the tax reductions, deregulation, and slashing of social programs for which Bush would take credit. As a presidential candidate, Bush boasted about education reform—his favorite topic as governor—but during his term, spending and achievement in low-income school districts largely declined. The Texas political commentator Molly Ivins, one of Bush's most scathing critics, argued that from the governor's record "it appears that he doesn't know much, doesn't do much, and doesn't care much about governing. . . . In fact, given his record, it's kind of hard to figure out why he wants a job where he's expected to govern."[11]

Even Ivins, though, conceded that Bush is "a likeable guy; you'd have to work at it to dislike him." She also disputed the common criticism that Bush was lazy, noting that "you get no sense of laziness from watching him—if anything, he seems to have a rather short attention span and often seems impatient to move on to the next topic or project, leaving an impression of restless energy." Nevertheless, Bush regularly took "a couple of hours off in the middle of the day to work out and play video games." The governor was charismatic in person, the journalist Frank Bruni noted, but he lacked the "electricity of bearing that undulates across a large room . . . or crackles through the television set. Bush's wattage was more modest and quirkier."[12] Nor did Bush seem self-disciplined or determined enough to launch a bid for the White House. But as Rove realized and even Ivins grudgingly admitted, Bush had the intelligence and the energy to play the role of candidate effectively and, if necessary, to rise to new challenges along the campaign trail.

The Bush presidential effort in 2000 proved to be a monumentally expensive effort, overseen by Rove but aided by many other hands, which in the end nearly met with failure. More than two years before the election, veterans from his father's administration such as Dick Cheney and Condoleezza Rice made their way to Austin to give seminars on policy for the governor. He retained only the general outlines of their lessons. When Bush, as a candidate, displayed ignorance of the identity of world leaders and geography, specialists diagnosed possible dyslexia and other handicaps. To the governor himself, though, as well as to Rove, it was beneficial to boil the campaign down to simplicities. Bush felt that he "had a clear vision of where to lead" the country if elected, while Rove's first rule was that "a campaign's essential argument must be easily understood, capable of being widely disseminated, backed by evidence, and authentic. . . . That theme needs to be structured and delivered in a way that resonates with the information that voters carry around in their heads."[13] The campaign raised over $200 million, an unprecedented sum, to get the clear message across. The message it promoted was that George W. Bush was a "compassionate conservative."

Yet in his first national campaign Rove made costly errors. Taking the opposition of John McCain too lightly, the Bush camp suffered a landslide defeat in the New Hampshire primary. The next battle, in South Carolina, got off to a poor start when Bush gave his main speech at Bob Jones University, an evangelical school known for its racially discriminatory policies. Undoubtedly with Rove's blessing (although he denies it), the local heirs of the late Lee Atwater aided Bush in the Palmetto State by running a vicious telephone campaign that accused McCain of fathering interracial children and called his wife a drug addict. McCain had made his own mistakes, criticizing evangelical Christians a bit too stridently, but opposition dirty tricks ensured his loss to Bush, which forced the senator to quit the race. Bush and Rove, meanwhile, took the high road, exemplified by a new allit-

erative slogan that declared the candidate to be "a reformer with results."
The general election campaign against Al Gore featured a similar mixture of
high and low tactics, abetted by Gore's stiff performance on the trail and in
debates. In the end, Rove confidently told Bush on the morning of Election
Day that he would beat Gore by 6 percent of the popular vote. His statistical
modeling failed him spectacularly; Bush instead trailed the vice president by
half a percentage point, and Rove endured "thirty-six days in political
hell"—the Florida recount.[14]

Emerging triumphant in mid-December 2000, Bush had to make a rapid
transition into the White House. Fatefully, this transition was largely controlled by the vice president–elect, Dick Cheney. The affable, good-humored,
and occasionally goofy Bush contrasted strongly with Cheney, who was
quiet, uncharismatic, and dour. The former chief of staff in the Ford
White House, an able lieutenant of President Reagan's in Congress, and
George H. W. Bush's secretary of defense, Cheney had been head of Bush's
vice-presidential selection process, which many believe he manipulated to
win the second spot on the ticket for himself. To the press especially, Cheney
symbolized the return of the Republican establishment, especially in foreign
policy, after eight years of Clinton's presidency. In reality, though, the vice
president seized control of personnel and policy, especially in energy and
foreign affairs, leaving Bush to supervise domestic initiatives such as education and assistance to faith-based charities. Karl Rove—now a counselor in
the West Wing, recovered from his embarrassment on Election Day—joined
Cheney in persuading Bush to be not a timid, minority-vote president, but
a brusque leader who would achieve long-sought and controversial conservative goals. As at other times in his life—but never more fatefully than now
—Bush allowed others to determine his initiatives and intellectual focus.[15]

As Cheney accumulated power with a disregard for popular opinion and
planned for an eventual invasion of Iraq to topple Saddam Hussein—in his
view, unfinished business from a decade before—perhaps half of the electorate grew alienated from Bush's administration. This polarization at best
posed a challenge to the president's image makers, but at its most extreme,
it reflected their own rejection of the emotive and empathetic image of the
chief executive that had predominated in the 1990s. Due likely to both his
family's patrician background and his Texas cultural roots, Bush did not

share Bill Clinton's fascination with the achievements and style of successful film figures. According to Karl Rove, when the candidate attended a social event at the Bel Air, California, home of the Warner Brothers executive Terry Semel, the liberal film icon Warren Beatty "watched Bush circulate through the room and answer questions. You could tell the star was impressed. Bush didn't reciprocate. Hollywood never impressed him."[16]

Perhaps, but Rove nevertheless helped to ensure that a well-staffed White House communications office would smoothly and regularly craft the presidential image along its own cinematic lines, making Bush effective in the mass media. Dan Bartlett, the office's director, was a young Bush aide from Texas with no background in communications, but he supervised three skilled veterans of TV production: Scott Sforza, Bob DeServi, and Greg Jenkins. Their most evident innovation in presenting the president was the "message board," a monochromatic backdrop to a Bush speech carrying numerous iterations of the day's high concept. It did not matter that the slogans were almost unreadable to those who viewed the events in person; the fonts, and the materials on which they were printed, were chosen to show up vividly on television. After the president's former leading corporate benefactor, Enron, collapsed in scandal, he appeared before a blue message board saying CORPORATE RESPONSIBILITY; his next address took place in front of a red backdrop with the message STRENGTHENING THE ECONOMY; a later set read HELPING SMALL BUSINESS. When Bush took his frequent vacations in Crawford, Texas, Bartlett ensured copious coverage of the president's vigorous brush-cutting and leisure activities. The early White House "spin" of the nearly accidental president obviously emulated the poses of a predecessor who had won two clear-cut election victories, Ronald Reagan. In Bush's first eight months in office, such imagery especially helped him to maintain his hold on his conservative base.[17]

This condition—and much more—changed drastically on September 11, 2001. Informed of the first air attack in New York City as he walked into an elementary school classroom in Sarasota, Florida, Bush decided (he later claimed) to "project calm."[18] As the teacher read the story *My Pet Goat* to the class, Bush sat for twenty minutes while aides whispered in his ear news of each fresh atrocity. Captured on videotape, his rigid, inactive staring in this instance perplexed many Americans, but it offered a rare glimpse of an unscripted president acting on his own without coaching or directing. Perhaps it showed Bush as he claimed to be, as well as how he often seemed to be—an earnest, even capable, individual who tended to react simply and impulsively to new challenges. After he finally left the school that morning, the scale of the terrorist attacks became clear: thousands had died, and more attacks might be coming. Bush allowed his advisers to fly him to bases in Louisiana and Nebraska, hesitating until the midafternoon to insist that he be taken back to Washington. His itinerary that day also generated controversy. By then, though, he had reached another clear-cut conclusion: America was at war, and his administration would henceforth be defined by his effort to protect the homeland and win the struggle against terror.

The next few weeks were the most successful of Bush's eight years in office, mostly due to the unanimity of anger, fear, and yearning for leadership felt by the American people. The "end of the age of irony" proclaimed by Graydon Carter, editor of the often ironic magazine *Vanity Fair,* proved to be fleeting, but for a time 9/11 silenced the cynical humor that had long shaped public perceptions of Washington.[19] The catastrophe also provided a virtually perfect moment for the cinematic presentation of the chief executive. The destruction of the World Trade Center towers, the tallest in New York City, struck many as strangely and powerfully aesthetic. Only a few intellectuals, such as Susan Sontag and Karlheinz Stockhausen, dared to perceive elements of courage or beauty in the act, and they were criticized widely for their statements. Many others, though, likened the attacks to film scenes. The destruction of the World Trade Center had been simulated with the use of special effects in movies ranging from the remake of *King Kong* (1975) to *Deep Impact* (1998). As Brigitte Nacos has noted, "in search of box-office hits, Hollywood had already produced for many years a steady stream of disaster movies and thrillers, often based on best-selling novels, which used just such images." After a tour of the devastation, Governor George Pataki of New York told reporters, "I remember seeing one of these Cold War movies and after the nuclear attacks with the Hollywood portrayal of a nuclear winter. It looked worse than that in downtown Manhattan; and it wasn't some grade 'B' movie. It was life. It was real." Even the novelist

John Updike, who saw the attacks from his apartment in Brooklyn, fell back on his TV-watching sensibility: "as on television, this was not quite real, it could be fixed; the technocracy the towers symbolized would find a way to put out the fire and reverse the damage."[20]

Acts of terrorism, as Nacos notes, have almost always been theatrical, floridly deceptive displays of power committed by rather powerless individuals or groups. But the scale of the 9/11 attacks showed the criminals' grotesque flair for replicating the villainous, high-casualty assaults on large-scale infrastructure found in modern movie thrillers. Now President Bush had the opportunity to match them with a cinematic gesture of his own. Appearing amid the smoking rubble of the towers on September 14, Bush greeted exhausted and traumatized relief workers. Karl Rove trained his director's eye on a crushed truck lying on its side and asked a city firefighter to test the stability of its fender. While the fireman was still atop the truck, the president mounted the fender, put his arm around the other man, and rallied the rescue workers, speaking through a bullhorn. Like Bill Clinton's mourning at Oklahoma City, the gesture at Ground Zero was plain and easy enough for almost any president to make, but like Clinton, Bush's particular grace at that moment seemed to epitomize his charismatic qualifications for the contemporary presidency. Especially for those who had supported Bush in 2000, his character and persona were now fixed. For Rove, the moment especially provided the all-important clear message. "Atop a crushed fire truck, amidst the rubble of shattered towers, Bush showed moral clarity and courage that were to prove vital to confronting this enemy."[21]

The next week Bush followed his Ground Zero appearance with an address before Congress, which effectively stated the nation's united desire to punish Al Qaeda and its host nations. The president's sincere plea for respect for the Muslim faith also won the respect of fair-minded citizens. Most of them continued to approve of Bush's performance when a small CIA-led force entered Afghanistan within weeks and sent the ruling Taliban and the guest Al Qaeda leadership into hiding (though Osama bin Laden escaped).

At this crucial point, weeks after 9/11, Bush's team made its sole effort to enlist Hollywood as a regiment in the war on terrorism. The chief executive may have cared little for Hollywood personally, as Karl Rove argued, but the enmity was mutual. Before the terrorist attacks, liberals in the industry had made no secret of their disdain for the president. A short-lived television show, *That's My Bush!,* created by Matt Stone and Trey Parker (who originated the caustic animated comedy *South Park*), was designed mostly to parody situation comedies in a White House setting—Stone and Parker had also sketched an Al Gore version of the program, in case he had won—but the barbed assaults on conservative positions made its political stance plain. After the show was canceled owing to low ratings, Parker and Stone began work on an action-film parody, *George W. Bush and Secret of the Glass Tiger,* which was scheduled to begin production before 9/11 caused its cancellation as well.[22] Yet after the attacks a rapprochement between the White House and Hollywood seemed sensible to many. The initiative came from two political conservatives, the director and screenwriter Lionel Chetwynd and the producer Craig Haffner, who contacted White House aides about a meeting. Higher powers in Hollywood and Washington took interest, and a "summit" between leading figures from both towns was scheduled.[23]

On November 11 Karl Rove met with more than forty Hollywood executives at a hotel in Beverly Hills. Paramount chairwoman Sherry Lansing and Viacom Entertainment Group chairman Jonathan Dolgen, "two stalwarts of liberal Hollywood," and eighty-year-old Jack Valenti, president of the MPAA, hosted the meeting. Valenti and Rove both insisted that the studios were not being asked to produce propaganda films. "Content is off the table," Valenti had announced earlier. However, Rove proceeded to encourage Hollywood to use its special skills to help sell the United States' war aims in other ways. He hoped that short films, public service announcements, and personal appearances by stars might convey a few messages valued by the Bush administration: that the war was against terrorism, not Islam; that Americans were being called to serve; that troops and their families would be helped; and that "it is a fight against evil rather than a disagreement between nations." "The war effort needs a narrative that should be told," Rove said. The Hollywood executives then pitched some ideas. Bryce Zabel, head of the Academy of Television Arts and Sciences, recommended "ask[ing] some of our very best filmmakers to do a three-minute piece on the theme 'My Country 'Tis of Thee,' and then compile them together on video and airdrop them over areas hostile to us." The executives vowed to create a "Hollywood 9/11" working group to realize these ideas.[24]

Creative personnel had been excluded from the Rove meeting, and some of them aimed to put content back on the table by offering to make propaganda movies for, and perhaps even with, the government. Lionel Chetwynd, an originator of the gathering, did not hesitate to seek Washington's consent and assistance in making propagandistic films. Chetwynd interviewed administration officials, and in 2003 he produced and directed a cable television film, *D.C. 9/11: Time of Crisis,* depicting a thoroughly heroic George W. Bush responding to the events of that day. Timothy Bottoms, the lookalike actor who had starred in the 2001 parody *That's My Bush!,* also played the president in this film, which was a critical and ratings failure. Meanwhile, the Army-funded Institute for Creative Technologies at the University of Southern California hosted a series of "brainstorming sessions," in which screenwriters such as John Milius (*Apocalypse Now*) and Steven de Souza (*Die Hard*) tried to script the next episodes in the war on terror pondering, for the benefit of Pentagon planners, Al Qaeda's likely motivations and schemes.[25]

Some filmmakers forthrightly defended the exploitation of the moment for its entertainment value, as a respite from real-life news and as a satisfyingly violent wish fulfillment. Only weeks after 9/11, the producer Lawrence Kasanoff, who attended the Rove meeting, had sped to Jordan with a multinational film crew to shoot scenes for the movie *Mortal Kombat II: Annihilation.* "I worried about what if someone was hurt or killed," Kasanoff recalled, "but I also worried about what if we didn't go?" His opinion echoed that of many Americans in those days: "it's extremely important for the whole country to continue doing what we normally do—laughing, going to the movies, watching TV, playing sports—whatever makes life enjoyable. If we give up even some of our daily activities, we are letting the terrorists win. . . . These days, I think escapist entertainment is a very good idea." The expensive, popular, and critically acclaimed television series *24,* about an intelligence agent's frantic attempts to halt terrorist actions (often with the help of the West Wing), had originated before 9/11, and it could claim a liberal producer (Brian Grazer) and a right-leaning network (Fox, owned by Rupert Murdoch) among its progenitors. Agent Jack Bauer's retaliatory violence against suspected terrorists was toned down in the initial episodes, which appeared in November 2001, but it was enhanced in later shows by popular demand. The show's depictions of suspects being tortured as time bombs ticked were cathartic and even instructive fantasies. Republican members of Congress and military and CIA interrogators were heard to approve of the use of the harsh, even sadistic, methods dreamt up by 24's script writers.[26]

Tensions between Rove and liberal-leaning Hollywood lay close to the surface of the November 11 meeting, and the cultural divide between the two camps reemerged soon afterward. The producer Lynda Obst, who did not attend the meeting, scoffed, "we are already propaganda experts. . . . the veritable American Dream Machine. We hardly need any instruction from Karl Rove in this area." A "well-known actor-director" who attended the Rove meeting derided it as "little more than a jerk-off session," while the movie critic John Powers called it "the usual boring Washington-Hollywood dumb show. They pretend they are going to do something important, knowing full well nothing will ever come of it."[27]

Such cynicism reflected the dissolution of the short-lived 9/11 consensus among the electorate. As before, liberals came to disdain Bush's single-minded simplicity. His references to "evildoers" in Al Qaeda derived from the Old Testament, while his pledges to "smoke them out" and capture them "dead or alive" recycled the Man on Horseback presidential rhetoric of TR and Reagan. Such primitive language delighted traditionalists, but it led others to doubt again whether Bush could master the complex challenge he faced, or even comprehend the scope of his own government's operations. The Justice Department and the CIA rapidly expanded surveillance on citizens and foreigners, incarcerating and torturing suspected Al Qaeda members and holding them indefinitely without cause in locations around the world. At the urging of administration lawyers, Bush created signing statements, attached to the bills he allowed to become law, explaining the circumstances under which he would not be bound by them. Neoconservative ideologues led by Cheney and Defense Secretary Donald Rumsfeld spread the war on terror to Iraq, a disarmed nation since the Persian Gulf War which had no apparent involvement in the 9/11 attacks. Cheney and others, we now know, had planned the Iraq War from the outset of the Bush administration, and 9/11 became their excuse to launch it.[28] In 2002 the administration waged an intense public relations campaign to increase public support for the invasion. The administration's PR campaign for war in Iraq became an issue in its own right, and it resulted in vendettas and court cases that would linger for years. These policies caused extraordinary political and social tension.

As a result, during this time—especially after Operation Iraqi Freedom was launched in early 2003—Bush's image makers went to unprecedented lengths to create the illusion of support and unity in America for his administration's costly and often brutal efforts. As Frank Rich has noted, the administration benefited from the fact that since the late 1980s, "entertainment giants" had acquired television networks, putting news organizations on tight budgets and requiring that they attain high viewer ratings. Time Warner, Viacom, and Disney owned CNN, CBS, and ABC, respectively, while General Electric positioned NBC similarly within its communications holdings. Rupert Murdoch's News Corporation owned Fox Television, which influenced the programming found on its newer sister station, the Fox News Channel. "In this new mediathon environment," Rich writes, "drama counted more than judicious journalism; clear-cut 'evildoers' and patriots were prized over ambiguous characters who didn't wear either black or white hats."[29] Fox News, under the guidance of the veteran political consultant Roger Ailes—a producer, not a journalist—became an extension of the White House's message machine, leading the cheers for "compassionate conservatism" and the Iraq War.

Encouraged by media specialists in the Pentagon early in the war, Fox and other news organizations played up *Wag the Dog*–style stories of heroic soldiers. These included the tale of Jessica Lynch, a private wounded, taken prisoner, and rescued in Iraq, and the saga of Pat Tillman, a football star turned soldier who was killed in action in Afghanistan. Initially at least, the government wagered that an end to irony had indeed come—that the cynicism about mass media narratives of patriotism and sacrifice, expressed during the Clinton years, had been swept away. The gung-ho soldiers' stories became elements of the "narrative that should be told," the fables of "moral clarity" that the Administration sought to convey.[30]

This effort also meant that more than any other president before him, a heroic image of George W. Bush was manufactured—one that was almost a caricature of the cinematic leader-figure produced by earlier West Wing

PR efforts. In 2002 and 2003, the communications office continued to
meticulously prepare each of Bush's major speaking appearances. As the
office's head, Dan Bartlett, explained, "Americans are leading busy lives. . . .
If they have an instant understanding of what the president is talking
about by seeing 60 seconds of television, you accomplish your goals as
communicators." Bartlett's media specialists posed the president at one
event at Mount Rushmore so that his profile fell into line with the like-
nesses of the great leaders carved into the mountain. Bob DeServi, an expert
in lighting, shipped a battery of high-powered Musco lamps across Europe
to illuminate Bush during an appearance in Romania. The team went to
particular pains for the speech marking the first anniversary of the 9/11
attacks, delivered by Bush on Ellis Island in New York harbor, with the
Statue of Liberty in the background. Three barges loaded with DeServi's
Muscos lit the statue from torch to toe. A year later, during the Iraq War,
Bush made a secret visit to Baghdad to greet American soldiers while they
ate their Thanksgiving dinner. The payoff for the expensive and logistically
challenging trip was the photograph of Bush in a Norman Rockwell pose,
holding a traditional holiday turkey on a platter before a table full of beam-
ing troops. The turkey was a prop—the troops ate meat served out of steel
tubs—part of an elaborate photo opportunity arranged by the Pentagon
contractor Halliburton KBR.[31]

The apex of these image making efforts had come earlier, on May 1, 2003,
when President Bush was a passenger on a Navy fighter plane which landed
on the deck of the *USS Abraham Lincoln*. Bush emerged from the cockpit
wearing a full flight suit, carrying his helmet under his arm. After a long
delay, the president reemerged from his quarters, now dressed in a business
suit, and delivered a speech under a banner reading "Mission Accomplished" hanging from the aircraft carrier's command tower. The White
House's Scott Sforza had spent days aboard the ship, planning the flight and
the ceremony and hanging the banner. The *Lincoln*'s arrival home, after a
year abroad, had been delayed one day for Bush's appearance; the craft was
turned around so that it would appear in news video to be far out to sea, not
near the San Diego coast; and the crew waited for three hours for the speech,
so that it would take place during "magic hour," bathed in the golden light
of the setting sun favored by Hollywood film crews.[32]

The event yielded the flawless and impressive images that had been hoped for. "This was fantastic theater," a Fox News commentator claimed, while the notably nonpartisan journalist David Broder of the *Washington Post* crowed that "this president has learned how to move in a way that just conveys a great sense of authority and command." Few matched the approving words of Michael Deaver, Ronald Reagan's innovative event planner: "They understand the visual as well as anybody ever has. . . . They watched what we did . . . and they've taken it to an art form."[33] Appropriately, Bush's flight inspired comparisons to *Top Gun,* the 1986 movie about Navy fliers that virtually epitomized the application of the high concept to big studio productions. The high concept of victory in Iraq had found its depiction in the presidential carrier landing.

Within days of the USS *Abraham Lincoln* event, though, as the anticipated American victory in Iraq degenerated into a chaotic and tenuous occupation, the Bush image making apparatus began to come under criticism. The "Mission Accomplished" banner became a target of critics who now foresaw a long and painful US presence in Iraq, and the Bush administration distanced itself from an event about which it had formerly boasted. The President told reporters that his advance man Scott Sforza was "[not] that ingenious," and the White House insisted that it had only produced the banner at the insistence of the ship's staff (to celebrate the completion of the *Lincoln*'s mission, not the Iraq War). Karl Rove now shrugged off the matter; "I wish the banner was not up there. I'll acknowledge the fact that it has become one of those convenient symbols." Incredibly, Rove ignored the event completely in his memoirs, published in 2010. Dan Bartlett confessed that the event "set the wrong tone for what became a protracted, difficult mission. If there was ever a do-over, that would be it." And George W. Bush himself admitted in his memoirs, "our stagecraft had gone awry. It was a big mistake."[34]

Other war fictions were deconstructed. Even as the story of Private Jessica Lynch went into development as a standard heroic television movie, the Army's official account came under dispute. Lynch, eyewitnesses testified, was less seriously wounded, in less danger, and more easily rescued than early news stories had claimed. Pat Tillman's death in Afghanistan, portrayed initially as a heroic demise at the hands of the enemy, was in fact a more prosaic (and embarrassing) "friendly fire" incident; the difficulties his parents endured in uncovering the truth illustrated the Pentagon's tenacity in promoting gung-ho stories for the sake of public relations. The Bush administration kept trying to mold a positive American image in the Middle East, founding an office of Global Communications which was eventually headed by the president's confidante, Karen Hughes. Meanwhile, a bipartisan group of public figures took the matter into their own hands and recruited Hollywood professionals to create Al Haqiqa (The Truth), a video news service designed to promote American perspectives in the Middle East. Among the patrons of Al Haqiqa was the president's own father, George H. W. Bush.[35]

Outrage over the Bush administration's extreme fictionalizing grew— and not just among Democrats. The overreaching of neoconservatives helped to drive the US government into massive deficits, and it mired military and civilian contractors in a hazardous rebuilding effort in Iraq that did nothing to redress the 9/11 attacks. Controversy grew over the apparent nonexistence of weapons of mass destruction in Iraq, the growing civil war there, the atrocities committed by US troops in Baghdad's Abu Ghraib prison, and the victimization of the CIA agent Valerie Plame for her diplomat husband's criticisms of the war. Revelations about the extent of the administration's twisting of the truth multiplied. In 2005 it was revealed that a man with no journalistic credentials, employed by a conservative news service, had been admitted to White House press conferences for two years, and that press secretaries and the president habitually turned to him for easy and flattering questions that cut off more hostile lines of inquiry. The administration also used public money illegally to pay large fees to a conservative radio host, Armstrong Williams, to promote its education policy among African Americans.[36]

In 2004 Karl Rove met the tall challenge of reelecting George W. Bush by enforcing a campaign of extreme discipline and simplicity of message, portraying the president as a strong war leader and exploiting his elaborate data models brilliantly to locate and commit every possible sympathetic voter. The myth of Bush's leadership strength was especially developed, to keep the GOP base excited; this tactic was successful, but it also helped to make nonbelievers even more hostile. Surrogates tossed mud at the Vietnam War record of the Democratic candidate, the highly decorated veteran Senator John Kerry. During the campaign, even more than before, Bush seemed to disappear into the clear and simple role that Rove had scripted for him. Opinion polls showed the contest virtually even, but in the end Rove's Herculean get-out-the-vote effort produced a second term for his president.[37]

———

Liberals could only shake their heads at the resiliency of Bush's brazenly duplicitous, widely criticized presidency. The filmmaker Michael Moore raged at Bush as a "fictitious president" at the Academy Awards and, in his documentary *Fahrenheit 9/11*, sought to expose the Bush family's deep ties to Islamist Saudi Arabia. The historian Neal Gabler developed a more nuanced appreciation of the administration's fictitiousness, concluding that its success was only due to its full absorption of the Hollywood mythologizing of Ronald Reagan. Since Reagan, Gabler argued, "conservatism has become a Hollywood movie, liberalism has become literature. Like the movie blockbusters, contemporary conservatives centralize action, extol the power of the individual to bend the world to his or her will, demonize enemies . . . , operate from an absolute confidence in the hero's rightness while treating opposition to it as a form of treason, and promise the comforting catharsis of eventual victory that confirms everything that has gone before." Introspective liberals, by contrast, had forgotten the narrative skill and exuberance of FDR and JFK, and like novelists they now "centralize thought and deliberation rather than action, fasten on human interconnectedness and the inability of any one individual (or nation) to command events, attempt to understand the complexity of life, . . . [are] wary [of] absolute certainties, and promise no final victories." Gabler advised Democrats that "it's time to go back to making movies."[38]

Yet in any era, making movies—either literally or in Gabler's sense, that of constructing compelling political narratives—was difficult to do. It was especially challenging in the 2000s, when the power of the movie narrative in American culture began to wane in curious ways. The conservative "Hollywood movie" Gabler divined was largely a product of the past. Its *Top Gun* aspects aside, even at the height of Bush's cinematic image in 2003, the heroic figure celebrated by conservatives was a heavily nostalgic one, derived from characteristics found in decades-old movies. Stylistically, the journalist Bill Keller noted, Bush looked backward, but rather than emulating his own father, he aspired to be "Reagan's son," a ranch-owning, plainspeaking champion of capitalism and democracy for a new generation.[39]

For the American audience in the 9/11 era, though, such a traditional leading man had lost much of his traditional symbolic power. For half a century television had emulated the movies in producing elaborate fictional features and had served as a training ground for future film stars. In the late 1990s, though, the broadcast networks dropped many series and curtailed the making of made-for-TV features and miniseries in an effort to cut costs. Inspired by British successes, US networks turned to "reality" programming, which featured non-actors in largely unscripted situations. This was done in part to save money, but reality TV also betrayed programmers' growing realization that their medium was not well suited to the mythologizing, high-concept plotting found in theatrical films. As politicians had long realized and regretted, TV cut people down to size, mercilessly exposing their tics and foibles. Shows such as *Survivor*, *The Bachelor*, and *Big Brother* depicted people failing to impress each other or to overcome their weaknesses. Even *American Idol*, which annually anointed a star of the future, gained high ratings in its early rounds by displaying the judges' ritualistic humiliation of the least talented aspirants. In a natural extension of the culture of narcissism, viewers increasingly used television to watch people like themselves becoming famous on the basis of their mediocrity, pettiness, and vulgarity. Some of these resoundingly average folk—Jon and Kate Gosselin, the Kardashian sisters, and the cast of *Jersey Shore*—became the new television stars, acquiring agents, gaining endorsement contracts, and becoming the subjects of regular coverage in celebrity magazines and tabloids.[40]

Meanwhile, theatrical films lost some of the simplistic heroic quality that had predominated during the high-concept heyday of the 1980s and 1990s. Movie screens and large-screen home theaters continued to offer platforms for outsized film personas, but performers and viewers gravitated more often to theatrical depictions of flaws and vulnerability. Traditional male box office leads such as Tom Cruise and Leonardo DiCaprio now regularly took on somber and conflicted roles that contrasted sharply with their earlier, sunnier star turns. Other leading men, such as Brad Pitt and the versatile

Johnny Depp, gravitated more often to character-type roles, transforming the dramatic lead into a farcical or quirky persona. As the critics Manohla Dargis and A. O. Scott noted in 2011, "The golden age of Hollywood may have passed, but these are boom times for great character actors." They noted that some of these actors, ironically, also found comfortable niches on the handful of cable TV channels that continued to produce fiction films and series. "On the big screen and the small, in movies and in television, beautiful sad sacks like Paul Giamatti, Bryan Cranston and Steve Buscemi are running away with some of the best roles and lines going." Scott notes that "television has eroded movies' monopoly on talent and prestige. We have more kinds of celebrities than we used to, and also more platforms for actors who want creative challenges and a measure of artistic control as well."[41] Curiously, it might be said that these actors were embracing the introspection and subtlety of literature that Neal Gabler, in his classification of contemporary political thought, associated with liberalism.

The most reliable male box office attractions now were comic actors (and television graduates) such as Adam Sandler, Jim Carrey, and Will Ferrell, who in their roles seemed ignorant of old-fashioned masculinity and trapped in boyish forms of arrested development. (This persona evoked the fun-loving side of George W. Bush, who was a fan of such films.)[42] The highly "bankable" Will Smith was a versatile actor, and notable for being an African-American star, but like that of Sandler and the others, his popular persona continued to be rooted in his early comic roles (as well as hip-hop music). As in the studio era, some male stars seemed to have achieved fame almost accidentally, but now their success illustrated the quirks and happenstance that seemed to dominate contemporary Hollywood. The young actor Shia LaBeouf, who gained fame in the *Transformers* action movies, confessed that he did not "understand what it is I do that people want. I don't know what an actor does. I have no credentials. I don't know what I'm doing. To my mind, talent doesn't really exist. Talent is like a card player's luck. . . . I think acting is a con game."[43]

Perhaps the most traditional male lead actor of the decade was George Clooney, who wore his mantle in a politically revealing way. After an early flirtation with camp as the star of the disastrous *Batman and Robin* (1997), Clooney cultivated restraint in both his dramatic and his comic roles. While

his characters were often also emotionally conflicted, they moved authori-
tatively across the screen and usually commanded admiration from those
around them (especially lead female characters). The critic Terrence Rafferty
considered Clooney to be the best modern exemplar of "movie-star performing," "a peculiar, poorly understood subset of the art of acting [that]
relies on a certain constancy of personality, on the ability to seem at all times
as if you were simply playing yourself and to give the audience the illusion
that they, somehow, know you—you the person, not just you the character."
Off the screen, Clooney's comfort in tuxedos, strolling down public red
carpets, helped to revive the male tradition of Hollywood glamour. To
match this look, Clooney shed an early reputation for callous abrasiveness
to recast himself as a sober humanitarian, using his celebrity to draw the
world's attention to the suffering millions in Sudan's Darfur region. As
a result of this, some liberals encouraged the actor to emulate his father,
the journalist Nick Clooney, who had run for Congress in 2004. Clooney
rejected such entreaties: "I didn't live my life in the right way for politics,
you know. I fucked too many chicks and did too many drugs, and that's the
truth."[44]

Partly as a result of the new brittle moodiness of most male lead actors,
by the 2000s it became less certain that screen stardom might ease an actor's
path to political leadership. In 1987 Jesse "The Body" Ventura and Arnold
Schwarzenegger had co-starred in a successful action film, *Predator,* as soldiers of fortune in a jungle battling an elusive alien monster. More than a
decade later, Ventura and Schwarzenegger each were elected governor of a
state. Each, though, found his celebrity to be of little help in overcoming
political challenges. Ventura, a professional wrestler turned actor, was the
surprise winner of a three-way battle for governor of Minnesota in 1998. He
thus became the highest-ranking candidate of the Reform Party, Ross
Perot's short-lived organization, ever to win office. Ventura entered office
unprepared, and even in a time of prosperity he found his duties to be vexing. Within two years he began moonlighting as a football broadcaster, and
he did not seek reelection.[45]

Arnold Schwarzenegger's odyssey was far more consequential—it is, indeed, one of the major episodes in the history of Hollywood's interaction with
US politics—but, in the end, his failure was more complete than Ventura's.

Schwarzenegger was not just a well-known actor; by the 1990s he was the most popular movie star in the world, noted for his muscular presence in violent action films, which he leavened with touches of humor. (One of his rare missteps was to play George Clooney's antagonist, Mr. Freeze, in *Batman and Robin*.) His rise to fame was a colorful recapitulation of many past stories of immigrant success in Hollywood. Schwarzenegger grew up obscure and unhappy in a lonely corner of Austria, but he worked with weights and took anabolic steroids to develop a massive physique. Billed as "the Styrian Oak," he moved to America, won Mr. Universe titles, and even managed to earn a college degree. Charismatic despite his heavy accent and bulging form, Schwarzenegger kept enlarging his goals, and in the early 1980s he achieved action-movie stardom. He then turned his sights to politics. The actor made appearances for Republican candidates, befriending President George H. W. Bush, but he also married into the Kennedy family, winning the hand of the broadcaster Maria Shriver. After his marriage Schwarzenegger remained an inveterate womanizer, and rumors of continued steroid use persisted (though he denied these charges), but as he aged and his box office allure began to fade, he plotted a run for office with characteristic common sense and daring. The recall election of the unpopular California governor Gray Davis in 2003 gave Schwarzenegger a perfect opportunity. After mounting a well-organized campaign, he easily finished first in the crowded race to choose Davis's successor.

His foreign birth precluded an eventual run for the White House, but otherwise Schwarzenegger's breathtaking rise resembled that of his hero, Ronald Reagan. Like Reagan, as governor of the largest state he faced numerous crises, but his fate in office was less pleasant than his predecessor's. Reagan had confronted stormy cultural upheavals in the 1960s and 1970s, but he did not attempt to reform the fundamental workings of California's state government. By contrast, Schwarzenegger—a far more successful film star than Reagan had ever been—swaggered in his new job, cigar in mouth, happily adopting the persona of the "Governator" and resorting to weight-room trash talk, dismissing Democratic legislators as "girlie men." Facing enormous budget deficits, he sought constitutional reforms and massive program cuts.

Repeatedly, though, Schwarzenegger found that even a flamboyant "people's governor" could not overcome entrenched interests in both parties and in the capitol's army of lobbyists. As he later admitted, "The bottom line is, even me as a celebrity governor—even with that, I can't penetrate through certain things." In Karl Rove's judgment, Schwarzenegger committed the cardinal error of not being clear and consistent, instead shifting his ideology to align himself with fickle popular opinion. In 2007 a recession set in, California's budget deficit worsened, and the governor became deeply unpopular. Beyond personal bravado and a willingness to listen to all sides, Schwarzenegger brought few cultivated skills to the job of governing, and in the end suffering citizens found little to admire. His successor, Democrat Jerry Brown, had also succeeded Ronald Reagan as governor in 1975. Brown then had been a rather flamboyant young man who dated pop singers and made quixotic runs for the presidency. Now he was in his seventies, a dutiful veteran of many elected positions and a candidate who deliberately lowered the public's expectations, pushing for the painful budget choices that his predecessor had avoided. In the process he became the anti-Schwarzenegger: a humble public servant in the old republican mold.[46]

Meanwhile, on the national scene, the chief executive found his image irreparably tarnished. George W. Bush's lack of involvement in guiding his administration led to disaster early in his second term. In August 2005 Hurricane Katrina and the resulting floods devastated New Orleans, in what was likely the first occasion since the Civil War on which a US president might be blamed for the destruction of a major American city. The almost non-existent federal response reflected the disinterest of Bush and his top aides in the crisis and in the living conditions of urban minority groups, as well as their earlier gutting of domestic preparedness programs. The president's claim to be a "compassionate conservative" could never be taken seriously after Katrina. Bob DeServi's usual blazing Musco lights, deployed for the speech Bush gave in New Orleans during his eventual visit to the region, now only served to illuminate Bush's disconnection from the grim reality surrounding him. More generally, within his administration personal tensions between top advisers, especially regarding foreign policy, now led them to argue openly. Bush's inability to quell internecine staff fights had serious consequences, as Dick Cheney, Condoleezza Rice (the new secretary of state), and Donald Rumsfeld fell into steady disagreement. Damning reminiscences by former staff members began to appear. Former press secretary Scott McClellan wrote that Bush was "a leader unable to acknowledge that he got it wrong, and unwilling to grow in office by learning from his mistakes," a man with a "fear of appearing weak." "As far as Bush and his advisers (especially Karl Rove) were concerned," McClellan argues, "being open and forthright in such circumstances was a recipe for trouble."[47]

Bush's sole successes in his second term were the well-designed "troop surge" in Iraq and his AIDS initiative in Africa, which may have saved millions of lives. But the image making machinery had broken down. In his memoirs, Rove significantly does not even mention the AIDS effort, likely because it was of little interest to US conservative voters. After barely avoiding indictment in the Valerie Plame scandal, Rove left the White House, and in its last two years the administration's message and imagery drifted. The president went through the motions, but the cinematic glory of the early years could not be regained. Even if his remaining major speeches had received glossy and elaborate production, they could not have hidden the fact that Bush's high concept, the war on terror, had been tarnished. High deficit spending, corrupt defense contracting, and abuses of executive power increased public disapproval, even among conservatives. Manufactured Hollywood-style presidential image making might be an extra benefit in times of crisis leadership, but it could not obscure the hard realities witnessed and felt by the public. The growing retrospective disapproval of Bush gives the lie to claims that citizens want only to be entertained or cannot discern reality from make-believe. As before, they struggled to reconcile hard realities with their dreams of an easy and fulfilling life, but they could no longer maintain any illusions.

———

Bush's final crisis, the recession and Wall Street crash of autumn 2008, ensured the election of Democratic senator Barack Obama as his successor. Obama's unlikely rise on the one hand shows a resurgence of the liberal/charismatic tradition of cinematic-style leadership, but it was also a unique instance of audacious individual image making on the political stage.

For most of his early life, Obama's building of his own image seemed to have little or nothing to do with self-preparation for the presidency. The lackadaisical young George W. Bush was passively exposed to a kind of training for his future position, through the constant example of his politician father. The son was deeply ambivalent about following this example, but he kept returning to it as a model, and eventually succumbed to the blandishments of Karl Rove and others to run for office.

Barack Obama had no comparable model before him. His father, a visiting graduate student from Kenya, had left his white American wife and their infant son in Hawaii so that he could attend Harvard University. The senior Barack Obama soon abandoned his quest for a Harvard doctorate in economics and returned to Kenya, divorcing Barack Jr.'s mother in the process. He would see his son only once again, during a brief visit. The elder Obama aspired to reform Kenya's government, but the corrupt and violent regime then in charge excluded him from influence. An alcoholic and an erratic driver, he was killed in Nairobi in 1982 when he drove his speeding car into a tree. Barack Senior plainly had provided his son with no blueprint for American political advancement. His mother, Ann Dunham, who soon remarried an Indonesian man and moved with her son to Jakarta, was an inquisitive anthropologist-in-training who inspired her son to appreciate the world's diversity and to excel in school. But young "Barry" enjoyed almost none of the benefits of many earlier presidents-to-be: a family political tradition, powerful connections, wealth, and Man on Horseback good looks that might catch the eye of campaign entrepreneurs. Like other Horatio Alger figures in presidential history such as Lincoln, Hoover, and Nixon, Obama would have to cobble together the building blocks of his own success story.

Furthermore, he was of mixed race. As he reports in his memoir *Dreams from My Father,* during his lonely time at a prep school in Honolulu, when he lived with his mother's parents, Obama gravitated toward an African-American personal identity. His love for playing basketball, and the male friendships it encouraged, helped to solidify this identity. As a college student in Los Angeles and New York City, and especially afterward, when he began to work as a community organizer in Chicago, he labored to be accepted in established black communities. "If I had come to understand myself as a black American, and was understood as such," he recalled, "that understanding remained unanchored to place. What I needed was a community, I realized. . . . A place where I could put down stakes and test my commitments."[48]

As his memoir barely notes, though, at Harvard Law School (where he excelled and became the first African-American president of the law review) and in Chicago, Obama came into contact with influential and admiring white members of the power structure. Academically gifted, smiling and glib yet also serious and articulate, Obama had mastered what one of his professors called "the cheerful impersonal friendliness—the middle distance— that marks American sociability." He gained as mentors the Harvard law professor Laurence Tribe and the Chicago political figures Newton Minow and Abner Mikva. *Dreams from My Father* ends with Obama's embrace of his father's extended family and Luo tribal culture during a five-week trip to Kenya in 1988. Obama, however, apparently relegated this homecoming to his psychic background in the next decade, as he now worked to launch a successful political career in multiracial America. As Obama's friend Cassandra Butts put it, "as a biracial person, he has had to come to an understanding of the two worlds he's lived in. . . . His role is as an interpreter, in explaining one side to the other."[49]

Like other American kids of his generation, Obama (born in 1961) was raised on a diet of network television, and he also saw his share of movies. Children of the late Baby Boom, though, shared little of the naïve fascination with screen and video entertainment that their parents, or even their older siblings, might have experienced. ("I've always felt a curious relationship to the sixties," Obama has written.)[50] "Generation X," born in the 1960s, was saturated by large and redundant amounts of mass media imagery, and after the social and political disappointments of the Watergate era, the connection between movie dreams and real-world improvement seemed tenuous. They grew up noting that films in the 1970s were critical of both society and Hollywood genre formulas, while movies in later decades tended to be slick, cynical, overblown renditions of high concepts. In reaction, the independent film movement rejected studio practices and nurtured a quirky and brittle new generation of actors. In politics, while the old movie imagery could still sway a conservative audience, as the Bush administration's image makers proved, it held little attraction for introspective younger students of society such as Barack Obama.

At least that is the impression one receives from *Dreams from My Father*. Obama makes no mention of the possible impact of his charisma on others. Biographer David Remnick, though, clearly shows that he struck many people as a uniquely attractive political figure. Obama's special ability to motivate listeners was barely perceptible in the 1980s, but the African-American oratorical tradition inspired him to craft his speaking into an effective asset a decade later, when he entered politics. A Harvard classmate found Obama to be professorial but also personally magnetic, "the most impressive person [I] had ever met in [my] life," while a professor recalled that "he seemed so centered that, in combination with his evident intelligence, I just wanted to buy stock in him. I knew the capital gains would be enormous." Abner Mikva, a veteran of Illinois politics, considered him "the most talented politician in fifty years." Obama himself later would admit, simply, "I have a gift." In his first races, though, Obama struggled to persuade African-American voters in South Chicago that he was one of them, that he understood their problems. He won their support in 1996 for a seat in the state senate, but he did not get it four years later, when he ran for the US House. Almost subliminally he learned to speak in the rhythms of the South Side, and even walk in "an adaptation of a strut that comes from the street," as his nemesis in the House race, Congressman (and former Black Panther) Bobby Rush, recalled.[51]

His loss to Rush in the Democratic primary for the House seat, coupled with his dislike of legislative duties in Springfield, compelled Obama to reexamine his influences and resources and reinvent himself once again. As Rush put it, "you cannot deny Obama's brilliance, his disciplined approach. He is a very political guy, very calculating." After he lost the race for Congress, Obama worked harder in the state senate, softened his professorial demeanor, and toured farms and small towns. He was surprised to find that rural white Illinoisans often seemed to enjoy his company. Post-9/11 events then provided Obama with an opportunity. At a rally in Chicago in 2002 against the impending war in Iraq, he gave a terse, carefully rehearsed denunciation of the Bush administration's policies that earned him national headlines. As his acquaintance William Ayers (a former 1960s radical) recalled, "I remember Obama's speech vividly because it was all done in the cadence of the black church. 'I'm not against all wars, just a foolish war. . . .' That's so Obama: smart, unifying, and very moderate."[52]

Obama's years of networking and self-reinvention paid off. His victory in the 2004 US Senate primary in Illinois was in part due to luck, as his main opponents fell victim to scandals, but his talents were on display as well. Presidential nominee John Kerry met Obama then and was moved to remark, "this guy is going to be on a national ticket someday." Kerry picked him to be the keynote speaker at the Democratic National Convention. "A super-star is born," a Chicago columnist exulted after the speech, echoing the general reaction of moderate and liberal listeners.[53] His designated Republican opponent also fell to scandal, and Obama coasted to victory in November. Presidential rumors were already rife.

Obama's basic appeal lay neither in the traditional heroic profile favored by conservatives nor in the image of the empathetic public servant typified on the left by Bill Clinton. In the dichotomy proposed by Neal Gabler in 2004, it seemed as if the senator-elect had maintained his faith in a liberal's literary form of introspection, thoughtfully parsing ideological, racial, and social divisions in his speeches and writings. The heart of his convention keynote address was a critique of the notion that the United States was divided into conservative "red" and liberal "blue" halves. Four years later, during his presidential campaign, the novelist Claire Messud noted that "seen up close, the attraction of Barack Obama as a candidate has less to do with the cut of his suits or the fact that he's championed by hip rock singers than with an almost geeky earnestness, a decency and sobriety that he projects when speaking to a crowd. A large part of his mystique lies in his insistence on his message, and on the complexity of that message; and in his old-fashioned, almost stern will to cut the flim-flam."[54] The candidate was given a nickname by his staff that, in the annals of presidential campaigns, was uniquely antitheatrical: No-Drama Obama. Nevertheless, as biographers such as Remnick have shown, Obama had also learned to sweeten his thoughtful and analytical speaking with smiles, good listening, and a relatively easygoing manner.

As a US senator, Obama worked diligently on some foreign policy and domestic issues, but he disliked being a legislator in Washington as much he had in Springfield. Already possessing a lucrative book contract, he was more of a celebrity than virtually any other member of Congress, but with his limited experience, what could he do next? After characteristic deliberation and wide consultation, Obama decided to seek the Democratic presidential nomination in 2008. *The Audacity of Hope,* the book he published shortly before making his decision, was a canny, superficially modest blueprint for the campaign he now proposed to run. On the basis of a very thin political resume, but with great confidence in the political climate, the demographic and emotional makeup of the 2008 electorate, and his own intellect and speaking ability, Obama launched an audacious campaign.

His main opponent for the nomination, Hillary Rodham Clinton, was also a political celebrity and best-selling author challenging the white male dominance of the presidency. Having spent years as a highly political First Lady and a US senator, Clinton had more national experience than Obama; she had also spent the two preceding decades as a nationally known attorney and child-welfare advocate. Clinton's campaign excited many female activists and voters, particularly fellow Baby Boomers who had grown up inspired by the Women's Movement. Female governors and senators were now commonplace, and the recent ascension of Democrat Nancy Pelosi to the speakership of the House was a good portent for Clinton's effort. Many voters, though, identified Clinton with her husband's controversial presidency and felt that she had used her unelected position as First Lady to acquire power. Some liberals, furthermore, did not forgive her for voting in 2002 in support of Bush's invasion of Iraq. Behind the scenes, Clinton's top advisers fought among themselves and never agreed on a theme for the campaign. Clinton, unlike Obama, missed the Senate and came to despise the rigors of the primary campaign trail; it seemed as if her heart was not in the race. Obama's success against Clinton also illustrated how firmly the liberal charismatic tradition remained in male hands. Clinton's star power often seemed more evident to female voters, while male supporters tended merely to be respectful of her. Obama's dismissive, offhand comment in one debate—"You're likable enough, Hillary"—seemed to sum up this particular dynamic.[55]

Obama's campaign meticulously prepared for the first contest, the Iowa caucus vote in January 2008, and it won a convincing victory there. Despite his loss to Clinton days later in the New Hampshire primary, Obama's

superior national organization ensured that he would win more future contests. A bruising battle in South Carolina ended anticlimactically, with Obama
easily defeating Clinton. Almost all African-American voters now embraced
him, and as the Super Tuesday primary night in early February neared, the
full flush of "Obamamania" descended. Stephen Heine, a Republican voter
from Ohio, wrote in a *New York Times* blog during these days, "these are not
ordinary times given the momentum and psychology of the Obama band-
wagon. It certainly is impressive, but to me it seems to be morphing into a
bizarre, almost cult following of a charismatic leader. History teaches us
that we must look for more than charismatic speeches and promises." Joel
Rittenhouse, a college student from the same state, disagreed: "I just hope
that all this momentum is going to come to fruition. I hope that the change
of which Mr. Obama speaks so elegantly is real. I hope he really can offer the
opportunity for the people to take back their government. I hope this all
isn't a dream. I hope we really are the change we've been waiting for." Press
accounts played up the frenzy that greeted Obama at large gatherings in
primary states, which notably resulted in a rash of faintings. The incidents,
some observers pointed out, were common at all candidates' rallies, where
attendees often stood for hours without nourishment waiting for the candidate to appear, and they accused Obama of exploiting them by calling for
medical help and bottles of water.[56]

The epic primary battle continued throughout the spring. African-
American voters no longer questioned whether Obama was "black enough,"
but when indictments of white America by the Reverend Jeremiah Wright
of Chicago—Obama's pastor—became widely circulated, the candidate faced
the opposite charge: that he too might be a disaffected, angry black man. The
senator countered the charge effectively enough to win the majority of delegates and the presidential nomination.[57]

Barack Obama eventually won the general election against John McCain,
the Republican opponent, by a comfortable margin, scoring historic victories in battleground states. His tally of sixty-nine million votes was the largest in US electoral history. McCain, a Vietnam War hero a quarter-century
Obama's senior, had sought to mock his opponent's fame, especially after
Obama made a short summer trip to Europe and spoke before enormous
and adulatory crowds. A McCain ad denigrated him as "the world's biggest

celebrity," and the Arizonan privately complained that the news media had preordained his opponent's victory by making him the symbol of America's multiracial future. As in his elections to the Illinois and US senates, Obama benefited from lucky breaks. McCain's running mate, Governor Sarah Palin of Alaska, had first helped to narrow the race with her own youthful, charismatic presence, but she soon embarrassed the ticket by displaying a lack of preparation for the vice presidency. The Wall Street crash in September further discredited the Bush administration and burdened McCain with another major disadvantage. Obama basked in joyous celebrations on election night and inauguration day and took legitimate pride in surmounting historic racial barriers, but in the end it had been his opponent's errors and bad fortune, not the aura of his own special charisma, that had decided the election in his favor.

Nevertheless, in the first year of his presidency, elements of that aura persisted. Obama treated Hollywood with a studied reticence. The television star Oprah Winfrey, a racial pioneer in her own right, had campaigned enthusiastically for Obama, but he never greeted her support with any real amazement or relish. Such mild-mannered hauteur only seemed to make show people value him more, as if he had put himself above other politicians who craved to be associated with famous actors. Thus Sean Penn, winning an Oscar in 2009 for his portrayal of the pathbreaking gay politician Harvey Milk, accepted the award by praising "a country that is willing to elect an elegant man president." The young Indian American actor Kalpen Modi (billed in movies as Kal Penn) temporarily abandoned his career to work in the Obama White House's Office of Public Engagement (like the communications office, an invention of the Nixon administration). Modi assisted in the administration's intensive Internet operation, which posted online numerous short films that were designed to land at the top of "Obama" search hits on YouTube and Google. Circumventing TV news organizations, Obama's team "produc[ed] and distribut[ed] more video (by far) than any past administration."[58]

Obama's staff, like those of earlier presidents, exploited every available tool to try to shape the flow of daily news. In the process they repeated some of the disturbing fictionalizing of the preceding administration. As Dana Milbank of the *Washington Post* noted, Obama's first televised afternoon news conference featured a series of easy and flattering questions by obscure journalists who, it turned out, had been invited and prompted by the White House staff. "Yesterday wasn't so much a news conference as it was a taping of a new daytime drama, 'The Obama Show,'" Milbank wrote. "This is Barack Obama, and these are the Days of Our Lives. . . . Missed yesterday's show? Don't worry: On Wednesday, ABC News will be broadcasting 'Good Morning America' from the South Lawn (guest stars: the president and first lady), 'World News Tonight' from the Blue Room, and a prime-time feature with Obama from the East Room." Perhaps inevitably, Obama became the first chief executive to land on *Forbes* magazine's "Celebrity Power 100" list, in forty-ninth place. "Obama is hands-down the most famous person in the world," *Forbes* claimed. "His historic presidential run helped him sell more than a million copies of his books; he landed on many magazine covers. There is a real interest in him as a president, a family man, a celebrity."[59] When the Nobel Peace Prize committee named Obama as the recipient in late 2009, it was in fact celebrating his global appeal as a potential force for peace in the near future, since he had accomplished very little in this regard to date.

By this time, though, persistent conservative hostility to Obama's economic stimulus plan and proposed universal health insurance, as well as general fears about the weak economy and the continuing war in Afghanistan, eclipsed his glowing mass media image. A year into his presidency he faced the outright hatred and veiled racism of a resurgent right wing, as well as dismay from progressives who lamented his tolerance of persistent financial skullduggery on Wall Street and his continuation of the war. In the face of this opposition and a persistent economic recession, Obama may perceive the need to reinvent himself further as an African-American public servant with a vision for the nation. Claire Messud's perception in 2008 remained relevant: "Obama, arisen at breakneck speed from the common mass, faces the task of creating his own authority, of convincing voters of his forcefulness simply by showing that, as his team's chant would have it, 'Yes, We Can.' To create his charismatic authority, Obama has had to work a storyteller's magic, making of his peculiar biography an iconic narrative."[60] Like critics of earlier presidents, though, others perceived even Obama's image making efforts as insufficient. The Canadian columnist Rex Murphy complained that Obama's "set speeches have a peculiar detached quality about them, a touch of the professional actor's proud ability to find all the right tones and gestures regardless of the quality or content of a given script. They don't so much convince as impress. They beguile rather than reveal. They are dazzlingly—it's almost a paradox—competent."[61]

———

At this writing, Barack Obama remains the antithesis of George W. Bush in his approach to the presidency, as a candidate, an individual, and an executive. Still, like Bush, he struggles with the office's limitations and the inability of his image making to overpower difficult conditions and implacable opposition. Both recent presidents illustrate a recurring fact in US history: presidential performance in the Hollywood style can entertain and enlighten, but it cannot provide the last measure of power that can accomplish great things for the American people.

CONCLUSION

In the afternoon of May 1, 2011, top military and diplomatic officials, including the vice president and the secretary of state, joined President Barack Obama in the White House Situation Room, beneath the West Wing. The staff brought beverages and sandwiches to the twenty leading policymakers, who huddled at one end of the cramped room to watch a live video feed on a television monitor. The image came from a computer-operated spy camera mounted on a pilotless drone, circling 15,000 feet above Abbottabad, Pakistan. Shrouded by a moonless night, twenty-two Navy SEALs had traveled from the US base in Jalalabad, Afghanistan, to a walled-off mansion in Abbottabad. Years of intelligence work revealed that the building was most likely the hideout of Osama bin Laden, the instigator of the 9/11 attacks and the world's most wanted outlaw. Neptune's Spear, as the operation was code-named, aimed to locate and to kill Bin Laden.

Obama, Joseph Biden, Hillary Rodham Clinton, and the others squinted at the infrared video images and listened as sporadic audio communication from the SEALs provided narration. The drone's images provided a distant bird's-eye view, and contrary to early news reports, the SEALs did not wear helmet-mounted cameras that might have provided viewers with a perspective from the ground. Disaster seemed imminent when one of the two helicopters carrying the SEALs toppled in the building's courtyard and crippled its propeller blades. "There was a time period of almost twenty to twenty-five minutes where we really didn't know just exactly what was going on," CIA director Leon Panetta later recalled. The accident required the crew to destroy the damaged helicopter to thwart looters and the Pakistani government—an uneasy ally of the US, filled with Al Qaeda sympathizers, which had not been told of the raid—but none of the SEALs was injured, and the mission proceeded according to plan. In the next few minutes, the troops killed a guard and entered the house. A contingent of SEALs located Bin Laden, unarmed, in the private suite on the top floor. "For God and country—Geronimo," one SEAL shouted, and the contingent killed Bin Laden with two rifle shots. "Geronimo E.K.I.A."—enemy killed in action—a soldier then reported, indicating the success of the mission. The group at the White House breathed freely and said prayers; "we got him," Obama said quietly. In the next hour, a rescue helicopter helped the remaining original aircraft evacuate the SEALs. They took with them Bin Laden's body, destined for a secret burial at sea later that night, as well as computer data found in his rooms.

As the journalist Nicholas Schmidle later reported, news of the helicopter's crash brought the tensest moment in the Situation Room. A special-operations officer told Schmidle that "eternity is defined as the time between when you see something go awry and that first voice report." The officials who had gathered at the White House similarly "viewed the aerial footage and waited anxiously to hear a military communication." Inevitably, one of the leading officials who spoke off the record with Schmidle—Clinton, perhaps, or Biden, or even Obama—"compared the experience to watching 'the climax of a movie.'"[1]

Contemporary Americans would register little surprise in response to this last statement. Like many aspects of the contemporary presidency, the capture of Bin Laden has been filtered through our long exposure to motion pictures. Crisis monitoring via remote satellite feed was dramatized in 1990s action movies such as *Patriot Games* and *Air Force One*. The scene in the Situation Room that day was similar to a movie screening in a well-appointed home theater, albeit with inferior picture quality. The powerful group in the room huddled together in casual clothing and nervously consumed snacks and drinks as they watched the drama unfold. As with the bombings of Al Qaeda sites ordered by Bill Clinton in 1998 (the *Wag the Dog* incident), the rescue of Private Jessica Lynch in Iraq, and numerous other recent military actions, the mission presented a narrative fraught with

suspense and an uncertain outcome. Enhanced video and satellite technology heightened the experience by providing live sound and pictures to the
White House (as well as CIA headquarters in Langley, Virginia, and command centers in the Pentagon and Islamabad, Pakistan). One military officer
in charge of planning the mission had survived the notorious "Black Hawk
Down" incident in Mogadishu, Somalia, in 1993, when two US helicopters
were shot down during a mission to capture advisers to a Somali warlord,
and a mob of residents and guerrilla soldiers killed and desecrated the bodies of American servicemen. The incident had been depicted in a big-budget
movie made in 2001 by the stylish director Ridley Scott. *Black Hawk Down*'s
jittery camera work, jarring violence, and grimy urban-desert setting in turn
molded the look of military narrative simulations, created for video game
platforms, which in the 2000s transformed action movies into interactive
living-room entertainment. The veteran of Somalia, along with other planners of the Bin Laden mission, had feared a repeat of the Black Hawk Down
incident, which was now enshrined in American popular culture.

In addition, as George W. Bush had done beginning in 2001, the planners
of Neptune's Spear laid the template of the western movie over the US's
military adventures on the dusty high plains of South Central Asia. "Before
the mission commenced," Schmidle writes, "the SEALs had created a check-
list of code words that had a Native American theme. Each code word represented a different stage of the mission: leaving Jalalabad, entering Pakistan,
approaching the compound, and so on. 'Geronimo' was to signify that bin
Laden had been found." That evening Barack Obama, ever the temperate
leader, made a happy yet terse announcement of the mission's success from
the White House. Within minutes of his announcement, far less restrained
demonstrations erupted across the United States, in which some individuals
exulted as if they had just triumphed in a video game. Inebriated young men
at a few universities got carried away with their celebrations and rioted,
destroying campus property and getting themselves arrested. Within weeks,
reports indicated that at least three Hollywood producers were planning
cinematic re-creations of Operation Neptune's Spear.[2]

———

This book has suggested that in moments such as the capture of Bin Laden, motion pictures mediated Americans' perception of real-life events and helped them to perceive these events as drama and as entertainment. As part of this mediation, movies transformed political leaders into leading men, figures who could fulfill voters' wishes and summon some of the charisma displayed by the best male film stars. The widely circulated image of the group in the Situation Room that day, taken by White House photographer Pete Souza, showed Obama hunched over in expectation among his circle of advisers. The president's characteristically cool appearance before the cameras that evening, as he announced the death of Bin Laden, encapsulated the image of leadership that his staff wanted to convey. Since the identity of the SEALs taking part in the mission remained secret, the president assumed his expected place in the spotlight. Ray Price's words in his memo for the Nixon campaign in 1967, labeling the chief executive as "a combination of leading man, God, father, hero, . . . and just a touch of the avenging Furies thrown in," has rarely seemed as applicable as in this instance.

Movies have played a crucial role in updating techniques that leaders in the West—assisted by aides and complicit subjects—have employed for millennia to glorify and memorialize themselves and to fortify their rule against political opposition. In the proudly republican new United States, George Washington and his supporters wove the mystique of monarchy into his public self-presentation as the first chief executive. Although later presidents, especially Thomas Jefferson and Andrew Jackson, democratized the etiquette of the office, its grandeur lived on in the columns and state rooms of the White House and stirred to life when enterprising occupants (such as Jackson and Lincoln) utilized their electoral mandates powerfully to transform the nation. In the self-consciously democratic times beginning in the 1830s, the less lofty grandeur of modern celebrity, and of fame on the popular stage, also proved attractive to both voters and leaders. Presidents as a result became enamored of actors' techniques of audience persuasion and were drawn into social acquaintance with some leading performers. Lincoln's fatal shooting by John Wilkes Booth in Ford's Theater, Grover Cleveland's hobnobbing with Edwin Booth at the Players Club, and Woodrow Wilson's private mimicking of vaudeville acts all illustrated this trend, which joined a theatrically conscious presidential image to the classical, monumental pose that had been originated by Washington and John Adams. By the 1920s the culture of fame had produced its own professional class—public relations experts—whose cynicism about the mass public and its alleged gullibility steadily grew into a maxim of campaign strategy.

Motion pictures rose to extraordinary early heights in the 1920s through the same fame-building techniques that originated in ancient politics, were exploited by the theater business, and were now managed by PR and advertising professionals. But the movies provided something powerful and new: an immediate apparent realism, a lens that seemed to illuminate the zenith (as well as the nadir) of the human soul. Charismatic stars, propelled by Hollywood narrative strategies, suddenly possessed the power to teach Americans how to move, talk, and translate their thoughts into action. A fan such as Franklin Roosevelt, motivated strongly by his need to masquerade as a leader who could stand and march at the head of the nation, learned crucial performing tips from movies, and in gratitude he enhanced the Oval Office's social and political ties to Hollywood. Like their peers, presidents of the generation that followed FDR, especially John Kennedy and Richard Nixon, were socialized from a young age by the movies.

The 1960s were central to the cinematic presidential image. Kennedy and Nixon applied the techniques and general mentality of Hollywood make-believe to their political careers, with wildly contrasting results. Each posed himself carefully in the White House and produced spectacles made for television. TV fixed a new image of the president as a man of the white middle class, capable of both casual familiarity and commanding toughness. Unlike their elder predecessors, Truman and Eisenhower, who struggled with the petty challenges of appearing on TV, presidents in the 1960s made their on-the-air effectiveness a major priority. By the time of the administrations of Ronald Reagan, the quintessential acting president, and Bill Clinton, the quintessential First Fan, the public had come to expect that the president would speak in quips, appear in photo opportunities, and generally conduct his work with narrative panache—in short, would give the kind of unified "performance" that Hollywood leading men had provided for decades, on and off the movie set. After 2001 the discredited cosmetics of George W. Bush's war on terror made these publicity techniques ring hollow and lose their persuasive force among voters—an outcome that inspired a backlash that elected a very different kind of leading man in 2008. Barack Obama benefited from a unique personal charisma that blended African-American urban style, a professorial demeanor, and cautious rhetoric. While I have argued here that Obama's appeal may signal a decline in the traditional cinematic presidential image, time may instead reveal it to be but a new version of that image, more subtle and culturally diversified than any of the variations that preceded it.

In this book, space and time have permitted us to explore only the most notable confluences of America's public and fantasy lives. I have attempted to sketch the contours of the realm of cultural perception that resulted. In this realm, leading men rule, and dreams and national goals merge and fictional narratives and official accounts blend into a single myth. Presidents helped to create this realm, but they were also acted upon by the evolving institutions, opinions, demographics, and technologies that shaped government and entertainment. It is my hope that *The Leading Man* will inspire further explorations of this realm.

One topic that needs much more definition is the peculiar power of movies —the qualities that differentiate them from other mass entertainment and make their impact on public life unique. As psychologists beginning with Hugo Münsterberg in the 1910s noted, the carefully constructed and artificial plotting of feature films (especially Hollywood's influential products) have encouraged us to view real life in new ways. Movies entice us with neat narrative sequences, simplified causes and effects, and an appealing emotionalism that might trump a critically rational approach to experience. This powerful influence reshaped the political perceptions of viewers, for example leading them to seek clear explanations for chaotic national events, as well as a straightforward cast of characters and transparent accountability that might clarify the tangled mess of government. As Münsterberg put it in 1916, in motion pictures "the massive outer world has lost its weight, it has been freed from space, time, and causality, and it has been clothed in the forms of our own consciousness. The mind has triumphed over matter and the pictures roll on with the ease of musical tones. It is a superb enjoyment which no other art can furnish us. No wonder that temples for the new goddess are built in every little hamlet."[3] In order to understand this "triumph" of fantasy over reality in political terms, historians must dig deeper, to explore what movies and movie stars mean to people and society.

The appeal of movies is elusive and ambiguous. It is revealing, for example, that even Hollywood studio executives barely understood why their films held such power over viewers. In the 1930s they turned for answers to the nascent field of market research and allied academic disciplines such as psychology and sociology. The studios founded the Audience Research Institute, employing such instruments of measurement as the Lazarsfeld-Stanton Program Analyzer (courtesy of Columbia University), the Cirlin Reactograph, and the Hopkins Electric Televoting Machine to test viewers' immediate reactions to films, scenes, and stars. As Leo Handel pointed out in 1950 in his survey of the Institute's work, audience studies offered provocative insights into the impact of movies. One analysis of juvenile viewers, for example, concluded that they "imitate the action of movie stars; that movies are apt to produce heightened emotions of fear, sorrow, and passion, but at the same time may produce an opposite reaction of detachment and boredom; and that movies may produce for certain children a whole new, and perhaps false, view of the world." Handel cautioned, however, that these explanations might be gravely limited. "We have no way of determining whether the differences observed [in clothing, behavior, attitudes, etc.] actually result from movie attendance or from some prior cause that itself determines moviegoing." At the very least, though, movies reinforced existing views of the world and heightened viewers' existing tastes and attitudes. Audience research during the 1940s had already appreciated the challenge of diversity, showing how male, female, juvenile, and African-American audiences reacted very differently to themes in movies. For studio executives as well as politicians, the audience was not a single mass public, but rather a kaleidoscopic moving target, full of contrasting hopes and fears.[4]

In other ways, audience studies told the studios that common attitudes united the national audience. In the late twentieth century, business researchers perceived that the majority of moviegoers sought a generalized, apolitical pleasure, what Jehoshua Eliashberg and Mohanbir S. Sawhney in 1994 called "hedonic consumption experiences." Newer audience measurement instruments—quasi-medical detection devices such as polygraphs and galvanic skin response sensors—found that movies appealed seductively to viewers, in the same way that advertising often did. These tools found their way into voter research as well. Political consultants tested focus groups with skin gauges and preference dials, seeking data on individuals' immediate reactions to the appearance and utterances of a politician. The search for common impulses and reactions among both viewers and voters is one illustration of the mating of politics and the movie industry.

———

Further investigation will confirm, I believe, that movie stars have functioned as important matchmakers in this mating process. The star's look, behavior, and role in his or her most typical kind of movie brought specificity and clarity to the vague desires shared by members of the mass audience. For centuries in the West, subjects and citizens had been conditioned to view monarchs and presidents as embodiments of both individual wishes and national identities. The tools of celebrity culture—including newspapers (later tabloids), gossip columns, fan magazines, and newsreels—reduced rulers to the status of well-known people in the arts and other endeavors. Celebrities became average people's famous acquaintances. The movie actor extended and deepened this acquaintance. He or she could present a personality more fully than any other medium had yet allowed, and viewers could spend two hours watching this personality interact with a seemingly authentic world, full of real-looking pleasures and perils. No monarch of the past could have pretended to be such a companion and confidant of the people.

The movie star's political importance may lie in his or her ability to dramatize the daily needs and wants of contemporary audience members. Through their performances on and off the screen, stars elevate these concerns to the status of public issues. Individuals in the national audience thus share notions of how their present condition ought to be changed, and how in the near future they might be happier, more successful, more loved, and more sexually attractive. As Richard Dyer, a leading cultural historian of stardom, has put it, "stars articulate what it is to be a human being in contemporary society. . . . [They] matter because they act out aspects of life that matter to us," and they "get to be stars when what they act out matters to enough people." In particular, stars "express the particular notion we hold

of the person, of the 'individual.' . . . they articulate both the promise and
the difficulty that the notion of individuality presents for all of us who live
by it." Dyer notes that the intense individuality of the star's persona nevertheless can have a wide social impact: "The private/public, individual/society
dichotomy can be embodied by stars in various ways; the emphasis can fall
at either end of the spectrum, although it more usually falls at the private,
authentic, sincere end." Gifted stars can explore important cultural concerns
in their performances. For example, "in the fifties," Dyer notes, "there were
specific ideas of what sexuality meant and it was held to matter a very great
deal; and because Marilyn Monroe acted out those specific ideas, and
because they were *felt* to matter so much, she was charismatic, a centre of
attraction who seemed to embody what was taken to be a central feature of
human existence at that time."

Like Monroe herself, the authority wielded by a movie star can be volatile
and fragile. In Dyer's view, this is due to the fact that stars are promoted by
an "aspect . . . of modern life that is . . . associated with the invasion and
destruction of the inner self and the corruptibility of public life, namely the
mass media."[5] The exploitative nature of movies might pollute the appeal
and the cultural messages projected by a star. Hollywood films, for example,
have abused their cultural authority by depicting racial minorities and idealized body types in ways that have harmed nonwhite and female moviegoers
psychologically and socially.[6]

Like films themselves, the appeal of stars is often elusive and difficult to
quantify as a social or political force. Leo Handel noted that 1940s audiences
disagreed sharply about the effect of smoking and drinking by stars in movies.
Decades later, though, as the health dangers of cigarettes and alcohol became
better known, moviemakers exploited the mixed reputations of these addic-
tive substances to achieve dramatic effect. Cigarettes in a movie, researchers
in the 1990s found, "can help create an aura of sexiness and sophistication,
for example, or convey an image of someone caught in the grip of addiction,
self-abuse, or neurosis. . . . the contradiction between what we now know
about the health effects of tobacco and the reality of continued use open up
new possibilities for character depiction. Smoking can now communicate
such personal qualities as inner dissonance or psychological inconsistency."[7]
Like voter opinion, viewers' reactions to ambiguous and contested aspects of

culture depicted in movies may be difficult for scholars to decipher. It is not always easy to discern the appeal of stars, just as it is often hard to determine why a particular citizen might vote a certain way or hold certain opinions.

Nevertheless, as *The Leading Man* on occasion shows, movies can also clearly demarcate divisions, eras, and mentalities in the American past. Since 1920, Hollywood films with contemporary settings have evolved in a rough approximation to changes in social and political conditions and controversies. Melodramas depicting the social mores of the 1920s and economic suffering during the Great Depression gave way to the war films and home-front comedies of the 1940s. Film noir explored latent social, sexual, and economic tensions in the postwar era, offering a prelude to films of the 1950s and 1960s that challenged the Production Code and depicted subversive behavior in American society. The high-concept blockbuster of the 1970s signaled a conservative reaction to such rebelliousness, initiating an era of big budgets and big profits. Independent films then offered a counter-reaction to the high-concept movie. Hollywood's films could be described as a stylized depiction of public opinion that evolved through the decades, tacking to the left and the right as the national audience's concerns shifted.

These shifts of opinion illustrated the powerful, subterranean impact of national politics on the movie business. Fundamental national currents shaped industry politics—and real politics—in Hollywood and helped to dictate the ideological content of films. The studios' antitrust battles, post-1935 labor conflicts, and use of the blacklist implicated them fully in major trends in US politics, as did the executives' and the stars' involvements in political fundraising and campaigning. As we have seen, these events and activities created structural alliances between Hollywood and Washington that persist to this day. The relationships of individual politicians with Hollywood, inevitably, have varied greatly in nature. Politicians who have been highly attuned to popular sentiments have tended to learn from Holly-wood's leading men about how to present themselves and articulate their messages. Candidates who borrow clumsily from movies risk stoking the scorn of voters who tend to question the authenticity and honesty of politi-cians. Nevertheless, these same voters might also respond most positively to public figures who can communicate smoothly in the mass media, in the manner of the skilled entertainer.

Candidates, campaigns, and administrations do their best to try to control leaders' public images, but such control is difficult to achieve. Individuals and groups, motivated by significant cultural trends that elude a national campaign's notice, might perceive a candidate's image in ways that PR advisers cannot anticipate. They mold what they believe to be positive profiles for candidates, built up along conventional lines of image making, only to see them become unexpected targets of ridicule and invective. Michael Dukakis's 1988 tank ride is a notable example.

Today the foibles of political image making continue to demonstrate that star power is as difficult to quantify in politics as it is on the silver screen. In 2010 the journalist Julia Baird detected a trend among writers and bloggers —presumably representative of a larger voter population—of characterizing female conservative politicians and political pundits in demeaning sexual terms. "There seems to be an insistent, increasingly excitable focus on the supposed hotness of Republican women in the public eye, like Sarah Palin, Michele Bachmann, Michelle Malkin, and Nikki Haley—not to mention veterans like Ann Coulter." Baird disapproves, concluding with the familiar admonition that "we need properly scrutinized candidates, not circus performers." The spate of articles in mainstream magazines with titles such as "Is Sarah Palin Porn?" cited by Baird might have been a collective reaction to a new phenomenon in conservative politics: a large group of conventionally attractive, young-looking women competing seriously for state and national office. The ogling of female Republican candidates descends in part from behavior and roles that were established by Hollywood, which since its genesis has famously exploited the sexual allure of actresses. The politicians mentioned by Baird undoubtedly received fashion and cosmetic cues from contemporary movie actresses such as Jennifer Aniston, but in an ironic and unpleasant twist, the widespread denigration of those actresses as sex objects eventually victimized politicians as well. Such volatile dynamics typify the continuing conflation of Hollywood and Washington in today's media and in voters' perceptions.[8]

———

This conflation also encourages us to explore how movies fit into the public sphere, in the daily transactions of national political life. As vehicles for charismatic stars, movies could be seen as the antithesis of rational models of political behavior. Max Weber recognized this in his writings on charismatic political leadership, which he starkly contrasted with rationalized bureaucratic government. In recent decades another German thinker, the philosopher Jürgen Habermas, has tenaciously studied and argued for the need to recover and value the rational bases of political life. Habermas is the champion of communicative rationality, advocating for a public discourse based on logical and dispassionate argument. His arguments, like Weber's, tend to deal loftily with ideal social types, but they have fueled sharp attacks by others against the alleged harm done to the public sphere by "irrational" mass entertainment. Reviving the hostility to popular culture expressed by Habermas's early mentor, Theodor W. Adorno, these critics occasionally equate the impact of Hollywood on politics with that of Joseph Goebbels's film propaganda on behalf of the Nazi regime.[9]

Such criticism deserves attention, but like American conservatives' tirades against modern popular culture, it tends to presuppose—as even Habermas does—that rational discourse once ruled politics, and that recent generations of Westerners are fallen sinners who have deserted this ideal. As Michael Schudson and others have pointed out, though, with respect to the United States it is difficult to find a past golden era in which rational speech dominated and in which irrational depictions of leaders and issues did not warp political culture. Schudson has argued that "the idea that a public sphere of rational-critical discourse flourished in the eighteenth or early nineteenth century . . . in the American instance . . . is an inadequate, if not incoherent, notion. Its empirical basis . . . seems . . . remarkably thin." In Massachusetts from 1760 to 1830, according to the historian Ronald Formisano, "apathy prevailed among citizens until they perceived a threat to their immediate interests." In the words of the historian William Gienapp, before the 1830s, when political parties utilized the mass media to excite white male voters, "few men were interested in politics, and fewer still actively participated in political affairs. Politics simply did not seem important to most Americans." Habermas himself concedes that the modern public sphere in Western Europe has in fact been the "popular public sphere," which "emerged only in competition with the literary public sphere of the late eighteenth century."[10]

On the basis of that observation, it might be suggested that in the trans-atlantic world in the late 1700s and the early 1800s, modern rational discourse arose in concert with the promotional machinery that gave rise to modern celebrity culture, in the common incubator of urban journalism.[11] This is not to suggest that tabloids and celebrity worship, past or present, should be equated with rational political argument. Further investigation might reveal, though, that the mass media that nurtured celebrities in the nineteenth and early twentieth centuries also helped to socialize average people to become more aware and more critical of governments and leaders. Suggestive evidence in this regard includes Thomas Nast's newspaper cartoons, which helped to send Tammany Hall boss William Tweed to jail; Upton Sinclair's novel *The Jungle,* which helped to launch consumer protection laws; and the movie version of *All Quiet on the Western Front,* which contributed to American isolationism in the 1930s. The debate over how Hollywood has affected the public sphere, and what that sphere consisted of before movies began to alter it, has not yet been won by champions of a lost golden age of rationality. It may be that the emotional and narrative richness of movies has enabled contemporary citizens to gain a clearer and more emotionally intelligent understanding of basic issues in the current political discourse. The distillation of these issues by politicians and their advisers into gestures, slogans, and styles that mimic Hollywood may represent a peculiar new variety of communicative rationality, not its refutation.

In the meantime, as the last chapter of this book suggests, recent developments indicate that we might be entering a post-entertainment phase in our political life. A weary and media-aware public now regularly criticizes or shuns elements of showmanship in politics. People today are perhaps more conscious than any previous generation of the ephemeral and disposable nature of news as well as entertainment. It would be difficult, though, to discern in this attitude any shift toward a new appreciation of civic virtue or a realization of Habermas's ideal of communicative rationality. Instead, it may represent voters' fundamental disillusionment with both politics and entertainment. The columnist Mark Morford noted in 2011 "how insanely fast we forget about all" news stories of the moment. "No sooner are we all aflutter, enraged and atwitter over one issue or conflict, then we shrug it off and leap onto the next Incredibly Important Thing, barely remembering what all the fuss was about in the first place. . . . All those events and spectacles we think are so imperative at the time, so mandatory to our very survival, vanish in almost an instant."[12] Such disillusion echoes other eras of deep uncertainty in US history, such as the 1880s, when farmers despaired of political culture before the advent of Populism, or the late 1940s, when Americans, shaken by World War II and the coming of the Cold War, mistrusted political speech on television, developed the cynicism that helped nurture McCarthyism, and voted in low numbers. In the most pessimistic reading of today's uncivil political discourse, rationality has fallen prey to harsh invective and strident ideological division, plagues unleashed by the Internet and cable television. Among other evidence, ugly depictions of President Obama in the blogosphere, racist and otherwise, suggest that many citizens have little faith in the communicative power of language and reason, or in the emotional unity that can be created through powerful cultural narratives such as have been found in movies. The pessimists foresee a bleak future for politics, in which there is neither rational content nor elegant style.[13]

Or, perhaps, the current bleak situation represents a trough in our political life, which will be overcome in a future cyclical rebound. In this regard one might compare the 2010s to the early 1920s, an era dominated by crude partisan caricatures and anti-intellectual voter debates, or even to the political muddle that occurred in the uneasy years of transition between the first and second party systems, in the 1810s and 1820s. Given our enormous contemporary investment in education, though, the idea that we have fallen into such a trough today, even temporarily, might itself be a cause for despair.

I also believe it is instructive to point out that the history of the cinematic presidential image has not generally been cyclical in nature. The image arose gradually beginning in the 1920s and 1930s and reached peaks in the 1960s, 1980s, and 1990s. While the cult of the Leading Man may now seem to be taking a beating, its long and robust history suggests that it is the product of persistent and significant long-term forces. Hollywood has enjoyed staying power as a shaper of American culture, and while its influence has often been attacked, movies have often brought vigor, excitement, and vivid communication to politics, relating a powerful optimism through an apparently undying faith in the happy ending. Ronald Reagan built his entire political career, rather easily, on the transmittal of that faith to the public sphere. This long tradition of optimistic, vigorous cultural narrative cannot be easily erased from politics or entertainment, and it suggests that sympathetic and gifted public leaders in the future might be able to harness the tools of cinematic vision in beneficial ways. Ronald Reagan's "morning in America" and Bill Clinton's "place called Hope" are vague notions, but they remain adaptable to any promising trend in our public life that a future president might hope to advance.

NOTES

INTRODUCTION

1. Henry R. Luce, oral history transcript, 11 November 1965, John F. Kennedy Library, 13, http://www.jfklibrary.org; Jeffrey Schmalz, "Resurgent Waterbury Prepares to Greet Candidate Reagan," *New York Times* (19 September 1984), B1; David M. Lubin, *Shooting Kennedy: JFK and the Culture of Images* (Berkeley: University of California Press, 2003), 124–25; Mary Evertz, "Charm Takes Over in Tampa," *St. Petersburg Times* (11 November 1999), http://www.sptimes.com/News/111199.

2. Seymour Hersh, "Darker Than We Want to Know" (8 January 1998), www.theatlantic.com; Richard Reeves, *President Kennedy: Profile in Power* (New York: Simon and Schuster, 1993), 291; Tony Alessandra, "Why Charisma Matters," www.frugalmarketing.com/dtb/charisma.shtml.

3. Mario Puzo, *The Last Don* (New York: Random House, 1996), 27.

4. Norman Mailer, "Superman Comes to the Supermarket," *Esquire* (November 1960), http://www.esquire.com/features. A ferocious attack on the modern notion of charisma, which is found to be antithetical to its classical religious formulation, is Philip Reiff, *Charisma: The Gift of Grace, and How It Has Been Taken Away from Us* (New York: Pantheon, 2007).

5. Grace de Monaco, oral history transcript, 19 June 1965, John F. Kennedy Library, 3, http://www.jfklibrary.org.

6. Jack Valenti, "The Unpredictable World of Politics: Lessons I Have Learned," lecture, San Marcos, Texas, 3 April 1997, http://www.txstate.edu/commonexperience/pastsitearchives/2008-2009/lbjresources.

7. Leo Braudy, *The Frenzy of Renown: Fame and Its History* (New York: Oxford University Press, 1986), esp. parts 1 and 5.

8. Fred Inglis, *A Short History of Celebrity* (Princeton, NJ: Princeton University Press, 2010), esp. chaps. 3 and 4. See also Braudy, *Frenzy of Renown,* part 5.

9. My research on Walker for a previous book helped inspire me to explore the impact on the presidency of mass entertainment. Burton W. Peretti, *Nightclub City: Politics and Amusement in Manhattan* (Philadelphia: University of Pennsylvania Press, 2007), chap. 2.

10. Ronald Brownstein, *The Power and the Glitter: The Hollywood-Washington Connection* (New York: Pantheon, 1990); Kathleen Hall Jamieson, *Packaging the Presidency: A History and Criticism of Presidential Campaign Advertising,* 3d ed. (New York: Oxford University Press, 1996); Alan Schroeder, *Celebrity in Chief: How Show Business Took Over the White House* (Boulder, CO: Westview Press, 2004).

CHAPTER 1: "THE TORMENTS OF DESIRE"

1. Michael Kammen, *A Machine That Would Go of Itself: The Constitution in American Culture* (New York: Knopf, 1986).

2. Ernst H. Kantorowicz, *The King's Two Bodies: A Study in Mediæval Political Theology* (Princeton, NJ: Princeton University Press, 1970).

3. James Thomas Flexner, *Washington: The Indispensable Man* (New York: Collins, 1976).

4. Robert H. Wiebe, *The Opening of American Society: From the Adoption of the Constitution to the Eve of Disunion* (New York: Vintage, 1985), 115; Dumas Malone, *Jefferson the President: First Term, 1801–1805* (Boston: Little, Brown, 1970), 170–175, 378–385.

5. Carl Sferrazza Anthony, *First Ladies: The Saga of the President's Wives and Their Power, 1789–1961* (New York: Morrow, 1990), parts 2 and 3.

6. Karen Halttunen, *Confidence Men and Painted Women: A Study of Middle-Class Culture in America, 1830–1870* (New Haven, CT: Yale University Press, 1983), chap. 3; Fred Inglis, *A Short History of Celebrity* (Princeton, NJ: Princeton University Press, 2010), esp. chap. 3.

7. Anthony, *First Ladies,* 126–134.

8. Daniel Walker Howe, *The Political Culture of the American Whigs* (Chicago: University of Chicago Press, 1979), 89; Abraham Lincoln, "Address to the Young Men's Lyceum of Springfield, Illinois, January 27, 1838," in Don E. Fehrenbacher, ed., *Abraham Lincoln: Speeches and Writings* (New York: Library of America, 1989), 1:34.

9. Samuel Kernell and Gary C. Jacobson, "Congress and the Presidency as News in the Nineteenth Century," *Journal of Politics* 49 (1987): 1016–1035; Sean Wilentz, *The Rise of American Democracy: Jefferson to Lincoln* (New York: Norton, 2005), esp. chaps. 9, 11, and 16; Daniel Walker Howe, *What Hath God Wrought: The Transformation of America, 1815–1848* (New York: Oxford University Press, 2007), chap. 7, 543–546.

10. See for example Mary P. Ryan, *Civic Wars: Democracy and Public Life in the American City during the Nineteenth Century* (Berkeley: University of California Press, 1998).

11. Henry Adams, *The Education of Henry Adams,* rept. ed. (Boston: Houghton-Mifflin, 1961), 266; Henry Adams, *Democracy: An American Novel,* rept. ed. (New York: Airmont, 1968), 50.

12. James Bryce, *The American Commonwealth,* 2d ed. (New York: Macmillan, 1889), chap. 8. See also Ari A. Hoogenboom, *Rutherford B. Hayes: Warrior and President* (Lawrence: University Press of Kansas, 1995) and Charles W. Calhoun, *Benjamin Harrison* (New York: Times Books, 2005).

13. William Allen White, *Masks in a Pageant* (New York: Macmillan, 1928), 155.

14. On mid-1800s fashion see Halttunen, *Confidence Men and Painted Women,* esp. chap. 3; Leo Braudy, *The Frenzy of Renown: Fame and Its History* (New York: Oxford University Press, 1986), esp. part 1.

15. Jonas Barish, *The Anti-Theatrical Prejudice* (Berkeley: University of California Press, 1981); Jay Fliegelman, *Declaring Independence: Jefferson, Natural Language, and the Culture of Performance* (Stanford, CA: Stanford University Press, 1993); Timothy Raphael, *The President Electric: Ronald Reagan and the Politics of Performance* (Ann Arbor: University of Michigan Press, 2009), 22–27.

16. Thomas A. Bogar, *American Presidents Attend the Theatre: The Playgoing Experiences of Each Chief Executive* (Jefferson, NC: McFarland, 2006), 5; Fliegelman, *Declaring Independence,* 24.

17. Bogar, *American Presidents Attend the Theatre,* 22–28, 44–49.

18. Anthony, *First Ladies,* 130–134; Bogar, *American Presidents Attend the Theatre,* 73–75.

19. Elise Kirk, *Music at the White House: A History of the American Spirit* (Urbana: University of Illinois Press, 1990), 69, 75–76, 84–85; Joseph A. Mussulman, *Music in the Cultured Generation: A Social History of Music in America, 1870–1900* (Evanston, IL: Northwestern University Press, 1971).

20. Braudy, *Frenzy of Renown,* 72–78, 151–152, 499–500; Neal Gabler, *Life, the Movie: How Entertainment Conquered Reality* (New York: Knopf, 1998), 99.

21. Arthur Schlesinger Jr., *The Age of Jackson* (Boston: Little, Brown, 1945), 51.

22. Richard J. Ellis, *Presidential Travel: The Journey from George Washington to George W. Bush* (Lawrence: University Press of Kansas, 2008), 69, also esp. chaps. 2–3; see also Fletcher M. Green, "On Tour with President Andrew Jackson," *New England Quarterly* 36 (1963): 209–228.

23. Bogar, *American Presidents Attend the Theatre,* chap. 8.

24. Francis Bicknell Carpenter, *Six Months at the White House with Abraham Lincoln: The Story of a Picture* (New York: Hurd and Houghton, 1866), 49–52, 58, 162; Michael Rogin, *Ronald Reagan, the Movie: And Other Episodes in Political Demonology* (Berkeley: University of California Press, 1988), chap. 2.

25. John Rhodehamel and Louise Taper, eds., *Right or Wrong, God Judge Me: The Writings of John Wilkes Booth* (Urbana: University of Illinois Press, 2000), 154.

26. Benjamin McArthur, *Actors and American Culture, 1880–1920,* rept. ed. (Iowa City: University of Iowa Press, 2000), 76–84.

27. Brenda Murphy, *American Realism and American Drama, 1880–1940* (New York: Cambridge University Press, 1987). On realism generally see David E. Shi, *Facing Facts: Realism in American Thought and Culture, 1850–1920* (New York: Oxford University Press, 1996).

28. Daniel Czitrom, "Underworlds and Underdogs: Big Tim Sullivan and Metropolitan Politics in New York, 1889–1913," *Journal of American History* 78 (1991): 542.

29. Czitrom, "Underworlds and Underdogs"; Burton W. Peretti, *Nightclub City: Politics and Amusement in Manhattan* (Philadelphia: University of Pennsylvania Press, 2007), chap. 2; Neal Gabler, *An Empire of Their Own: How the Jews Invented Hollywood* (New York: Crown, 1988), part 1.

30. The best recent survey is Michael McGerr, *A Fierce Discontent: The Rise and Fall of the Progressive Movement in America, 1870–1920* (New York: Oxford University Press, 2005), esp. chap. 1.

31. On Chautauqua see Charlotte Canning, "The Platform versus the Stage: The Circuit Chautauqua's Antitheatrical Theatre," *Theatre Journal* 50 (1998): 303–318, and Andrew C. Rieser, *The Chautauqua Moment: Protestants, Progressives, and the Culture of Modern Liberalism* (New York: Columbia University Press, 2003).

32. Edward Wagenknecht, *The Seven Worlds of Theodore Roosevelt,* rept. ed. (New York: Lyons, 2008), 89–90.

33. Braudy, *Frenzy of Renown,* 492; Karen Miller Russell and Carl O. Bishop, "Understanding Ivy Lee: Newspaper and Magazine Coverage of Publicity and Press Agentry, 1865–1904," *Public Relations Review* 35 (2009): 92–95.

34. Greg Goodale, "The Presidential Sound: From Orotund to Instructional Speech, 1892–1912," *Quarterly Journal of Speech* 96 (2010): 164–184; on Roosevelt and manliness, see Sarah Watts, *Rough Rider in the White House: Theodore Roosevelt and the Politics of Desire* (Chicago: University of Chicago Press, 2003), esp. 116–118.

35. Wagenknecht, *Seven Worlds of Theodore Roosevelt,* 124–127.

36. Goodale, "The Presidential Sound"; Carol Gelderman, "All the President's Words," *Wilson Quarterly* 19(2) (Spring 1995): 68–79; Robert A. Kraig, *Woodrow Wilson and the Lost World of the Oratorical Statesman* (College Station: Texas A&M University Press, 2004), 99–100; see also Mary Stuckey, "Establishing the Rhetorical Presidency through Presidential Rhetoric: Theodore Roosevelt and the Brownsville Raid," *Quarterly Journal of Speech* 92 (2006): 287–309.

37. James Bradley, *The Imperial Cruise: A Secret History of Empire and War* (New York: Little, Brown, 2009), 167–168; Anthony, *First Ladies,* chaps. 33–39.

38. Joseph P. Tumulty, *Woodrow Wilson as I Know Him* (New York: Literary Digest, 1921), chap. 4.

39. Kraig, *Woodrow Wilson and the Lost World of the Oratorical Statesman,* 4.

40. Elmer E. Cornwell Jr., "Wilson, Creel, and the Presidency," *Public Opinion Quarterly* 23 (1959): 190.

41. Elmer E. Cornwell, Jr., "Coolidge and Presidential Leadership," *Public Opinion Quarterly* 21 (1957): 265–278.

42. Larry Tye, *The Father of Spin: Edward L. Bernays and the Birth of Public Relations* (New York: Picador, 2002).

43. Edward Bernays, "Breakfast with Coolidge" typescript (1924), book file, carton 457, Edward L. Bernays Papers, Library of Congress, http://www.memory.loc.gov.

44. "Trusts 'Giants Not Ogres,'" *Boston Evening Transcript* (9 January 1926), clipping in box 89, Commerce files, Herbert Hoover Library, West Branch, Iowa (hereafter HHL); Tye, *The Father of Spin*, 63–69.

45. Herbert Hoover, "The Public Relations of Advertising," address at the Associated Advertising Clubs of the World Annual Convention, Houston, 11 May 1925, folder 25, box 2, Commerce files, HHL (emphasis added).

46. Advertisements and correspondence from folders 24A, 25, 26, 27, box 2, Commerce files, HHL.

CHAPTER 2: THE STUDIOS' GOLDEN AGE
AND THE WHITE HOUSE, 1929–1945

1. Robert Sklar, *Movie-Made America: A Cultural History of American Movies*, rev. ed. (New York: Vintage, 1994), part 1; Neal Gabler, *An Empire of Their Own: How the Jews Invented Hollywood* (New York: Anchor, 1988), part 1.

2. Richard Abel, *Americanizing the Movies and "Movie-Mad" Audiences, 1910–1914* (Berkeley: University of California Press, 2006), chaps. 1–2; David Bordwell, Janet Staiger, and Kristin Thompson, *The Classical Hollywood Cinema: Film Style and Mode of Production to 1960* (New York: Columbia University Press, 1985), esp. chaps. 1–3.

3. Hugo Münsterberg, *The Photoplay: A Psychological Study* (New York: Appleton, 1916), 47.

4. Leonard J. Leff and Gerold L. Simmons, *The Dame in the Kimono: Hollywood, Censorship, and the Production Code,* rev. ed. (Lexington: University Press of Kentucky, 2001), chaps. 1–3; Francis G. Couvares, ed., *Movie Censorship and American Culture* (Washington, DC: Smithsonian Institution Press, 1996); Sklar, *Movie-Made America,* chap. 10.

5. Louis B. Mayer to Herbert Hoover, 2 September 1924, and Hoover to Mayer, 28 November 1927, Mayer folder, box 388, Commerce files, Herbert Hoover Library (hereafter HHL). See also Ronald Brownstein, *The Power and the Glitter: The Hollywood-Washington Connection* (New York: Pantheon, 1990), chap. 1.

6. Mayer telegram to Hoover, 28 August 1928, box 47; George Akerson telegram to Hoover, 24 October 1928, box 41; Ida R. Koverman to Lawrence Richey, 27 January 1929, box 41, Campaign & Transition files, HHL.

7. 1926 correspondence, Mayer folder, box 388, Commerce files, HHL; see also Louis B. Mayer file, box 172, Presidential Subject files, HHL, and Brownstein, *The Power and the Glitter,* chap. 1.

8. Ed Jacobs telegram to White House, 25 May 1929; Rodney Dutcher, "Talking Films Shown Twice a Week for President Hoover," *Washington Daily News* (9 July 1929); and other clippings and correspondence in Motion Pictures file, box 198, Presidential files, HHL.

9. Joseph P. Kennedy, ed., *The Story of the Films* (New York: Shaw, 1927), 11; Richey to Abram Meyers, 7 September 1929, Motion Pictures file, box 198, Presidential files, HHL.

10. On Hoover's career at Commerce see Lynn Dumenil, *The Modern Temper: American Culture and Society in the 1920s* (New York: Hill and Wang, 1995), 36–54; Will H. Hays folder, box 1045; Akerson to Hoover, 19 August 1931, box 198, Presidential Subject files, HHL; Dorothy M. Brown, *Mabel Walker Willebrandt: Power, Loyalty, and the Law* (Knoxville: University of Tennessee Press, 1984), chap. 8.

11. Film and photograph available at the Hoover Library website, http://www.hoover.archives.gov.

12. Correspondence from Motion Pictures folders (1929–1932), box 198, Presidential Subject files, HHL.

13. Benjamin McArthur, *Actors and American Culture, 1880–1920,* rept. ed. (1984; Iowa City: University of Iowa Press, 2000), 173–176; Roberta E. Pearson, *Eloquent Gestures: The Transformation of Performance Style in the Griffith Biograph Films* (Berkeley, CA: University of California Press, 1992), chap. 3; Sklar, *Movie-Made America,* chap. 4.

14. Jeanine Basinger, *The Star Machine* (New York: Knopf, 2007), 405.

15. Robert S. McElvaine, *Down and Out in the Great Depression: Letters from the Forgotten Man* (Chapel Hill: University of North Carolina Press, 1983); Lawrence W. Levine and Cornelia R. Levine, *The People and the President: America's Conversation with FDR* (Boston: Beacon, 2002).

16. Alice Kaplan, *The Collaborator: The Trial and Execution of Robert Brasillach* (Chicago: University of Chicago Press, 2001); David Welch, *Propaganda and the German Cinema, 1933–1945,* rev. ed. (London: Tauris, 2001); Greg Mitchell, *The Campaign of the Century: Upton Sinclair's Race for Governor of California and the Birth of Media Politics* (New York: Random House, 1993).

17. Boxes 18, 70, 93, and 103, Office of Social Entertainments papers, box 8030; President's Personal Files, Franklin D. Roosevelt Library (hereafter FDRL); "Screen News Here and in Hollywood," *New York Times* (14 May 1942), 23; Alan Schroeder, *Celebrity in Chief: How Show Business Took Over the White House* (Boulder, CO: Westview, 2004), chap. 1.

18. Schroeder, *Celebrity in Chief,* 18.

19. Brownstein, *The Power and the Glitter,* chap. 3.

20. Helen Gahagan Douglas to Eleanor Roosevelt, 22 November 1944, box 7371, President's Personal Files, FDRL.

21. Douglas Fairbanks Jr., *The Salad Days: An Autobiography* (New York: Doubleday, 1988), esp. 289, 305–309; Nicholas J. Cull, "Overture to an Alliance: Propaganda at the New York World's Fair, 1939–1940," *Journal of British Studies* 36 (1997): 335n29; correspondence between Fairbanks and FDR is in box 7130, President's Personal Files, FDRL.

22. Sumner Welles to FDR, 24 January 1941, box 68, Welles Papers; Welles to Douglas Fairbanks Jr., 3 February 1941; further correspondence is in the same location and in box 7130, President's Personal Files, FDRL. See also Douglas Fairbanks Jr., *A Hell of a War* (New York: St. Martin's, 1993).

23. Louis Pizzitola, *Hearst over Hollywood: Power, Passion, and Propaganda in the Movies* (New York: Columbia University Press, 2002), esp. chaps. 11–13; David Nasaw, *The Chief: The Life of William Randolph Hearst* (Boston: Houghton Mifflin, 2000), 279–268, 446–466.

24. Cari Beauchamp, *Joseph P. Kennedy Presents: His Hollywood Years* (New York: Knopf, 2009). The celebrated motion picture *Citizen Kane* (1941) indirectly linked Kennedy with Hearst. Orson Welles's film, which infuriated the publisher because it was based in part on his life, was produced by RKO (Radio Keith Orpheum) Studios, a company that Kennedy created in 1929 and briefly owned.

25. Joseph Kennedy quoted on the web site of the John F. Kennedy Library, http://www.jfklibrary.org.

26. Jean Edward Smith, *FDR* (New York: Random, 2007), 234–235; H. W. Brands, *Traitor to His Class: The Privileged Life and Radical Presidency of Franklin Delano Roosevelt* (New York: Doubleday, 2008), 318.

27. Smith, *FDR,* 402–406; Conrad Black, *Franklin Delano Roosevelt: Champion of Freedom* (New York: Public Affairs, 2003), 906–908.

28. Documents and transcripts from "Senate Subcommittee Movie Investigation" folder, Lowell Mellett papers, box 1, Official Correspondence 1938–1944, FDRL.

29. FDR message to Motion Picture Producers Association, 23 February 1938, Will Hays folder, box 1945, President's Personal Files; committee transcript, 1023, Mellett papers, box 1, Official Correspondence 1938–1944, FDRL.

30. Deborah Carmichael, "*Gabriel over the White House* (1933): William Randolph Hearst's Fascist Solution for the Great Depression," in Peter C. Rollins and John E. O'Connor, eds., *Hollywood's White House: The American Presidency in Film and History* (Lexington: University Press of Kentucky, 2003), 159–179.

31. Alfred Haworth Jones, *Roosevelt's Image Brokers: Poets, Playwrights, and the Use of the Lincoln Symbol* (Port Washington, N.Y.: Kennikat Press, 1974); Frank McGlynn, *Sidelights on Lincoln* (Los Angeles: Wetzel, 1947).

32. Michael P. Rogin and Kathleen Moran, "Mr. Capra Goes to Washington," *Representations* 84 (2003): 213–248.

33. Elmer Davis to Harry F. Byrd, 19 November 1942, Lowell Mellett papers, box 1, Official Correspondence 1938–44, FDRL.

34. Sally Stein, "The President's Two Bodies: Stagings and Restagings of FDR and the New Deal Body Politic," *American Art* 18 (Spring 2004): 32. Stein's title derives from the classic study of Ernst H. Kantorowicz, *The King's Two Bodies: A Study in Mediæval Political Theology* (Princeton, NJ: Princeton University Press, 1970).

35. Brands, *Traitor to His Class,* 776–77.

36. David M. Kennedy, *Freedom from Fear: The American People in Depression and War* (New York: Oxford University Press, 2001), 117; Stein, "The President's Two Bodies," 32–36.

37. Brands, *Traitor to His Class,* 777; Edward Wagenknecht, *The Seven Worlds of Theodore Roosevelt,* rept. ed. (New York: 2008, Lyons), 112.

38. Black, *Franklin Delano Roosevelt,* 394–396, 589–591, 601–602.

39. Stein, "The President's Two Bodies," 33, 36.

40. Brands, *Traitor to His Class,* 776.

41. Black, *Franklin Delano Roosevelt,* 994; John Morton Blum, *V Was for Victory: Politics and American Culture during World War II* (Boston: Houghton Mifflin, 1976), 8.

42. Materials from Presidential Portrait folder, Stephen T. Early papers, box 33, Official Correspondence 1938–44, FDRL.

43. James Agee, *Agee on Film* (New York: McDowell Oblensky, 1958), 146–148.

CHAPTER 3: THE OLD MAN AND TV,
1945–1960

1. Lauren Bacall, *Lauren Bacall: By Myself* (New York: Ballantine, 1985), 176–177; another eyewitness account is Peter Andrews, "My Brush with Betty," *American Heritage* 45 (1994): 39–40.

2. Bacall, *Lauren Bacall,* 115–121.

3. David O. Selznick telegram to James Forrestal, 13 April 1945; Will Hays letter to Harry S. Truman, 16 April 1945; Harry Warner letter to Truman, 27 April 1945; Samuel Goldwyn letter to Truman, 16 September 1947; memo re Infantile Paralysis luncheon, 30 January 1946, Motion Pictures files, box 418, Official Files, Harry S. Truman Library (hereafter HSTL).

4. Charles G. Ross letter, 23 November 1945; George Dorsey (RKO studio) to White House, 8 April 1946; Carter Barron (MGM) to White House, 12 March 1946; Art Baker to Truman, 7 January 1947; Truman to Baker, 14 January 1947; Mabel Shank to Truman, 11 March 1947; White House memo re Samuel Bronston, 11 March 1946, Motion Pictures files, box 418, Official Files, HSTL. Bronston would not produce *John Paul Jones* until 1959.

5. Harry H. Vaughn to Jack Warner, 12 April 1949; John Steelman to James Stewart, 6 April 1948, Motion Pictures files, box 418, Official Files, HSTL; David Clark, "Truman and the Rich and Famous," PowerPoint presentation, n.d., HSTL. The Dewey campaign produced a biographical film about its candidate, which compelled newsreel companies to compile *The Truman Story* free of charge for the president's campaign, to provide balance in the nation's theaters. David McCullough, *Truman* (New York: Simon and Schuster, 1992), 684–685.

6. On union issues, see 1945 folder, Motion Pictures files, box 418; Helen Gahagan Douglas telegram to Truman, 6 October 1945, Motion Pictures files, box 418, Official Files, HSTL; Garry Wills, *Reagan's America: Innocents at Home* (Garden City, NY: Doubleday, 1987), 272–275; and *New York Times* (5 October 1945), 1. On the foreign earnings issue, see Will Hays to Franklin D. Roosevelt, 4 July and 5 July 1942, Hays file, box 1045, President's Personal File, Franklin D. Roosevelt Library, and correspondence in Motion Pictures files, box 418, Official Files, HSTL. On the rise of independent producers, see Thomas Schatz, *The Genius of the System: Hollywood Filmmaking in the Studio Era* (New York: Simon and Schuster, 1988), 381–393, 420–427, and Denise Mann, *Hollywood Independents: the Postwar Talent Takeover* (Minneapolis: University of Minnesota Press, 2008).

7. Society of Independent Motion Picture Producers telegram to Truman, 10 September 1948; Cecil B. DeMille to Truman, n.d. (1949); Truman to DeMille, 18 April 1949, Motion Pictures files, box 418, Official Files, HSTL; Schatz, *Genius of the System,* 411–413.

8. John Steelman to Charles Speer, 10 January 1951, Television files, box 698, Official Files, HSTL.

9. Memos and correspondence, Television 1945–49 folder, box 697, Official Files, HSTL.

10. Ross letter, 24 July 1947; William A. J. Dean to Truman, 31 October 1948; Westervelt Romaine to Truman, 26 October 1947; letter to Truman, 18 December 1948; Eben A. Ayers to Woodrow McAllister, 13 April 1949, Television 1945–49 folder, box 697, Official Files, HSTL.

11. Truman to Hal W. Lanigan, 25 August 1940, quoted in Lanigan letter to Truman, 25 October 1948; Merriam Smith memo to Truman, 30 September 1947; memo, 29 June 1948; E. F. McDonald to Truman, 25 January 1949; White House memo, 2 June 1949, Television 1945–49 folder, box 697, Official Files, HSTL.

12. Numerous requests for Fireside Chats are in Television folder 1, box 697, Official Files; Hal Styles to Truman, 29 May 1951, box 233, President's Personal Files, HSTL.

13. Memos in Television 1950–53 folders, boxes 698 and 699, Official Files; finding aids to Charles W. Jackson and John R. Steelman papers, HSTL. Scripts for *Battle Report: Washington* are in the Jackson papers.

14. E. I. Kaufmann telegram to Herbert Hoover, 19 August 1931; George Akerson note, n.d. (August 1931); Shelby O'Neal to Lawrence Richey, 6 May 1931, Motion Pictures files, box 198, Presidential Papers, Herbert Hoover Library.

15. Eugene G. Rochow to Truman, 27 July 1949, Television 1945–49 folder, box 697, Official Files; Thomas J. Dunphy to Truman, 20 July 1950, 7–8; Irving C. Hodlick to Ross, 4 July 1950; Richard Krolik to Matthew J. Connelly, 6 September 1950, Television 1950 folder, box 698, HSTL.

16. Irving Perlmeter letter, 24 March 1952; Truman note on letter from CBS, 21 July 1950; George Elsey memo, 6 February 1951; Television 1950 folder, box 698, Official Files; Jed Johnson memo, 11 October 1947, Television 1945–49 folder, box 697, Official Files, HSTL.

17. Kenneth Lynn, *Hemingway* (New York: Simon and Schuster, 1987), 565–569; Alan Nadel, *Containment Culture: American Narratives, Postmodernism, and the Atomic Age* (Durham, NC: Duke University Press, 1995), chap. 4.

18. Sigurd Larmon, "The Eisenhower Campaign," typescript, 8 January 1952, box 1, Young & Rubicam papers, Dwight D. Eisenhower Library (hereafter DDEL). SHAEF was the headquarters of the Allied command in the European theater during Word War II.

19. James A. Hagerty, "'A Serenade to Ike' is Theme at Rally," *New York Times* (9 February 1952), 1, box 1, Young & Rubicam papers, DDEL.

20. Robert Montgomery, "The Time is Now," typescript, 13 November 1951, staff files, box 1, Young & Rubicam papers; see also Montgomery speech text, 24 March 1954, box 2141, White House Central Files, DDEL.

21. Thomas A. DeLong, *John Davis Lodge: A Life in Three Acts* (Fairfield, CT: Sacred Heart University Press, 1999), 119 and passim; also John D. Lodge radio speech script, 5 February 1952, staff folder, Young & Rubicam papers, DDEL.

22. DeLong, *John Davis Lodge*, 121–122 and passim.

23. Stephen E. Ambrose, *Nixon: The Education of a Politician 1913–1962* (New York: Simon and Schuster, 1987), 284; see generally 276–294.

24. Ambrose, *Nixon: The Education*, 290.

25. On the 1952 campaign see Kathleen Hall Jamieson, *Packaging the Presidency: A History and Criticism of Presidential Campaign Advertising*, 3d ed. (New York: Oxford University Press, 1996), chap. 2; Stephen E. Ambrose, *Nixon: The Triumph of a Politician 1962–1972* (New York: Simon and Schuster, 1989), 364.

26. William J. Bailey and Rufus Nelson, letters to White House, 8 May 1953; Blanche Young to Dwight D. Eisenhower, 2 February 1953; James Connelly to Eisenhower, n.d. (February 1953), box 151; Matthew Epstein to Mamie Eisenhower, 2 February 1955; Ellen Henderson to Eisenhower, 6 June 1954, box 152, Central Files, DDEL.

27. Various correspondences, box 151, Central Files, DDEL.

28. Craig Allen, "Robert Montgomery Presents: Hollywood's Debut in the Eisenhower White House," *Journal of Broadcasting and Electronic Media* 35 (1991): 431–448.

29. *New York Times* (10 January 1954), E5; also 7 January 1954, 20; 29 January 1954, 28.

30. Eisenhower memo to Montgomery, 16 March 1954, box 7, DDE Diary Series, DDEL.

31. William L. Klein to Eisenhower, 22 March 1954, box 152, Central Files, DDEL.

32. Mrs. M. M. Robertson to James Hagerty, 16 April 1954, box 152, Central Files, DDEL.

33. Fred Tew, "TV Aides Put Ike on the Skids," n.d. (April 1955), newspaper clipping; "Let Ike Be Himself," n.d. (April 1955), newspaper clipping, box 152, Central Files; Gertrude Roberts to Eisenhower, 21 September 1954, box 610, President's Personal Files, DDEL.

34. Newspaper clipping, n.d. (April 1955); Tew, "TV Aides"; E. C. Mills to Eisenhower, 15 October 1954, box 152, Central Files, DDEL.

35. Tew, "TV Aides"; Mills letter, 15 October 1954; clipping, n.d., box 152, Central Files, DDEL.

36. Robert Montgomery, *Open Letter from a Television Viewer* (New York: Heinemann, 1968), 62–63; memorandum by Hagerty, 18 July 1958, folder N, box 120, Central Files, DDEL.

37. Montgomery, *Open Letter,* 68–70; Eisenhower to Montgomery, 22 December 1956, folder A, box 49, President's Personal Files, DDEL; Allen, "Robert Montgomery Presents," 443–444.

38. Schatz, *Genius of the System,* 458.

39. Ibid., 472–473.

40. Leonard J. Leff and Jerold L. Simmons, *The Dame in the Kimono: Hollywood, Censorship, and the Production Code,* rev. ed. (Lexington: University Press of Kentucky, 2001), chaps. 8–9.

CHAPTER 4: CHARISMA'S HOUR, 1960–1969

1. Pierre Salinger, *With Kennedy* (Garden City, NY: Doubleday, 1966), 102–104.

2. Kathleen Stewart to Warner Brothers, 9 March 1961; Pierre Salinger to B. Pearson, 27 October 1961; Maureen O'Sullivan Farrow telegram to Salinger, 16 May 1962 and Salinger response, 21 May, box 811, White House Central Files, John F. Kennedy Library (hereafter JFKL). See also PT 109 correspondence folders, box 132, Personal Secretary Files, President's Office Files, and various correspondence, boxes 811–813, Central Files, JFKL.

3. Salinger to Eugene L. Wyman, 25 April 1963 and various correspondence, box 813, Central Files, JFKL.

4. Marshall McLuhan, *Understanding Media: The Extensions of Man* (New York:

NAL, 1964); Guy Debord, *Society of the Spectacle,* trans. Fredy Perlman and Jon Supak (1967; New York: Black and Red, 1970).

5. Norman Mailer, "Superman Comes to the Supermarket," *Esquire* (November 1960), http://www.esquire.com/features.

6. Ibid.

7. Richard Reeves, *President Kennedy: Profile in Power* (New York: Simon and Schuster, 1993), 476, 480, 538.

8. David Kaiser, *American Tragedy: Kennedy, Johnson, and the Origins of the Vietnam War* (Cambridge, MA: Belknap Press, 2000), 265.

9. Mailer, "Superman Comes to the Supermarket."

10. William K. Goolrick, "Jack Kennedy Takes Two Tough Tests," *Life* (27 April 1959), 47–51; Robert Dallek, *An Unfinished Life: John F. Kennedy, 1917–1963* (Boston: Little, Brown, 2003), 225.

11. Jon Goodman et al., *The Kennedy Mystique: Creating Camelot* (Washington: National Geographic, n.d. [2006]), 11; Alan Schroeder, *Celebrity in Chief: How Show Business Took Over the White House* (Boulder, CO: Westview, 2004), 276; see also Reeves, *President Kennedy,* 64.

12. Clinton P. Anderson, oral history transcript, 14 April 1967, JFKL, 4, http://www.jfklibrary.org; Nigel Hamilton, *American Caesars: The Lives of the Presidents from FDR to George W. Bush* (New Haven, CT: Yale University Press, 2010), 163–164.

13. Mailer, "Superman Comes to the Supermarket."

14. Benjamin C. Bradlee, *Conversations with Kennedy* (New York: Norton, 1975); Benjamin C. Bradlee, *A Good Life: Newspapering and Other Adventures* (New York: Simon and Schuster, 1996), 217, 270–271; Theodore H. White, *The Making of the President, 1960* (New York: Atheneum, 1961); Hugh Sidey, *John F. Kennedy, President: A Reporter's Inside Story* (New York: Scribner, 1963).

15. Daniel Boorstin, *The Image: Or, What Happened to the American Dream* (New York: Atheneum, 1962), chap. 1. (In 1971 Boorstin changed the subtitle of this book to *A Guide to Pseudo-Events.*) Leo Braudy, *The Frenzy of Renown: Fame and Its History* (New York: Oxford University Press, 1986), 9.

16. David S. Brown, *Richard Hofstadter: An Intellectual Biography* (Chicago: University of Chicago Press, 2006), 131.

17. Andrew Hacker, "When the President Goes to the People," *New York Times Magazine* (10 June 1962), 13ff.

18. Carl Sferrazza Anthony, *First Ladies: The Saga of the Presidents' Wives and Their Power, 1961–1990* (New York: Morrow, 1991), chaps. 1–4.

19. Goodman, *Kennedy Mystique,* 94–95; David M. Lubin, *Shooting Kennedy: JFK and the Culture of Images* (Berkeley: University of California Press, 2003), 280–283.

20. Kathy Peiss, *Hope in a Jar: The Making of America's Beauty Culture* (New York: Metropolitan, 1998).

21. Geoffrey Perret, *Jack: A Life Like No Other* (New York: Random House, 2001), 237; Dallek, *An Unfinished Life,* 494.

22. *From Max Weber: Essays in Sociology,* trans. and ed. H. H. Gerth and C. Wright Mills (New York: Oxford University Press, 1946), chaps. 9–10.

23. Barry Schwartz, "George Washington and the Whig Conception of Heroic Leadership," *American Sociological Review* 48 (1983): 18; Robert J. House, William D. Spangler, and James Woycke, "Personality and Charisma in the U.S. Presidency: A Psychological Theory of Leader Effectiveness," *Administrative Science Quarterly* 36 (1991): 370–371.

24. Gerth and Mills, *From Max Weber.*

25. Brown, *Richard Hofstadter,* 129–130.

26. James C. Davies, "Charisma in the 1952 Campaign," *American Political Science Review* 48 (1954): 1087; William H. Friedland, "For a Sociological Concept of Charisma," *Social Forces* 43 (1964): 18–26; also see James Q. Wilson, "Two Negro Politicians: An Interpretation," *Midwest Journal of Political Science* 4 (1960): 346–369, and Edward Shils, "The Concentration and Dispersion of Charisma: Their Bearing on Economic Policy in Underdeveloped Countries," *World Politics* 11 (1958): 1–19.

27. C. L. Sulzberger, "It's Charisma That Counts in the End," *New York Times* (7 November 1960), 34.

28. Alan Schroeder, *Presidential Debates: Forty Years of High-Risk TV* (New York: Columbia University Press, 2000), 137.

29. Nigel Hamilton, *JFK: Reckless Youth* (New York: Random House, 1992), 380–381 (emphasis in original); Dallek, *An Unfinished Life,* 83, 152. Joseph Kennedy alluded to his sons Joe and John's fascination with movies in Joseph P. Kennedy, ed., *The Story of the Films* (New York: Shaw, 1927), 17.

30. Hamilton, *JFK,* 777–779.

31. Bradlee, *Conversations with Kennedy,* 27; Lubin, *Shooting Kennedy,* 127–128; Lee C. White to Kenneth B. Wilson, 12 April 1962, box 812, Central Files, JFKL.

32. Seymour M. Hersh, *The Dark Side of Camelot* (Boston: Little, Brown, 1997), esp. chap. 15; Reeves, *President Kennedy,* 707; Perret, *Jack,* 344–349.

33. Otto Preminger to Salinger, 13 July 1961, box 811; Salinger to Allen Drury, 6 January 1962, box 812; Joseph R. Vogel telegram to John F. Kennedy, 6 October 1961, box 811; Curtis Bernhardt to Salinger, 16 August 1963, box 813; Marvin Chomsky to Andrew Hatcher, 15 August 1963, box 813, Central Files, JFKL.

34. Pierre Salinger dissembled publicly about Kennedy's liking for Fleming's novels. Memo n.d. (circa April 1963, listing *From Russia with Love* as one of JFK's favorite books); Sandy Bonar to JFK, 24 September 1963; Salinger to Bonar, 24 October 1963 (denying that JFK liked Fleming); Salinger to Herb Caen, 28 October 1963 (stating that Kennedy "has read all of the Ian Fleming books"), box 722, subject files, Central Files, JFKL; Bradlee, *Conversations with Kennedy,* 224.

35. On *Spartacus* and *The Alamo,* see Russell Birdwell telegram to JFK, 10 February 1961; T. J. Reardon to William Gordon, 13 February 1961; and John Dungey to JFK, 5 March 1961, box 811, Central Files, JFKL. On *Operation Abolition,* see correspondence in ibid. On Murrow and Stevens, see Murrow memo to Salinger, 2 March 1961; Murrow memo to JFK, 24 July 1961; and Donald M. Wilson to Salinger, 26 May 1961, box 810, Central Files, JFKL.

36. Lester Cowan to Salinger, 3 April 1962, box 810; Cowan to Salinger, 23 November 1962, box 812; Cowan to Salinger, 14 February 1963, with attached correspondence, box 813, Central Files, JFKL; Vincent Canby, "Schlesinger Will Write Story for Film on President's Lives," *New York Times* (10 February 1966), 32; Lester Cowan obituary, *New York Times* (23 October 1990), 9.

37. Cowan to Salinger, 23 November 1962, box 812, Central Files, JFKL.

38. Lubin, *Shooting Kennedy,* 28–36, 163–171; Hamilton, *JFK,* preface.

39. Peter Biskind, *Easy Riders, Raging Bulls: How the Sex-Drugs-and-Rock 'n' Roll Generation Saved Hollywood* (New York: Simon and Schuster, 1998), 35, 47; Peter Biskind, *Star: How Warren Beatty Seduced America* (New York: Simon and Schuster, 2010), chaps. 3–5; Ronald Brownstein, *The Power and the Glitter: The Hollywood-Washington Connection* (New York: Pantheon, 1990), 240–249.

40. Donald Smith, "The Camelotians," *New York Times Magazine* (4 November 1973), 38, 137.

41. Jay Walz, "Canada: Trudeau for the Liberals," *New York Times* (14 April 1968), E10.

42. *Esquire* (February 1972), cover and 17; Jack Rosenthal, "McCloskey's Primary Campaign Has Its Ups and Downs," *New York Times* (5 March 1972), 38.

43. Tom Lehrer, "George Murphy," *That Was the Year That Was,* Reprise RS-6179, 1965. Reprinted by permission of Tom Lehrer.

44. Jacques Leslie, "John Tunney, Kennedy's Friend in Muskie's Corner," *New York Times Magazine* (26 December 1971), 6–7, 10–14; R. W. Apple Jr., "Reagan Is Far Ahead," *New York Times* (30 September 1970), 28.

45. Thomas M. Brown and Martin Smith, " . . . and the Main Event West," *New York Times Magazine* (31 October 1976), 17–18.

46. Robert A. Caro, *The Path to Power* (New York: Knopf, 1982), 73, 118, 303; "The Hoblitzelle & Interstate Theater Collection," http://www.hrc.utexas.edu/collections/film/holdings/interstate/; Kaiser, *American Tragedy,* 287.

47. On Carey and Wayne, see Garry Wills, *John Wayne's America: The Politics of Celebrity* (New York: Simon and Schuster, 1997), 101–121.

48. Robert A. Caro, *Means of Ascent* (New York: Knopf, 1990), 318–339; Caro, *Path to Power,* 155.

49. Caro, *Means of Ascent,* xxv.

50. Schroeder, *Celebrity in Chief,* 278.

51. Ibid., 31–33, 78, 140, 278.

52. Ibid., 214.

53. Brownstein, *Power and the Glitter,* 179–181, 188–202.

54. Ibid., 181–188, 212–224; Robert Dallek, *Flawed Giant: Lyndon B. Johnson and His Times, 1961–1973* (New York: Oxford University Press, 1999), 452; Connie Bruck, *When Hollywood Had a King: The Reign of Lew Wasserman* (New York: Random House, 2003).

55. Jack Valenti, *This Time, This Place: My Life in War, the White House, and Hollywood* (New York: Crown, 2007), esp. chaps. 10–11.

CHAPTER 5: ENTER STAGE RIGHT, 1969–1989

1. Stephen E. Ambrose, *Nixon: The Education of a Politician 1913–1962* (New York: Simon and Schuster, 1987), 69–70, 92–93, 97.

2. Stephen E. Ambrose, *Nixon: The Triumph of a Politician 1962–1972* (New York: Simon and Schuster, 1989), 10, 412.

3. David Greenberg, *Nixon's Shadow: The History of an Image* (New York: Norton, 2003), 154.

4. Ibid., 3.

5. Joe McGinniss, *The Selling of the President [1968],* rept. ed. (1969; New York: Penguin, 1988), epigraph.

6. Greg Mitchell, *Tricky Dick and the Pink Lady: Sexual Politics and the Red Scare, 1950* (New York: Random House, 1998).

7. Norman Mailer, "Superman Comes to the Supermarket," *Esquire* (November 1960), http://www.esquire.com/features.

8. Nixon to H. L. Hunt, 28 March 1963, box 22, White House special files, Richard M. Nixon Library (hereafter RNL).

9. Ambrose, *Nixon: The Education,* 652; Nixon memo to John Ehrlichman, 9 January 1969, box 1, White House special files, RNL.

10. Garry Wills, *Nixon Agonistes: The Crisis of the Self-Made Man* (Boston: Houghton Mifflin, 1969), 406; Nigel Hamilton, *American Caesars: The Lives of the Presidents from Franklin D. Roosevelt to George W. Bush* (New Haven, CT: Yale University Press, 2010), 116; David Greenberg, "Nixon Speaks," *Chronicle of Higher Education* (16 November 2011), http://www.chronicle.com/article/Nixon-Speaks/129791.

11. Patrick Buchanan memo to Nixon, 15 November 1967, 4–5 (emphasis in original), box 35, White House special files, RNL.

12. McGinniss, *Selling of the President,* 194 (emphasis in original).

13. Ibid., 187–188, 207, 210, 213.

14. Rick Pearlstein, *Nixonland: The Rise of a President and the Fracturing of America* (New York: Scribner, 2008), 83, 184.

15. McGinniss, *Selling of the President,* chap. 1.

16. Ibid., xiv; see also Kathleen Hall Jamieson, *Packaging the Presidency: A History*

and Criticism of Presidential Campaign Advertising, 3d ed. (New York: Oxford University Press, 1996), chap. 6.

17. Leonard Garment, *Crazy Rhythm: From Brooklyn and Jazz to Nixon's White House, Watergate, and Beyond* (New York: Times Books, 1997), 100; Ambrose, *Nixon: The Education,* 411. See also Greenberg, *Nixon's Shadow,* 140–144.

18. Pearlstein, *Nixonland,* 148, 252; Nixon memo to H. R. Haldeman, 17 September 1968, box 35, White House special files, RNL; *Esquire* (May 1968), cover (the designer was George Lois).

19. Haldeman memo to Nixon, 9 June 1968, folder 7, box 35, White House special files, RNL.

20. See for example Hamilton, *American Caesars,* 126–128, and Ambrose, *Nixon: The Triumph,* 200–204.

21. Stephen J. Whitfield, "Richard Nixon as a Comic Figure," *American Quarterly* 37 (Spring 1985): 114–132; Pearlstein, *Nixonland,* 372; Herbert Klein, *Making It Perfectly Clear* (Garden City, NY: Doubleday, 1980), 298; H. R. Haldeman, *The Haldeman Diaries: Inside the Nixon White House* (New York: Putnam, 1994), 60–61.

22. Klein, *Making It Perfectly Clear,* 203; Richard M. Nixon, *RN: Memoirs of Richard Nixon* (New York: Grosset and Dunlap, 1978), 355; Pearlstein, *Nixonland,* 363.

23. Pearlstein, *Nixonland,* 361 (emphasis in original); Ambrose, *Nixon: The Triumph,* 297, 372; Klein, *Making It Perfectly Clear,* 340; Robert Locander, "Modern Presidential In-Office Communications: The National, Direct, Local, and Latent Strategies," *Presidential Studies Quarterly* 13 (Spring 1983): 247.

24. Pearlstein, *Nixonland,* 664.

25. Ambrose, *Nixon: The Triumph,* 298; also Haldeman, *Diaries,* 58.

26. Haldeman, *Diaries,* 59, 73.

27. Klein, *Making It Perfectly Clear,* 188; Pearlstein, *Nixonland,* 361.

28. Klein, *Making It Perfectly Clear,* 351.

29. Pearlstein, *Nixonland,* 381; Haldeman, *Diaries,* 52; Robert B. Semple Jr., "Nixon Calls Manson Guilty, Later Withdraws Remark," *New York Times* (4 August 1970), 16.

30. Pearlstein, *Nixonland,* 472–482.

31. Hamilton, *American Caesars,* 271–272.

32. David Gergen files, finding aid, Gerald R. Ford Library, http://www.fordlibrary museum.gov/library/guide.asp.

33. Gerald Rafshoon, exit interview with David Alsobrook, 12 September 1979, Jimmy Carter Library, http://www.jimmycarterlibrary.gov/library/exitInt/Rafshoon .pdf. Rafshoon never made the Lee miniseries.

34. See for example Pearlstein, *Nixonland.* A dissenting view is Sean Wilentz, *The Age of Reagan: A History 1974–2008* (New York: Harper, 2008), xv.

35. Lou Cannon, *President Reagan: The Role of a Lifetime* (New York: Simon and Schuster, 1991), 73–74.

36. Ibid., 52–53; Timothy Raphael, *The President Electric: Ronald Reagan and the Politics of Performance* (Ann Arbor: University of Michigan Press, 2009), 132–133.

37. Garry Wills, *Reagan's America: Innocents at Home* (Garden City, NY: Doubleday, 1987), chaps. 28–29.

38. George Murphy and Victor Lasky, *Say . . . Didn't You Used to Be George Murphy?* (New York: Bartholomew, 1970).

39. Richard Reeves, *President Reagan: The Triumph of Imagination* (New York: Simon and Schuster, 2005), xv.

40. Heston's political career was both typical of film stars' activism in the post-1960s era—in that he spoke out in favor of causes, but avoided running for public office—and an atypical instance of one actor striving for a quasi-presidential real-life role. The star of *The Ten Commandments* and *Ben-Hur* adapted his portentous acting style to the post of president of the National Rifle Association. During the impeachment of Bill Clinton, Heston's public profile inspired thousands of NRA members to proclaim on bumper stickers "My President is Charlton Heston." Emilie Raymond, *From My Cold, Dead Hands: Charlton Heston and American Politics* (Lexington: University Press of Kentucky, 2006).

41. Sally Ogle Davis, "Battling It Out in Hollywood," *New York Times* (25 April 1982), 38–42; David Burnham, "Reagan Role in F.C.C. Case Assailed," *New York Times* (4 February 1984), 46.

42. Cannon, *President Reagan*, 51–52; see also Alan Nadel, *Flatlining on the Field of Dreams: Cultural Narratives in the Films of President Reagan's America* (New Brunswick, NJ: Rutgers University Press, 1997), 16–17.

43. Cannon, *President Reagan*, 51.

44. David Gergen, *Eyewitness to Power: The Essence of Leadership, Nixon to Clinton* (New York: Simon and Schuster, 2000), chaps. 5–7; Cannon, *President Reagan*, 497–501, 644–645.

45. Gergen, *Eyewitness to Power*, 186; Michael K. Deaver and Mickey Herskowitz, *Behind the Scenes* (New York: Morrow, 1988), 140–141.

46. Deaver, speaking circa 1989, quoted in William F. Eadie and Paul E. Nelson, *The Changing Conversation in America* (Thousand Oaks, CA: Sage, 2001), 27–28.

47. Wills, *Reagan's America*, 316–326; "Michael Evans, Photographer of Ronald Reagan, Dies at 61," *New York Times* (2 December 2005), 25.

48. Nadel, *Flatlining on the Field of Dreams*, preface and chap. 1.

49. "Films President and Mrs. Reagan Viewed," Ronald Reagan Library, http://www.reagan.utexas.edu/archives/reference/filmsviewed.html.

50. William A. Henry III, *Visions of America: How We Saw the 1984 Election* (New York: Atlantic, 1985), 39.

51. Cannon, *President Reagan*, 58–60; Wills, *Reagan's America*, 196.

52. Cannon, *President Reagan*, 57–58; Stephen Vaughn, "Spies, National Security,

and the 'Inertia Projector': The Secret Service Films of Ronald Reagan," *American Quarterly* 39 (1987): 355–380.

53. Barber quoted in Reeves, *President Reagan,* 8; Tom Wicker, "The Hollywood Touch," *New York Times* (20 May 1987), 31.

54. Wills, *Reagan's America,* 25–33; Michael Rogin, *Ronald Reagan, the Movie: And Other Episodes in Political Demonology* (Berkeley: University of California Press, 1986), chap. 1.

55. Ron Reagan, *My Father at 100* (New York: Viking, 2011), 217–218.

56. On *Taxi Driver,* see Peter Biskind, *Easy Riders, Raging Bulls: How the Sex-Drugs-and-Rock 'n' Roll Generation Saved Hollywood* (New York: Simon and Schuster, 1998), 299–307; "John Hinckley, Jr." Wikipedia, http://en.wikipedia.org/wiki/John_Hinckley.

57. Rogin, *Ronald Reagan, the Movie,* 24–27.

58. Attentive readers will note that the 1981 film *The Fan*—starring Harry Truman's former piano mate Lauren Bacall—should not be confused with the 1996 film of the same name, which happened to star Robert De Niro in the John Hinckley–style title role.

59. Gil Troy, *Morning in America: How Ronald Reagan Invented the 1980s* (Princeton, NJ: Princeton University Press, 2007), 338; Wilentz, *The Age of Reagan,* 25.

CHAPTER 6: HOLLYWOOD WAGS THE DOG,
1990–2000

1. Frank Bruni, "Wagging Tongues in 'Incredibly Cynical Times,'" *New York Times* (21 August 1998), 1; also James Bennet, "Clinton, Dogged by Scandal, Juggled Politics and Bombing," *New York Times* (22 August 1998), 1.

2. Neal Gabler, *Life, the Movie: How Entertainment Conquered Reality* (New York: Knopf, 1998), esp. 136–138; Shawn J. Parry-Giles and Trevor Parry-Giles, *Constructing Clinton: Hyperreality and Presidential Image-Making in Postmodern Politics* (New York: Peter Lang, 2002); Caryn James, "Postmodernism Goes to the Movies," *New York Times* (23 July 1990), C11.

3. Nigel Hamilton, *Bill Clinton: An American Journey, Great Expectations* (New York: Ballantine, 2003), 391.

4. P. David Marshall, "Introduction," in P. David Marshall, ed., *The Celebrity Culture Reader* (London: Routledge, 2006), 5.

5. For a general survey of the topic, see Peter Biskind, *Easy Riders, Raging Bulls: How the Sex-Drugs-and-Rock 'n' Roll Generation Saved Hollywood* (New York: Simon and Schuster, 1998).

6. David Denby, "Star Wars," *New York* (2 June 1977), 45; Biskind, *Easy Riders, Raging Bulls,* 338.

7. Jim Collins, Hilary Radner, and Ava Preacher Collins, eds., *Film Theory Goes to*

the Movies (New York: Routledge, 1993), 23; Kristin Thompson, *Storytelling in the New Hollywood: Understanding Classical Narrative Technique* (Cambridge: Harvard University Press, 1999), 152; David Bordwell, *The Way Hollywood Tells It: Story and Style in Modern Movies* (Berkeley: University of California Press, 2006), 5 and passim.

8. Thompson, *Storytelling in the New Hollywood,* esp. chaps. 1–2; Bordwell, *The Way Hollywood Tells It,* esp. chaps. 2–4.

9. Screenwriting guides that emphasize the hero's journey include Christopher Vogler, *The Writer's Journey: Mythic Structure for Writers,* 3d ed. (Studio City, CA: Michael Wiese, 2007) and Stuart Voytilla, *Myth and the Movies: Discovering the Myth Structure of 50 Unforgettable Films* (Studio City, CA: Michael Wiese, 1999).

10. Jameson quoted in Parry-Giles and Parry-Giles, *Constructing Clinton,* 24; Marshall, "Introduction," 5.

11. Christopher Lasch, *The Culture of Narcissism: American Life in an Age of Diminishing Expectations* (New York: Norton, 1978), 59.

12. See for example Sarah Z. Wexler, *Living Large: From SUVs to Double Ds—Why Going Bigger Isn't Going Better* (New York: St. Martin's, 2010), chap. 1.

13. Hamilton, *Bill Clinton: An American Journey,* 561.

14. Amitai Etzioni, *Spirit of Community: The Reinvention of American Society* (New York: Crown, 1993); William J. Bennett, *The Book of Virtues: A Treasury of Great Moral Stories* (New York: Simon and Schuster, 1993); Shelby Steele, *The Content of Our Character: A New Vision of Race in America* (New York: St. Martin's, 1990); Gail Sheehy, *Character: America's Search for Leadership* (New York: Morrow, 1988); Edmund Morris, *Dutch: A Memoir of Ronald Reagan* (New York: Random House, 1999), 639. *Newsweek*'s cover story, "George Bush: Fighting the 'Wimp Factor'" (19 October 1987), popularized this labeling of the candidate.

15. Kathleen Hall Jamieson, *Packaging the Presidency: A History and Criticism of Presidential Campaign Advertising,* 3d ed. (New York: Oxford University Press, 1996), 465.

16. See for example Vincent Canby, "Villains of the World! Hollywood Beckons," *New York Times* (24 September 1989), H1, H15; Bernard Weinraub, "Despite Clinton, Hollywood Is Still Trading in Violence," *New York Times* (28 December 1993), A1, C22.

17. Jamieson, *Packaging the Presidency,* 472 (emphasis added); William F. Lewis, "Telling America's Story: Narrative Form and the Reagan Presidency," *Quarterly Journal of Speech* 73 (1987): 280–302; Paul Waldman, "The Power of the Campaign Narrative," *American Prospect* (July 18, 2007); William Safire, "Narrative," *New York Times Magazine* (5 December 2004), 34. On screenplays and haiku: Allen B. Ury, *Secrets of the Screen Trade* (Los Angeles: Lone Eagle, 2004), 152; and Amnon Buchbinder, *The Way of the Screenwriter* (Toronto: Anansi, 2005), 193–195.

18. Gabler, *Life, the Movie,* 88–90.

19. Lawrence Stone, "The Revival of Narrative: Reflections on a New Old History," *Past and Present* 85 (November 1979): 3–24.

20. Hamilton, *Bill Clinton: An American Journey*, 227.

21. Ibid., 226, 228.

22. Ibid., 319.

23. Nigel Hamilton, *Bill Clinton: Mastering the Presidency* (New York: Current Affairs, 2007), 28.

24. George Stephanopoulos, *All Too Human: A Political Education* (Boston: Little, Brown, 1999), 5.

25. James Bennet, "Clinton Lawyer Will View Deposition in Paula Jones Suit," *New York Times* (11 August 1998), 16; Mark Katz, "President Clinton: the Screenplay," *New York Times* (25 August 1998), 17; Maureen Dowd, "Truth or Dare," *New York Times* (12 August 1998), 19.

26. Alan Schroeder, *Celebrity in Chief: How Show Business Took Over the White House* (Boulder, CO: Westview, 2004), 48–52.

27. Bernard Weinraub, "Among Hollywood Democrats, President Is Supported as One of Their Own," *New York Times* (29 September 1998), 19; Hamilton, *Bill Clinton: Mastering the Presidency*, 382.

28. Paul Begala, "I Miss Bob Dole," *Newsweek* (25 July 2011), 6; R. N. Smith, "Let Us Entertain You," *New York Times* (12 March 1998), 27.

29. Julia Anderson Miller and Bruce Joshua Miller, *Dreams of Bill* (New York: Citadel, 1994).

30. Michael Wines, "Hollywood Finds a Presidential Role Model," *New York Times* (12 November 1995), H1, H40. See also Loren P. Quiring, "A Man of His Word: Aaron Sorkin's American Presidents," in Peter C. Rollins and John E. O'Connor, eds., *Hollywood's White House: The American Presidency in Film and History* (Lexington: University Press of Kentucky, 2003), 234–250.

31. Bernard Weinraub, "All the President's Men . . . and Women," *New York Times* (26 September 1999), 56–58.

32. Dierdre Carmody, "Early Signs Are Promising for George Magazine," *New York Times* (29 January 1996), 5.

33. See Stephen Morewitz, *Sexual Harassment and Social Change in American Society* (San Francisco: Austin and Winfield, 1994) and Timothy M. Phelps and Helen Winternitz, *Capitol Games: Clarence Thomas, Anita Hill, and the Story of a Supreme Court Nomination* (New York: Hyperion, 1992).

34. Timothy Eagan, "With Spotlight Shifted to Them, Some Simpson Jurors Talk Freely," *New York Times* (5 October 1995), B18.

35. Maureen Dowd, "Choking on Lust," *New York Times* (28 February 1999), 19.

36. Hamilton, *Bill Clinton: An American Journey*, 557.

37. Dowd, "Truth or Dare," 19.

38. Jim Yardley, "No Introductions Were Necessary," *New York Times* (8 March 1998), WK2.

CHAPTER 7: THE TWIN TOWERS, 2001–2009

1. Marshall Sella, "The Stiff Guy vs. the Dumb Guy," *New York Times Magazine* (24 September 2000), 96. Years afterward Bradley maintained his sober approach to politics, encouraging Democrats to focus on less glamorous tasks such as grassroots organization and developing ideas. He insisted that "a party based on charisma has no long-term impact." Bill Bradley, "A Party Inverted," *New York Times* (30 March 2005), 23.

2. "Hot Politics in the Snow," *New York Times* (30 January 2000), WK14.

3. Transcript, *Larry King Live*, CNN (13 March 2000), http://transcripts.cnn.com/TRANSCRIPTS/0003/13/lkl.00.html.

4. David Plotz, "Dead Air," *New York Times Magazine* (13 August 2000), 17–20.

5. George W. Bush, *Decision Points* (New York: Crown, 2010), 19; Frank Bruni, *Ambling into History: The Unlikely Odyssey of George W. Bush* (New York: Harper-Collins), 25–26.

6. Bush, *Decision Points*, 46–47.

7. Karl Rove, *Courage and Consequence: My Life as a Conservative in the Fight* (New York: Simon and Schuster, 2010), 39; Nicholas Lemann, "The Controller," *New Yorker* (12 May 2003), 69; James Moore and Wayne Slater, *Bush's Brain: How Karl Rove Made George W. Bush Presidential* (New York: Wiley, 2003), 137.

8. Rove, *Courage and Consequence*, 67.

9. Moore and Slater, *Bush's Brain*, 53–58; Rove, *Courage and Consequence*, 60–61.

10. Moore and Slater, *Bush's Brain*, 154; Lemann, "The Controller," 77; Rove, *Courage and Consequence*, 58.

11. Molly Ivins and Lou Dubose, *Shrub: The Short but Happy Political Life of George W. Bush* (New York: Random House, 2000), xvii.

12. Ivins and Dubose, *Shrub*, xvii, xxi; Bruni, *Ambling into History*, 33.

13. Bush, *Decision Points*, 36; Rove, *Courage and Consequence*, 66–67.

14. Rove, *Courage and Consequence*, chaps. 12–13.

15. Shirley Anne Warshaw, *The Co-Presidency of Bush and Cheney* (Stanford, CA: Stanford University Press, 2009); Barton Gellman, *Angler: The Cheney Vice Presidency* (New York: Penguin, 2008), chaps. 2–3.

16. Rove, *Courage and Consequence*, 135–36.

17. Frank Rich, *The Greatest Story Ever Sold: The Decline and Fall of Truth from 9/11 to Katrina* (New York: Penguin, 2006), 53, 57; Elisabeth Bumiller, "Keepers of the Bush Image Lift Stagecraft to New Heights," *New York Times* (16 May 2003), 1.

18. Bush, *Decision Points*, 129.

19. David D. Kirkpatrick, "Pronouncements on Irony Draw a Line in the Sand," *New York Times* (24 September 2001), http://www.nytimes.com/2001/09/24/business/.

20. Brigitte L. Nacos, "Terrorism, the Mass Media, and the Events of 9-11," *Phi Kappa Phi Forum* 82 (2002): 13.

21. Ibid., 13–14; Bush, *Decision Points,* 148–49; Rove, *Courage and Consequence,* 519.

22. "Comedy Central Votes 'Bush' Out," *E! Online* (3 August 2001), http://www.treyparker.info/archives.

23. Marc Cooper, "Lights! Cameras! Attack! Hollywood Enlists," *Nation* (10 December 2001), 13.

24. Cooper, "Lights! Cameras! Attack!" 13; Rick Lyman, "Hollywood Discusses Role in War Effort," *New York Times* (12 November 2001), B2.

25. Cooper, "Lights! Cameras! Attack!" 13.

26. Ibid.; Paul Bond, "Lending a Hand: Hollywood Helping at Studio and Individual Levels (One Year Later)," *Hollywood Reporter* (11 September 2002), 18ff; Michael Goldman, "A New Role for Hollywood?" *Millimeter* (1 December 2001), 30.

27. Cooper, "Lights! Cameras! Attack!" 13.

28. See for example Jane Mayer, *The Dark Side: The Inside Story of How the War on Terror Turned into a War on American Ideals* (New York: Doubleday, 2008).

29. Rich, *Greatest Story Ever Sold,* 224–225.

30. Rich, *Greatest Story Ever Sold,* 80–82, 123–124.

31. Bumiller, "Keepers of the Bush Image," 1; Rich, *Greatest Story Ever Sold,* 57, 110.

32. Dale McFeatters, "Mission Accomplished," *Naples Daily News* (30 October 2003), http://www.naplesnews.com/news/2003/oct/30.

33. Rich, *Greatest Story Ever Sold,* 88–91; Bumiller, "Keepers of the Bush Image," 1.

34. David Paul Kuhn, "'Mission Accomplished' Revisited," *CBS News* (30 April 2004), http://www.cbsnews.com/stories/2004/04/30; Robert Draper, "Last One Out, Turn Off the Lights," *Gentlemen's Quarterly* (July 2007), http://www.gq.com; Bush, *Decision Points,* 257.

35. *The Tillman Story,* DVD, directed by Amir Bar-Lev (2010; Culver City, CA: Sony Pictures Home Entertainment, 2011); Nina Teicholz, "Privatizing Propaganda," *Washington Monthly* (December 2002), 16.

36. Rich, *Greatest Story Ever Sold,* 167, 171–173.

37. Rove, *Courage and Consequence,* 363, 394–398.

38. Neal Gabler, "Liberalism's Lost Script," *American Prospect* 15 (2004), 49–50.

39. Bill Keller, "Reagan's Son," *New York Times Magazine* (26 January 2003), 26; also Bruni, *Ambling into History,* 127–128.

40. See for example Susan Murray and Laurie Ouellette eds., *Reality TV: Remaking Television Culture,* 2d ed. (New York: New York University Press, 2008).

41. Manohla Dargis and A. O. Scott, "The Name Might Escape, but Not the Work," *New York Times* (18 September 2011), AR 31, and "The Good, the Bad, Not the Ugly," *New York Times* (11 August 2011) (blog), http://www.nytimes.com.

42. Bruni, *Ambling into History,* 26.

43. Dotson Rader, "The Mixed-Up Life of Shia LaBeouf," *Parade* (14 June 2009), 4.

44. Terrence Rafferty, "Being Clooney: Not as Easy as It Looks," *New York Times* (8 January 2010), VIII:9; Jon Avlon, "A 21st-Century Statesman," *Newsweek* (20 February 2011), 19.

45. See Tom Hauser, *Inside the Ropes with Jesse Ventura* (Minneapolis: University of Minnesota Press, 2002). A third cast member of *Predator,* Sonny Landham, ran unsuccessfully for governor of Kentucky.

46. Mike Leibovitch, "Who Can Possibly Govern California?" *New York Times Magazine* (5 July 2009), 26; Rove, *Courage and Consequence,* 68; Gary Indiana, *Schwarzenegger Syndrome: Politics and Celebrity in the Age of Contempt* (New York: New Press, 2005).

47. Scott McClellan, *What Happened: Inside the Bush White House and Washington's Culture of Deception* (New York: Public Affairs, 2008), 207, 209.

48. Barack Obama, *Dreams from My Father: A Story of Race and Inheritance* (New York: Times Books, 1995), 115.

49. David Remnick, *The Bridge: The Life and Rise of Barack Obama* (New York: Knopf, 2010), 186, 190.

50. Barack Obama, *The Audacity of Hope: Thoughts on Reclaiming the American Dream* (New York: Vintage, 2006), 36.

51. Remnick, *The Bridge,* 217, 305, 316–317.

52. Ibid., 331, 347.

53. Ibid., 387, 401.

54. Claire Messud, "Some Like It Cool," *Newsweek* (1 September 2008), 46–47.

55. On Clinton, see John Heilemann and Mark Halperin, *Game Change: Obama and the Clintons, McCain and Palin, and the Race of a Lifetime* (New York: Harper-Collins, 2010), 180 and chaps. 1, 3, 9.

56. "Open Caucus," *New York Times* (3 October 2008), http://www.nytimes.com; "Swooning Supporters Fainting for Obama," *WorldNetDaily* (16 February 2008), http://www.wnd.com/index.

57. Remnick, *The Bridge,* chaps. 8, 15.

58. Virginia Heffernan, "The YouTube Presidency," *New York Times Magazine* (10 April 2009), http://www.nytimes.com; "Kal Penn Joins Obama's Staff," *New York Times* (9 July 2009), 3.

59. Dana Milbank, "Stay Tuned for More of 'The Obama Show,'" *Washington Post* (24 June 2009), http://www.washingtonpost.com; Jui Chakravorty, "Obama, in Another First, Named 'Power' Celebrity," *Reuters* (2 June 2009), http://www.reuters .com.

60. Messud, "Some Like It Cool," 49.

61. Rex Murphy, "We Still Can't Read Obama," *Toronto Globe and Mail* (11 April 2009), http://www.theglobeandmail.com.

CONCLUSION

1. Nicholas Schmidle, "Getting Bin Laden," *New Yorker* (8 August 2011), http://www.newyorker.com/reporting/2011/08/08/.

2. Maggie Lange, "Hollywood Chases Bin Laden Capture," *Thompson on Hollywood* (27 June 2011), http://blogs.indiewire.com/thompsononhollywood/bin_laden_capture_to_become_graphic_novel. In 2009, Geronimo's ancestors sued Obama and other officials to reclaim the skeleton of the Apache warrior, which they alleged had been stolen from its grave in 1918 by Yale student Prescott Bush. Bush, they claimed, deposited the skeleton at Yale's elite Skull and Bones Society. Bush, his son George H. W. Bush, and his grandson George W. Bush all belonged to Skull and Bones. The case was dismissed in court. "Bush and Geronimo, and Skull & Bones," *ABC News* (19 February 2009), http://abcnews.go.com/blogs/headlines/2009/02/.

3. Hugo Münsterberg, *The Photoplay: A Psychological Study* (New York: Appleton, 1916), 220–221.

4. Jehoshua Eliashberg and Mohanbir S. Sawhney, "Modeling Goes to Hollywood: Predicting Individual Differences in Movie Enjoyment," *Management Science* 40 (1994): 1151–1173; Leo A. Handel, *Hollywood Looks at Its Audience: A Report of Film Audience Research* (Urbana: University of Illinois Press, 1950), 177, 180.

5. Richard Dyer, *Heavenly Bodies: Film Stars and Society* (New York: St. Martin's, 1986), 8, 15, 18–19. See also Richard Dyer, *Stars* (London: British Film Institute, 1979); Christine Geldhill, *Stardom: Industry of Desire* (Oxon, UK: Routledge, 1991); and Danae Clark, "The Subject of Acting," in Lucy Fischer and Marcia Landy, eds., *Stars: The Film Reader* (London: Routledge, 2004), 13–28.

6. See for example Emily Fox-Kales, *Body Shots: Hollywood and the Culture of Eating Disorders* (Albany, NY: SUNY Press, 2011), chap. 1.

7. David L. L. Shields, Julia Carol, Edith D. Balbach, and Sarah McGee, "Hollywood on Tobacco: How the Entertainment Industry Understands Tobacco Portrayal," *Tobacco Control* 8 (1999): 380.

8. Julia Baird, "Too Hot to Handle: Stop Ogling Republican Women," *Newsweek* (12 July 2010), 37.

9. See Aleš Debeljak, *Reluctant Modernity: The Institution of Art and Its Historical Forms* (Lanham, MD: Rowman and Littlefield, 1998), 28, and Laura Langman, "The Dialectic of Selfhood," *Current Perspectives in Social Theory* 26 (2009): 273–274.

10. Michael Schudson, "Was There Ever a Public Sphere? If So, When? Reflections on the American Case," and Jürgen Habermas, "Concluding Remarks," in Craig Calhoun, ed., *Habermas and the Public Sphere* (Cambridge, MA: MIT Press, 1992), 146, 149, 465. See also Leo Braudy, *The Frenzy of Renown: Fame and Its History* (New York: Oxford University Press, 1986), introduction.

11. See also Fred Inglis, *A Short History of Celebrity* (Princeton, NJ: Princeton University Press, 2010), part 1.

12. Mark Morford, "The Great Impending OMG of 2011," *San Francisco Chronicle* (5 January 2011), http://www.sfgate.com/cgi-bin/article.cgi?f=/g/a/2011/01/05/.

13. On the Obama images, see Leslie Lindenauer and Marcy May, "'The Most Badass President Ever': Gender and Image in American Civic Life," and Marcy May, "The Body Politic: The Corporeal Construction of Political Manhood in Postwar America," unpublished papers, Historians of the Twentieth Century United States annual meetings (Brighton and Oxford, UK), July 2010 and July 2011, respectively.

INDEX

All titles listed are those of films unless otherwise indicated.

Murnau, F. W., 63
Murphy, George, 187, 226; political career
of, 152, 188
Murphy, Rex, 278–279
Murrow, Edward R., 142, 147
Music Corporation of America, 117–118,
159. *See also* Universal Pictures
Mussolini, Benito, 139
Myers, Dee Dee, 227

Nacos, Brigitte, 255, 256
Nadel, Alan, 100
narrative, in contemporary politics, 210,
223–224, 242, 245, 247, 257, 264, 278,
281–282
Nast, Thomas, 292
National Foundation for Infantile
Paralysis, 69–70, 91
National Lampoon's Animal House, 212
Nelson, Donald M., 99
Neptune's Spear, Operation (2011),
280–283
Nessen, Ron, 184
Newman, David, 210
Newman, Paul, 157–158, 228
newspapers, 4, 5, 8, 9–10, 17, 26, 31, 38,
110, 135, 287, 292; Coolidge and, 44–45;
JFK and, 142; Nixon and, 179
newsreels, 10, 60, 64, 68, 75, 87, 91, 97, 101,
287
New Wave, French, 210, 212
Ney, Bob, 204
Nguyen Van Thieu, 176
Nichols, Mike, 210, 214
Nicholson, Jack, 222–223, 230
9/11 terrorist attacks (2001), 204, 246,
254–256
Nixon, 230
Nixon, Pat, 106, 182; and acting, 162, 166
Nixon, Richard Milhous, 72, 110, 122,
194–195; as actor, 162, 182, 184, 190–191;
background of, 165–166; and Checkers
speech, 104–106; image making of, 10,
161, 164, 168–169, 170, 175, 177, 178–182,
198, 202, 206; and JFK, 167, 182, 284;
and movies, 7, 163, 182–184, 284; and
1960 campaign, 129; and 1962 campaign
for governor, 105, 167–168; and 1968
campaign, 170–177; personality of, 163,
169–170, 175; presidency of, 151, 162–163,
169, 191; and Reagan, 164–165, 185–186,
189, 201; and television, 168, 170,

173–174, 176, 179; and Watergate,
177–178, 184
Nolan, Christopher, 214
North, Edmund S., 183
Novak, Kim, 117
Nye, Gerald, 77

Obama, Barack Hussein, 271
Obama, Barack Hussein, II, 5; back-
ground of, 271–274; as celebrity, 11;
generation of, 272–273; image making
of, 247–248, 270, 274, 276–277, 278, 283,
293; presidency of, 277–279, 280–281;
and race, 271–272, 273, 276; and
television, 277–278; and 2008 campaign,
275–277
O'Brien, Pat, 69
Obst, Lynda, 259
O'Daniel, Wilbert "Pappy," 70, 71
O'Donnell, Kenneth, 148, 150
Office of War Information, 81
Of Thee I Sing (play), 78
O'Hara, Maureen, 70
Old Man and the Sea, The (novella), 100,
113
Onassis, Jacqueline Kennedy. *See*
Kennedy, Jacqueline
101 Dalmatians, 241
Operation Abolition, 146
oratory, 24; and Chautauqua, 36;
instructional style of, 40–41, 42, 81–82;
Nixon's, 165–166; politicians and, 4,
26–27, 28, 35; and television, 95, 98–99,
110
O'Sullivan, Maureen, 125

Packwood, Bob, 238, 239
Paine, Thomas, 24
Palin, Sarah, 277, 290
Panetta, Leon, 280
Parallax View, The, 150
Paramount Pictures, 59, 60, 92, 102, 115,
155, 211, 257
Parker, Trey, 257
Parry-Giles, Shawn and Trevor, 207
Parsons, Louella, 187
Pataki, George, 255
Patriot Games, 281
Patton, 183–184
Pearlstein, Rick, 178, 180
Peck, Gregory, 147, 157–158
Pelosi, Nancy, 275

ABOUT THE AUTHOR

Burton W. Peretti is a professor of history at Western Connecticut State University. He is the author of four other books, including *The Creation of Jazz: Music, Race, and Culture in Urban America* and *Nightclub City: Politics and Amusement in Manhattan.*